Shared Idioms, Sacred Symbols, and the Articulation of Identities in South Asia

Shared Idioms, Sacred Symbols, and the Articulation of Identities in South Asia

Edited by

Kelly Pemberton & Michael Nijhawan

Routledge
Taylor & Francis Group
New York London

First published 2009
by Routledge
270 Madison Ave, New York, NY 10016

Simultaneously published in the UK
by Routledge
2 Park Square, Milton Park, Abingdon, Oxon OX14 4RN

Routledge is an imprint of the Taylor & Francis Group, an informa business

Typeset in Sabon by IBT Global.

Library of Congress Cataloging in Publication Data

Shared idioms, sacred symbols, and the articulation of identities in South Asia / edited by Kelly Pemberton & Michael Nijhawan.
p. cm.—(Routledge studies in religion ; 11)
Includes bibliographical references and index.
1. Group identity—South Asia. 2. Symbolism—South Asia. 3. Political culture—South Asia. 4. South Asia—Civilization. I. Pemberton, Kelly. II. Nijhawan, Michael.
HM1753.S53 2008
305.0954—dc22
2008028826

ISBN10: 0-415-95828-8 (hbk)
ISBN10: 0-203-88536-8 (ebk)

ISBN13: 978-0-415-95828-8 (hbk)
ISBN13: 978-0-203-88536-9 (ebk)

Contents

Part II: Landscapes of Ritual Performance: Ritual, Agency, and Memory in Focus

Acknowledgments

When we first conceived the idea of editing a volume on identity in the South Asian context, we had little sense of how long, and sometimes frustrating, the journey to completion would be. While the idea came from our participation on a conference panel, "'Hindu Na, Nahin Musulman': Shared Idioms of Piety and Sanctity," at the Association for Asian Studies annual meeting in 2002, our work in individual chapters, and on the volume as a whole, has moved far beyond the aims and vision of that panel. In the interim, we have acquired a more nuanced understanding of the questions of identity (as a field of study) and identification (as a process of articulating the self) this volume investigates. While we, the editors, have benefited from extended conversations with each other by e-mail and phone, our study has been enriched far more deeply by conversations and collaborations over the years with colleagues and friends who have challenged us to think beyond our initial concepts and assumptions and to push the question of identity—and identifications—much further. In that respect, we have a few people to single out for special thanks. Tony Stewart and Joyce Flueckiger provided initial encouragement and advice (and the requisite warnings) for embarking on this project. Jack Hawley, Amina Yaqin, Jenny Takhar, and Huma Dar provided valuable input on the theoretical framework for this volume in the early stages of its composition. Our friends and family provided moral and emotional support through the years we spent revising and seeking publication for this volume, and we thank them, too. Finally, thanks are also due to Erica Wetter, our editor at Routledge, New York, to Debbie Ruel, our copyeditor, and Terence Johnson, our production manager at IBT Global, and to the anonymous readers who critiqued individual chapters and the volume as a whole. While the work has been significantly enriched by their comments and support, we assume full responsibility for the ideas—and errors—found in the pages of this volume.

Introduction

Toward an Integrative Hermeneutics in the Study of Identity

Kelly Pemberton and Michael Nijhawan

Over the past quarter century, numerous volumes that take up the question of identity have been published, and indeed, identity has become a question of central importance within the field of South Asian studies, as in the human and social sciences more broadly.[1] Some have addressed the question on epistemological or ideological terms, privileging the role of institutions and other structuring entities (such as the state or the market place) upon constructions of identity. Recent studies of the middle classes in India, for instance, have debated their characterization as a product of consumerism and/or market forces, of emerging forms of political culture, or of a Westernized subculture that enjoys privileged access to global transnational capital (or information) flows. Others have sought to remedy this problem by prioritizing empirical and experiential evidence over purely structuralist frameworks of analysis.[2]

In some cases, historical (text-critical) and anthropological (participant-observation) research has yielded rich portraits of encounters between diverse socio-cultural groups in the Subcontinent, with emphasis in recent decades on how locally embedded forms of practice and dominant representations of what is "normative" stand in relation to each other. Post-modern hermeneutic methods[3] typically characterize these encounters in two ways. First, the relationship between dominant representations and local "micronarratives" is couched in the language of conflict, particularly where a struggle over resources or desire for access to certain forms of power (e.g., economic resources, control over symbolic capital, or influence within or over institutions of governance) is apparent. Second, where they involve "fruitful encounters"—particularly at the level of the so-called "popular" or "vernacular" religious experience—this relationship is often depicted as one of syncretism.

Several recent studies of "Hindu–Muslim" conflict implicate the political order in sustaining "communal violence" and, concurrently, in mobilizing the power of rhetoric to both create and interpret riots as evidence of the incompatibility of the two groups.[4] More often than not, such works obscure the permeability of such boundaries, and offer little substance for understanding the place of contingent factors in the production, reconfiguration, or transformation of knowledge and action. Furthermore, such a methodological position forces one to resort to notions of "the state" as a self-evident category that is imposed on everyday spheres of action, and works to obscure how, specifically under conditions of violence, the multifaceted aspects of state power (perceived both as a threat to and as a guarantor of security) mediate forms of local agency. Scanning the landscape of new anthropological and sociological work on violence and identity formation, one notices the importance given to the production of voice and agency in everyday realms of life, precisely because it is in those heterogeneous everyday worlds that we can observe both the ability of symbols to mobilize actors along lines of exclusion and the persistence of shared idioms that allow for processes of recuperation and recovery.[5] This recent work affords greater possibilities for charting the shared worlds of everyday practice in a range of other areas of social and cultural production in South Asia. Our focus on "shared idioms" indexes this broader preoccupation within contemporary scholarship on South Asia. This task assumes crucial importance in a time of renewed violence in that region, as around the world, sustained by ongoing processes of "re-essentialization" and boundary-drawing along sectarian, political, religious, and ethnic lines. Furthermore, these processes are now often produced within a broader transnational dynamic in which (e.g., the Gujarat riots in 2002) diasporic organizations provide an organizational and ideological component of fundamental importance.

The other oft-cited model of social relations in South Asia, syncretism (or hybridity), is employed in a pejorative, neutral, or meliorative manner to designate the intermixture of two or more different religions. The premises of this model rest on an intrinsic view of religion as a bounded system of signs, symbols, and set(s) of meaning(s), which the syncretized variant draws upon to forge something that is neither wholly the original nor wholly the "Other." As an interpretative model, syncretism fails to offer an adequate explanation of the confluence of factors that make up, and affect the articulation of, identities; rather, it underscores an oppositional framework between official/hegemonic and popular/subaltern religion. In so doing, syncretist interpretive models offer explanations of identity and experience that make possible a number of troubling presumptions: one, the existence of a "pure" (and thus somewhat "hegemonic") hybridized variant (as opposed to the cultural borrowing that is germane to most forms of religious, social, ritual, and literary expression), two, the essentially transgressive nature of this variant, and three, the "privileged" position of syncretism in relation to identities that do not define themselves along such lines.[6]

TRANSLATION REGIMES

A more promising suggestion for conceiving these relationships is suggested by Tony Stewart in his essay "In Search of Equivalence," which calls attention to the practical notion of "strategizing"—through the use of the local vernaculars—on the part of the early Bengali Muslim writers in the endeavor to understand and be understood by the Hindu "Others" they encountered and sought to translate into an Islamic perspective.[7] This analytic framework incorporates a theory of linguistic and cultural translation that, in our view, brings us closer to some of the actual strategies, narrations, and creative forces depicted in the chapters that comprise the first part of this volume. The chapters by Amy Bard and Valerie Ritter, and Arvind Mandair carry forward some of the concerns raised by Stewart's discussion of translation, demonstrating the transformative potential of discursive resignifications, and thus highlighting several key operative variables within processual modes of identification and naming, or the means and mechanisms by which identification or naming is carried out. These include the influence of common structuring elements, the ends sought by interlocutor(s), and the impact of critical moments in time.

The challenges of interpreting acts of literary production are highlighted in Bard and Ritter's chapter, "A House Overturned." This study demonstrates how shared linguistic signifiers—as marshaled in the translations of the small-town pandit "Hariaudh" (1865–1947)—can actually work to produce difference. As the authors suggest, the translation of an early-twentieth-century *marsiyah*, or mourning poem, dedicated to the memory of the massacre of the Prophet Muhammad's grandson and his entourage on the battlefield of Karbala, from Urdu into Hindi's literary Braj Bhasha dialect, was no mere adaptation. Drawing upon two closely related notions of affect—one (epistemological) in which authors consciously work to produce an emotional sense within their audiences, and the other (literary) in which existing local perceptual frames themselves can produce particular responses to narrative performances—the authors argue that the process was one that involved an intense engagement with similar evocations and meanings, purported to be experienced "differently." The very fact that the *marsiyah* genre in Urdu, which is associated with a world-transforming stage in Islamic history, could be used by the architects of such processes to differentiate and distill a separate Hindi (and Hindu) identity from a fairly plural linguistic and literary landscape, suggests that the range of vocabulary and imagery available to early-twentieth-century writers of Hindi was still quite broad, indeed, and that the esteem with which the Urdu and Persian literary forms were held by the learned classes was slow to disappear even after the Hindi language movement took hold.

In Mandair's chapter, difference figures as a catalyst for the creation of a master narrative of "Sikh religion" by the noted ideologue Bhai Vir Singh. Bhai Vir Singh's narrative seeks to seamlessly weave divergent concepts of divinity into a coherent whole by collapsing earlier strands of theological inquiry by leading Sikh interpreters with Sikh commentaries on the translation of Sikh scripture by the nineteenth-century German linguist Ernest Trumpp. Mandair argues that despite the obvious flaws and implicit prejudices in Trumpp's (eventually debunked) translation project (with its denial of a Sikh monotheism separate and distinct from premodern Indic narratives of a Supreme Being), it drew renowned Sikh commentators into a kind of theological discourse that led them to repress any connection to broader Indic beliefs and practices (such as idol worship) and work to prove the monotheistic nature of Sikh religion. The intriguing fact about Mandair's approach is that it deftly sidesteps a constructivist argument that would posit a syncretist origin (as contrasted with a purified version) of Sikh identity, instead crafting a convincing case for rethinking the translatability of such concepts as religion, God, and theology—as they have emerged from Western intellectual traditions—into Indic contexts. In so doing, Mandair simultaneously highlights the "symbolic violence" that is committed toward any notion of Sikh tradition when transcendence is collapsed and subsequently used to blur the boundaries between the idea of God (a transcendent entity) and a method of inquiry (universalizing, or seamless translation across cultural boundaries).

As with these two chapters, an emphasis on process, rather than identity or community as such, allows several other contributors to this volume to point to group activities in which essentialized class-based, ethnic, caste, religious, sectarian, or ethnic monikers of collectivity are transformed into persuasive mobilizers for group action. Consequently, our sense of "sacred symbols" is not intended as a reification of the religious (a category, as we argue further, that has itself come under scrutiny), but draws upon the power of symbols to catalyze groups along exclusivist lines of identity and belonging. Here a distinction between intention and effect must be taken into consideration, since the anticipated consequences of acts of identification and naming, particularly when carried out by the state or by social elites, are not necessarily realized or even adopted by the targeted social actors.

We see this outcome in the chapter by Amina Yaqin on the makers of Pakistan's national identity. In her chapter, Yaqin discusses the state's strategic appropriation of signifying discourses about the Pakistani nation. By sponsoring the textual productions of three iconoclastic "national" poets and literary icons—Faiz Ahmad Faiz, Jamil Jalibi, and Fahmida Riaz—Pakistan sought to transform the fragments of the nation into a cohesive, loyal whole by delineating a unique and homogenous Pakistani self that was predicated upon both its putative difference from the Indian Other and the minimization of ethnic and regional differences among the nation's citizens. Notably, many of the signs and signifiers these poets used as tools of identification and naming were interwoven, intersected, and clashed with interpretations of Islam in the country and city, state and nation. Yaqin argues that whether they situated themselves within or outside of the hegemonic narrative of the nation as articulated by the state, these three authors were stymied by their own myth-making efforts, while their cultural productions worked in quite opposite fashion to underscore the continued ability of regional and ethnic loyalties to operate as centrifugal forces, undermine the state's efforts at homogenization, and ultimately expose the state's inability to contain and channel those forces.

The contradictions engendered by efforts to re-envision the nation have frequently produced violent outcomes in the case of Indian Muslims, according to Huma Dar. Taking as her point of departure a reading of the poem "Farewell" by the Pakistani poet Agha Shahid 'Ali, Dar argues that portrayals of Indian Muslims in popular film, literature, and narrative are all too often inscribed with the uneasy tension between India and Pakistan, and with a "tyrannical" discourse that is reflective of anti-Muslim pogroms in India. In her assessment of cultural constructions of the Indian Muslim, Dar unapologetically criticizes the self-conscious "liberalism" of many Indians today as being limited in its willingness to protest the continued vilification—and persecution—of Indian Muslims. Through the works she surveys, Dar identifies and deconstructs several key tropes that reinforce some of the stereotypes that emerged from the early days of Indian cinema: the rapacious feudal lord, the underworld gangster-terrorist, the hypersexualized courtesan, and the oppressed, veiled, yet sensual female. Drawing upon three important discourses of naming that have appeared in recent Hindi films, Dar provides a nuanced perspective on the continued suspicion of Indian Muslims in India today. Dar's stark commentary on depictions of Muslim Indians in a select group of historical, poetic, and literary pieces, and documentary and feature films, lays bare the lasting effect of Partition for constructions of the Indian Muslim "Other" and calls into question the ability of liberal Indians—and the state—to overcome these effects within the current cultural and political landscape.

Admittedly, despite the promise that these critical approaches hold for shattering essentialist notions of identity as a coherent category, in the world out there we often find a fusion of flexible and primordial identifications. This, of course, has been observed before, and the question has been raised whether a constructivist position (especially a radical postmodern position) has maneuvered itself into a paradox of argumentation.[8] In the words of the sociologist Rogers Brubaker and the historian Frederick Cooper, "a constructivist notion of identity leaves us without a rationale for talking about 'identities' at all and [is] ill-equipped to examine the 'hard' dynamics and essentialist claims of contemporary identity politics." The conflation of 'identity' as social and analytical category would result in an "uneasy amalgam of constructivist language and essentialist argumentation," which is not just "a matter of intellectual sloppiness" but instead "reflects the tension between the constructivist language that is favored in the current academic climate, and the foundationalist or essentialist message that is important to acknowledge if appeals to 'identity' are to be effective in practice."[9]

IDENTITY TALK

The work of Brubaker and Cooper provides us with a conceptual toolkit that splits up the identity category into a range of more manageable terms (such as "bounded groupness," "self-identification," and "narratives") that can perform the work of analysis effectively. We certainly agree that one should try not to collapse different levels of analysis into one broad category (identity) without taking into account the multi-sited, historically and culturally shifting parameters of identity formations. This should be evident from the different approaches taken in each individual chapter. However, Brubaker and Cooper articulate a deeper concern about the possible erosion of a classical standpoint of social science theory through explorations of identity formation. The continued engagement of scholarly practices in "identity talk" could eventually lead, they propose, to a weakening of analytical precision, which is foundational to any sociological, anthropological, and historical inquiry.

While there is no easy response to the question of how best to avoid "identity" as a foundationalist category, contributions to this volume seek to offer more nuanced approaches to the problem, in part through an orientation towards the realm of practical experience, consciousness, and politics and in part through a questioning of the very metaphysics of identity. Two issues should be clarified here at the outset. First, as with many other categories in the social sciences and humanities that are of immediate relevance in practical terms, the idea of a completely detachable and objectivist use of these categories outside of the realms of practice stipulates a false image of separateness that we cannot subscribe to. Far from describing Brubaker and Cooper as naïve "positivists," we nonetheless believe that part of their argumentation draws a false distinction between the realms of theory and practice. This, indeed, is a crucial issue that begs the question of the translatability of epistemological categories between theory and practice (and Western and non-Western discourse, one might add) and that poses another set of questions related to how to conceptualize the notion of agency.

As a way to start thinking about this problematic, we take terms such as "ritual," "religion," or "community" and consider how these have shaped the self-understanding of social actors and interpreters of "tradition" in South Asia and elsewhere, with careful attention to the relationship between the symbolic and material conditions of self-identifications, on one hand, and the forces that can override, mediate, or modify these self-identifications, on the other. In so doing, we seek to understand the genealogy of those terms—without ascribing them foundationalist status—by considering regimes of translation that mediate between different discursive realms in each case. Srilata Raman, for instance, demonstrates how narratives of identity can be constructed both discursively and materially by instigating processes of self-fashioning through reiterated bodily practices. In her work on Maraimalai Adigal, a Tamil scholar and

Dravidian ideologue who wrote extensively on Tamil culture in the early twentieth century, Raman demonstrates how racial ideologies have served as a blueprint for narratives of Tamil identity that hinged on the politics of linguistic nationalism. Adigal's *Velala Civilization* delineates a distant, classical Tamil past that is both an archaic and an arcadian landscape, a community rather than a state or a nation, governed by reciprocal relationships, by food and diet, and demonstrating the features of an organic society. This society is a crucible for certain moral values, and the Velala, the high-caste non-Brahmin with traditional ties to the land, embodies these values and is both the creator and the lynch-pin of this society. The "hard" and "soft" historiographical practices which underlie Adigal's vision rely almost overwhelmingly on then-extant, dominant Orientalist idioms of "Aryan" and "Dravidian." Yet, as Raman argues, even while Adigal's historiography exists within such a dominant tradition and even shares some of the latter's fundamental methodological practices and assumptions, its emancipatory potential arises out of what might be called a "critical-political hermeneutics" which marks its departure from the shared idiom. Such a hermeneutics enables, in turn, the development of a parallel historiography situated in a space between social suffering and social assertion, between shame at the present and pride in a past, between a caste-based and egalitarian society and between an irretrievable lost past and utopian future world.

The regimes of translation that inform modes of social interaction between researchers and interlocutors and the broader (geo)political discourses in which these are embedded have been amply analyzed,[10] and only a few of our chapters address this concern directly. The crux of the matter, however, is that academic reasoning is, by the very nature of its endeavor, implicated in a complex discursive process of translation. Having acknowledged the intricacies (and universalizing tendencies) of identity discourse in history and religious studies approaches, we must be similarly concerned with issues of representation in our work. In our ethnographic chapters in particular, we might also unwittingly sustain relations of dominance and subordination in our "innocent" efforts to "articulate the other" for the benefit of a (largely) academic audience. And so it is clearly important that we emphasize what others before us have brought up as a critique of this discourse of detached objectivism: a move from "speaking for the other" to "speaking with and listening to the other" necessarily involves the idea of transformative knowledge that has potential implications for both sides of the dialogue. Thus, we recognize the need to move beyond mere definition and naming that obscures more than it reveals, and worse, silences the voices of those we claim to present, refashioning them to our own liking. Heeding the words of the feminist philosophers Maria Lugones and Elizabeth Spelman, we seek to develop the tools to learn to hear the voices of others who do not speak like us, and in so doing, to avoid "reducing to ourselves" those we seek to understand.[11]

For contributors to this volume, exploring the genealogy of the politics of identity formation in modern South Asia represents more than an academic endeavor; it also reflects a serious commitment to the lives of the people we are concerned with and to which we are connected in a number of ways. By marshalling (and interrogating) key theoretical developments while seeking to situate our analyses in contemporary examples of social, political, and religious forms of life, and in bringing together scholars from a range of sub-disciplines within the field of South Asian Studies, the chapters in this book thus want to push current debates on identity forward. We seek to accomplish this task not merely by interrogating the usefulness of identity as an analytical construct as such, but by simultaneously seeking to capture the complex processes through which we come to understand emergent forms of sociality and community formation, focusing our lenses on two areas in particular. First, we consider those translational and transgressive moments in which essentialized, bounded symbols of group belonging are mobilized into action. Second, we investigate the many everyday worlds of life in which such symbols are reworked, cracked open, resignified, and resituated within a broader, shared universe of social interaction and ethical orientation. This is important precisely in the moment in which the re-essentialization of identities manifests itself in the scenarios of political violence and urban riots in recent decades.

Indeed, much of this can be understood as a product of hard-core nationalisms and exclusivist identity politics, which today are also connected to globalization and the uncertainty this process has induced.[12] As we shall further argue, these processes unfold in a context in which the shared social, cultural, and religious worlds of everyday life are under constant transformation, with deep repercussions on the form and meaning of boundaries existing between groups and individuals. And yet, it is precisely here in these "messy scenes" of identity politics that we must intervene without just refuting the use of "identity" as a category of inquiry. When we therefore evoke the notion of "shared idioms" of everyday cultural and religious conduct, we reflexively point to those vital elements of identity formation as an ongoing process and the historical product of creative human interventions. The dilemma for us becomes one of how to talk reasonably about identity as something that is simultaneously grounded in the everyday, historically conditioned, and susceptible to change and (re)interpretation. This question is taken up more pointedly by the chapters in Part II of this volume.

AGENCY, RITUAL, AND NAMING

In the second part of this volume, identity emerges even more as "a moveable feast" than as a classification that is tethered to the notion of a unitary, bounded self.[13] This fluidity is captured by the interplay between the oral and the written in the crafting of the South Indian Marathi Varkari tradition as taken up by Christian Lee Novetzke. His study highlights the ways in which individual and group activities (and, more specifically, their memorialization—both literary and praxis-oriented)—can transform monikers of collectivity into what Bruce Lawrence and David Gilmartin have called "mobile collective identities," which index repertoires of language, behavior, knowledge, and "voice" that transcend both externally imposed and self-imposed definitions.[14] Looking largely through the lens of the "Jnandev Samadhi," a narrative describing the self-entombment of the thirteenth-century Marathi saint Jnandev, in the Maharastrian town of Alandi, Novetzke uncovers how time, place, objects, performances, dreams, and the written word have all converged to memorialize this important saint of the Varkari religious tradition. These elements came together in the sixteenth century, largely through the efforts of the Varkari Brahmin scholar-saint Eknath, who rediscovered the site of Jnandev's *samadhi* with the aid of a dream, re-inaugurated the ritual remembrance of this event, and, according to many, edited the textual record of "Jnandev's Samadhi." The multiple meanings of the Jnandev memorial, described as a "scriptural tomb" by Novetzke, are reflected in the term *samadhi* itself. It refers to the ritual act of self-entombment which Jnandev performed as a result of his desire to enter the permanent meditative state of *sanjivan samadhi*; the place where Jnandev is believed to still reside, deep in this meditative state; and the text that memorializes both the ritual act and the place where it occurred. According to Novetzke, text, event, performance, and place in this tradition stand at a critical juncture in the intersection of the worlds of memory and history.

Drawing primarily from rich ethnographic materials, the other chapters in the second part of the volume also set out to examine social actors' ability to fashion their individual and collective selves. They do so by fleshing out domains of relative autonomy at critical moments in the articulation of identity. This domain can be conceptualized in distinctively different ways, as all four chapters in this section demonstrate. As a general point of departure, many would agree today with a notion of agency that results from a dialectic of constraining and enabling forces as they are built into historically emergent and culturally varying forms of life. No matter what example we look at, individual or group proclivities do not represent a closed system of signs and meanings, but rather, reflect the practical functions of language, its signs, and its signals (as distinct from its "structure"). Apparently, the term "relative autonomy" recalls Pierre Bourdieu's now classical notion of habitus. In Bourdieu's work, habitus occupies a space between the reproduction of an objective "field of relations" of which, Bourdieu would argue, people are inevitably a part, and the culturally formed and embodied patterns of social action within "systems of durable, transposable dispositions."[15] Habitus, which according to Bourdieu resides in human institutions, representations, and practices, and emerges as meaning, perception, and action/reaction, is regulated by structuring forces (and itself may act as a structuring force) without amounting to mere obedience to established "rules." His understanding of the effect of structuring forces upon human action rejects overly deterministic, mechanistic explanations of social action, but it also rejects the idea of intentionality (or strategizing) as an adequate explanation for human action.

Bourdieu's important insight into the relationship between human action, on one hand, and the mechanisms that produce and regulate them, on the other, has provided some fodder for theorizing the dialectic between structuring mechanisms and the conditions under which these mechanisms engender blueprints for action. It has been observed that his theoretical model of action privileges the actor's "practical" logic and experience of reality, coupled with ingrained knowledge (learned since childhood) of "recognized" beliefs and practices (that is to say, "recognized" within his or her own cultural and social location). There are merits and shortcomings to this view. Yet, through the notion of habitus, we can locate a relatively autonomous domain of action that is both structured by external, antecedent structuring forces, and capable of re-structuring (or reinterpreting) those forces.

This interplay is suggested in Diane D'Souza's chapter on the emergence of female orators (*zakira*s) among Indian Shi'ah Muslims. Their contemporary role as purveyors of collectively shared and experienced memories of faith, suffering, and resilience may challenge dominant discourses about gender roles and women's leadership, but it has also helped Shi'ah women exercise self-confidence and feelings of self-worth in their everyday lives. According to Shi'ah sacred history, the precedent of a woman reciting the events that led to the martyrdom of the Prophet Muhammad's grandson, Husayn, on the battlefield of Karbala can be found in the original recitation performed by Husayn's sister Zaynab shortly after this tragic episode in Islamic history, although women orators were largely unknown until the late nineteenth century. Rather, women tended to participate in such assemblies as interested spectators and organizers; this was true even for all-female gatherings, where men would act as reciters of the Karbala events. D'Souza speculates that the growth in numbers of female *zakira*s occurred because of several factors that encouraged this development: the influence of Muslim reformers who sought greater rights and opportunities for women to participate in the larger public arenas of activity; an extant tradition of poetry recitation; and the growth in numbers of educated women. Unlike among Sunni Muslims, the rise of gender justice issues to the wider realm of public discourse did not seem to produce a crisis of conscience among Shi'is in India. In fact, D'Souza maintains, far from being a mere sound piece for the performance of ritualized mourning, the *zakira* has come to be seen as voicing the collective memory of the Shi'ah community. This includes not only the events at Karbala, but also the intricacies of Shi'ah tradition, belief, and history. As such, the figure of the *zakira* has come to embody the strength and importance of women's leadership among Shi'ah today.

Even though Bourdieu successfully theorized the dispositional aspects of social actions, his model is still rooted in a framework that prioritizes class positioning and allows for little variation within the circumscribed field of a specific cultural habitus. Habitus alone seems rather inadequate to conceptualize agency as a process that operates discursively and self-reflexively. Furthermore, the notion tends to ignore that, even within a confined socio-cultural domain, there might exist convergent modes of self-fashioning and self-cultivation that sometimes overlap and sometimes consciously counteract.[16] Anthony Giddens' work was instrumental in posing a process of self-reflexivity as central to a notion of agency.[17] While drawing upon a notion of (virtual) structure as both impeding and enabling independent action, he has also introduced a concept of intentionality that drives the constant flow of social conduct. According to his "double hermeneutic," established social concepts tend to filter back into society, where they affect individual (and social) thinking. Because individuals are increasingly capable of and inclined toward self-reflexive thinking, they monitor the flow of human activities and its products, and adapt their own individual actions to their evolving understandings of these activities and products. This potentially transformative capability is both a consequence and a diagnostic of power.

We see this process in action in all of the chapters in this part of the volume. The authors' observations suggest a self-reflexive motive for such adaptation, but it is also one that is deeply embedded in social practices and institutionalized forms of cultivating the self (e.g., through "idealized" personalities and modes of "performance") as understood by the subjects who are discussed in these chapters, and as articulated by the authorizing discourses that seek to name those subjects (or, more precisely, those speaking as their representatives). While denying primacy to either institutional structures or the agency of those venerating sacred texts/sites, these chapters suggest that processes of naming and identification are better understood in terms of a dialectic of individual choice on one hand, and the structures, influences, and predispositions that constrain and shape them, on the other, than as a conflict between these variables. In that sense, there is a resonance of Giddens' insights into how actors are capable of assessing and reinterpreting structural constraints *in the very process of action*. Unlike Bourdieu, who addressed this problem as a dialectic between habitual practice and strategically organized (if not always strategically intended) conduct, Giddens relocated processes of reflexivity in the discursive realm. Human conduct, Giddens argued, is above all characterized by modes of discursive transformation and (moral) orientations around questions of accountability.[18]

However, this begs the question as to how Giddens would conceptualize the relationship between discourse and practice in the context of formally prescribed and stipulated acts of ritual practice, where the question of form, aesthetics, and ethics is intrinsically linked to the very understanding of agency as a culturally specific and effective form of (social, self-) transformation. As all of the chapters in Part II are centrally concerned with a discussion of identity in the disputed terrains of ritual conduct and performance, it is worthwhile to take up this specific point. For it seems to us that notions of agency are even more complex to fathom than it is indexed in Giddens' theory of action that, despite its universal claims, rests on a particular notion of self and subject that is not necessarily shared by the subjects in our encounters.

Scanning the academic literature on ritual, it appears that conceptualizations of ritual for considerable time went hand in hand with attempts to demonstrate the capacity of ritual to create and reassert group cohesion. Because of the sweeping claims that have resulted from such approaches in ritual studies, scholars have more recently re-interpreted the notion of ritual in the context of performance theory, in the context of a theory of embodiment, or dismissed the "mega-category of ritual" altogether (reminding us of Brubaker and Cooper's critique of such broad categories lacking analytic value).[19]

Webb Keane has convincingly argued that rituals are intrinsically linked to understandings of agency, while they do not necessarily correspond with a Western rational subject as the sole author and agent behind rituals as meaning-generating and socially transformative acts. He also shows that ritual complexes, especially if they entail the transaction (or expenditure) of material goods (such as animal sacrifice), become key sites for understanding the contest over boundaries of putatively hegemonic discourses on religious and national identity. This does not suggest that a new, "imaginary" (understood in the specific sense of connotatively "inauthentic") quality of the ritual practices is necessarily being "re-invented" in every case. Rather—and this is something the chapters in this volume highlight as well—ritual practices may serve as empowering mechanisms (for individuals or for sub-groups within a larger collective) even as they appropriate the language of subservience.

Empowerment in this context can be understood in terms of the ability to project new meanings of selfhood that acquire extrinsic, as well as intrinsic value, symbolic as well as economic capital. To that end, all of the chapters in this part of the volume emphasize the agentive component of ritual praxis, which serves as a point of engagement for the acceptance—or rejection—of an actor's symbolic communication of authenticity, sincerity, and spiritual or moral authority by others, and the reflexive nature of ritual, which serves to orient the individual (or group) to particular productions of subjectivity that may appropriate the language of a more dominant group, philosophy, or worldview. Rituals as bodily practices might underscore sincerity of purpose and mark piety; they help forge new, economically and spiritually lucrative relationships; they underscore connections with the past, enabling a sense of rightful belonging; and they facilitate the emergence of well-respected players in highly charged, emotive practices that encapsulate the worldview of a group self-identified as a faith community.

In the case of Sufi mystics, a sense of Muslim "self" in relation to others can appear rather more ambiguous, if ritual performances that simultaneously draw upon devotion to "Islamic" (i.e., grounded in notions of Islamic Shari'a) and "universal" moral and ethical visions of faith are any indication. Particularly in recent decades, such performances may serve to maintain or open avenues for group cohesion and redefinition, as the chapter by Kelly Pemberton demonstrates. For the "servants" (*khadims*) of the renowned shrine of the Sufi saint Mu'in ud-din Chishti in the northwest Indian state of Rajasthan, acts of identification and naming carried out by them serve to cultivate relationships of sacred exchange. Calling these acts "rhetorical strategies," Pemberton argues that by highlighting or de-emphasizing the aspects of Mu'in ud-din's identity that evoke themes of communal harmony, the *khadims* are able to acquire, retain, and meet the needs of the diverse pool of clients who visit the shrine seeking the favors of the saint. They are also able, with these strategies, to reinforce their claims of spiritual authority and qualification to represent the saint and mediate competing claims of "authenticity" in order to distinguish themselves as "good" Muslims in response to Islamic reformers' criticisms of contemporary Sufi shrines and their servants. Pemberton's chapter lays out a number of variables to highlight the ambivalence that characterizes attempts on the part of the *khadims* to balance their own sense of Islamic propriety with their obligation to serve the needs of pilgrims, many of whom are not Muslim. She argues that in the case of the Chishti servants of Mu'in ud-din's shrine, notions of "Islamic," "authentic," and "universal" values are articulated in response to strategies for cultivating and sustaining relationships of sacred exchange, and that the *khadims* must be able to deftly shift among all three concepts in order to remain effective and convincing to their clients. At the same time, she sees these acts of identification as producing a kind of dissonance among the *khadims*, who are in fierce competition with each other for clients and other resources, who remain keenly aware of their status as a controversial minority among Muslims, and whose ranks are plagued by corruption.

Sharing this perspective on the practical mastery of ritual and its multiple implications for the process of identity formation, the chapter by Michael Nijhawan highlights processes of contestation and internal ambiguity when deliberating on the production of alternative discourses within a particular field of religious practice. While the *dhadi* singer-performers and orators with whom Nijhawan interacted often characterized their community's voice as one that has been devalued under the contemporary system of patronage, Nijhawan warns against viewing such discontent simply as the staging grounds of resistance to the "normative" values of Sikhi. Nijhawan's hermeneutic pivots upon two key problematics: one, an interrogation of the conceptual frameworks of reflexivity and agency as destabilizing mechanisms vis-à-vis fixed notions of community identity, and two, an evaluation of subjective processes of self-identification as mechanisms that transform and are transformed by subjects' perceptions of the inherent potentials of religious languages and practices. Nijhawan argues that the connections between *dhadi* singer-performers and Sikh patrons can be characterized in part through prevailing idioms of hegemonic relations. *Dhadi* discourse and practice has increasingly come to be identified with a particular version of Sikh Khalsa identity. Adopting Sikh principles of moral authority and pious conduct along with outward markers of Sikh identity (such as the adoption of the symbols of Khalsa) has become instrumental to the performance of Sikh dhadi. Nonetheless, the *dhadi* performers' criticisms of Sikh disdain toward their community is often cast in a language of servitude that is reminiscent of traditional patron–client relations in Punjab, in which the bard occupies the position of the low-caste *mirasi*. Yet the language of social orphanage, Nijhawan argues, is translated into a reflexive and affirmative form of self-identification that transcends the notion of subjugation, by making use of what Nijhawan refers to as the "emancipatory potential" of the language and idioms of the dominant Sikh model. Looking at performative contexts through the lens of the "performative voice," Nijhawan sees some of the connections between performance and social power as indexing a process of self-assertion: Social differences between the *dhadi* and other groups within the Sikh community are subsumed under a more encompassing (and potentially self-transforming) concept of morality and piety through which *dhadi* performers are able to reassert their centrality in the Sikh domain.

A FINAL WORD

The written and the oral; the performed, embodied, and articulated; localized, nationalized, and universally conceived notions of belonging: the chapters brought together in this volume are motivated by a common interest in exploring some of the intricacies of these relationships. The twin notions of "shared idioms" and "sacred symbols" that shape this volume suggest both a search for common ground and boundary-drawing processes at work in the articulation of identities, while individual chapters seek to locate "sites" of these two modes of identification and some of the conditions that give rise to them. The rubric that frames this volume ultimately seeks to accomplish this task by highlighting and problematizing the truth-claims of unitary, coherent markers of community and tradition. While exposing the ways in which language, history, historiography, poetry, and other forms of literature can be used to challenge artificial separations between cultural and religious realms of activity, and sources of received tradition, it also suggests ways in which political and sectarian uses of language and literature (especially those that seek to evoke visions of the "nation" as a unitary bloc) can reveal persistent tensions—or ongoing re-imaginings—within communities often conceived as homogeneous, coherent entities with a common orientation and worldview. Finally, our individual and collaborative modes of investigation seek to contribute to the pool of current debates about the emergence of strategies of cultural reproduction during periods of rapid or significant social and political change while also suggesting an alternative order of knowledge and thought that calls into question the characterization of "tradition," or "traditional knowledge," as a field of unchanging (or, alternatively, finite) topoi.

NOTES

1. New contributions in the area of South Asian studies include Bidyut Chakraborty, ed., *Communal Identity in India: Its Construction and Articulation in the Twentieth Century* (New York: Oxford University Press, [2003] 2005); Laura Dudley Jenkins, *Identity and Identification in India: Defining the Disadvantaged* (London: Routledge/Curzon, 2002); David Gilmartin and Bruce B. Lawrence, *Beyond Turk and Hindu: Rethinking Religious Identities in Islamicate South Asia* (Gainesville: University Press of Florida, 2000). On the notion of identity in social theory, see Stuart Hall and Paul du Gay, *Questions of Cultural Identity* (London: Sage, 1996), and Peter Wagner, *A Sociology of Modernity: Liberty and Discipline* (New York: Routledge, 1998).
2. See, for example, Leela Fernandes, *India's New Middle Class* (Minneapolis: University of Minnesota Press, 2006); Carol A. Breckenridge, ed., *Consuming Modernity: Public Culture in a South Asian World* (Minneapolis: University of Minnesota Press, 1995); Bernard S. Cohn "The Census, Social Structure, and Objectification in South Asia," in *An Anthropologist Among the Historians and Other Essays, ed.* Bernard S. Cohn (Delhi: Oxford University Press, 1987): 224–254.
3. The difficulty, if not impossibility, of defining "postmodern" is one we acknowledge. We signal, by our use of the term, a set of critical analyses that employ concepts such as difference, articulation, strategic, contingency, and agency in order to to call into question ideas such as identity, homogeneity, essential, and (unequivocal) meaning.
4. See, for instance, Paul Brass, *The Politics of India Since Independence* (Cambridge: Cambridge University Press, 1994), and *The Production of Hindu–Muslim Violence in Contemporary India* (Seattle: University of Washington Press, 2003); Bankey Bihari Misra, *The Indian Middle Classes: Their Growth in Modern Times* (London: Oxford University Press, 1961); Pranab Bardhan, *Scarcity, Conflicts, and Cooperation* (Cambridge, MA: MIT Press, 2005); Thomas Blom Hansen, *Wages of Violence: Naming and Identitiy in Postcolonial Bombay* (Princeton, NJ: Princeton University Press, 2001).
5. See, in particular, Veena Das, *Life and Words: Violence and the Descent into the Ordinary* (Berkeley, CA: University of California Press, 2007), as well as Roma Chatterji and Deepak Mehta, *Living with Violence: An Anthropology of Events and Everyday Life* (London/New York: Routledge, 2007).
6. A number of works have enumerated the problems with these concepts. See, for instance, Talal Asad, *Genealogies of Religion* (Baltimore: Johns Hopkins

Press, 1993); Charles Stewart, "Syncretism and Its Synonyms: Reflections on Cultural Mixture," *Diacritics* 29, no. 3 (1999): 40–62; and Charles Stewart and Rosalind Shaw, *Syncretism/Anti-Syncretism: The Politics of Religious Synthesis* (London, New York: Routledge, 1994). Other works have suggested ways in which the syncretism/hybridity hermeneutic might be useful for theorizing about socio-cultural admixtures. See, for instance, Homi Bhabha, *The Location of Culture* (London, New York: Routledge, 1994); Vassilis Lambropoulos, "Syncretism as Mixture and Method," *Journal of Modern Greek Studies* 19, no. 2 (2001): 221–235; and Pnina Werbner and Tariq Modood, ed., *Debating Cultural Hybridity: Multi-Cultural Identities and the Politics of Anti-Racism* (London: Zed Books, 1997).

7. Tony Stewart, "In Search of Equivalence: Conceiving Hindu–Muslim Encounter Through Translation Theory," *History of Religions* 40, no. 3 (Feb 2001): 260–287.
8. Rogers Brubaker and Frederick Cooper, "Beyond Identity," *Theory and Society* 29 (2000): 1.
9. Ibid., 6
10. For this point, see Asad, *Genealogies of Religion*, and his *Formations of the Secular: Christianity, Islam, Modernity* (Stanford: Stanford University Press, 2003); and Chandra Mohanty, *Feminism Without Borders: Decolonizing Theory, Practicing Solidarity* (Durham, NC: Duke University Press, 2003); Naomi Sakai, *Translation and Subjectivity: On "Japan" and Cultural Nationalism* (Minneapolis: University of Minnesota Press 1997); Gayatri Chakravorty Spivak, "Translating into English," in *Nation, Language, and the Ethics of Translation,* ed. Sandra Bermann and Michael Wood (Princeton, NJ: Princeton University Press, 2005), 93–110.
11. Maria C. Lugones and Elizabeth V. Spelman, "Have We Got a Theory for You! Feminist Theory, Cultural Imperialism, and the Demand for 'The Woman's Voice'," *Women's Studies International Forum* 6, no. 2 (1983): 573–581.
12. See Arjun Appadurai, "Dead Certainty: Ethnic Violence in the Era of Globalization," *Public Culture* 10, no. 2 (1998): 225–247.
13. Stuart Hall, "The Future of Identity," in *Modernity and Its Futures*, ed. Tony McGrew and Stuart Hall (Cambridge: Polity Press, 1992), 274–316.
14. Gilmartin and Lawrence, *Beyond Turk and Hindu Identities in Islamicate*, 2.
15. Pierre Bourdieu, *Outline of a Theory of Practice* (Cambridge: Cambridge University Press, [1977] 2004), 72.
16. For this critique of the habitus and the notion of self-cultivation, see Saba Mahmood, *Politics of Piety: Islamic Revival and the Feminist Subject* (Princeton, NJ: Princeton University Press, 2005).
17. Anthony Giddens, *Central Problems in Social Theory: Action, Structure and Contradiction in Social Analysis* (Berkeley: University of California Press, 1979).
18. In Giddens' view, people do not simply self-reflexively draw on multiple discourses or registers already extant within social structures when speaking about themselves or others. Rather, there are a limited variety of processes of identification and naming available to the social actor that may evolve or be modified with time and circumstance (as experiences, values, and the influences that shape them shift), that are sometimes accessible outside of any particular set of conditions or forces that gave rise to them, and that shape, as well as refract, those forces. In Giddens' framework this is not to deny a role to unconscious, or "unreflected" action, but rather to call attention to the reflexive "monitoring" of action in everyday life: the ability to anticipate

the arrival of new (whether unexpected or expected) "information" while simultaneously relating it to older ingrained, innate, or otherwise internalized "information."

19. A discussion of the newer and intriguing developments in ritual theory is beyond the scope of this edited volume. We can tentatively define ritual as a performative act framed by social convention and consisting of various forms of symbolic communication that are to different degrees formalized, iterable, and/or dramatic (as they are embedded in a field of power relations in which the potentials and risks of social transformation materialize). Nonetheless, the precise question of how ritual informs processes of identity formation largely depends on the particular school of ritual theory to which one subscribes. Thus, in a neo-Durkheimian perspective, rituals are explained in their mimetic function in relation to the social collective as a whole; Batesonians instead consider the relational aspects of ritual form, defining "identity" (of ritual participants) as a result of the differential effects of ritual processes. Anthropologists in the tradition of the Manchester school point to the fundamental social conflicts that underlie the performance of ritual and thus imagine identity and its contestation as being the result of ritual drama, while in performance theory, ritual acts constitute social identities through their illocutionary force, that is, their capability to create and transform social relations and reassert social entities in repeated practical (linguistic and symbolic) enactments. For further discussion, see in particular Catherine Bell, *Ritual Theory, Ritual Practice* (Berkeley: University of California Press, 1992) and Caroline Humphrey and James Laidlaw, *The Archetypal Actions of Ritual: A Theory of Ritual Illustrated by the Jain Rite of Worship* (Oxford: Oxford University Press, 1994).

Part I

Landscapes of Translation

Linguistics, History, and Culture in Focus

1 A House Overturned

A Classical Urdu Lament in Braj Bhasha

Amy Bard and Valerie Ritter

"The specific tension between father and sons, earlier and later texts, suggests the model of translation itself:* the carrying over of the text in a way that may be blatantly imitative, disguised, misguided, misread, reread, recreated, or intentionally mistranslated."*

Opening verse of an Urdu marsiyah poem by Mir Babar 'Ali Anis	**"Verses on the Topic of Offspring," from the Braj Bhasha by Hariaudh**
1. There's no better wealth in the world than a son.	Once you've seen a succulent fruit, no other taste can appeal [like it again].
There's no better comfort than repose for the heart.	Once you've known the soft flower, no fragrance can appeal [like it again].
There's no better taste than a succulent fruit's.	There is no other happiness like a joyful heart.
There's no better fragrance than the aroma of a fresh rose.	There's no wealth better in the world than a son.
For the crippled heart under assault, only he is a cure.	When assaults fall upon the wounded heart, he alone is the pleasing cure.
Only he is sustenance, he satisfaction, he the soul.	He alone is the body and soul, he alone the lotus flower, he alone the essence of soma.

INTRODUCTION

This chapter is a case study of linguistic and cultural transformation at the turn of the twentieth century, and of the process and products of translation. The reformist literary undertaking we examine, an early twentieth-century Indian "lament" adapted from Urdu into Hindi's literary Braj Bhasha dialect, demonstrates how translation sometimes illustrates the dialectics of writing as fascinatingly as "the paradigm of original creation itself."[1]

The versatile writer Ayodhyasimh Upadhyay "Hariaudh" (1865–1947), in one of his many ingenious literary projects, artfully showcased the "difference-in-sameness" that has always characterized the continuum of Hindi and Urdu language and literature, yet he produced this difference in specific ways. Hariaudh, a Hindu writer of Hindi, engaged intensely with Urdu and Urdu poets. His "Verses on the Topic of Offspring," in *The World*[2] *of Love: A Collection of Poems on Love* ("Santanvishayini kavita" in *Premprapanc arthat premsambandhi kavitavali*),[3] document his literary encounter with famed Urdu *marsiyah*-writer Mir Babar 'Ali Anis (1802–1874). This endeavor of Hariaudh's is a particularly intriguing case of the "double authorship" that is inherent in literary translation, and especially, as comparative literature scholar Willis Barnstone points out, in poetry with its many layers of "aesthetic, phonic, and expressive" meaning.[4] Launching his lament from a formulaic and lachrymose Urdu *marsiyah* poem, Hariaudh certainly "recognizes and resurrects" the Urdu text's author, Anis, but also "actively determines our understanding, reception, and evaluation of the source in a re-creation that ultimately vies with the 'original' for authority and originality."[5]

In the nineteenth and early twentieth centuries, impassioned recitations of *marsiyah*s, often at least an hour long, with their battles, long drawn-out death scenes, and families riven apart, were the centerpiece of Shi'i Muslim mourning assemblies commemorating the martyred Imam Husain. The genre entered the Urdu literary canon largely because of the virtuosic contributions of Anis. *Marsiyah*s still remain a staple of the religious observances of *Muharram*, although today's performances feature a scaled-down role, curtailed length, and simplified diction. How did Hariaudh reinterpret this Arabic- and Persian-inspired South Asian genre rooted in Shi'i Muslim rituals, and in the process confront the linguistic and literary quandaries of Hindi and Urdu's historical status as "one language, two scripts"?[6] At the heart of this experiment is Hariaudh's reconstruction of certain thematic and stylistic features of Anis's work into Braj Bhasha as Hinduized (but perhaps also universal) verses on grief. The result can be read, one on hand, against the rest of Hariaudh's oeuvre and the concerns of modern Hindi canon-building, and on the other, against the religious and performative context of Anis's original narrative work as it was known to its late nineteenth-century audience.

2. Only he can make the parents' hearts bud profusely	Only by having a son will the bud of the parents' heart bloom.
He's the flower to make a household the envy of a rose-garden	The garden looks into the home and is put to shame by this flower alone.
He alone is the making of comfort and repose	From him alone is the abundance of happiness and enjoyment.
He stands as the people's crown of humanity	From him alone shines the abode, the image of the glory of man.
How can the heart bloom if one lacks vital organs?	How much is the heart bloomed, if love for the son doesn't remain?

A home is worse than the grave if it lacks a son	A house is worse than a cremation ground, without a son; people in the world reckon thus.

Anis's and Hariaudh's poems creatively manipulate affective and artistic responses to the broadly resonant sentiment of parental love. Hariaudh's "Verses on the Topic of Offspring," however, are probably notable more for their quirky stylistic and linguistic elements than for their emotive qualities. While Hariaudh was far from the only Hindu poet or Hindi poet of his era to delve into ritualized Shi'i lament genres, his treatment of the *marsiyah* is unique for its almost complete excision of Urdu vocabulary and overtly Islamic characters.[7] In one example, upon which we will elaborate here, Hariaudh replaces the Qur'anic Jacob and Joseph of Anis's original work with King Dasarath and Ram of the Hindu *Ramayana*:

7. Ask its master about what it's like when a well-filled home is overturned.	Approach and ask the father of a full house about its demise.
Ask the members of that household about what it's like when they're scattered apart.	Ask the people of the house about the sadness inside it
Ask a mother and a father about what it's like when fortune's laid waste.	Ask the parents about the ruination of their fate.
Ask Jacob about what it's like when Joseph's torn away from him.	Ask King Dasharatha about the separation of Ram's banishment.
May God not let us see sorrow over the light of our eyes.	Hariaudh says, may God not ever show me grief for a beloved son.
For it'll then be the blood of the heart and soul that flows from our eyes.	The blood of the heart, the whole body, flows through the eyes.

Examined together, Anis's and Hariaudh's poems illuminate the range of vocabulary and imagery available to Hindi and Urdu writers of the early twentieth century, the Hindi movement's willful alignment of lexicon and diction with religious identity, and the processes whereby readers, including but not limited to literary translators, become interpreters and authors of texts.

HINDI AND URDU

Hindi and Urdu are Modern Indo-Aryan languages that emerged in the area around Delhi in the eleventh and twelfth centuries CE. Persian and Turkic newcomers to India—including employees of the Sultanate rulers who participated in an enduring "ethnic and linguistic pluralism"—adopted the language of the capital to communicate with the local inhabitants, and quickly added to it a vast stock of Persian and Arabic words.[8] The resulting common core of spoken Hindi-Urdu, sometimes called Khari Boli ("standard," "standing" speech) is one justification for considering Hindi and Urdu one language. The historical contours and defining points of the Hindi–Urdu continuum, though, remain matters of dispute and scholarly discussion, complicated by the rather flexible usages of several nomenclatures.

"Hindi," written in a Devanagari script derived from Sanskrit, is now a national language of India, and "Urdu," with its Perso-Arabic script, is the national language of Pakistan. Linguist Colin P. Masica notes succinctly in his *Indo-Aryan Languages* that the two are "based on the same linguistically-defined subdialect [i.e., Dehlavi, a.k.a. Khari Boli]. At the colloquial level, in terms of grammar and core vocabulary, they are virtually identical. . . . At formal and literary levels, however, vocabulary [differs] . . . to the point where the two languages/styles become mutually unintelligible."[9] The languages, then, share a foundation of Indic grammar, with many Sanskritized elements in written and the higher spoken register of Hindi, and Persio-Arabic elements in Urdu. Today, the vocabulary, diction, and sayings that are largely common to Hindi and Urdu form the spoken vernacular of North India and Pakistan and the language of the popular culture typified by Bollywood films. The British administrator John Gilchrist was said to have coined the term "Hindustani" for the colonial-era version of this widely spoken tongue in the late eighteenth century, though there are scattered earlier references to it.[10]

In India, native speakers employed other labels rather fluidly, with discrete categories emerging only in the nineteenth century. The word "Hindi" comes from an early term for the Indus River, and as "India" was referred to as "Hind" in Persian, "Hindi" often simply designated something "Indian." The term "Urdu" derives from the Turkic word for the army camp where the spoken vernacular is supposed to have largely developed. As late as the eighteenth and nineteenth centuries, however, poets referred to what would now be called "Urdu" as *rekhta*, which distinguished their highly Persianized literary language from Persian itself, and probably also from the colloquial Hindi or Urdu that "smacked of the bazaar and rough uncultured armies."[11]

A number of pre-modern North Indian dialects, including Hindavi and Braj Bhasha, also lent themselves to poetic production, especially expressions of *bhakti* (devotionalism). Braj Bhasha, for example, was associated with works about the god Krishna, and it was not unusual for Muslim Mughal rulers to patronize its poets. At the same time, by the late fourteenth century, *bhakti* poets had been influenced by the Persian genres of mystical Islam, and Sufi poets were composing in Indian vernaculars as well as in Persian, giving rise to a literary tradition that, according to Aditya Behl, "marks the full indigenization and assimilation of Islam into an Indian cultural landscape."[12] The texts related to this tradition, especially Sufi romances (*masnavis* and *prem-kahanis*) were long written in both Devanagari and Persio-Arabic scripts. Many writers, whether "Hindu" or "Muslim," drew on conventions from both Indic and Persian literary legacies to represent the human relationship with the divine. Several *bhakti* poets (notably Kabir and Nanak), however, whose works date to the late fifteenth and sixteenth centuries, "distanced themselves from distinctive Hindu and Muslim symbols" by emphasizing worship of a formless (*nirguna*) god.[13]

In the 1860s, with various strains of nationalism on the rise and regional linguistic movements, religious reform movements, and an agitation for vernacular education all gaining impetus in India, there were pronounced moves to distinguish Indic from Islamic, and Hindi from Urdu. Hariaudh's elaborate re-casting of Anis's *marsiyah* poem points up how an earlier "Hindustani" lingua franca, written in either script (although the Urdu script was dominant), and without regard to any politics of etymological provenance, underwent a transformation in the late nineteenth century. "Hindi" became associated with the classical and ritual language of Sanskrit, the Devanagari script, as well as the variety of religious practices known as "Hinduism," in contradistinction to "Urdu," associated with Persian, Arabic, a modified Persian script, and Islam. Hariaudh's transcreation was a very concrete literary example, even a culmination, of this trend.

His effort, especially his choice of a religiously imbued text to translate, is also a startling testament to the way in which languages, as Sumathi Ramaswamy puts it, "attract multiple, even contrary imaginings" as they "are subjected to the passions of all those interested in empowering them."[14] The substitutions and excisions Hariaudh made even provide an intriguing foreshadowing of modern national products such as the Sanskritized Hindi television news, which Indians often joke cannot be easily understood by ordinary Hindi speakers. In Hariaudh's own literary realm, this transcreation was one of a number of projects that recycled Persianate genres for the Hindi movement. Significantly, despite Hariaudh's Sanskritized product, his verses here are quite faithful in spirit—and sometimes in verbal detail—to their Urdu original, much more so than better-known Hindi appropriations such as Maithilisaran Gupta's Urdu-inspired *Bharat-Bharati*, or the early Hindi bestseller, *Candrakanta*, based on the *dastan* genre.[15]

To complicate our analysis of "difference-in-sameness," Hariaudh's poem is written in the Braj Bhasha dialect (often called "Braj" for short) alluded to previously. The closest ancestor in Devanagari script of modern Hindi, Braj Bhasha was a cosmopolitan poetic register with earthy, folksy undertones, utilizing motifs from Hindu devotionalism and Sanskrit poetics, and having distinctive phonological and grammatical traits. Braj became a literary dialect of the regional and Mughal courts, and was used widely from the sixteenth to the twentieth century, at which point poetry began to be written in a modern register of Hindi that followed spoken Hindi-Urdu grammar and more proper Sanskrit phonology. Hariaudh was one of the last poets of Braj Bhasha, which in the late nineteenth century began to represent the "Hindi" poetic tradition for Hindi supporters in the Hindi-Urdu language debates. Hence, Hariaudh's translation from Urdu was actually into Braj Bhasha, but a Braj Bhasha that signified the Hindi/ Hindu equivalence to its early twentieth-century audience.

AYODHYASIMH UPADHYAY "HARIAUDH" AND THE HINDI MOVEMENT

Hariaudh, a small-town pandit born in 1865, was part of the early group of followers of the Hindi movement, a political movement for public instruction and regional administration in the Devanagari script, which was allied with Hindu objection to Muslim politico-cultural power. The Hindi movement began in the 1870s with the leadership of the "Father of Hindi Literature" himself, Bharatendu Hariscandra of Varanasi,[16] and it flourished with the establishment of an institution for the cause in Varanasi in 1893. Hariaudh was an early member of this Society for the Promotion of Nagari (Nagari Pracarini Sabha), whose library and publications remain primary resources for the study of modern Hindi literature.[17]

Hariaudh himself was a bit of a backwater fellow. He was a schoolteacher and registrar of land accounts ("registrar *qanun-go*") for most of his life in the district town Azamgarh, about sixty miles—at least a day's carriage ride—from Varanasi. Later he moved to Varanasi to teach at the famous Banaras Hindu University, the brainchild of the nationalist leader Madan Mohan Malaviya. By then he was famed as an author in *shuddh* (pure) Sanskritized Hindi, by dint of his 1914 *Priyapravas*, a *mahakavya* poem in modern Hindi, but in Sanskrit meters, and with hardly any Persian vocabulary.[18] He died in May of 1947, shortly before India's Independence and Partition. In 1950, the Constitution of India established Hindi in the Nagari script as the official language of the Union, giving realization to the goals of the Hindi movement. Hindi literary curricula expanded throughout India, and Hariaudh has remained a part of this canon to the present day.

Hariaudh's relationship to Urdu literature was complex and profound, although few of the details of his connection to Urdu survive in the Hindi canonical consciousness. He lived in the time of the Hindi–Urdu controversy and must have imbibed the rhetoric of "Hindi for Hindus" and of "purification" from "foreign elements" in language and culture, for the cause of a Hindu nation. He was one of the Brahmans who, Alok Rai has shown, felt there was something to gain by legislating the use of Sanskrit's Nagari script.[19] However, the complexity of the Hindi–Urdu debate was demonstrated by at least one anecdote from Hariaudh's own life. He composed a poem for recitation at the NPS's celebration of its new facilities in 1904, but this Hindi poem drew criticism for its Urdu metrical form, exemplifying the difficulties of extricating "Hindi" from "Urdu" in this period.

Hariaudh came to the Hindi movement as a young man. His hometown of Azamgarh was a center of Urdu poetry, led by the critic Muhammad Shibli Nu'mani (1857–1914), whom he knew; Hariaudh had also trained in Urdu and Persian for his employment. In 1889 Hariaudh published a Hindi translation of an Urdu translation of Shakespeare's *Merchant of Venice*, as *Venis ka banka* (*The Dandy of Venice*) out of a Hindi press in Kolkata.[20] The circumstances of the creation of this translation are of note: Hariaudh made this translation into "pure Hindi" from an "Urdu" translation of this work in a recent magazine at the request of the district Deputy Inspector of Schools, Syam Manohar Das. Hariaudh reported his response to this request, and his interchange with Das, as follows:

> "Urdu is itself a version [*rupantar* (difference of [visible] form)] of Hindi, what would be a translation of it?!" [Das] said, "I desire that all Persian and Arabic words in the Urdu translation be changed, and that those sentences that are formed in the style of Urdu be given the color of Hindi."[21]

Thus, it appears that Hariaudh's introduction to the Hindi movement, and likely his "conversion" to it, occurred with this Sanskritized Shakespearean translation. From this narrative, it seems he inherited also the current notional idea that Urdu had a particular grammatical style, which according to modern Hindi norms, involved "syntactic inversions."[22]

In this same year, Das procured a job for Hariaudh at the district collector's office in Azamgarh, and during his years of government service, his career as a writer began to flourish. In the next fifteen years he published twenty works of collected poetry, dramas, novels, and translations. In 1900, Hariaudh published a trilogy of poetic volumes with publisher Khemraj Krshnadas of the Sri Venkatesvar Press of Mumbai, publisher of Hindi and Sanskrit works distributed throughout India and even worldwide.[23] These were a "water of love" series: *The Current of the Water of Love, The Flowing of the Water of Love,* and *The Ocean of the Water of Love* (*Premambu pravah, Premambu prasravan,* and *Premambu varidhi*). All three expressed conventional devotional sentiments for Krishna in the various metrical forms of Braj Bhasa verse, and displayed various literary sentiments such as the pain of separation (*viraha*), the entreaty or rebuke of God (*vinaya*), and poems depicting the pitiful and peaceful sentiments (*karuna* and *santa rasa*s), which literary "moods" were in fashion of late. The Braj Bhasa that Hariaudh used was, as has been mentioned, a linguistic register identified with "Hindi" as opposed to "Urdu" in a generic sense. At the turn of the century, Braj was still considered a viable medium for modern literature.

Concurrently with the *Water of Love* trilogy, Hariaudh produced a "transcreation" of Urdu verse through this same Mumbai press. In yet a fourth title on the topic of love in this year 1900, Hariaudh published our text at hand, *The World of Love*, comprised of translations into Braj Bhasa of verse by the Urdu authors Mirza Rajab 'Ali Beg "Surur" (1787–1867) and Mir Babar 'Ali Anis (1802–1874). This work's register, structure, and voice featured a most unusual amalgam of literal translation and authorial license. The first section was a translation of the couplets interspersed in Surur's 1824 Urdu fantastical narrative, the *Tale of Wonders* [*Fasana-eajaib*], and the second section, which concerns us here, was a translation of verses by Anis. Both sections appended verses of Hariaudh's own composition.

The publication of *The World of Love*, while ostensibly an ecumenical pursuit translating across lines of script/language/religion, in fact helped to create divisions. The introduction had an extremely Sanskritized lexicon, such that it practically represents an ideological statement of the identity of Hindi with the Hindu. While Hariaudh's introductions in the preceding *Water of Love* series were formal but generally plain-speaking, here, the *tatsama* Sanskrit words abound, and he also invokes a common Hindi chauvinist argument that not all of the original verses of Surur were fit to translate because of occasional "obscenity" [*aslilbhav*].[24] This represents a view quite consonant with the common insinuation by Hindi proponents of the moral decadence of the culture of Urdu poetry, and Islam by extension.[25] But more than "cleaning up" these Urdu verses, Hariaudh may have wanted to prove the worth of Braj as a medium "in the league" of Urdu, as well as prove its difference from Urdu. His words on these verses follow:

> There are two subjects worthy of consideration in this work: One, is the sweetness of Braj distinct from the sweetness of Urdu or not? Two, despite the spoken form of Urdu and Hindi being almost the same, how much difference is there in the language of the poets of both languages, and how separate are the particular styles of both of them?; when the gentlemen connoisseurs of Bhasha[26] compare [these with] the Urdu versions, they will be amazed in this regard.[27]

> . . . here and there in the translation there is the defect of stiltedness and elsewhere, the feeling of Urdu is put into the translation. . . . the connoisseurs of Bhasha will see how our dear Braj Bhasha can make room for the mannerisms of another language excellently, in its beautiful and noble manner.[28]

Hariaudh clearly perceives his translation project as one of possible equivalence—making room for Urdu's mannerisms—but one bridging profound difference—the "sweetness" (the commonplace term for the beauty of a language) of Braj and Urdu, respectively, differs. His impetus in transcreating remains puzzling; did he want to show the undervalued Braj "competent to" the task of equaling Urdu and its sweetness and its mannerisms, or to prove Braj not only distinct but also superior in its "noble manner"?

Hariaudh likely found a certain universality in motif and affect across the Urdu and Braj poetic traditions. The verses he translated from Surur's *The Tale of Wonders* in the main body of his *World of Love* were not unlike those from his previous *Water of Love* works, in that they abound with the pangs of love in separation, the cruelty of the beloved, and other aspects of separation, or *viyog*. Certain of the verses had been "Hinduized" with mention of the Hindu mythological characters Sita, Ravana, and Rukmini, implying a certain equivalence between the characters of Hindu and Muslim mythologies.[29] The appended verses from Anis, "concerning offspring," in the original elaborate the importance of the son for the family legacy. In Hariaudh's transcreation, they lie nearer to the *vatsalya bhava* often found exemplified in poetry on the child Krishna, the affective state of feeling parental love for a child in the practice of devotion for Krishna, as elaborated in Chaitanyite Vaishnavism.[30] Consonant with the other verses in this volume, he Hinduized the Qur'anic Jacob and Joseph with the *Ramayana*'s Dasaratha and Ram. The verses also ring true to the categories of *sokgit*, songs of grief, and *vilap*, lamentation, both of which appear in Sanskrit literature onwards. Notably, the category of *sokgit* had come into prominence in late nineteenth-century Bengali with several publications engaging with English lyric elegy modes in the voice of a bereaved widow or widower, or friend.[31] The *vilap*, or lamentation, which had so often been the mode of lovers in separation, was soon incorporated into the vocabulary of nationalism in the early decades of the twentieth century, with lamenting widows and mothers of heroes peopling the pages of Hindi poetic texts. Thus, Hariaudh wrote this transcreation in a trans-regional literary atmosphere that valued the poetics of mourning.

THE URDU MARSIYAH TRADITION

In creating the verses, Hariaudh drew upon a fundamentally Islamic—and specifically Shi'i Muslim—*marsiyah* tradition that immortalizes the valiant deaths of members of the Prophet Muhammad's family at a desolate site in what is now Iraq. *Marsiyah*s can be poems of tribute and lament upon the death of a family member, friend, or patron, but most Urdu *marsiyah*s describe the sufferings of the third Shi'i imam, Husain, and his family at Karbala in 61 A.H./680 C.E. Taken as a corpus of poems, the genre relates the entire chain of events surrounding the "great sacrifice"(*qurbani-e 'azim*) offered by Husain, the grandson of Prophet Muhammad. Whereas Ibrahim (Abraham), a primary and potent figure in Islamic narratives, displayed a devoted willingness to sacrifice his beloved son but was spared from doing so in the end, it was Husain's destiny to fulfill that spirit of sacrifice, and give up all of his family members, and his own life, for a higher cause.

Shi'i Muslims commemorate Husain's story and its moral lessons through processions, self-flagellation, acts of obeisance to sacred objects, and highly structured mourning assemblies during the month of Muharram, which has also become the name for these observances themselves. For Shi'ahs, the battle between Husain (626–680) and Yazid the Umayyad Caliph (d. 683) defines good, evil, and even true Islam, by revealing the extraordinary virtues of their revered *imams*, leaders of Muhammad's blood. Imam Husain refused to swear allegiance to Yazid or ignore cruelties that Yazid perpetrated in the name of Islam, although he foresaw that in the course of the conflict in the Karbala desert, he, his children, and his companions would be slaughtered, and his female relatives imprisoned.

Mu'awiyah, an erstwhile governor, had assumed the Muslim Caliphate once Husain's father 'Ali and his brother Hasan had been deposed and murdered. Yazid, Mu'awiyah's son, whom Shi'ahs characterize as a drunken reprobate, came to power upon his father's death in 60A.H./680 C.E. The political and spiritual conflict between Husain and Yazid eventually came to a head at Karbala, where Yazid's enormous army ultimately massacred Husain, his male relatives (including young children), and his small band of fighters. Husain was at the time journeying to Kufah in response to a request for his leadership from Muslims disenchanted with Yazid. After Husain's enemies beheaded him as he bowed in prayer, the general Ibn Sa'd paraded the women of the imam's household, unveiled, to Damascus.

Shi'ahs, those who identify with the supporters of Husain and his father (and their descendants) in the early generations of Islam, have for centuries related the whole Karbala story in minute detail; their renderings encompass the majesty and the human frailty of Husain as he fought tirelessly in the face of certain defeat, willingly sacrificed his life, and witnessed the painful persecution of every member of his family. Shi'i mourning assemblies (*majalis*; sing. *majlis*) even today replay this conflict, recounting the feats and trials of Husain and his companions through sermons, short dirges, and several genres of religious poetry, including the *marsiyah*. *Marsiyahs* first appeared in India as short, simple laments around the fifteenth century, but by the nineteenth century they were elaborate narrative poems of up to two hundred verses that incorporated vivid descriptions of desert heat and details of expert swordplay by Husain's men, as well as pathos-saturated scenes of warrior martyrdom, family partings, and small children tortured by Yazid's brutal henchmen.

One of the *marsiyah*'s most popular episodes, Husain's loss of his young, virile son 'Ali Akbar when Akbar is just at the cusp of manhood, of an age to marry and perpetuate the Prophet's lineage, is showcased in the original poem that Hariaudh re-works. Akbar's death is frequently presented in *majlis* literature as a final, devastating blow to Husain; once he searches out his beautiful, bloodied child on the battlefield and carries him back to camp, Husain's only desire is to join the boy in martyrdom. Mir Babar 'Ali Anis, the master poet of the *marsiyah* tradition and, according to some critics, one of the four greatest Urdu poets of all time, wrote dozens of *marsiyah*s about Akbar's martial feats and gruesome death, including the *marsiyah* Hariaudh adapted.

With decades of patronage by the Shi'i dynasty of Avadh kingdom, the enormous nineteenth-century gatherings in which Anis and his rival Dabir read their *marsiyah*s became as much poetry contests as religious rituals. Hariaudh would have been a child during Anis's later years, and because of the Hindi writer's later involvement with Urdu literary figures, especially Shibli, he undoubtedly knew Anis's reputation for eloquence and "natural" language. When it came to the intense competition fomented by admirers of Anis and Dabir, Shibli took a nuanced and influential pro-Anis stance in an early-twentieth-century opus that compared the two poets.[32]

REFORMISM AND EXPERIMENTATION IN LITERARY CRITICISM

The idea of Anis as an exponent of colloquial language and straightforward emotional expression may well have influenced Hariaudh when he selected a *marsiyah* for translation. The *marsiyah* in general was also known for a moral tone felt to be absent in the best-known Urdu genres, notably the popular *ghazal* love-lyric, and we have already seen how Hariaudh engaged with the contemporary discourse about Urdu's decadent or even "obscene" tendencies. As Ram Babu Saksena—one of many critics of the later twentieth century who still at times seemed to despise the very tradition they wrote about—put it, the *marsiyah* " . . . is a pleasant welcome from the revolting sensualism of the court muse. A *marsiya* howmuchsoever inferior it may be in point of artistic workmanship, is moral in its tone and Urdu poetry much needed this corrective."[33]

Hariaudh's other works also show that the notion of a poetry that was "natural" in terms of depictions of nature, or of "real life," and poetic styles considered free from artifice appealed to him. A preoccupation with reforming Indian poetry to make it more "natural" colored both Urdu and Hindi literary criticism in Hariaudh's era. Urdu scholar Frances Pritchett demonstrates how literary reformers such as Altaf Husain Hali and Muhammad Husain Azad advocated naturalism partially as a response to colonial critiques of sensual, artificial qualities in Urdu poetry (especially the *ghazal*) and in the "decadent" sensibility of the Indo-Muslim elite more broadly. Indeed, "natural poetry" (*necharal sha'iri* or *necharal po'itri*) became something of a watchword for much of nineteenth- and twentieth-century Urdu criticism.[34] The *marsiyah* held a particular attraction in this effort because of its basis in a historical event. Accordingly, while surreal or supernatural descriptions and narrative embellishments are actually some of the most distinctive and interesting aspects of the genre, Urdu critics like Qamar Azam Hashmi tend to argue for the *marsiyah*'s "realism," based on the historical core of the Karbala story:

> *Marsiyah* presents the events of Karbala, and all of the Karbala events are historically documented and preserved. The *marsiyah*-writer doesn't enjoy the convenience of being able to omit or add events or characters according to his will, to display the force of his imaginative powers, or to exhibit his quick wit and continually meddle with or edit fixed historical events.[35]

In the Shi'i context, the pride and loyalty, and the grief, that listeners express over the Karbala tragedy through weeping and breast-beating are communally oriented, ritualized, yet also intense and often internalized. *Marsiyah* had long attracted interest beyond the Shi'i community for these emotions that it depicts and elicits, which may partially account for why Hariaudh, proponent of a Hindi movement that denigrated Urdu, and a Brahman *pandit* to boot, might think to translate *marsiyah* verses. This inherent affective appeal ties in with a historical and biographical picture that illuminates and expands what might seem to be narrow social categories. "Hindus" participated in Muharram throughout decades of communalization.[36] Some Karbala-related laments in Avadhi (a folk and courtly literary "Hindi" dialect) still performed today across communal and sectarian lines almost certainly extend back into Hariaudh's time and social context. Finally, Hariaudh's religious background as a *sahajdhari* Sikh[37] would have entailed a *nirguna* theological context including a certain rejection of both Brahmanical and Islamic ritual—although obviously his own family's status as practicing Brahman would mitigate this principle for him in practice.

Literarily speaking, aside from Hariaudh's irrepressible urge toward experiment, we might posit two principles at work: (a) that he assumed a universality of the appeal of this genre—that is, that it was "worth translating," and (b) that a translation would produce something pleasurable—from the standpoint of either novelty or intellectual gaming—and perhaps useful for Hindi movement politics. He may have taken inspiration from an 1876 lamentation of Dasaratha by the famed litterateur Hariscandra himself.[38] At least partly, he must have been attracted to Anis's purported realism and natural qualities in vogue at the time. In the process of creation, he participates in the construction of Urdu poetry as "Other," while writing in a dialect of Hindi that would suggest a range of Hindu cultural associations, but would be less comprehensible, less decipherable, to its audience than its Urdu linguistic counterpart. We might say that Hariaudh's translation of Anis's *marsiyah*, although appealing to a universality of grief, actually *produces* difference between Urdu and Hindi, Muslims and non-Muslims.

THE PRODUCTION OF DIFFERENCE

On one level, Hariaudh appears to invoke an idea of literary and/or affective universality simply by dint of the possibility of translation of this text. By using a religiously marked genre such as the *marsiyah*, while obviously being quite aware, and perhaps protective, of his own difference from the Muslim community, Hariaudh seems to suggest that there is an inner core of the elegy that transcends religious community.[39] Some phrases that enter into Hariaudh's text, which are *not* translations from Anis, support this supposition. In verse 2, for instance, there is the broad claim that "people in the world reckon thus" (*jaga jana ganai*, 2.6), in reference to the statement that "the house is worse than a cremation ground, without a son" (this cremation ground [*masana*], though, is an alteration of the "grave" [*qabr*] of Anis's original, reflecting a "Hinduization" of the text). Other verses, such as verse 8, "let no one's tree be leafless" (*apata nahoya kamana taru kahuko*), also suggest a certain invocation of universal human pain, as do his repeated injections of "in the world" into his adaptation. The poem appears to be a meditation on the experience of grief for a son, in his death *or* in his absence, evident in the scene from the *Ramayana* invoked in verses seven and ten, of Ram's departure for his banishment in the forest. Here, this oft-remembered, emotionally charged moment signals a certain abstraction of grief from the *marsiyah* context per se.

The cast of Krishna devotion (the standard topic of Braj poetry) is unmistakable in the last verse and couplet, as Hariaudh states, "there is no wealth you can have, but that love toward the dear one." The consistent use of *lal* as the term of endearment in the poem, and playing on its homonym term "ruby"—and this is present in both the Urdu original and Hariaudh's version—suggests immediately the scores of poems in Braj Bhasha centered on the child Krishna, in which he is called "*lal*." The ending couplet begs to be read as an invocation of "The Child," that is, the child Krishna of much mythological and iconographic elaboration, the vision, or *darsan*, of whom can deliver salvation itself:

> Compared to all those who are called children, this child
> Surpasses, as you gaze at him, the body and soul, even one's own salvation.

Overall, however, in his almost platitudinous tone, Hariaudh seems to suggest a secular view of literature, presenting the *marsiyah* genre as a basically literary representation of a universal affect that is generically re-presentable in other religio-cultural contexts.

The particular *marsiyah* Hariaudh chose facilitated his project as few other poems of the genre would have. It features a slightly unusual introduction that catalogues, with an insistent, repetitive simplicity, the virtues of male offspring and the son as a source of pride and security for his parents. More commonly, *marsiyah*s directly reference in their initial lines a specific episode, even a distinct moment, from Husain's tragedy, signaling the ritual logic that transports listeners across space and time to Karbala. Some sample *marsiyah* titles/first lines are, for instance, "When the Bereft Zainab's Sons Fought in the Battlefield," and "When the Tormented Captives Set Off From Karbala, Robbed of All."[40] While about half of the best-known *marsiyah*s also allude in their first lines, by name or by epithet, to the main character they will feature, this work by Anis does not even name 'Ali Akbar until the eighth verse (and as it is not referenced in Hariaudh's poem, this verse is not included in the translation presented here). Urdu readers or listeners familiar with the context of the mourning assembly would still know instantly upon hearing the first line, "There is No Better Wealth in the World than a Son," that the eighteen-year-old 'Ali Akbar will be the poem's subject. It is, though, the generalized sentiments Anis invokes in the introduction that Hariaudh capitalizes on when he extracts this introduction from a Karbala context saturated with powerful personalities and specific, minutely chronicled events in the lives of the Prophet's descendants.

Hariaudh's work consists of seven *chappay* verses that are fairly close translations of the first seven verses of Anis's 180-verse poem, and an additional four verses of his own invention in a similar vein, followed by a closing couplet (*doha*).[41] In the original *marsiyah*, when Anis mentions the hero 'Ali Akbar for the first time, he launches immediately into a description of the series of farewells Akbar faces as he takes leave of his family and prepares for battle.[42] The hero, the battle, the laments of specific characters pivotal to the Shi'i tradition, and a whole technique of narrative are all set into motion here, but none of these hold interest for Hariaudh, and it is at this point that he instead grafts his own verses onto the piece.

In overall structure the Hindi poet echoes, but significantly alters, the Urdu form. In the translated stanzas, he employs a six-line *chappay* verse form that provides a good counterpart for the Urdu *musaddas* stanza; both verses are conceived as quatrains plus a couplet, though the metrical systems for Hindi and Urdu are, importantly, different.[43] As has been pointed out, Hariaudh also excises the words in these verses that would be primarily associated with Islamic contexts, or even with Indo-Persian poetry very broadly. Anis compares Akbar to a "fresh rose" (the ubiquitous symbolic love object in Persian and Urdu poetry), while Hariaudh's plant imagery incorporates the *soma* plant used in Vedic rituals. The Hindi poet sometimes re-orders lines, but it is a testament to how faithful he is to most of Anis's individual lines that these inversions are immediately apparent.

One of the most striking of the re-orderings is in the first verse itself. Anis's original reads:

There's no better wealth in the world than a son.
There's no better comfort than repose for the heart.

There's no better taste than a succulent fruit's.
There's no better fragrance than the aroma of a fresh rose.
For the crippled heart under assault, only he is the cure.
Only he is sustenance, he satisfaction, he the soul.

An Urdu poem's first line (the *matla'*) is crucial both in terms of aesthetic impact and categorization: It is the basis for listing the poem, and determines its placement in a written work. In literary collections, the rhyme scheme exemplified in the first line is the ordering principle, while *marsiyah* anthologies used for recitations during Muharram are often organized according to the character or event referenced in the *matla'*. In oral references to a work as well, this first line operates as the poem's "title." As we have already mentioned, Shi'i listeners would almost certainly know from Anis's first line that this is an Ali Akbar poem.

Hariaudh, however, begins by displacing the human center of the poem with the list—virtually parallel to Anis's—of qualities and metaphors associated with the male child. In so doing, instead of paraphrasing, paralleling, or elaborating on a clearly stated subject line, as Anis does, he builds towards the revelation of a son's value as the crux of the verse in line 4. This is, significantly, the only verse in which Hariaudh does not retain Anis's first line as the basis for his own translated first line.

Once you've seen a succulent fruit, no other taste can appeal [like it again].
Once you've known the soft flower, no fragrance can appeal [like it again].
There is no [other] happiness like a joyful heart.
There's no wealth in the world better than a son.
When assaults fall upon the wounded heart, he alone is the pleasing cure.
He alone is the body and soul, he alone the lotus flower, he alone the *soma*'s essence.

For the reader of the Braj poem, then, the subject of a beloved son, though hardly an unusual topic of passionate interest in the culture, will come as something of a surprise. Hariaudh's phrasing here also interestingly imparts a gentle feeling of loss or melancholy, even as it celebrates the perfection of a son, with the subtle suggestion that not only does nothing compare to a son, but the whole world would be tasteless and colorless without one. In the case of the *marsiyah*, since the poetic form by definition bewails death and bereavement even as it asserts moral victory, a sense of doom is always assumed in the background of the work. Because it operates within the conventions of the martyrological form, then, Anis's opening verse, despite the layered feelings of love and loss it evokes, lacks the slight emotional suspense of Hariaudh's.

Grammatically speaking, the Urdu text is consistent with spoken forms of Hindi/Urdu, and Hindi prose literature. The Braj Bhasha translation, on the other hand, was grammatically distinct from the Khari Boli of Anis,[44] and it would have become increasingly less comprehensible to the Hindi reading public of 1900 and beyond, who were turning away from this literary dialect toward prose literature and journalism.[45] Certain lexical choices reflect the stylistically inflected effect of Braj Bhasna as a mode of "rustic" speech or courtly renderings thereof.

The notion of Hindi–Urdu differences in syntax order is displayed in particular syntactic reversals of postpositional phrases. In verse two, Hariaudh inverts the end rhyme of the Anis, *hai isi se* [it is from this very thing], into *yahisom* at the beginning of the lines. Similarly, in verse three, the *jahisom*, equivalent of the Khari Boli/Urdu *jis se*, migrates towards the beginning of the lines, although interestingly retaining some inversion within the postpositional phrase itself. Certain lexical items remain the same, and Hariaudh does not always discriminate on the basis of a word's etymological heritage. For that matter, there are also some acceptably Hindi words present in the Anis original: *lal* for son/ruby, as mentioned earlier (3.6 and 4.4), and in the final verse, *ghar* (house, home; 7.1); *ujar-* (to be overturned, 7.1) and *bigar-* (to be despoiled; 7.3). Basic elements of Hindi-Urdu grammar remain, such as *hai*, the present tense of "to be," many pronomials, and some adverbs.

Here, a few examples of the linguistic changes incurred through translation are given (see Appendix 2, at the end of this chapter, for English translation):

Bold: phonetically similar lexeme/s for the same signified meaning in both versions

Bold and italics: same word in both versions

(N.B.: The lines from Anis are above, lines from Hariaudh below; the verses from Hariaudh are transliterated with end-final "a," reflecting Braj meter and recitation conventions)

1.1 (in Hariaudh, 1.4)
Daulat **koi** duniya **men** pisar **se nahim** behtar
Kou dhanahai bhalo **nahim** sutas**om** jaga**mahim**
1.6:
Raiham hai ***yahi***, rah ***yahi***, ruh **yahi** hai
Tana prana ***yahi*** sarasija ***yahi*** somalatarasahai **yahai**
2.3:
Sab rahat-o-aram **ka** saman ***hai*** isi se
Yahi**som** ***saba*** sukhapramoda**ki** ***hai*** adhikai
3.6:
Moti bhi luta dete haim is **lal ke** badle
Badikai badalai ya **lalake moti** dehim lutaya nita

4.1:
Saulat ***yahi***, shaukat ***yahi***, ijlal ***yahi hai***
Teja ***yahi*** bala ***yahi*** prabala paratapa ***yahihai***
4.2:
Sarwat ***yahi*** hashmat ***yahi*** iqbal ***yahi***
Opa ***yahi*** duti***yahi*** pati ***yahi*** dapa ***yahi*** hai
4.3:
Sarmayah ***yahi*** naqad ***yahi mal yahi hai***
Vibhava ***yahi*** vita ***yahi*** dhana ***yahi mala yahihai***
4.4:
Gauhar ***yahi*** yaqut ***yahi lal yahi***
Hira ***yahi*** mani***yahi*** amolaka ***lala yahi***hai
4.6:
Kuch ***pas*** **nahim** gar ***yah*** raqam ***pas*** nahim ***hai***
Kachu ahai ***pasa*** **nahim** jo na ***yaha*** caru padaratha ***pasahai***
6.2:
Voh ***cain hai*** rahat ki ghari **rehti** hai jis **se**
So su***caina hai*** **rahata** sukh ghati ja**som** age
7.2:
Ghar**valom se** is tafirqah paR jane ko **pucho**
Punchahu ***ghara*****varanasom** yahi antara dukhakamhim

Hariaudh's faithfulness to Anis is illustrated by the semantic dependence on the original of much of these first seven verses. Several of the Braj verses are virtually nonsensical without an understanding of Anis's original Urdu; they strangely rely on Anis's poem, or at least on the particular kinds of statements made in *marsiyah*s, in order to make sense in the Braj linguistic context. Because of this, these verses present in a more extreme form the usual difficulty in Braj poetry of inexplicit semantic connections: You simply have to know of what the verse speaks to know what is the agent, the object, an adverbial, etc. in a semiotic world that is not universally obvious.[46] It appears that this translation would have presented a special case of interpretive difficulty. While Hariaudh's literate Hindi-speaking audience *did* probably generally know what to expect from a *marsiyah* in terms of its tropes, almost any readership would likely find these more abstract verses, transposed into a Hinduized Braj context, somewhat difficult to decipher. Poetry on Krishna or Ram did not include such repeated exclamations of the value of a son, etc.; such statements would appear unexpectedly within conventional Braj meter, while they would have seemed more natural in their home context of Urdu laments.

The result is that these verses, grammatically and semantically, confound the definition of translation itself. Hariaudh's "Verses on Offspring" exist somewhere in between Roman Jakobsen's three ordained forms. The commonality of grammar and lexemes between Anis' and Hariaudh's verses would suggest an intralingual translation or mere rewording; their grammatical and lexical differences would suggest an interlingual translation, as in a translation between two utterly foreign languages, and their differences in reference (Hindu vs. Muslim characters, etc.) would suggest an intersemiotic translation. But none of these quite captures the grammatical and semiotic dependency of Hariaudh's verses upon Anis' original.[47] Further, Hariaudh's choice of verses also complicates the picture.

The texts of this *marsiyah* of Anis's that Shi'i reciters have actually used for mourning assemblies since at least the 1930s move directly from this first verse to verse 7, excluding the somewhat repetitive material in between, and then into the final scene from the full-length *marsiyah*, which details Akbar's gory wounds and his death.[48] Hariaudh, then, has focused expressly on the very verses, 2 through 6, that seem to have received limited attention or appreciation from listeners in the mourning assembly. Having addressed those verses largely in terms of the linguistic features of Hariaudh's poem, we will now discuss verse 7 as the pivotal one in both Anis's original *marsiyah* and in Hariaudh's poem:

> Ask its master about what it's like when a well-filled home is overturned
> Ask the members of that household about what it's like when they're scattered apart
> Ask a mother and a father about what it's like when fortune's laid waste
> Ask Jacob about what it's like when Joseph's torn away from him
> May Allah not let us see grief over the light of our eyes
> For it'll then be the blood of the heart and soul that flows from our eyes

In Anis, the devastation in this verse prefaces Akbar's own story of heroism and tragedy. In the Braj Bhasha piece, it precedes the despairing verses of Hariaudh's own creation on the loss of a child, the section that might be conceptualized as exemplifying *karuna rasa*, the emotional/aesthetic category of sorrow and compassion, in a despairing version of the *vatsalya bhava* of Hindu poetry.[49]

In both works, however, the earlier lavish praises of strength and support, of satisfaction and comfort, and the flow of poetry itself, are abruptly overturned as the prosperous household is torn asunder. In a way, this upheaval is the very essence of the *marsiyah*. Key to its emotional texture is the play between the respect and affection shared within the noble family of the Prophet and the oppression they suffer as a result of their virtuous refusal to compromise. The more Husain, Akbar, and the other Karbala characters reveal their exceptional moral qualities, the more their craven enemies attack them, reinforcing the basic polarity between good and evil.

Anis finishes off his list of tragedies with the oft-used but powerful motif of the father–son relationship between beautiful exiled Joseph and Jacob grieving over him. The Urdu poetic convention is that though Jacob cried himself blind over Joseph, his love imparted to him a miraculous vision of his imprisoned son; this lends continuity and intensity to the last couplet of the verse (especially since Anis has made reference in verse 5 to the "wondrous vision" bestowed by the son on an aging father):

> Ask Jacob about what it's like when Joseph's torn away from him
> May Allah not let us see grief over the light of our eyes [the son]
> For it'll then be the blood of the heart and soul that flows from our eyes

It is here that Hariaudh replaces these Quranic figures with King Dasarath and his son Ram from the Indian epic the *Ramayana*:

> Ask King Dasarath about the separation of Ram's banishment.
> Hariaudh says, may God not ever show me grief for a beloved son.
> The blood of the heart, the whole body, flows through the eyes.

As in Anis, the ideas of loss, exile, and paternal enfeeblement are invoked in a shorthand manner through well-known mythological figures, and Hariaudh even expands on Dasarath's grief in verse 10, one of the last verses he appends to the translation. There we find Dasarath throughly distraught, and, although Prince Ram is exiled rather than killed like Husain, the father's life is not worth living once the son is gone. In fact, in the *Ramayana*, Dasarath ultimately dies of his grief. Husain's anguish over Akbar finishes him off in a sense as well, though it is in the imam's case the final spur to an ill-fated battle in which he must engage for lofty moral reasons.

What remains most similar between the two lexically differing poems is ultimately a rhetorical device: the emphatic iterations, "from he alone," "by him alone," "he alone is . . . ," and the litany of qualities given in Anis's original, despairing ruminations on the profound importance of a son to one's emotional and practical livelihood. The poetic strategies of iteration and enumeration, traces of the original, remain unchanged after Hariaudh's lexical and syntactic ministrations, perhaps pointing to what appeared to Hariaudh as a core of elegy, whether *vilap* or *marsiyah*.

INDIC AND ISLAMIC POETIC LEGACIES: A COMPLEX LITERARY ENCOUNTER

The next year after the publication of *The World of Love*, Hariaudh published a popular translation, *The Flower of instruction, a translation into vernacular of the eighth chapter of the* Gulistam (*Upades kusum arthat ashtam bab Gulistam ka bhasanuvad*), a translation into Braj verse and Hindi prose of the eighth chapter of the *Gulistan* by Sa'adi, a thirteenth-century Persian instructional text on the subject of personal conduct. As in *The World of Love*, the introduction of *The Flower of Instruction* displayed extremely Sanskritized language, and Hariaudh explained that he transcreated the text such that *bhasharasiks* (lovers of the vernacular, that is, Braj/Hindi) would not be "inconvenienced by reading of the matters and sayings of the Muslim religion."[50]

Again, Hariaudh here pointedly differentiates himself and his social group from Islam and the Islam-associated Persian language, although the choice for translation of this text itself bespeaks the long-established integration and importance of Persian literature among learned classes in India. The position of the Hindi movement as a "grassroots" movement of Hindus desiring more cultural authority was thus ironically furthered by these kinds of re-productions, or perhaps appropriations, of well-known literary works of Urdu and Persian. Hariaudh would later become famous for his epic length poem *Priyapravas*, his pièce de résistance in Khari Boli Hindi and Sanskrit meters, in which he virtuosically avoided the use of Perso-Arabic words, and which in subsequent editions he further Sanskritized such that the text has become a model of "pure Hindi." In the 1920s, Hariaudh continued with long and elaborate experiments with Urdu verse forms in Khari Boli Hindi, which received little interest from the literary public, by and large committed to an idea of Hindi poetry that excluded Urdu/Persian lexicon and genres. The *marsiyah* genre is now practically a footnote in literary histories of the Hindi-language elegy or lament, folded into the category of *karuna rasa* (the pitiful sentiment), and considered much less influential on Hindi elegiac poetry than even Thomas Gray's "Elegy."[51] However, aspects of the poetry of Maithilisaran Gupta (1886–1964) would bear comparison to the *marsiyah* genre,[52] and folk performances of Shi'i laments continue to incorporate both Hindus and "Hindi" forms. Hariaudh himself would later cite Anis as one of the great teachers (with the Hindu-marked term *acarya*) of *karuna rasa* in his 1927 work on Hindi poetry in "the way of speech."[53]

In one sense, it may not seem surprising that as a Hindu poet of Braj Bhasha, Hariaudh excises not only the specifics of the Karbala tragedy and the personality of its characters, but allusions to Allah and to figures such as Jacob and Joseph. To take his experiment as indicative of literary boundaries between Hindi and Urdu in North India, however, could prove quite misleading. Despite emotional debates about the political status and religious affiliations of Hindi and Urdu from the 1860s on, and attempts to differentiate them definitively, both literary traditions could offer forums to Hindu or Muslim poets, and both often drew their symbols as readily from the world of Hindu temples, statues of deities, and festivities as from figures like Joseph or world-altering tragedies like that of Karbala. In the *marsiyah* world, when Anis and Dabir render scenes like the heart-rending marriage of Husain's nephew Qasim right before he dies in battle, the garb, the ceremonies, and the terminology (especially that alluding to the blessed state of marriage and the inauspicious state of widowhood) are undeniably Hindu-inflected Indian, as opposed to Middle Eastern.

The very engagement of other non-Muslim poets with the Karbala tragedy, and the plentitude of works in Hindi about the Karbala characters testify to how unusual Hariaudh's particular undertaking is. As long as Muharram has been observed in India, there seem to have been at least several well-known Sunni Muslim or Hindu poets and reciters of the *marsiyah* in every generation. Around the time Hariaudh lived, Munshi Channoo Lal Lakhnavi, whose pen-name was "Dilgir," produced *marsiyahs* in classical Lucknow style that even Anis is said to have admired, and that are widely anthologized today. Nineteenth- and twentieth-century Hindu writers who made names for themselves as *marsiyah* poets employed a lexicon, range of episodes, and verse forms similar to those used by the famous poets Anis and Dabir, and many even spoke of a personal devotion to one or another of the Shi'i imams.[54]

While the works of Dilgir and other non-Shi'i *marsiyah* poets are peppered liberally with Arabic and Persian words and look to classical Urdu models, another kind of poem loosely incorporates the *marsiyahs*' narrative themes, but shares little or nothing of its formal structure, and expresses these themes in overtly Hindi vocabulary or diction. One such north Indian poem, an example of a genre called *dah* (derived from the Persian word for "ten," for the ten days of core Muharram observances), refers to Husain playing the flute on the riverbank like Lord Krishna. Such poems often have rural origins, and are often simple, musical, and rooted in very localized interpretations of the Karbala tale. In another poem from rural Uttar Pradesh, Husain's wife Bano is described in lines entirely, or almost entirely, lacking in Urdu words, such as: "Bano dukhyari rovat hai: 'Hai Husain'" ("The sorrowful Bano weeps, 'Alas, Husain!'"). These works differ dramatically from Hariaudh's verses in their direct focus on the personalities and activities of the Karbala characters, and in their role in inclusive, inter-religious commemorations of Karbala. In such songs, as in virtually any lament or elegy, the writer performs an act of remembrance, whether by actually reciting and weeping, by depicting bereaved characters, or by moving listeners to sorrowful response to a tragic death. In the *marsiyah* tradition, all three possibilities are usually realized, while Hariaudh's "verses concerning offspring" idealize the wonders of a son in a disembodied, aestheticized way. It is not just the linguistic common ground with Urdu that disappears in the Braj "lament," but the theme and tones of remembrance itself.

Remember Hariaudh's own comment, "Urdu is itself a version of Hindi, what [would be] a translation of it!" We, in our turn, might well ask what a *marsiyah* becomes when certain of its refrains, words, and structural features are retained (in translation), but its basic context is eliminated. In Anis's opening verses, the generalized fondness for a son is effective in part because it forms a part of both a ritual remembrance that bestows spiritual merit, and a specific, detailed narrative that has great power to craft and reinforce community identity. Also, although this surprisingly repetitive piece isn't Anis's most inventive or stirring, it has an attractive, flowing, musical quality (*ravani*), which complements the grammatical simplicity of the poet's litany of filial attributes and capitalizes on deceptively simple alliteration.[55] What stands out in Hariaudh's work, by contrast, is a punctilious artistic virtuosity that also testifies to the writer's deep knowledge of Urdu and Urdu poetry. Though his lines occasionally use internal rhyme, meter, and alliteration to charming effect, the aural impact is anything but smooth and flowing.

The outcome of Hariaudh's careful reworking of Anis is oddly parallel to what so many early twentieth-century Urdu critics did in their efforts to reform their literary tradition. While they held up the martial, moral *marsiyah* as an antidote to the sensual *ghazal*, they often omitted its extended depictions of women's laments over fallen heroes and of the warriors themselves weeping. In a sense, Hariaudh was one of many "reformers" who extracted isolated bits of this long genre and displayed them in an uncontextualized way. Approved excerpts of Anis's "realistic" depictions of the morning or of nature, which are approximately the length of Hariaudh's poem, can be found in Urdu literature textbooks even today. Yet Hariaudh culls from Anis so selectively that he eschews entirely the battle of good and evil that so many who have cited the *marsiyah*'s "universal appeal" see as its basis; without the evil, hypocritical Yazid and his henchmen ever present in the background of the poem, it is fate, seemingly, rather than forces of vice and virtue, that infuse Hariaudh's work with sadness. What the Hindi writer's poem does retain is much of the same interplay between abundance or satisfaction and its destruction that pervades the *marsiyah* tradition. In Hariaudh's project, then, translation impinges on the realm of affect as well as that of lexicon and word order. If this is an aspect of an "inner core of the elegy," then perhaps Hariaudh has been successful in universalizing it, but he seems to have chosen the *marsiyah* as much "because it was there" and available to be converted to his Hindi movement agenda as because a broadly appealing tragic sense gripped his imagination. At any rate, with the passage of time, the audience for his experiment—readers who would have understood something of the conventions of both a changing Braj Bhasha and of Shi'i laments—would soon become rather narrow.

The "Verses Concerning Offspring" of *The World of Love* and Hariaudh's other translations from Urdu speak directly to the problem of what comprises the difference between these two languages, besides the usual socio-linguistic litmus tests of script and explicitly Muslim and Hindu religious genres. Certainly, lexicon was a main focus of Hariaudh's transcreation. But more important was the medium of Braj poetry itself, with its metrical cadences and associations with Hindu-inflected devotional affects of inconsolability, via the banished Ram or the elaborated concept of motherly love among some Krishna devotees. By extension, this suggests that the defining process of Hindi itself, by its promoters, was a project of evocations as much as script or lexicon, in a sort of willed exertion of a homology of identity and language as if to say, "We understand the world differently than it is presented in Urdu." Hariaudh's translated verses, more than a transposition of signs, suffering from inevitable inexactitude, are actually seeking out that difference. In the process of doing so, they reveal how translations can create national identities "through a specular process in which the [audience] identifies with cultural materials that are defined as national and thereby enable a self-recognition in a national collective,"[56] and how problematic is Benedict Anderson's assumption, made in much scholarship on linguistic nationalism, that languages have "singular, homogenous, and stable identities that their speakers carry with them from mother's knee to the grave."[57] In this case, a "Hindi" identity rooted in Hindu myth and the folksy sounds of Vaishnava poetry is very consciously constructed out of the relatively plural linguistic and literary world of late nineteenth-century North India. Hariaudh acknowledges and draws from this pool of pluralism to produce difference, almost as though casting a preemptive strike at the now ubiquitous, almost hectoring Indian national slogan, "unity in diversity" (*vibhinnta me(n) ekta*).[58]

Nevertheless, like a refrain, the affect of grief and its myriad North Indian expressions recur. Incorporations of death-of-a-son laments in high Hindi literature suggest that Urdu's classical elegy had a formative and profound role in modern Hindi literary production. Hariaudh's strange distillation of Anis' *marsiyah* bears testament to the analytical challenge presented by literary and linguistic experiments of the Hindi movement era. And the poem Hariaudh produces, and that *we* now read/interpret/translate, is more than a quirky artifact of a particular politics, historical moment, and individual literary virtuosity. Translation, in practice and in theory, wrangles with "the relation among authors, texts, and the degree to which the translator-author and new text in each instance lie close to or go creatively far from prior author and source."[59] The new text that Hariaudh makes of the lament of another, then, embodies preoccupations of translation, but these feed into questions of textual lineage and intertextuality, originality and imitation, that recur in literary theory more generally.

APPENDIX 1: EXACT TRANSLATION OF ORIGINAL URDU LINES

Urdu *marsiyah* poem by Mir Babar 'Ali Anis	"Verses on the Topic of Offspring," from the Braj Bhasha by Hariaudh
1. There's no better wealth in the world than a son.	Once you've seen a succulent fruit, no other taste can appeal [like it again].
There's no better comfort than repose for the heart.	Once you've known the soft flower, no fragrance can appeal [like it again].

There's no better taste than a succulent fruit's.	There is no other happiness like a joyful heart.
There's no better fragrance than the aroma of a fresh rose.	There's no wealth better in the world than a son.
For the crippled heart under assault, only he is a cure.	When assaults fall upon the wounded heart, he alone is the pleasing cure.
Only he is sustenance, he satisfaction, he the soul.	He alone is the body and soul, he alone the lotus flower, he alone the essence of soma.
2.Only he can make the parents' hearts bud profusely.	Only by having a son will the bud of the parents' heart bloom.
He's the flower to make a household the envy of a rose-garden.	The garden looks into the home and is put to shame by this flower alone.
He alone is the making of comfort and repose.	From him alone is the abundance of happiness and enjoyment.
He stands as the people's crown of humanity.	From him alone shines the abode, the image of the glory of man.
How can the heart bloom if one lacks vital organs?	How much is the heart bloomed, if love for the son doesn't remain?
A home is worse than the grave if it lacks a son.	A house is worse than a cremation ground, without a son; people in the world reckon thus.
3.He is the staff that keeps the old young.	A son is the staff by which one remains young in old age.
He is that well-set jewel that ensures enduring fame.	He by whom the breathing of the breath of life remains is called a pearl.
He is the lamp that lights the house.	He is that sign through which one's name remains in the world.
He is the pearl that anchors life's strands.[60]	He is that lamp of the house which remains lit.
One would rather lose gold and goods than this wealth.	Hariaudh says: no one would lose the wealth of this treasure [the son] for worldly wealth.

Better to have even pearls stolen than this ruby.	Rather than have harm come to that ruby, always give pearls away for nothing.

4.He alone is vigor, he alone is glory, he alone magnificence.	The son alone is energy, he alone is power, mighty valor is he alone.
He alone is prosperity, he alone is dignity, he alone felicity.	Luster is he only, radiance is he alone, one's good name/honor is he alone, pride is he alone.
He alone is money, wealth, and goods.	He himself is might, he himself is money, he himself is wealth, he himself is the asset.
He alone is the pearl, the garnet, the ruby [or dear one, *lal*].	He alone is the diamond, the jewel, the priceless ruby [or dear one, *lal*].
If one has a heart-cherished son by one's side, then sorrow stays away.	Hariaudh says: if your son is near, then the abode of sorrows is far away.
And if one doesn't have this item, one doesn't have anything.	You don't have anything if you don't have this agreeable object.

5.A mother and father's assurance and comfort reside in a son.	From the child comes the parents' happiness and hope
There is a sweetness to living, even in bitter adversity, through a son.	From the child comes the fund of hope despite sorrow in life.
There's blood in the body, wondrous vision for the eyes, from a son.	From the child is the light in the eyes, the blood in the body.
Even in one's weakest days, one has strength, through a son.	From the child comes strength for the heart, even having become old.
He is repose for the emotions, strength to the heart, comfort to the spirit.	He is ease of the mind, delight of the heart, nourisher of the spirit.
In senescence one has this strength: that one's son is young.	Hariaudh says: in old age this strength remains, that my son is a young man.

6.He is the thing that keeps happiness astride one's threshold.	He remains the wonderful thing from which everyone will get joy.
He is the peace that assures moments of comfort.	He remains the great ease from which happy moments will come.

He is the gem that keeps hope bright.	He remains the jewel by which the hope of life is filled.
He is the pearl that makes life worth living.	He remains a pearl from which life [goes on].
He conveys repose for the heart, strength and power.	Hariaudh says: happiness, power, and strength of the heart are always with him.
Wherever he roams, all the strands of life follow.	That direction in which he sets off, life takes up that very road.

---

7. Ask its master about what it's like when a well-filled home is overturned.	Approach and ask the father of a full house about its demise.
Ask the members of that household about what it's like when they're scattered apart.	Ask the people of the house about the sadness inside it.
Ask a mother and a father about what it's like when fortune's laid waste.	Ask the parents about the ruination of their fate.
Ask Jacob about what it's like when Joseph's torn away from him.	Ask King Dasharatha about the separation of Ram's banishment.
May God not let us see sorrow over the light of our eyes.	Hariaudh says, may God not ever show me grief for a beloved son.
For it'll then be the blood of the heart and soul that flows from our eyes.	The blood of the heart, the whole body, flows through the eyes.

---

	8. O Lord, let not anyone's tree of desires be leafless.
	Let no one's house ever be without light.
	May the child never be born again separate from the parents [i.e., die].
	Nobody longs for separation from the son, upon [his] leaving the world.
	That which is without a cure in the world, is only the scar of grief upon the heart.
	That house is worse than a cremation ground, where there is not the lamp of life.

9. Separation from the son in the world is understood to be [like] an enemy.

May nowhere a home under any religion be laid waste.

There are all kinds of pain, but there is none [like] pain of the heart.

O Hari, without the light of one's eyes, nobody hopes for anything.

Hariaudh says: even if you reign over the three worlds, then it's just dust [i.e., nothing]

Life is pointless [dried up] in all ways if there isn't the source of happiness that is a son.

10. When the dear hero of the Raghus [Ram] was separated from [his father] King Dasharatha

[There was] only one other son remaining, the one dear to the heart was gone.

All happiness was forgotten from grief, life in old age was defeated.

Alas, separated from the child, Dasharatha looked at him and called out to him many times.

Peace didn't come in the day, he didn't get sleep at night.

The heart was wandering aimlessly from grief, the stinging pain in his gut remained.

11. Although how could the world ever be of use to this child [anyway]?

And [still] for him, the parents have so much grief.

But there is this, that sign, by which the name remains alive in the world.

[If] the beloved child is away for a moment, life burns up from sorrow.

Don't ever, being disappointed in what you have earned [for your years of love, etc., for the son], turn away from him.

Hariaudh says, there is no wealth you can have, but that love toward the dear one.

12. Compared to all those who are called children, this child

Surpasses, as you gaze at him, the body and soul, even one's own salvation.

APPENDIX 2: EXAMPLES OF PATTERNED CHANGE AND CONTINUITY IN HARIAUDH'S POEM

1.1 (in Hariaudh, 1.4)
Daulat **koi** duniya **men** pisar se **nahim** behtar
Kou dhanahai bhalo **nahim** suta**som** jaga**mahim**
There's no better wealth in the world than a son.

1.6:
Raiham hai ***yahi***, rah ***yahi***, ruh **yahi** hai
Tana prana ***yahi*** sarasija ***yahi*** somalatarasahai **yahinai**

He alone is the body and soul, he alone the lotus flower, he alone the essence of soma.

2.3:
Sab rahat-o-aram ***ka*** saman ***hai*** isi se
Yahi**som** ***saba*** sukhapramoda***ki hai*** adhikai
From him alone is the abundance of happiness and enjoyment.

3.6:
Moti bhi **luta dete** haim is ***lal ke*** **badle**
Badikai **badalai** ya ***lalake moti*** **dehim lutaya** nita

Rather than give up this ruby [or dear one, lal], always give up your pearls to plunder instead.

4.1:
Saulat ***yahi***, shaukat ***yahi***, ijlal ***yahi hai***
Teja ***yahi*** bala ***yahi*** prabala paratapa ***yahihai***
The son alone is energy, he alone is power, mighty valor is he alone.

4.2:
Sarwat ***yahi*** hashmat ***yahi*** iqbal ***yahi***
Opa ***yahi*** duti***yahi*** pati ***yahi*** dapa ***yahi***hai
Luster is he only, radiance is he alone, one's good name
honor is he alone, pride is he alone.

4.3:
Sarmayah ***yahi*** naqad ***yahi mal yahi hai***
Vibhava ***yahi*** vita ***yahi*** dhana ***yahi mala yahihai***

He himself is might, he himself is money, he himself is wealth,
he himself is the asset.

4.4:
Gauhar ***yahi*** yaqut ***yahi lal yahi***
Hira ***yahi*** mani***yahi*** amolaka ***lala yahi***hai

He alone is the diamond, the jewel, the priceless ruby [or dear
one, *lal*]

4.6:
Kuch ***pas*** **nahim** gar yah raqam ***pas*** nahim ***hai***
Kachu ahai ***pasa*** **nahim** jo na yaha caru padaratha ***pasahai***
And if one doesn't have this item, one doesn't have anything.

6.2:
Voh ***cain hai*** rahat ki **ghari** ***rehti*** hai **jis se**
So su***caina hai rahata*** sukh **ghati jasom** age
He remains the great ease from which happy moments will come.

7.2:
Ghar**valom se** is tafirqah paR jane ko **pucho**
Punchahu ***ghara*****varanasom** yahi antara dukhakamhim

Ask the people of the house about this sadness of separation [or
of the heart, antar]

NOTES

* Willis Barnstone, *The Poetics of Translation: History, Theory, Practice* (New Haven: Yale University Press, 1993), 22–23.

1. Michael Joseph Gillespie, discussing Harold Bloom's approach to translation, in "Translation, Reading, and Literary Theory" (Ph.D. diss., Indiana University, 1987), 95.
2. The term *prapanc* has a variety of meanings, ranging from "the visible world" and its connotative meanings of "illusion" and "error," to "that which derives from the five elements" with its sense of "expansion," or "diffusion." The

term has been used to signify the genres of drama and compendia; it is the latter genre that is evoked here, with the literal translation "world."

3. Mumbai: Khemaraj Srikrsnadas, Srivenkatesvar Steam Press, 1900.
4. Willis Barnstone, *The Poetics of Translation: History, Theory, Practice* (New Haven, CT: Yale University Press, 1993), 4.
5. Ibid., 8.
6. As in the title of Christopher R. King's work on the Hindi movement, *One Language, Two Scripts: The Hindi Movement in Nineteenth Century North India* (Mumbai: Oxford University Press, 1994).
7. For contrasting examples of non-Muslim poets who have worked within more standard *marsiyah* conventions, see, for example, Mujavar Husain Rizvi, "Urdu marsiye ke ghair muslim shu'ara" [The non-Muslim poets of Urdu *marsiyahs*], in *Urdu marsiyah: seminar mem parhe ga'e maqalat,* ed. Sharib Rudaulvi (New Delhi: Urdu Academy, 1993).
8. See Barbara D. Metcalf and Thomas R. Metcalf, *A Concise History of India* (Cambridge: Cambridge University Press, 2002), 5.
9. Colin P. Masica, *Indo-Aryan Languages* (Cambridge, UK: Cambridge University Press, 1993), 27. A popular Hindi textbook concurs, " . . . at the everyday spoken level, Hindi and Urdu are virtually identical, and you should not be surprised if you are complemented on your spoken 'Urdu' when you complete this course in 'Hindi'!" Rupert Snell with Simon Weightman, *Teach Yourself Hindi* (London: Hodder & Stoughton Educational, 2003), 1.
10. See, for example, Ram Babu Saksena, *A History of Urdu Literature* (Lahore: Sang-e Meel, 1996), 7.
11. Saksena, *History*, 8.
12. Metcalf and Metcalf, *History*, 13–14; Aditya Behl, "Desire and Narrative in a Hindavi Sufi Romance, circa 1503," in *India's Islamic Traditions, 711–1750,* ed. Richard M. Eaton (New Delhi: Oxford University Press, 2003), 180.
13. Metcalf and Metcalf, *History*, 13. Also see John Stratton Hawley and Mark Juergensmeyer, *Songs of the Saints of India* (Oxford and New York: Oxford University Press, 1988).
14. *Passions of the Tongue: Language Devotion in Tamil India, 1891–1970* (Berkeley and Los Angeles: University of California Press, 1997), 22.
15. Maithilisaran Gupta, *Bharat-bharati* [The voice of India] (1912–14; thirty-seventh ed., Jhansi: Sāhitya-Sadan, 1991) and Devakinandan Khatri, *Candrakanta* (1892; Delhi: Navacintan Sahitya, 2004). Such borrowings and adaptations were not uncommon but not legion either. On the *musaddas* form, and the Urdu work that inspired *Bharat-bharati*, see Christopher Shackle and J. Majeed, trans., Hali's *Musaddas*: The Flow and Ebb of Islam (Delhi: Oxford University Press, 1997). On *dastan* as a performance and print genre, see Frances W. Pritchett, ed. and trans., *The Romance Tradition in Urdu: Adventures from the* Dastan *of Amir Hamzah* (New York: Columbia University Press, 1991).
16. See Vasudha Dalmia, *The Nationalization of Hindu Traditions: Bharatendu Harischandra and Nineteenth-century Banaras* (Delhi: Oxford University Press, 1997).
17. For the early history of this organization, see King, *One Language.*
18. Hariaudh [Ayodhyasimh Upadhyay], *Priyapravas: Khari-Boli ka sarvasresth mahakavya* [*The Absence of the Beloved*: the Best Poems of khari-Boli] (1914; revised 1941; 23rd printing, Varanasi: Hindi Sahitya Kutir, 1996). Mahakavya is a Sanskrit term denoting a poem of considerable length and with several distinct features of meter and content.

19. Alok Rai, *Hindi Nationalism* (Vol. 13 of *Tracts for the Times*; Hyderabad: Orient Longman, 2001).
20. *Venis ka banka* [The dandy of Venice] (Kolkata: Aryavarta Press, 1889; second edition, Varanasi: Pathak and Son Bhasha Bhandar Pustakalay, 1928).
21. Hariaudh, Introduction to the second edition of *Venis*, 3.
22. This distinction, which has not to our knowledge ever had much popular force, is noted by Sir George Grierson in reference to Hariaudh's novel *Theth Hindi ka thath, arthat theth Hindi mem likhi gai ek lubhanevali kahani* [A framework of authentic Hindi, or a charming story in authentic Hindi]: "This, like the 'Kahani theth Hindi mem' of Insa Allah [Khan], is in pure Hindi. . . . Unlike the older work, the idiom is that of Hindi, rather than that of Urdu. This is most noticeable in the order of the words." ("A Bibliography of Western Hindi, Including Hindostani [*sic*]," *Indian Antiquary* Vol. 32 (1903): 160–179, esp. 166. In a cursory examination of these texts, we found the differences in word order minor, consisting of the use of dangling postpositional phrases in the section headings of Khan's early nineteenth-century story (e.g., *Kahani Rani Ketaki ki*).
23. This publisher is still in existence, and was a major publisher of Hindi and Sanskrit publications in India, and via export to Indians abroad, etc. See http://www.khemraj.com.
24. Hariaudh, Introduction to *World*, 3.
25. This phenomenon is epitomized by the personification of Urdu as a courtesan commonly featured in poetry and pamphlets of the era. In contrast, a chaste and simple woman in distress embodied Hindi. See King, pp. 135–159, 184.
26. That is, "vernaculars," Indic languages related to but excluding Sanksrit.
27. Hariaudh, Introduction to *World*, 4.
28. Hariaudh, Introduction to *World*, 6.
29. Here we might invoke the concepts of refraction and dynamic equivalence in translation theory, as Tony K. Stewart has explored in reference to an older and more complex text merging Hindu and Islamic theological concepts: "In Search of Equivalence: Conceiving Muslim-Hindu Encounter Through Translation Theory," *History of Religions* 40, no. 3 (Winter 2001): 261–288.
30. *Vatsalya bhava* in the poetry of Sur Das on the child Krishna is examined by Kenneth E. Bryant in *Poems to the Child-God: Structures and Strategies in the Poetry of Surdas* (Berkeley: University of California Press, 1978).
31. See Pratap Mukhopadhyay, ed., *Bangla sokakabya samgrah* [A collection of Bengali elegies] (3 vols; Kolkata: Praiti Prakasan, Paribesak, Pustak Bipani, 2001) for reprints of several late nineteenth-century elegies.
32. Muhammad Shibli Nu'mani, *Muwazanah-e Anis o Dabir* [A Comparative Study of Anis and Dabir] (Lahore: Maktabah-e Din o Duniya, 1964 [1907]).
33. Saksena, *History*, 149.
34. Frances W. Pritchett, *Nets of Awareness: Urdu Poetry and its Critics* (Berkeley: University of California Press, 1994), preface, 34–35, 38, 134–135.
35. "Marsiyah bataur razmiyah" The Epic *Marsiyah* (in Rudaulvi), 289. Amy Bard's translation.
36. See, for example, J. R. I. Cole, *Roots of North Indian Shiism in Iran and Iraq: Religion and State in Awadh, 1722–1859* (Berkeley: University of California Press, 1988), 92–119; Rahi Masum Raza, *AdhaGaon* [Half a village] (Delhi: Akshar Prakashan Private Ltd.,1966); and Amy C. Bard, "Turning Karbala Inside Out: Humor and Ritual Critique in South Asian Muharram Rites," in *Ritual Levity and Ritual Play in South Asia,* ed. Selva Raj and Corinne Dempsey (Albany: SUNY Press, forthcoming).

37. That is, a Sikh who does not meet the strict definition of Khalsa identity. See Harjot Oberoi, *The Construction of Religious Boundaries* (Delhi: Oxford University Press, 1994), 71 ff., on the "Khalsa/Sahajdhari duality."
38. "Dasaratha vilap" [The lament of Dasaratha], *Vidya-vinod* [Pleasures of Knowledge], Asvin, 1876, reprinted in Ayodhya Prasad Khatri, comp., *Khari Boli ka Padya: The Poetical Reader of Khari Boli*, ed. F. Pincott (London: W. H. Allen, 1888), 11–13. This poem also had an at least nominally Persianate cast to it, as proven by its inclusion in the "Maulvi style" section of the latter anthology. Also of note are two lines that evoke Anis' *marsiyah*: "Mera dhan lut karake kaun bhaga? / Mere ghar ko kis ne ujaRa? [Who has run off looting my wealth? / Who has overturned my house?] (Ibid., 12).
39. This universalistic idea is one that appears in various contexts in the Subcontinent in this era, and one that could have possibly European sources (personal communication, Michael Nijhawan). Certainly, this Hindu-inflected hint at universalism suggests also Paul Hacker's conception of Hindu inclusiveness as an expression of hierarchy; however, Hariaudh's verses remain very silent on the question of which theological world, Hindu or Muslim, encompasses the other.
40. These poems are included in many printed *marsiyah* collections, but are also known by these "titles" simply through oral transmission.
41. A six-line verse, with metrics as defined by Rupert Snell in *The Hindi Classical Tradition: A Braj Bhasa Reader* (New Delhi: Heritage Publishers, 1992), 23.
42. See Mir Babar Ali Anis, "Daulat koi duniya men pisar se nahin behtar" [There is no better wealth in the world than a son], in *Anis ke marsiye* [Marsiyahs of Anis], ed. Salihah 'Abid Husain (New Delhi: Taraqqi Urdu Bureau, 1990), 449.
43. The Braj meter in use here relies on a system based on units of time (*matra*) defined as measuring either one or two. See Part II of Snell *Reader*. Urdu prosody adapts Persian and Arabic meters with fixed feet of long and short syllables. Four or five such meters were frequently used in classical Urdu *marsiyah*s. The meter of the poem under discussion here (= =—/ = =—/= =—/= =, where = is a long and—a short syllable) is common in many of the *marsiyah*s that are recited melodically—as opposed to in declamatory form—even today. See Frances Pritchett and Khaliq Ahmad Khaliq, *Urdu Meter: A Practical Handbook* (Madison: South Asian Studies, University of Wisconsin, 1987). On the six-line *musaddas*, see, for example, Saksena, *History*, 10, 139.
44. Although it was clearly influenced by Khari Boli, indicating its late provenance and Urdu inspiration.
45. This difficulty was surely exacerbated by the unusualness of much of the content in Braj; poetry on Krishna or Ram did not include such repeated exclamations of the value of a son, etc.
46. Take for instance, the following line on the beauty of Krishna's face, in which modern editing has provided us with interpretive hyphens, commas, and word-breaks: *muni-mana harata, juvati-jana ketika, ratipati-mana jata saba khoi*. A word-for-word translation is as follows: "ascetic-heart / steals [or "is stolen"] / young woman-people / how many? / lord of Rati-pride / goes / all / lost." *Juvati-jana* (young women) seems to share the status of being the object of *harata* (steals), with the understanding that the young women's *hearts*, like the ascetic's, are stolen by Krishna's beauty. Metrical convention for caesurae, albeit malleable, would lead us to this sort of reading rather than another, in which the honor or pride of *juvati-jana ketika* (so many young women) might be read to have "gone away" along with that of god Kama, the lord of Rati. (Sur Das, *Sursagar: golokvasi Jagannath Das*

'Ratnakar' dvara samgrhit aur Sabha ko pradatt samagri ke adhar par sampadit [The Ocean of Sur: Compiled by the late Jagannath Das 'Ratnakar" and edited on the basis of materials given to the Sabha] [5th ed.; edited by N.D. Vajpeyi; Vol. 1; Nagaripracarini granthmala 25; Varanasi: Nagaripracarini Sabha, 1978], 828.3.)

47. Roman Jakobsen, "On Linguistic Aspects of Translation," from *On Translation* (1959), excerpted in *Theories of Translation: an Anthology of Essays from Dryden to Derrida,* eds. Rainer Schulte and J. Biguenet (Chicago: University of Chicago Press, 1992): 144–151, esp. 145.
48. See Shaikh Hakim Abul Qasim Husam, ed., *Hilal-e Muharram* [The Crescent Moon/Pangs of Muharram](Vol. 2; Hyderabad: Kutabkhanah Haidari, 1990).
49. Like many people of his time, Hariaudh had himself experienced the deaths of several of his child siblings and his own children; however, there is no indication that a personal event inspired this transcreation.
50. Hariaudh, *Upades kusum arthat ashtam bab Gulistam ka bhasanuvad* [Flowers of Instruction, A Translation into Vernacular of the Eighth Chapter of the *Gulistan*] (Allahabad: Indian Press, 1901), 2.
51. See Narbadesvar Ray, "Hindisokagiti: parampara aur pratiphalan [Hindi songs of grief: tradition and its fruition]," in *Magadh Bharati Sodh Granthmala,* ed. Vasudevanandan Prasad et al. (Allahabad: Abhinav Bharati, 1977), and the introduction to *Pratinidhi sokgit* [Representative songs of grief], ed. Ramanuj Lal Srivastav (Jabalpur: Lokcetana Prakasan, 1965).
52. Namely, the prominence of the lamentation over the dead Abhimanyu of *Jayadratha-vadha* [The Slaying of Jayadratha] of 1910 and the narrative content of *Kaba aur Karbala* [Kaba and Karbala] of 1942 (both Ciragamv: Sahitya-sadan). Neither of these obviously reference poetic features of *marsiyah,* however.
53. Hariaudh, *Bolcal* [The way of speech] (Bankipore: Khadgavilas Press, 1927).
54. See Sayyid Mahmud Naqvi, "'Ahd-e hazir ke ghair muslim marsiyah-go shu'ara" [Non-Muslim *marsiyah*-reciting poets of contemporary times] (in Rudaulvi).
55. In verse 1, for example, the final line uses three Arabic-derived words that not only alliterate, but share multiple letters (hardly a matter of chance): raihan *hai yahi,* rah *yahi,* ruh *yahi hai.* Anis has also selected a number of words in the verse that evoke a sense of bounty *(rahaan)* and/or of sensual pleasure (*samar,* fruit), but which also were actually used in Urdu to refer to offspring.
56. Lawrence Venuti, "Local Contingencies: Translation and National Identities," in *Nation, Language, and the Ethics of Translation*, eds. S. Bermann and M. Wood (Translation/Transnation Series; Princeton, NJ: Princeton University Press, 2005), 177–202, esp.180.
57. *Imagined Communities: Reflections on the Origin and Spread of Nationalism* (London: Verso, 1983), 140.
58. The first usage of this ubiquitous phrase (also a national motto in modern Indonesia) in the Indian context is murky and largely irrelevant, but it is attributed often to Tagore in a very early twentieth-century play, and even more often to its frequent user, Jawaharlal Nehru.
59. Barnstone, *The Poetics of Translation*, 22–23.
60. i.e. that ensures the continuance and prosperity of a lineage, in keeping with the metaphors for the son in the previous three lines. "rishta-e-jaan" may also refer to the life's breath, the reason for living, of the parent. The son, is also, then, the pearl that makes the continuance of life itself possible.

2 The Politics of Non-duality

Unraveling the Hermeneutics of Modern Sikh Theology[1]

Arvind Mandair

Few in Sikh or South Asian studies today would deny the importance of neo-colonial reform movements such as the Singh Sabha in transforming and eventually monopolising the interpretation of Sikh tradition. It is now increasingly accepted that the representation of modern Sikhism as an ethical monotheism owes much to the political activism and scholarly output of members of the Singh Sabha movement.[2] However, as a recent editorial introduction rightly points out, the scholarly work of the Singh Sabha is also

> responsible for a major obstacle to our understanding of the Sikh tradition, one which is rendered all the more serious by virtue of its being difficult to recognise. The obstacle derives from the remarkable measure of intellectual success achieved by a small group of Singh Sabha writers in formulating a distinctive interpretation of the Sikh tradition and in promulgating it as the only acceptable version . . . [M]en like Dit Singh, Vir Singh, Teja Singh, Kahn Singh of Nabha . . . were so successful in their attempt to reformulate the Sikh tradition that their general interpretation of the tradition acquired the status of implicit truth. That status it continues to hold to the present day.[3]

What exactly is this "major obstacle" in understanding Sikh tradition and why is it so "difficult to recognize"? Although it has not been considered in this way, some of the main consequences arising from the transformation of Sikh tradition during the colonial period—the redefinition of Sikh identity (McLeod 1989), the construction of religious boundaries (Oberoi 1994), the reinvention of Sikh martyrologies (Fenech 2001), the representation of Sikhism as a "world religion" (Dusenbury 1999), and not least the production of new commentaries on Sikh scripture (McLeod 1984, Singh 2000)—are indissociably linked to the formulation of a systematic concept of God and a redefining of the meaning of *gurmat* (lit. the teaching of the guru) as "Sikh theology." In many ways, the commentaries provide the core of the response by reformist Sikhs to the new regime of colonial translation brought into operation by the publication and endorsement of Ernest Trumpp's translation of the Adi Granth. The response to Trumpp from reformist Sikhs, which came almost fifty years later, appeared in the form of short treatises on Sikh history and longer, more systematic works of scriptural commentary which were of a broadly theological nature.[4] One of the more far-reaching effects of these commentaries is that they helped to crystalize a new and distinctive way of representing the central teaching of the Adi Granth. The central teachings (*gurmat*) came to be projected from a standpoint of a systematic concept of God or Ultimate Reality, based on which *gurmat*, theology and tradition come to be seen as synonymous. The idea that *gurmat* (= theology = tradition) can be represented in terms of a proper concept of God came to exert a hegemonic influence on the modern Sikh imaginary.

Surprisingly, however, the suggestion that the prevailing concept of God in modern Sikhism evolved under historical circumstances goes against the grain of conventional wisdom about Sikhism—both traditionalist and historical[5]—which assume that the commentaries of the Singh Sabha simply extracted and reproduced a theological hermeneutic that is intrinsic to the teachings of Guru Nanak as found in the central Sikh scripture the Adi Granth. The familiar narrative of traditionalist scholarship, for example, assumes that at the heart of Sikhism lies the mystical experience of Guru Nanak, an experience that is articulated through his own poetic compositions (*gurbani*) and his teaching (*gurmat*). The nature of this teaching conforms to a revealed theology grounded in the concept of a transcendent and immanent God. By way of comparison, the prevailing perspective in historical (and by self-definition "critical") Sikh studies as articulated by its most distinguished exponent, W. H. McLeod, considers Guru Nanak to be part and parcel of the devotional tradition of North India and specifically within the Sant lineage. The basis of Sant religiosity is *nirgun bhakti* or devotion to the Name of an ineffable transcendent being. Speculating elsewhere on the possibility of a Sikh theology for modern times, McLeod argues that, although strictly speaking theology is a Western discipline, Sikh tradition "as it has evolved" under the Singh Sabha is rendered "eminently suitable to a theological treatment." The idea of a Sikh theology can therefore be justified because theology encompasses both the "natural theology of Nanak's *bani*" and the evolution of a Sikh exegetical tradition in the hands of the Singh Sabha. Moreover, "theology is a suitable category in the sense that there is no essential distortion of scriptural meaning."[6] Hence, the word *gurmat* as used by the Singh Sabha is a suitably pragmatic translation for "theology." The only requirement today would be to modernize its mode of reception. Since this perspective is likely to be echoed by traditionalist scholars, there appears to be a consensus on one of the central points about the Sikh religion.

This chapter argues for a degree of vigilance to be exercised at precisely the point where there appears to be a fundamental link between these two otherwise divergent schools of thought. The link consists in a certain understanding of transcendence that refers simultaneously to the idea of a transcendent being and a method of inquiry. In this sense both narratives adhere to a preconceived notion of transcendence as universal or trans-cultural, which enables it to be used as both a theological and an anthropological tool in the conceptualization of religion. Though rarely understood, however, both "critical" and "traditionalist" narratives deploy two very different models of transcendence: epistemological transcendence and theological transcendence.[7] Despite differences, these two models have come to be confused and entangled with each other, resulting in a dialectical illusion which pretends to the transcendence of itself. This illusion has been most pervasive in movements such as phenomenology, systematic theology, and through them the comparative study of religion.[8] The result, broadly speaking, has been confusion between the conditions of possibility and their products. Such confusions commonly confuse the transcendental with the transcendent, performing a gesture that can be described as metaphysics or ontotheology.[9] Following Heidegger's pregnant suggestion that the basic constitution of metaphysics is ontotheological[10]—which means that, far from being a term that can be applied without prejudice to all cultures, metaphysics is rooted in a specific religio-cultural tradition whose contours reveal themselves through the combination and continuity of the Greek (*onto*), Christian-Scholastic (*-theo*), and secular-humanist (*-logical*) traditions—it is possible to uncover a somewhat uneasy intersection between post-colonial theory and recent continental philosophy of religion. This intersection questions the belief in unhindered translatability and/or universality of themes such as religion/God/theology into non-Western contexts. For cultural traditions such as the Indic, which have no exact referents for religion/God/theology, one cannot simply make such assumptions as "Sikh theology" unless one also assumes the existence of a transcendental subject—a subject who invokes the desire for "Sikh theology," and one that is necessary for there to be any historical—that is, epistemological—classification of Sikh theology as a phenomenon. It follows that the unhindered translatability or universality of terms such as religion/God/theology into non-Western contexts—specifically in this case for Indic traditions which have no exact referents for these terms—cannot simply be assumed. It is precisely through assumptions such as "Sikh theology," or a subject who naturally corresponds to the desire for "Sikh theology," that a metaphysical violence can be discerned at the heart of the hermeneutic that reconstitutes *gurmat* as a theological transcendence proper to the Sikh tradition. The term "violence" is appropriate here since the consensus over the existence of Sikh theology rests, it will be argued, on a failure to recognize a metaphysics that disguises the processes of change and transformation as the *continuity* of Sikh tradition. Violence, in other words, refers to the erasure of time in the reconstitution of *gurmat.*

From a post-colonial perspective it is more instructive to treat invocations of "Sikh theology" as a "performative utterance." Adapted from J. L. Austin's speech-act theory, the idea of "performative utterance" signifies a certain enunciation that may not necessarily have found articulation prior to the event of colonial translation, but which comes to realization after the imposition (and acceptance) of a certain regime of translation: in this case, the publication of Ernest Trumpp's "official" translation of the Adi Granth in 1877. Though rarely acknowledged, this event had far-reaching consequences for the emergence of modern Sikhism's religious ideology insofar as it helped to lay the conceptual groundwork for the reconstitution of gurmat (the Gurus's teachings) as "Sikh theology."

The theoretical strategy behind Trumpp's translation is contained in a prefatory chapter entitled "Sketch of the Religion of the Sikhs." Despite its brevity, this document exerted a profound impact on the minds of modern Sikh reformists. It would not be far from the truth to suggest that the vector informing the Sikhs' rejection of Trumpp's work, and subsequently their adoption of the conceptual medium of "theology" as the proper framework for representing the Gurus' teachings, is largely a *response* to Trumpp.

Trumpp's basic thesis was that although the "chief point in Nanak's doctrine" was the "Unity of the Supreme Being," there were no reasonable grounds for specifically differentiating the notion of God in the Adi Granth from orthodox Hindu philosophy. Clearly influenced by the Brahminical leanings of his Nirmala collaborators, Trumpp duly translated the first line of the Adi Granth by missing out the numeral "1," thereby rendering the opening syllable (*ik oankar*) as *om.*[11] Given that philosophers of Vedanta had long expounded the meaning of *om* in terms of the Hindu trinity (Brahma, Vishnu, Shiva), for Indologists and missionaries the word *om* represented Hindu pantheism; it was evidence of the Hindu mind's inability to transcend multiplicity. Trumpp therefore regarded the presence of the numeral '1' at the beginning of the Adi Granth as superfluous, an empty gesture on Guru Nanak's part since there was no conceptual correspondence between this '1' and the broader content of Sikh scripture. The numeral '1' could only imply one thing: transcendence of multiplicity and conceptual coherence which, for Trumpp, was absent in the hymns of Guru Nanak. Once a lack of theological transcendence was established, it was but a short step to designate the teachings of Nanak as akin to either Hindu pantheism or Buddhist atheism.

Trumpp's work not only threatened to displace the image of Sikhism in the minds of colonial administrators well below that of other Indic religions, it also suggested that early European accounts of Sikhs as a separate monotheistic or deistic religion within the Indic context were largely mistaken. According to Trumpp's evidence, the pantheistic nature of Sikhism could be found within Guru Nanak's own hymns which fundamentally *lacked* an adequate concept of God and consequently an adequate notion of the self. More important than the mere distinction between the categories monotheism and pantheism—what is in effect the *condition* for the validity of such categories—was that Trumpp managed to displace the conceptual framework for any future discourse about Sikh scripture into the domain of ontotheology, that is, towards a field of translation in which all statements and propositions about the Sikh religion were automatically routed through the question concerning the nature of God's existence. Thus the task for the Singh Sabha scholars was to disprove the reading of *gurmat* as pantheism and therefore to the signification of *lack* that pantheism implied.

In contradistinction to the view that Singh Sabha ideologues simply retrieved Guru Nanak's original intentions and seamlessly relocated them into a modern idiom (implying thereby the propriety of theological transcendence to the Adi Granth), I propose to read the emergence of Sikh theology in terms of a struggle to overcome the signification of lack. In this reading, the notion of lack becomes a critical hinge for any *post*-colonial reading of Sikh scripture insofar as it points to a fundamental resistance within the teachings of the Adi Granth—and therefore within any conceptualisation of *gurmat*—to what is known as metaphysics in Western philosophy and religion. Inevitably, such resistance also points to one of the more important though unresolved tensions in modern (neo-nationalist) representations of Sikh religiosity, namely, that *modern* Sikhism could only have come into being by repressing what is essentially non-modern. The non-modern refers to that which is incommensurable with the demands of modern consciousness such as contradictory and paradoxical notions of non-duality, identity and the self—modes of subjectivity that do not conform to the ego-cogito of the broadly Cartesian type.

Some important clues about this resistance can be gleaned by comparing the meanings of non-duality, self, and identity as we find it in the hymns of the Adi Granth with the meanings that come to be delineated in the commentaries. Consider, for example, the following verses from the hymn *Siddh Gost* which depicts a debate between the Siddhas (expert practitioners of Yoga belonging to the Gorakhnath sect) and Guru Nanak. Here we find Nanak evoking themes such as non-duality, self/ego/identity, and freedom but at the same time avoiding a direct metaphysical response to questions posed by the Siddhas:[12]

Siddhas

> What's the origin of the self? Where does it go? Where does it remain when merged? The teacher who can explain this mystery has indeed effaced all trace of desire.
> How can one love a reality that has no form or trace?
> Of itself the Absolute is the knower and the doer. How do you explain this, Nanak? 22

Nanak

Originating from nature's order, one returns to this order, remaining always indistinct.
Through the guru's instruction one practices truth to gain a measure of divine form.
As for the beginning, one can only speak in terms of wonder, for the One was absorbed in void.
Think of the ear rings as the uncontrived nature of the guru's wisdom: that all existence is real.
By means of the guru's word one spontaneously attains the limitless state and merges into it.
O Nanak, one who works and inquires genuinely will not take another path.
Wondrous is the divine way. This truth is known only to those who walk in its way.
Consider him a yogi who becomes detached by effacing self-love and enshrining truth within. 23
As pure form arises from infinite multiplicity, so existence becomes non-existence.
Through inner wisdom imparted by the guru one becomes attuned to the Name.
The ego's sense of difference is removed by recognizing the One truly as One.
He alone is a yogi who understands the guru's teaching and lets his lotus-mind bloom within.
Dying to the self everything becomes clear and one finds the source of all compassion.
O Nanak, by realizing the self's connectedness to all beings, honour is attained. 24.
The *gurmukh*'s self arises from truthful existence, then merges into its source, becoming identical with the One.
The self-centred beings come into this world yet find no place of rest.
Attached to a sense of otherness their coming and going continues.
Blessed by the guru's instruction one learns self-discrimination and this ceaseless wandering ends.
Man's congenital sickness is attachment to the other through which one forgets the Name's real taste.
He alone is aware who becomes aware without self-effort.
Through the guru's Word he is liberated.
Nanak, the mortal who effaces duality by stilling the ego,
Swims and helps others to swim across. 25

In verses such as these, the tenor of which is repeated throughout the Adi Granth, the non-duality of the Absolute is conceptually inseparable from the notion of freedom as found in the classic Indic theme of the polarity of fusion and separation. In conformity to broadly Indic patterns, knowledge of this Absolute is grounded in a state of existence that has realized this non-duality by relinquishing the individuality of the ego and merging itself into the Other. In this state of being, one instinctively resists representation and conceptualization in terms of subject-object duality. Such a realized individual (*gurmukh*) no longer represents the Absolute to himself since the distinction between self and other, I and not-I, disappears into a knowing that knows without immediately splitting into subject and object. Though caricatured on one hand as annihilation, dissolution, or depersonalisation, and on the other hand as an impractical ideal, the figure of the *gurmukh* and the kind of freedom associated with it is better seen as an intensely creative form of existence through which the world is perceived not as something outside of ourselves, to be recognized in detail, adapted, complied with, and fitted into our idiosyncratic inner world, but rather as an infinite succession of creative acts.

The resistance posed by such meaning reveals what could be termed as the "middle ground" of Sikh religiosity. This is a ground which, in the absence of a certain metaphysical violence, refuses a systematic *concept* of God, indeed, refuses the dominant form of conceptualization as it is understood in the Western philosophical traditions. Yet it would be a mistake to think of this "middle ground" as some kind of "original" Sikhism historically prior to colonialism and the nationalization of Sikh traditions. Whereas the term "original" remains connected to some kind of authorial intention or psychological state that can be retrieved from a standpoint of present self-consciousness, or perhaps a form of Sikh religiosity that was historically displaced, the term "middle ground" points to idioms, practices, forms, and strata of experience that are different from but also are broadly continuous with those of the wider North Indian devotional traditions. One could cite, for example, practices such as *kirtan* and *simran*, or themes such as *raga* and *rasa*, which evoke feeling and mood, or again themes relating to personal time and destiny such as *mukti*, *karma*, *and samskaras*. Despite the temptation to treat them as exotic or mystical, these themes comprise what Michel de Certeau termed the "practice of everyday life" in Sikh traditions. Yet with the emergence of a rationalized idiom characteristic of modern monotheistic Sikhism with its demand for uniqueness and clearly defined religious and cultural boundaries, the *articulation* of these non-modern modes of thinking and experience have undergone—indeed, continue to undergo—a certain repression. For the purpose of this chapter, the term "middle ground"—insofar as it refers simultaneously to a non-duality and subjectivity that is non-representational, non-conceptual, that cannot be theorized in terms of a subject that knows itself as an object nor reduced to the cognitive or the ethical—will provide a means for demonstrating continuities and transformations in the emergence of a "Sikh theology."

Not surprisingly, from the Western colonial perspective of translators such as Trumpp, this perspective on non-duality that I term as the "middle ground" came to be projected as a *lack* of a proper concept of God, a *lack* of ethical standpoint, and a *lack* of freedom in the religion of the Sikhs. In the commentaries one finds a treatment of non-duality that is responding to these accusations of lack, and insofar, begins to distance itself from the middle ground of the Adi Granth. Perhaps the best examples of this are the commentaries on the opening line of the Adi Granth which will be closely analyzed in the following section of this chapter. This opening line of the Adi Granth is better known as the *mul mantar* or the root mantra of Sikhism. For Sikhs the *mul mantar* serves as the creedal statement that expounds the central attributes of God: *ik oankar, satnam, karta purukh, nirbhau, nirvair, akal murat, ajuni, saibhang, gurparsad* (One God Exists, Truth by Name, Creative Power, Without Fear, Without Enmity, Timeless Form, Unborn, Self-Existent, By the Guru's Grace).[13]

In an effort to satisfy the perceived *lack* of an adequate conceptualization of God, Singh Sabha scholars invested a disproportionate effort to enunciate a precise and consistent meaning for the twelve or so words of the *mul mantar* since its meaning would reflect the meaning of the Adi Granth text as a whole. In what follows, I undertake a deconstructive[14] reading of the way in which *gurmat* (lit. teaching/instruction of the guru) is constituted as theology, that is, as a system of knowledge about God, a process that is linked to the work of imagining God's existence in a particular way. To illustrate how this new imagining is produced, it will be necessary to pay close attention to the hermeneutic strategies deployed by the various Singh Sabha scholars,[15] in particular their complex interweaving of time and ontology. Of the main commentaries, the commentary on the *mul mantar* by Bhai Vir Singh (hereafter BVS) is by far the longest, running into some thirty-six pages of dense exegesis. Unlike all other preceding commentaries in the Sikh tradition, BVS's text reads unmistakably like a systematic philosophical argument for the existence of God—indeed, a redefining of God's attributes "according to the guru's own instruction." My analysis in section two will therefore focus mainly on BVS's text and, for reasons that will become clear, on three terms in the *mul mantra*: *ik oankar* (One God Exists), *satnam* (Truth by Name), and *akal murat* (Timeless Form). In the third part of this chapter, I conclude by arguing that the Sikh reformist mode of thought, far from restating an original Sikh monotheism, actually makes a shift from previous Indic patterns of non-duality by importing a version of the ontological proof for God's existence.

READING THE SINGH SABHA'S EXEGESIS ON THE NON-DUAL ONE

God's Paradoxical Unity

A short and rather innocuous-looking footnote to the *mul mantra* by Teja Singh in his principal commentary the *Shabadarth Sri Guru Granth Sahib* summarizes the conceptual drive behind the reformists' exegetical project:

> *eh vartik rachna sikhi da 'mul mantra' hai. Arthat is vich oh bunyadi gallan dassian hoian han jinai dharm de neman di nih rakhi gai hai. Eh nih vahiguru di hasti di hai, us da sarup inhan lafzan vich ditta hoia he*. This verse composition is the '*mul mantra*' of Sikhi(sm); that is to say, within it are expounded those basic things upon which the foundations of religious faith (*dharam de neman di nih*) have been built. This foundation is the being or existence of God (*hasti*), whose configuration (*sarup*) is given in these words . . . (of the *mul mantra*).[16]

In three short points this statement outlines the circular hermeneutic of Singh Sabha theology: that scripture grounds the religious faith called Sikhism; that this ground is the existence of God; and that God's existence is configured or represented by the words of scripture. Yet the circularity of the statement also reveals a fissure which prevents any intended closure. This fissure is the difference between the being of God *as God* and the being of God as he comes to be *configured* or imagined in the commentary (*sarup, hasti, hond*)—a configuration which in turn points beyond its portrayal in scripture toward a logic of self-retrieval from which its originates. It is to the strategies of self-retrieval—disguised as an effacement or interiorisation of the self—that my reading will pay constant attention.

What is immediately noticeable about the commentaries on the meaning of the *mul mantra* and specifically the first syllable *ik oankar* (1E), is that they are rendered as a cleansing of authentic Sikh meaning by removing from it any association with the root mantra of Hinduism, namely the syllable *om*. Each of the Singh Sabha exegetes present short summaries of the syllable *om* as it has been understood in the Sanatana dharma, that is, in the Vedic and Puranic traditions, before contrasting it with the "true" Sikh interpretation which begins with the countering phrase: "But according to Gurmat . . ." (*par gurmat vich* . . .). The Sikh reformists justify their opposition to Vedic meanings by making a fundamental distinction between the Vedic *om* and the Sikh *ik oankar*. The Sikh syllable is differentiated from the Hindu by the numeral 1 (*ik*) which, they argue, is evidence for the monotheistic nature of Sikhism, its emphasis on the oneness of God, whereas in Sanatan tradition *om* symbolizes the pantheistic nature of the Hindu trinity of Brahma, Vishnu, and Shiva.

Paradoxically, though, the efforts of Sikh reformist scholars to remove Hindu influence led them to construct a system which, though outwardly monotheistic, could not avoid denigratory references to the ancient Vedantic metaphysics.[17] Consider, for example, the interpretations of Kahn Singh and Jodh Singh, which happen to be virtually identical: "But according to *gurmat* the numeral 1 is placed before the word *om* in order to clarify that the creator is one."[18] Here the Hindu word *om* is the same as the Sikh word *oankar*, except for its qualification by the numeral 1. Similarly, for Jodh Singh the matter is relatively straightforward where the numeral 1 serves to emphasize the essential quality of the being of God as unity: "that Being which is one only."[19]

Bhai Vir Singh's interpretation is more complex than either of the preceding. He comments at length on the separate components of the syllable *ik oankar.* According to BVS, the numeral 1 is not a quality that can be attributed to a being: "this '1' has not been used as a numerical attribute/quality but as a denotative."[20] The numeral "1" stands for "that which signifies his configuration, his name."[21] By naming the essence of God's being as oneness or unity (*ektav*), the numeral "1" is not the same as any other attribute. This "1" qualifies but is not itself qualifiable by any other quality except itself. By referring only to itself "1" denotes absolute identity and unity, pure oneness: *ektav.* Ironically, though, in the very first line of his commentary BVS is forced to speak about this ineffable "1":

> Oneness exists (the formless, who is in a state of indeterminate void)
> *ektav hai (nirankar, jo nantav vich)*
> There is existence (manifesting as form yet still oneness).
> *oankar (rup hoke phir ektav) hai.*[22]

In other words, BVS's need to account for the coming-into-form as a transition from pure oneness or indeterminate void, illustrates the aporia of any beginning—namely, that the first act is an act of translation, the translation from formlessness to form, from void to existence. Yet no sooner is the act of translation revealed than it must be denegated or foreclosed lest the movement of this translation be revealed as a movement of thought and therefore as an imperfection within this "One." I borrow the terms *denegation* and *foreclosure* from the vocabulary of Lacanian psychoanalysis. They refer to a peculiar strategy of repression in which, according to Lacan, "the ego rejects [an] incompatible idea together with the affect and behaves as if the idea never occurred to the ego."[23] The affect in question here is an anxiety concerning the disclosure of time at the heart of God's identity, his Oneness. The anxiety points to a potentially serious obstacle in any attempt to present a systematic theology and an ethically responsible subject—that is to say, a subject that is capable of successfully separating itself from the maternal (in this case "Hindu") body. In BVS's text, the work of denegation centers mainly around the polysemic nature of the word *nantav,* which occurs at key moments in the explication of *ik oankar* and specifically in the work of delimiting the precise nature of the oneness (*ektav*). Derived from the root *nan,* meaning nothing or negative, the term *nantav* refers to what is abstract, indeterminate, or devoid of form. At the same time—indeed, later in the very same commentary—*nantav* will also carry the meanings of multiplicity, differentiation, and diversity within the created expanse.

For Vir Singh:

> [T]his One which we speak of in periodic time as beyond the reach of mind or intelligence . without form, without sign or mark . . . (also happens to be) that which we perceive as abstract or indeterminate . . .

> [B]y further contemplating this aspect we perceive this aspect as diffused through all existent beings. What this means is that within His own oneness he always exists as one (*sada ik hai*).[24]

The word "always" indicates a refiguring of time that serves to suture any perceived difference between God's oneness and existence that may be implied through the polysemic term *nantav*: "When there is but the One then (He) exists as one. When perceived as indeterminate then he exists as diffused, but though diffused, his existence is not eclipsed by non-existence. In the state of abstraction also he remains but one."[25]

Clearly, Vir Singh's anxiety is linked to the possibility of mis-perceiving God's paradoxical oneness as a duality: there/not-there; existent/non-existent. Yet, for Vir Singh, the very suggestion that the "1" could signify non-existence is an anathema, tantamount to an imperfect concept of God. Indeed, only a few paragraphs later we come across an even stronger disavowal of non-existence:

> According to the instruction of the (10th) Guru the ground (*mul*) of this infinite (*anokha*) or abstract (*nantav*) or created (*sristi*) "1", whatever we call it, is not a zero or void (*shun*). It is not non-existence or negation (*anhond ya manfiat nahin*), rather [its ground] is existence which is "1" (*par hond hai jo ik hai*). The visible and invisible (*drishya andrishya*) are manifestations of this "one" unmoved being (*'iko' thir hasti*).[26]

To reinforce this, there follows a revealing footnote:

> The meaning of "shun" is non-existence (*sun da artha "anhond" hai*). But according to the teaching of the Guru "1" stands for "true existence" ("*yatharth hasti*"). Nothingness or non-existence ("*shun matar ya anhond*") is not *gurmat*. . . . Sometimes, though, the idea of "nothingness" has been used in explanations of the existence of the Supreme Being (*sun pad kai ver paramatman di hasti de arthan vich aya hai*). Consider, for example, Sankara's saying:
>
> *"ghambir dhiram nirvana sunyam / sansara saram nacha papa punyam."*
>
> Compare this to the Guru's own saying: "*Ghat ghat shun ka jannai bheo // adi purakh niranjan deo*", [in which] *shun* does not refer to nothingness or non-existence (*oh anhond nahin*) but to the primal being (*adi purakh hai*) who manifests to us as configuration / form (*prakash sarup hai*) . . . But here the meaning of *shun* is the Supreme Deity without sign or mark (*ithai sun da arth niranjan parmatman dev hai*).[27]

The strategy of denegation is just as evident in the explication of the letter *oankar* (E) which comprises the linguistic half of the symbol *ik oankar* (1E). Thus we read:

> From antiquity *om* has been a symbol for the supreme being (*paramesvar)* but in *gurmat* it is pronounced as *oankar*. It is the proper manifestation of the Supreme Being in which (his) *Nirgun* aspect and *Sargun* aspects are indiscriminately present and in which the dynamic and causal aspects are united.

> In the Upanishads *om* is the basis of the Nirguna and Saguna aspects of Brahman. The Puranic writers split (the word *om*) into the letters *a u m* indicating the three-fold division of the Hindu pantheon. But in *gurmat* there is no such division. *Om* is one letter and its meaning is Supreme Being. In its written form it conveys that *Nirgun*, who, becoming *Sargun*, yet remains one.[28]

Despite efforts to the contrary, the central issue that arises in BVS's treatment of *ik oankar* is an unmistakable tension between desire and fact. On one hand is the desire to know and therefore present God's identity as Absolute (as God exists in himself), an identity which cannot be represented except through number (*ek, ektav*) and negation (*nirgun*), which do not admit either attribute or relationality. On the other hand is the fact that, in speaking about God, duality and contradiction cannot be avoided. Indeed, the very movement toward speech about God must be represented as a difference between non-language and language, nothingness and existence, unknowable and knowable, non-time and time. To acknowledge this difference, however, is to acknowledge that time and/as movement relate "essentially" to God's Absoluteness. This means, paradoxically, that God cannot be Absolute. It is therefore the contradictory logic of this idea—where difference grounds the very possibility for presenting the identity of God—that Vir Singh and his fellow ideologues will be careful to avoid. Consequently, for them, number ("1") and word (*oankar*) cannot be admitted as different or as representing a difference in God's identity which is pure oneness (*ektav*). To admit such difference would inaugurate a translation from one mode ('1'=Nirgun=non-existence=unsayable) to another mode (E.=Sargun=existence=the sayable). The very idea of a passage from one to another would introduce contingency, nihilism, indeed uncertainty, at the ground of existence. God's identity might not then be Absolute. If so, could the entire message of the Sikh scripture (*gurmat*) have been unfolded on a nihilistic ground? Could impermanence be the proper ground of *gurmat*? A ground that, in its unfolding, automatically undermines itself?

It is to avoid this dangerous possibility that BVS et al. attempt to overcome the paradox at the heart of *ik oankar*. This is done by implementing a metaphysical assumption: that identity (*ektav*-oneness) is the condition for existence, and conversely that existence is the condition for identity. The intrinsic bond between identity and existence ensures that the division between *Nirgun* and *Sargun* will have been overcome, through a classic deployment of the law of non-contradiction (A = A). Thus, *Nirgun*—normally translated as ineffable—comes to be represented by an identity—the identity of *Nirgun* and *Sargun*—which is logically prior to the difference between them. However, the very resource for this identification can only come from the definition of being itself. This move (where the possibility of *Nirgun* as void/non-existence is circumvented by assuming that the identity of *Nirgun* and *Sargun* grounds any difference between them) actually takes place in the commentary on *satnam*.

Divine Stasis: Refiguring Time as Eternity

Although the conventional translation for the compound word *satnam* is "True Name," "Whose Name Is Truth," etc., the commentaries begin by separating its two component terms, *sat* (= being, existence) and *nam* (= name), and then focus almost completely on *sat* so that the meaning of this term becomes determinative for *satnam*. The commentaries read as follows:

> that being who remains of constant essence through the three modes of time
>
> *tin kal vich ik ras hon vala prsidh parbrahman.*[29]
>
> that (being) which endures as existing forever
>
> *sada kaim nahin vala. .*[30]
>
> whose name is the existent being
>
> *jis da nam hai hond vala.*[31]
>
> that being/existence who always remain
>
> *sada rahin vali oh hasti.*[32]
>
> That (being) which in time and eternity always remains stable/immutable"
>
> *jo kal akal sada hi thir rahe*
>
> Or that oneness which being an immutable oneness, whose name alone exists; '*satya*' in other words is that self-conscious being that remains always stable/immutable
>
> [*oh ektav*] *sada thir* [*ektav hai, us da*] *nam hi hai* [*sat(I) arthat sada thir rahin vala chetan vajud*].[33]

Consider the word "*sat*" to be an exposition of "1." The meaning of "1" is the one primal form which is one in every state of being, that is, which is immutable. Thus the meaning of word "*sat*" is that eternal (without break) form which remains always stable through the three states of time:

> *is vich sat pad "1" da hi mano tika hai | "1" da arth hai—ek hai mul hasti jo har haal "1" hai, arthat jo sada abdal hai. So "sat" pad da arth hai—trai kal abad rup jo sada thir hai.*[34]

Two things immediately strike us about these commentaries. First, there is almost complete unanimity in the way that exegesis on the name is subsumed into questions of time and ontology. Second, and what follows from the first move, is the repeated use of words which stress a particular mode of time where continuity is valued above change: *always* fixed (*sada, sada thir, sada hi thir*); of singular essence (*ek ras*); always remaining fixed (*sada thir hai*); always existing without change (*sada abdal hai*); eternal form (*abad rup*).

Contrary to appearances, these innocent-looking phrases suggest that the exegesis on *sat* is more than simply an extended exposition of the nature of "1," as BVS himself seems to suggest. In fact, the exegesis on *sat* is used to justify a particular reading of transcendence—one where the very meaning of transcendence is redefined in relation to the refiguration of time as eternity. The implication of this move can be usefully explained by way of comparison to Platonic metaphysics. Such a comparison is revealing in view of the dominant Western metaphysical context in which all Indian thinkers of the time were operating.

Plato's key statement on this matter derives from his theory of naming as given in the *Cratylus*.[35] His theory of naming is concerned with two things: (i) the distinction between name and thing, and (ii) that which is named in the thing. As a measure of correctness, the name names the essential being within a thing. This essential being is the locus of the thing's meaning, and by nature it must be fixed and of permanent duration. The very activity of naming, as the giving of a proper name, is therefore dependent on the assumption that what is named—essence as such—is "always such as it is." In turn, however, existence that is "always such as it is" depends on the distinction between two modes of temporality: the temporality of eternity as against the temporality of the present moment. This distinction is valid because things come into existence (they are created) and pass away (have a finite lifetime). But that which is *essential* being and thus "always such as it is," cannot by definition come into existence or pass away. It is eternal. There is no prior and no after to the creative event. The Platonic essential being, the 'always such as it is,' refers to the fact that what is named cannot be subject to change. Rather, what is named must be self-referring, always the same as itself, always identical. Hence the identity of the eternal: the eternally self-same as that which is always self-present.

Bhai Vir Singh's exegesis follows a very similar logic. For example, the distinction between time (*kal*) and not-time (*akal*) is effectively dissolved by grounding it in a being (*hasti, hond*) that is always stable (*sada hi thir*); stable because it admits of no change in essence. Which means that the point of difference between *kal* and *akal* (namely, the not, or the negative) is sublated into a moment that is eternally self-present. Governing the relation between time (*kal*) and not-time (*akal*) is the identity of God as eternal self-presence, which is indistinguishable from the notion of transcendence as absolute stability.

Ironically, though, the very possibility of division and duality raises further issues. If, as the commentary suggests, the truth of God's identity lies in its eternal self-presence, how is this identity to be conveyed to those who read the commentary? How is this Being of God, when God is *being* God, to be presented? What is the link between that which is to be *presented* (Truth, identity of God) and the *form* of the presentation? Will any presentation of the truth/identity of the divine not itself admit of an invasion of time into the eternal moment? Will there not have been a movement or transference from one moment to another, the well-known fall into time and contingency? Or, if the eternal moment must be preserved, will any presentation not be a virtual presentation, no more than a reflection of what is always-as-it-is? Will this transferential movement not risk the danger of being *mis*perceived, *mis*understood—which from the beginning it was the projected aim of these commentaries to avoid?

In short, the duality between the presentation and what is presented reveals one of the classic problems of religious knowledge: that there is an unavoidable discrepancy between the time of divinity (which the commentary seeks to present directly) and the time of the exegesis (which can at best re-present the divine). This discrepancy can only derive from a finite cognitive process, an act of imagining. How, then, to shift attention away from the operation of the imagination and by co-implication the identity of the thinker? This is the problem that BVS attempts to overcome (still within the exegesis of *sat*) by deploying a three-step strategy of self-effacement:

Step 1: BVS distinguishes two different kinds of cognition: the cognition of God as he is perceived by our empirical senses, versus the kind of cognition of God as Absolute which is intrinsic to the nature of the word *sat* (being). *Sat* is therefore a privileged word insofar as there is no change or variation in going from "1" to *sat*. *Sat* is not therefore based on a cognition *of* God, but constitutes the ground for cognition as such. The assumption here is that God's existence must first be guaranteed in order for there to be any possible cognition *of* God. This division of cognition is not entirely successful, however. Problems arise once we move beyond the essential word to a multiplicity of words, and consequently to manifold ways of perceiving and describing God. The *mul mantra* itself is an example of this, since the words *karta purukh, nirbhau, nirvair,* etc. can be regarded as different attributes of the same divine being.[36]

Step 2: In order to overcome the multiplicity inherent in sensible perceptions, BVS argues that it is necessary to cultivate a special type of cognition that stabilizes multiplicity into a unity. This special cognition he attributes to the practive of meditative repetition (*jap, simran*) which transcends time and the sensuous imagination.[37] Again, the kind of transcendence implied is one that immobilizes time, thus making it accord with the absolute immobilization of the eternal being of God. But, as Vir Singh realizes, the trace of the imagination cannot be effaced so easily. In order to argue for a shift toward repetition and remembrance, must he himself not rely on the very thinking he wishes to suppress? Doesn't the need to speak about God in terms of qualities and the fact that "we" can only perceive in multiple qualities (*gun/lacchan*) contaminate the divine with time?

Step 3: There follows a third move in which the notion of quality itself is further divided into two types: *sarup lacchan,* or qualities that give an understanding of form that is direct—that is, perceived by one's sense faculties—, versus tatsath lacchan, or qualities whose description of what is perceived transcends sense perception itself. *Tatsath lacchan* are privileged qualities that allow one to speak about God, or allow God to be configured, but which in the act of configuring, automatically negate or overcome any relation to the sensuous. For BVS, the *tatsath lacchan* par excellence is the word *karta* (Creator). *Karta* signifies a causation whose agency is not dependent on, or affected by, anything other than itself. Hence *karta* cannot simply mean Creator but *un*moved mover, *un*caused cause:

> Now the transcendent (in the sense of quality-less) quality (*tatsath lacchan*) which enables us to cognize the form of the formless divine is called : creator (*karta*).
>
> [*hun nirankar de sarup nu lakhan vale tatsath lacchan kahinde hain* 'karta'].
>
> Where this word '*karta*' is found in the *mul mantra* it gives the sense of the transcendent quality of the formless divine and operates as a causative *name (kirtam nam)*.
>
> [*jithe ih pad mul mantra vich pia hai uthai ih nirankar da tatsath lacchan hokai aya hai te kirtam nam hokai pia hai*].[38]

The aim of these *tatsath lacchan* is clearly to neutralize any threat to the transcendence of the divine by trying to remove—through a process of dematerialization—any link to time and world, to the Other, to the sensuous. By thus depriving any link to anything external, including being itself, what is ultimately effected is a pure self-positing, the self-movement of the form that is the subject. This pure subjectivity that defines the identity of God tries to efface every trace of the operation of imagining that might even hint at the existence of an *other* subject, that is, of alterity per se, since the presence of alterity would threaten the pure transcendence of this One.

TRACES OF IDOLATRY IN THE IMAGE OF THE ETERNAL

The commentaries on the phrase "*akal murat*" point to a convergence of the main anxieties outlined previously. Briefly, the commentaries on "*akal murat*" read as follows:

> (that being) whose installation/representation is not subject to time
> *jis di sthapana samai de bhed karke nahi.*[39]
> (that being) which is unaffected by time
> *us hasti pur samai da asar nahi.*[40]
> that being whose form (*sarup*) is beyond time i.e. whose body (*sarir*) is not subject to destruction.
> *jis da sarup kal to pare hai bhav, jis da sarir nas rahit hai.*[41]
> He is outside of time, yet being unaffected by time he is not non-existent, he exists as form/shape/image (i.e. He is in existence), meaning thereby that he has form (but) that form is not affected by time.
> *Oh akal = kal rahit hai, akal hokai oh anhond nahin, oh murat (= hond hai) arthat us da vajud ya sarup hai jo sarup kal to rahit hai.*[42]

In view of the previous effort to prove that God, though existent, cannot be limited by form or figuration, the presence of the word "*murat*"—which conveys the meanings of image, shape, form, picture, painting, idol, body, likeness, etc.—might have presented a more direct challenge to the reformists. Not least because one of the most important socio-political factors behind the divergence between reformists and traditionalists in colonial North India centered on the issue of the worship of images and idols (*murti puja*). As the Sikh reformist commentaries clearly admit, even within the *mul mantar* the word *murat* cannot easily escape a connection to time and world. But if the presentation of the formless divine "according to gurmat" was to avoid any association with "Hindu" idolatry, it would be necessary for the reformists to show: (i) that the word *murat* as used in Sikh Scripture and being qualified by *akal* has a very different signification to the "Hindu," and (ii) that there is no contradiction or inconsistency in placing *akal* and *murat* together.

On the first count, Bhai Vir Singh's remarks are fairly self-assured. *Akal murat,* he argues, takes its final meaning solely from the *mul mantra*. It does not correspond to images painted on paper, cloth, or on walls (*kagaz ke kaprai te kandan te chitarian murtian*), nor does it correspond to idols engraved in stone or cast in metal *(patharan te ukarian te dhatuan vich dalian murtian*).[43] According to the *mul mantra,* these are forbidden (*mul mantra de laksh hon to varjit ho gaian*). On the other count, regarding the consistency of meaning between *akal* and *murat*, there seems to be less certainty. The problem revolves around the semantic ambiguity of *kal* (time), which can have two different meanings depending on whether it is perceived subjectively or objectively. Thus, *kal* can be perceived subjectively as duration (*sama*) according to the threefold division of time (*trai vandan vich*) as beginning, middle, and end or past, present, and future (*aad , mad, ant*).[44] This is time as it is ascertained by the self, or to be more faithful to Bhai Vir Singh's text, it is the sense of time as the self *believes* time to exist (*aap nu partit karounda hai*).[45] Alternatively, time can be perceived objectively, as when it shows itself to our self from the perspective of the end of time, that is, teleologically (*kal jo "ant" vich apna ap nu dikhalda hai ta arth maut ho janda hai*).[46] Thus, if *kal* is taken objectively as "death," then *a-kal* can take on the meanings of immortal, eternal, that which always remains as it is. Hence, *akal murat* must mean the eternal form, the form that transcends time, and because it transcends time is able to transcend form itself. But, as Vir Singh explains, because the objective meaning of time as death/end is already contained within the subjective notion of time (*"kal" pad da arth "maut" arth "kal" pad de "sama" arth de antargat hai*), it is already part of a typically human understanding of time as a figure that is represented to a self who is always already present to itself. It follows, though, that the negation of this human time (*kal* as being-in-time) giving *a-kal* might imply a negation of the very mode of time whereby we conceive existence in general and the existence of all things. Which is to say that the logic of negation intrinsic to *akal* could be misunderstood as non-existence. However, it is, finally, to avoid this very possibility that Vir Singh will stress that it is perfectly correct to write *"akal murat"* (*"akal" kahkai murat pad nal likhna is vastai sahi hai*). By being *akal,* which also implies the negation of subjective human time, God does not become non-existent (*"akal" honai karke oh "an-hond" nahin ho janda*).[47]

Notwithstanding his efforts to find conceptual closure, Bhai Vir Singh's argument reveals gaps at the very point where claims to extreme transcendence appear to be strongest. An obvious flaw is the reliance on the metaphor of the sun to conceptualize divine transcendence of sensuous form and quality. Yet even this seemingly innocuous use of the metaphoric imagination is enough to preserve the effect of sensuous imagery while almost eliminating the threat posed by linking the sensuous to the divine. As one scholar (writing about a similar issue though in the very different context of early Christianity) has astutely noted, "In the all or nothing stakes implied by the extreme transcendence of the One . . . Even this tiniest residue [of the sensuous image] to which it inconspicuously but necessarily looks for support, is enough to compromise its avowed independence."[48] What begins as an assured strategy of the concept's upward movement turns into a rather uncertain trade-off: good metaphors for bad idols, good concepts for bad images; *akal murat* for *murati*, the external form for the perishable supplement. Yet the valuation of the "good" image of eternity will have been generated within a subjective standpoint, produced by a self whose primary mode of relationality is auto-affection—the production of the self by the self. Given that auto-affection is ultimately premised on a failure, in the sense that it can only work by subjecting time to a metaphysical figure of eternity, so also for

BVS, the eternal form (*akal murat*) can only be presented by thinking in and through form itself. It can only be imagined as a form in time: *sarir, sarup, hond, hasti.*

Ironically, therefore, attempts by the Singh Sabha writers to overcome idolatry and idolatrous notions of God by means of the elevated concept, have to admit the "tiniest residue" of idolatry into the process of cleansing *gurmat* (and therefore Sikhism) from any contamination by Hinduism. All along it seems, the Singh Sabha reformists were doing in their exegetical works precisely what they accused Hindus of doing in practice, which of course means that the project of constructing religious boundaries is compromised from the very outset. The question, however, is why, in a presentation where form simply replaces form, the trade-off could ever have been considered profitable? What is it that the reformists desired to gain? Or, inverting the question: What is it that the reformists thought they *lacked*?

ONTOTHEOLOGY AND THE ECLIPSE OF NON-DUALITY

To read the history of neo-colonial reform movements such as the Singh Sabha as the history of a perceived lack is to question some of the foundational assumptions on which modern knowledge about Sikhism is based. Sikh scholars in the reformist tradition have unanimously disavowed the relevance or necessity of formal theological proofs to Sikhism, preferring to argue that God and theology are naturally present in the Adi Granth. Writing within the conceptual framework set by Trumpp's translation, the Singh Sabha scholars needed to prove that Sikhism was not Hinduism by proving that the Sikh concept of God was not pantheistic but monotheistic. In short, they need to prove that God exists, that God's Name names this existence, and that the nature of this existence is an eternal identity, a static immutable One.

In view of its form and conceptual dynamic, however, it is difficult to deny that BVS's exegesis aspires to the status of a theological proof. Given that his commentary is structured not only by a dialectical chain of propositional statements about the nature of God, but by a conceptual dynamic that moves from the Oneness of God (*ektav*), through the Being of God (*sat*), to the Eternal as the Identity of God (*akal*), the *form* and *logic* of BVS's presentation bears a striking resemblance to the scholastic doctrine of *scientia dei,* the importance of which lies in its inseparability from the ontological argument.[49] However, one would need to qualify the statement that BVS's exegesis on the non-dual One *is* an ontological proof for the existence of God. Indeed, the appearance of such a proof is surprising for several reasons. First, although BVS received a secondary education in an Anglo-Vernacular mission school, there is no indication that BVS had detailed knowledge of Western philosophical theology and specifically not the history of the ontological proof. Second, prior to the Singh Sabha movement there is nothing akin to the ontological argument in the Sikh hermeneutic tradition.[50] Third, in the broader Indic context, though there are venerable traditions of analysis and argumentation about the nature and reality of "God," all of these traditions differ from the ontological argument as it is known in the West, in regard to at least one crucial point which can be explained in the following way.

Ordinarily, the ontological argument in its various statements revolves around the definition of God as "that Being than which nothing greater can be thought . . . He who understands that God exists cannot think of Him as non-existent." In short, God cannot be identified with nothingness. God is *not* nothing. Yet the matter can never end there. For hiding behind this rendering of the ontological argument is the presupposition that nothing exists without reason, known in the Western philosophical and theological tradition as the principle of reason.[51] The logic of this principle goes something like this: The reason why things exist rather than not exist resides in their cause. It follows that the first cause must also be the highest cause, a cause that towers above or transcends all others, namely, God. God's being thus transcends in the sense of being over-against and exceeding all conditioned beings. But although God is conceived as the highest being, such transcendence is still conceived from within the totality of all that exists. Which means that God, as with all other things that exist, remains subject to the principle of reason. God exists—indeed, knowledge about God exists—only insofar as the principle of reason itself holds. Stated differently, God exists only insofar as there is first a self-grounding cognition, a self-knowing-itself, which is able to present itself in the mode of an ego-cogito. It belongs to this self-presenting subject, which first and foremost *knows* itself, that it certify itself continually, which means as an identity.

In the *Metaphysical Foundations of Logic,* Heidegger argues that the subjective basis of theological knowledge remains hidden due to a long-standing confusion between two different ways of conceiving transcendence: epistemological and theological transcendence.[52] Though seemingly opposed, the standpoint of epistemology is in fact taken for granted in all theological reasoning resulting in the confusion between the transcend*ent* (the highest Being, first cause, God, etc.) and transcend*ence.* The latter term is crucial since its signification of passing beyond limits can be understood in very different ways. There is, for example, the metaphysical sense of being absolutely unaffected by time, in which case the meanings of transcendent and transcendence are conjoined to give what is known as ontotheology. This notion of transcendence has been characteristic of the tradition of Western philosophical thinking that continually grounds itself on the field of self-consciousness, the *ego-cogito* of the post-Cartesian tradition, but is largely absent from Indian and other Oriental forms of thinking.

The appearance of the ontological argument in BVS's commentary clearly suggests that the enunciation of *gurmat* as Sikh theology, or as monotheism, requires a fundamental departure from precolonial Indic ontologies and a concomitant accession to the ontology of modernity. Between any departure from one ontology and accession to another, lies the process of cultural translation that is experienced subjectively as a transformation. In-sofar as any accession to modernity requires a break with the pre-modern (this being the founding gesture of modernity), the translation/transformation process can also be regarded—as Peter Van der Veer rightly suggests—as a "conversion to modernity." The only difference here is that this process of translation/transformation was shown to occur seamlessly, without any hint of having been affected by anything foreign or external. To be more specific, the transformation of *gurmat* to monotheism, a process which happens to be disguised as the natural movement of tradition, involves the accession of *gurmat* into the comparative schema of "world religions."

As I argued elsewhere, however, the historical deployment of terms such as "monotheism" in context of Indic cultures must be viewed with caution.[53] Far from being 'natural' to the vocabulary of religions/theology, terms such as monotheism/pantheism/polytheism represent world-historical categories, which came to be invested with their present meanings in the context of political and intellectual encounter between West and non-West during the nineteenth century. Indeed, the rise of terms monotheism/pantheism/polytheism to world-historical status is inextricably linked to the advent of occidentalism and, along with this, the idea of the nation.

An important consequence of this was the evolution of the comparative enterprise. Driven by a Kantian logic of "cofiguration"—a rivalrous mode of comparison organized by an assumed belief in the symmetry and equivalence between autonomous entities—, the comparative enterprise can be seen as a process in which self (West) and Other (non-West) is automatically installed as the framework for thinking about the identity and difference between cultures, languages, and religions. Although scholars are now beginning to acknowledge that disciplines such as philosophy of religion and the history of religions emerged precisely as a result of this comparative enterprise, it is less well understood that the conceptual basis for comparative religions was and remains a version of the ontological proof for the existence of God. Given their conceptual similarity as modes of evaluating difference, the ontological proof can be regarded as a central mechanism, as it were, on one hand, for determining the theological identity or essence of a particular religion, and on the other for comparing religions in their totality through the schema called 'world religions' or the history of religions. Closely scrutinized, however, the source of comparativism can be traced to the very points where the identity of God (and by implication the identity of the Sikh subject) is delimited absolutely, which is to say, in terms of transcendence.

NOTES

1. This article has been previously published as: "The Politics of Non-Duality: Reassessing the Work of Transcendence in Modern Sikh Theology," *Journal of the American Academy of Religion* 74 (3) (2006), 646–73. Copyright and permission by Oxford University Press.

2. N. G. Barrier, *The Sikhs and Their Literature,* 1849–1919 (New Delhi: Manohar Book Service, 1970); W. H. McLeod, *Who Is a Sikh?: The Question of Sikh Identity* (Oxford: Clarendon Press, 1989); W. H. McLeod, "A Sikh Theology For Modern Times," in *Sikh History and Religion in the Twentieth Century,* eds. Joseph O'Connell et al. (New Delhi: Manohar, 1990); Harjot Oberoi, *The Construction of Religious Boundaries: Culture, Identity and Diversity in the Sikh Tradition* (New Delhi: Oxford University Press, 1994).
3. O'Connell et al., *Sikh History,* 1990.
4. McLeod 1990.
5. Though problematic, this distinction is best articulated by W. H. McLeod in his article "Cries of Outrage: History Versus Tradition in the Study of the Sikh Community," *South Asia Research* 14, no. 2 (1994): 121–135.
6. McLeod, "Sikh Theology," 1990.
7. Heidegger, *The Metaphysical Foundations of Logic*, 1992.
8. Land, *The Thirst for Annihilation*, 1991.
9. Caputo, *The Religious*, 2002.
10. Heidegger, *Identity and Difference*, 1969.
11. *Om* was also a focal point with the Indian philosophical traditions, especially in the two main forms of Vedanta (Advaita and Vishisht-Advaita) and Sankhya-Yoga. In the Vedantic systems *om* is the *sabdabrahman*, the word or symbol that stands for the supreme being (Brahman), which has two forms: *Nirguna* and *Saguna*. According to the standard accounts, the non-dualistic Advaita-Vedanta associated with the ninth-century Saivite ascetic Sankara, emphasized the Nirguna over Saguna aspect, with the result that sects and philosophies based on this system tended toward an abstract monism, metaphysical contemplation, or extreme asceticism. In contrast, the qualified non-dualism of Vishisht-Advaita Vedanta associated with the twelfth-century Vaisnavite thinker Ramanuja emphasized the Saguna aspect, resulting either in a defense of polytheism or as a definitive factor in the rise of the *bhakti* movement as rejuvenation of true Hindu religion.
12. *Adi Granth*, 940. Translation my own.
13. This is what I would call a typical Singh Sabha translation (especially "One God Exists"). Though it is now often replaced by "One Being", etc., still the intended meaning circulates within the same metaphysical form.
14. Despite the connotations of the word *deconstruction*—associated in particular with the work of Martin Heidegger and Jacques Derrida—this mode of regressive analysis is not intended to undermine tradition but to recall what it was about. Deconstruction here means finding the rule according to which the concepts were formed out of an experience of being, and then tracing backwards the motion of their genesis. Deconstruction thus involves a "double reading," which on one hand pays close attention to the texts of a particular tradition, but on the other hand, *in that very attention*, discloses a rupture in these texts which requires a radically different reading of it, thus destabilizing it and in the undecidability thereby created, opens the possibility of thinking differently.
15. I shall refer mainly to noted scholars such as Bhai Vir Singh, Kahan Singh Nabha, Teja Singh, Jodh Singh, and Sahib Singh.
16. Teja Singh, *Shabadarth Sri Guru Granth Sahib*, vol. 1. 8th ed. (Amritsar: Shiromani Gurudwara Parbhandhak Committtee, 1996), 1.
17. For Sikh reformists, however, it seems that the actual target of their critiques was not Vedanta as such. There is, for example, no sustained engagement with any Vedantic system. It is rather the influx of Vedantic ideas from Udasi and Nirmala schools throughout the nineteenth century and its effect on the interpretation of Sikh scriptures that appears to have been their real concern.

Under the patronage of Maharaja Ranjit Singh, many within the Udasi and Nirmala sects managed to establish themselves as readers of the Adi Granth or as attendants of Sikh *dharmshalas*. See Pashaura Singh, *The Guru Granth Sahib: Canon, Meaning and Authority* (New Delhi: Oxford University Press, 2000), 249–250. Notable Udasi scholars, such as Anandghan who had trained at centres of Hindu learning such as Kasi, wrote influential commentaries on the Japji. Despite certain differences with the Udasi sect, Nirmala scholars of the early to mid-nineteenth century such as Kavi Santokh Singh, Pandit Tara Singh Narotam, Giani Gian Singh, and Gulab Singh were equally inclined toward Vedantic interpretations of *gurbani*, maintaining that *gurbani* was essentially an expression of ancient Vedic teachings in the current vernacular. See Taran Singh, *Gurubani Dian Viakhia Parnalian* (Patiala: Punjabi University, 1980).

18. *Par gurmat vich om de mudh eka likhke sidh kita hai ki kartar ik hai.* See Kahn Singh Nabha, *Gurshabad Ratnakar (Mahan Kosh)* (Patiala: Bhasha Vibhag, 1981), 21.
19. *Oh hasti keval ik hai.* Jodh Singh, *Gurmat Nirnai,* 9th ed. (Ludhiana, Punjab: Academy Press, 1932), 1.
20. *Eh 1 "sankhya" vachik visheshan karke nahin vartain par 'sangya' karke vartaion hoi.* Bhai Vir Singh, *Santhya Sri Guru Granth Sahib* (New Delhi: Bhai Vir Singh Sahitya Sadan, [1958] 1997), 2.
21. *Jo us de sarup da likhayak us da nam hai.* Bhai Vir Singh 1997, 2.
22. Bhai Vir Singh 1997, *Santhya,* 1.
23. Laplanche and Pontalis 1974, *The Language of Psycho-Analysis,* 166–169.
24. *Thit duara updesh karde han man buddhi di paunch to parai hai . . . us da rup koi nahin, chhin koi nahin. . . . Ki jo nantav vich dekh rahe ho, is vich khoj kardian asi ghat ghat vich us nu dehia hai. Bhav ih hoia ki oh apni ektav vich sada ik hai.* Bhai Vir Singh 1997, *Santhya,* 2.
25. *Jad ik hai tan ik hai. Jad nantav vich dekho, tan ghat ghat vich hai, par oh ghat ghat vich hon karke pranchin nahin ho gia. Oh nantav vich bi aap ik da ik hi hai.* Bhai Vir Singh 1997, *Santhya,* 2.
26. Bhai Vir Singh 1997, *Santhya,* 3.
27. See footnotes to Bhai Vir Singh 1997, *Santhya,* 3.
28. Bhai Vir Singh, "Japji," in Panj Granthi Satik, 1-2. (Amritsar: Shiromani Gurdwara Pravandhak Committee)., 1-2. See also Bhai Vir Singh 1997, 10.
29. Kahn Nabha, *Gurshabad Ratnakar* (Mahan Kosh). Patiala: Punjab: Bhasha Vibhag [1931] 1981),148-149.
30. Teja Singh, *Shabadarth Sri Guru Granth Sahib,* vol. 1. 8th ed (Amritsar: Shiromani Gurdwara Pravandhak Committee, 1996), 1.
31. Sahib Singh, *Sri Guru Granth Sahib Darpan*, vol.1 (Jalandhar, Punjab: Raj Publishers 1962), 46.
32. Jodh Singh, *Gurmat Nirnai,* 9th ed. (Ludhiana, Punjab: Academy Press, 1932), 1.
33. Bhai Vir Singh 1997, *Santhya,* 1.
34. Bhai Vir Singh 1997, *Santhya,* 10–11.
35. See the "Cratylus," in *The Collected Dialogues of Plato,* eds. Edith Hamilton and Huntington Cairns (Princeton, NJ: Princeton University Press, 1961).
36. Bhai Vir Singh 1997, *Santhya,* 11.
37. When we shall begin to meditate upon these perceived qualities, then the tendency of consciousness to be dispersed will be reduced, unity will come about, and with attention fixed on the one eternal Being, union will be attained. (*Jad asin inhan lakhayak lacchan da, ya gurmantra da jap simran karange tan chit di birti da vikhep ghatega, ekagarta avegi te ik akal purakh vich birti da tikao hoke mel parapat hovaigi.*) See Bhai Vir Singh 1997, *Santhya,* 11.

38. Bhai Vir Singh, *Santhya,* 16.
39. Kahn Singh, *Gurshabad Ratnakar,* 36.
40. Jodh Singh, *Gurmat Nirnai,* 1.
41. Sahib Singh, *Sri Guru Granth Sahib Darpan*, vol. 1 (Jalandhar, Punjab: Raj Publishers, 1964), 46-47.
42. Bhai Vir Singh, *Santhya,* 1, 27.
43. Ibid., 27.
44. Ibid., 27-28.
45. The word *partit* means belief, faith, or trust. See Bhai Vir Singh *Santhya,* pp. 27–28.
46. See Ibid., 27-28.
47. Bhai Vir Singh, *Santhya,* 28.
48. Paulo Goncalves, "Vital Necographies: Deconstruction, God and Arche-Idolatry," in *Scottish Journal of Religious Studies* 19, no. 1 (1997): 90.
49. For details of this argument, see Heidegger, *Metaphysical Foundations,* 57-58.
50. For example, nothing like the ontological proof for God's existence can be detected in Taran Singh's analysis of the various streams of Sikh interpretive tradition (*Gurbani Dian Viakhian Prnalian*, Patiala, 1980).
51. Heidegger, , *Metaphysical Foundations,* 26–28.
52. Heidegger, *Metaphysical Foundations,* 161–162.
53. See A. S. Mandair, "What If *Religio* Remained Untranslatable?" in *Difference in Philosophy of Religion,* ed. Phillip Goodchild (Aldershot and Vermont: Ashgate Publishing, 2003).

3 Who Are the Velalas?

Twentieth-Century Constructions and Contestations of Tamil Identity in Maraimalai Adigal (1876–1950)

Srilata Raman

In the 1920s, the Tamil scholar and Dravidian ideologue Maraimalai Adigal[1] wrote a series of articles and short monographs on Tamil culture and "Velala" culture. Those were contentious times, when a new articulation of a Tamil, specifically anti-brahminical Dravidian identity had already emerged within the context of colonialism. There were several reasons for its emergence: British trade and colonial practices had brought economic opportunities and improved material prospects to the lives of many non-brahmin and subaltern communities; political debates, aided by the gradual spread of print culture, was conducted in a language of rights and liberalism; and these developments contributed to the formation of religious or caste associations which challenged or at least resisted existent power structures.[2] Particularly important in this context were the cultural and political tensions which had begun to emerge in the urban milieu of Madras between elite groups of brahmins and non-brahmins. The preponderance of brahmins in the civil administration of the Madras Presidency under the employment of the British was complemented by their successful and increasing acculturation to British manners, modes, and language. This, in turn, was reflected culturally in a new-found pride in an "Aryan" and Sanskritic past, an enthusiasm supported both by recent Orientalist scholarship as well as organizations like the Theosophical Society and its publications. These political and cultural developments, in the latter half of the nineteenth century, came to be strongly challenged by a non-brahmin elite through a re-articulation of what constituted authentic Tamil, "Dravidian" identity and religion. This identity and religion was increasingly located in the realm of the "non-brahmin," itself a newly constituted meta-category subsuming within it the heterogeneous caste-structure of those other than brahmins in Tamil society. The re-imagining of history played a vital role in this new articulation, and long-dominant or newly constituted elite histories and historiography were strongly contested, not just with the "hard" evidence of literature, inscriptions, and archaeology but through a "soft" and imaginative reclaiming of lost homelands of power, lost seemingly irredeemably from the perspective of the distressing present.[3] Maraimalai Adigal's short monograph *Velala Civilization* (*Velala Nakarikam*), standing for the Dravidian side of the debate, is characteristic of the blending of both hard and soft historiographical practices.

Maraimalai Adigal (1876–1950) had been born as S. Vedachalam in Nagapattinam, in the Madras Presidency, before he took on the Tamil version of his own Sanskritized name. As a young man he had acquired traditional learning both in Sanskrit and Tamil and had been, in fact, deeply religious in a conventional sense, with a belief in orthodox Vedanta. This was to gradually change when he came under the influence of Somasundara Nayakar (1846–1901), a Shaiva Siddanta scholar well-known for his polemics against both Vaisnavism and Vedanta. Through his studies with Somasundara Nayakar, Maraimalai Adigal acquired an uncompromising allegiance to Tamil Shaiva Siddhanta, which supplanted his earlier religious thinking. In 1906 he launched the first of a series of annual Shaiva Siddhanta conferences. Highly respected both for his erudition and his political engagement, he occupied an important place in the Saivite intellectual world. He wrote prolifically and lectured on Tamil culture and Shaiva Siddhanta and founded the "Pure Tamil Movement" which sought to return Tamil as a language to a state of pre-Sanskrit purity. A successful organizer, he also created several public organizations to sustain these numerous proselytising and publishing activities.[4] Indeed, the book *Velala Civilization,* a short monograph of no more than twenty-four brief chapters, had been written at the behest of some of his Sri Lankan admirers who had asked him to compose something on the Tamil Velala.[5]

Velala Civilization seizes upon a distant, classical past which is both an archaic and an arcadian landscape, a community rather than a state or nation, governed by reciprocal relationships, by food and diet, having the features of an organic society. Rural rather than urban, this society is a natural crucible for certain moral values. The Velala, the high-caste nonbrahmin individual with traditional ties to the land, embodies these moral values and is both the creator and the linchpin of this society.

Maraimalai Adigal had illustrious precedence for the topos of "the Velala as the archetypal Tamil," as expressed in classical and medieval Tamil literature. Yet, as I hope to show in this chapter, his vision of the Velala as part of a pure Tamil space, and as the bearer of a new Tamil ethics, was something new. It was new because for Adigal, Velala becomes, first and foremost, a political category constructed as a personification of "the Tamil," removed from the substantiality of caste or region and located in an imaginary lost landscape of the Tamil people, standing in opposition to everything which might signify Aryanism and Aryan-Brahminism. Further, Velala is also a social and moral category embodying essential Tamil virtues which become further ethicized and universalized in *Velala Civilization,* virtues which coalesce around the nature of food and the practice of vegetarianism. In this chapter, by exploring these particular themes and not others (such as Maraimalai Adigal's Shaivism), I further hope to show how major components of Velala identity are created and, as a result, become situated in a space between social suffering and social assertion, between shame at the present and pride in the past, between caste society and an egalitarian society, and between lost past and utopian future worlds.

TAMIL CIVILIZATION

Velala Civilization begins by exalting agriculture: The discovery and practice of agriculture alone generates the food surplus necessary for the creation and maintenance of a civilized society. The Velala man stands at the forefront of the effort to generate this food surplus and, hence, history in the Tamil region, in any meaningful sense, begins with him.

> In the times when one didn't know about agriculture and how to practice it successfully, people, poverty-stricken, lived without adequate food to eat or proper clothing to wear. They hunted and killed, with infinite sorrow, deer, sambur, porcupine, goats, and cows. They ate their flesh, as well as the fruits and tubers available nearby, wore bark and skins as clothing, and lived, devoid of civilization, on mountains and in the hollows of trees. There were times when their prey as well as fruits were scarce, however much they hunted. Then, there were many days of hardship when they had to endure being hungry.[6]

The Velala either enters this primitive landscape from outside or he is already the quick-witted inventor within it—this is not made clear in the book. Yet it is his virtues that make agricultural activity possible:

> Agriculture is a grievous profession. Only those who practise it know what sorrow is. One needs intellectual foresight *(nunnarivu)* in order to do it properly and successfully. Thus, only those who practise it possess an excellent intellect and the capacity to make use of it. For this reason compassion *(irakkam)*, intelligence *(arivu)* and generosity *(ikai)* are called the natural qualities of the Velalas.[7]

Let us register in these two passages Maraimalai Adigal's exaltation of the taming of primitive land, mountains, and the like, as well as the person who tames it. The perspective is romantic, lauding the urban intellectual, and links cultivation, economic improvement, and proprietorship in an inversion of the notion of progress: yearning for the pastoral in the aftermath of industrial modernity in the West.[8] The perspective focuses on the Velala who decides to cultivate the land, it is his "natural" acumen which makes the land yield lasting fruit; he alone has an inalienable right over it and by dint of it determines the course of society.

His superiority is assured by the fact that he alone does not rely on others to sustain him, but rather, he sustains others. He is not only the creator of food and stability, but also the first trader in this society: He trades his food for goods and does this through fair dealing, for he does not seek to exploit others. The Velala, thus, is both the landowner and the trader of Tamil society.[9]

In this account, we also see the attempt to construct a modernized Velala identity by someone who laid claim to being a Velala himself, at a critical juncture in the cultural politics of Tamil Nadu. Who are the Velalas he is referring to? The name derives from *Velalamai*, meaning cultivation and agriculture. References are plentiful in classical Tamil Cankam literature[10] to an elite social group, the tillers of the land (*ulavar*) as part of a rudimentary, hierarchical social order of cultivators, artisans, and hill people, of which they represented the summit.[11] Further, in the list of the innate qualities of the Velala let us pay attention, more closely, to generosity, or more precisely gift-giving or granting, *ikai*. This term, as well as its synonym, *kotai*, is central in classical Tamil literature, particularly as it refers to the gift-giving deeds of the hero. It is, moreover, associated with both excess and hierarchy.[12] The hero, like the king, generally, in the pan-Indian context, must give munificently, even while the specific term *ikai* refers to the largesse shown by a superior person to an inferior one.[13] The Velala, then, Maraimalai Adigal shows us through indirection, was the classical Tamil hero who was marked by his munificence toward others.

Yet his significance does not stop there. Rather, as we read further into the monograph and see how Tamil society comes to be constituted in these ancient times, we see that the power of the Velala extends naturally from that of feeding, trading, and sustaining society to determining and constituting it, even to a certain kind of cosmic leadership:

> . . . [Velalas], from ancient times, separated out a group from among themselves, gifted in intellectual foresight, in order to recite the sacred texts and to worship the divine within the temples. These, indeed, are the Tamil Brahmins, whom contemporary people call 'Aticaivas', ' Kurukkal', 'Pattar' and 'Nampiyar'. All the ancient temples in Tamil Nadu have been constructed by the Tamil people and belong to them. Hence, apart from this Aticaiva group which has been created from among the Velalas, no Aryan Brahmins (ariya parppanar) were permitted to touch and to worship the images within these temples.[14]

The next category of people, required for waging war and protecting the land, is chosen by the Velala to be kings. Still others were designated traders: their duty was to feed the brahmins, ascetics, and the poor of society, and to carry on trade. Those chosen for this hereditary profession were believed to have a good head for numbers and to be persuasive. Finally, the remainder of the Tamil peoples were allotted skills which were necessary for the functioning of any civilized society: blacksmiths, medicine men, launderers, minstrels—eighteen such professional categories in all. These eighteen groups followed the orders of the Velala and did their designated tasks in life faithfully. This, Maraimalai Adigal concludes, was the traditional Tamil social structure, created by the Velala. The sources for this vision of ancient Tamil society are not difficult to unearth, and the implicit equation of the Velala with the Tamil hero of the Cankam age guides us toward them. The vision derives from a discourse that was generated by the "discovery" and publication of Cankam literature through the pioneering work of C. V. Damodaran Pillai (1832–1901) and U. V. Swaminatha Iyer (1855–1942).[15] This discovery, in turn, fueled a modern re-crafting of Tamil literary and social histories[16] that derived much, if not all, of its understanding of ancient Tamil society from these works. As Sumathi Ramaswamy explains,

> These poems not only deepened the antiquity of Tamil literature, but quite as crucially, within a few years of their being made public, they came to be valorized as the repositories of an ideal and perfect Tamil society, prior to its colonization by either the British or, more enduringly, by the Brahmanical Aryans from the North. They were combed to generate nostalgic portrayals of an ancient Tamil people who were adventurous and heroic; who roamed the high seas in pursuit of gold and glory; who were "hospitable and tolerant in religion," "egalitarian" and "rationalist", fun-loving but contemplative and philosophical as well.[17]

In the same decades as Maraimalai Adigal was writing his treatise, M. S. Purnalingam Pillai, in his popular textbook, *A Primer of Tamil Literature*, had this to say about the society of the Cankam literature and "ancient Tamilaham":

> The Tamils were adventurous, and hospitable and tolerant in religion. They were civilized and polished and they had towns and forts, and arms and weapons, and drove a roaring trade.[18]

The social organization of this Tamil society was also depicted by scholars in lines similar to that described by Maraimalai Adigal. Thus Purnalingam Pillai says of ancient Tamil social stratification: "The Tamilar were of Eight Classes: Arivar, Ulavar, Ayar, Vedduvar, Kannalar, Padaiadchier, Valayar, and Pulayar," and adds, "The *Ulavar* or farmers were next in rank. Called also *Velalar* and *Karalar* or lords of the floods and seasons, they formed the landed aristocracy of the country."[19] Other scholars, such as Sesha Iyengar, who wrote *Dravidian India* (1925), or Kantaiyya Pillai, who wrote (Tamil Intiya) *Tamil India* in 1945, also agreed on this issue of the basic "class" division of ancient Tamil society, as well as the privileged and high status of Velalas within it,[20] even as they tended to assent, implicitly or explicitly, to the further assumption that this class society was different from "caste" society. It was different in the sense that class divisions were not religiously sanctioned, and in the way in which its structures of hierarchy were based on a natural division of labor and professional specialization and hence (according to these writers) were conflict-free and harmonious. In Maraimalai Adigal's own view this society was not free of hierarchy, since it was one in which the kings and the priests enjoyed high status and others who served them a lower one, yet this hierarchy was fundamentally different and more just than the Aryan one, with its reliance upon "alien" *dharma* texts for the ordering of social relations.[21] Here, we see a reinterpretation of caste as "division of labor" which is, nevertheless, fundamentally different from a brahminical model which does the same. For, as Pandian points out, "The Brahmins . . . , in order to render it modern and legitimate, claimed the caste system as an indigenous form of division of labour. But Adigal argued that caste was the corruption of a pre-existing form of the division of labour and an invention of Brahmins to dominate Tamils. In other words, while the Brahmin invoked the division of labour to legitimize caste, Adigal invoked it to discredit caste."[22] As depicted in *Velala Civilization,* the coming together of "Aryans" and "Dravidians" is a bitter tale of generosity betrayed.

The Aryans, in this work, come from somewhere outside the Tamil lands 5,500 years ago, having already experienced the high civilization of the Velalas who live in the north of India; they are received graciously by the southern Velalas. They repay the Velala kindness to them with treachery of a particularly distressful kind, through permanently degrading the status of the Velala within a caste hierarchy. Those who are most complicit in this act are those with the most to gain religiously: the Aryan Brahmins:

> Now, the good Tamil people, the Velalas, welcomed the Aryan Brahmins who had left their homes in order to survive. They received them with affection, gave them places to stay, food to eat and clothes to wear, assisted them in learning, did various acts of kindness and protected them. Instead of expressing gratitude these Aryan Brahmins resolved to degrade [the Velalas], much like a blade whose sharpness is tested on that very whetting stone which is used to sharpen it. Resolving to do this, they became audacious enough to shamelessly call the latter *sudras* at every opportunity which arose and, in all the Tamil and Sanskrit works which emerged after the period of Cuntaramurti Nayanar [the early *bhakti* period] they besmirched them by writing of them as *sudras*. In this later period the number of Velalas who were educated had become extremely scant due to the confusions which prevailed in the wake of Muslim rule. Thus, these Velalas, not understanding the meaning of the word *sudra* used derogatorily by the Aryan Brahmins, accepted the word and referred to themselves by that name.[23]

Maraimalai Adigal goes on to paint the consequences of this tragic history in light of his understanding of it as the result of duplicity, on one hand, and a naïve misunderstanding, on the other. The ensuing consequences occupy a space between the past and the present. The Aryan Brahmins, through their introduction of the caste system among a hapless

Tamil people, succeed in setting a once-harmonious society at odds with itself. They also categorize the rest of the populace according to the *varna* system, placing other, traditionally non-elite groups, into the categories of *kshatriya* and *vaishya* and, hence also the Velalas, who formerly stood among the ancient elite. In doing so, they generate new enmities among a people who had once co-existed peacefully with each other. Placing themselves above this manipulated and warring peoples the outsiders, the Aryan Brahmins, enjoy a prosperity even today which accrues to them alone.[24]

With this sharpened focus on an ancient Tamil "class" society as opposed to a modern Tamil "caste" society we also enter the second discourse of Dravidianism that polarized historiographic approaches to Tamil history in the first half of the twentieth century. This discourse cannot be disentangled from the first: the racial division of "Aryan" and "Dravidian" and the construction of the two races; so it is to that division that I now turn.

It is currently accepted that "Aryan" and "Dravidian" initially emerged in the late eighteenth to early nineteenth century British Orientalist and missionary scholarship, and first within the parameters of linguistic theories. Thus the discovery of the Indo-European family of languages, and subsequently the Dravidian, laid the foundations of comparative philology. Pioneers in this field were William Jones in Calcutta, whose discoveries regarding the former were made public in 1786, and Francis Ellis in Madras, who had anticipated the independent origin of the Dravidian family of languages (even though he did not use the word "Dravidian") in the early decades of the nineteenth century.[25] Trautmann has suggested that in the first half of the nineteenth century, the terms "Aryan" and "Dravidian" remained terms predominantly connected to different language groups and even when associated with different "races" the word "race" was understood most likely as coterminous with "Nation."[26] These relatively benign connotations were to change with the emergence of Aryan theories of race from the second half of the nineteenth century, where "race" is conceived in increasingly biological and somatic terms.[27] The most influential Orientalist theory of the second half of the nineteenth century which adumbrated "Dravidian" both as a family of languages as well as a "Race" was that of the Irish missionary Robert Caldwell (1814–1891).[28]

Much has been written about Caldwell's impact on Dravidianism.[29] It has been pointed out that Caldwell's own thoughts on the Tamil language followed in the footsteps of an older Protestant concern in South India with the defense and cultivation of the vernacular as the idiom of the "people," but his "genius lay in appropriating the history of Protestant lingualism to a theory of race and civilization."[30] Caldwell first developed his theories regarding "Dravidian" language and culture in his ethnographic work on the toddy-tapping caste, the Shanars, first published in 1849, and subsequently extended his observations to a grand theory of Dravidian language, religion, and culture in his *A Comparative Grammar of the Dravidian or South-Indian Family of Languages*, published in 1856. In it, Caldwell proposed that Tamil was part of the "Dravidian" family of languages, different and distinct from the Indo-European Sanskrit, with an antiquity and autonomy which rivaled that of the latter.[31] This antiquity, in turn, vouchsafed the existence of an ancient and egalitarian Tamil society free from the fossilizing effects of the caste system, albeit within a society which practiced a kind of primitive religion not far removed from demonolatry and Shamanism.[32] The Dravidians, according to Caldwell, had acquired a high civilization as well as the pernicious caste system through their colonization by the Aryans from the north. This colonization, as Caldwell depicted it, was a peaceful process and, in the final analysis, really a form of social and ideological self-colonization of a people who had been duped into accepting both Sanskritic values as well as the caste system by some clever brahmins: "The Brahmans, who came in 'peaceably, and obtained the kingdom by flatteries,' may probably have persuaded the Dravidians that in calling them Sudras they were conferring upon them a title of honour."[33] The enduring impact of Caldwell's work, as Nicholas Dirks[34] has recently suggested, is due to its ingenuous combination of philology, race theory, and a theory of cultural imperialism derived from a fierce anti-Brahminical critique. Thus, it became possible for Caldwell's perspective on the social history of the Tamils/Dravidians to lay the blueprints for a Tamil linguistic nationalism which was postulated on the ideological expulsion of the Brahmin from the Tamil "Race/Nation."

These broad contours apart, how in fact, Caldwell's views—and more generally, the Orientalist idioms of race, language, and culture—came to be incorporated, modified, and even transformed in post-Caldwellian, emic, Dravidian discourses is yet to be fully understood.[35] The problem can perhaps best be approached through looking, as this chapter does, at specific instances of literary appropriation and transformation in and through individual imaginings.

In Maraimalai Adigal's perspective on the "Aryan Brahmins" (*Ariya Parppanar*) and the "Velalas," we see clearly the Caldwellian discourses internalized and yet jostling, mingling, and even colliding with each other. On one hand, the distinction posed first by Caldwell between Aryan and Dravidian forms the basis of his understanding of ancient Tamil society. At the same time, this ancient society is divided into two ages: the hunter and gatherer versus the settled cultivator age. The former becomes synonymous with a primitive past inhabited by an unidentified group of *ur*-Tamils—and the life of the *ur*-Tamils is reminiscent, ironically, of Caldwell's own less-appreciated view among Dravidian circles of the primitiveness of Tamil society before the advent of the Aryans. This society is redeemed in Maraimalai Adigal's account, not from without by the Aryan brahmins, but from within, by the autochthonous Velala. And this settled cultivation stage, approximating to the *Cankam* age, forms, as it were, a paradisiacal interregnum between the primitive *ur*-Tamil and the caste

Aryan society. In other words, Maraimalai Adigal's version of the Aryan-Dravidian divide breaks up this dichotomy to produce a triad of the non-Velala and Velala Dravidians, on one hand, and the Aryan Brahmins on the other. Difference here, unlike in Caldwell, is also inscribed within the Dravidian fold, enabling a new, discursive structure which reconfigures Tamil society along the lines of other polarities relating to food: that of the vegetarian versus the meat-eater, the pure versus the impure.

FOOD

Let us recollect that the advent of the Velala not only enabled the suffering of the wild pre-existent population, the hunter-gatherers, to come to an end but the knowledge of agriculture brought or discovered by the Velala also provides this society, for the first time, with vegetable/vegetarian food on a sustainable basis. This, in turn, brings to an end the savage killing of animals: "Thus, it is only after the *Velala* started agriculture that the life of suffering, an affliction with regard to food, clothes and habitation came to an end. Murder of the animal species for the sake of food was stopped. . . ."[36] Implicit in this view is a kind of dietary determinism that links animal killing and its corollary, meat-eating, with barbaric practice and lowly food, the hallmarks of a lowly civilization in this configuration. The Velala represents the other end of this primitive pole, associated with vegetable food which equals high food and a high civilization of vegetarianism. Considering that the ingenuity of the Velala had already effected the transformation of *ur*-Tamil society from a low civilization to a high one, what, then, is the contribution of the outsider, the Aryan Brahmin to this society? In answering this question, *Velala Civilization* inverts Orientalist race theory in general through the metaphor of vegetarianism.[37]

Thus, Maraimalai Adigal draws upon contemporary Orientalist scholarship on Vedic religion to make a case for the primitiveness of Aryan religion and dietetics. The Aryans worship lesser gods such as Indra, Mitra, and Varuna, they make them offerings of *soma*, an intoxicant, and the flesh of animals which they have killed and which they will subsequently eat themselves. This depravity of the Aryan religion culminates in the horror of human sacrifice, which their own *Shatapatha Brahmana* vouches for. To sum up:

> In this manner, apart from exulting in such acts of possession involving drunkenness and killing, the Aryans' attitude did not go in the direction of abolishing such evil and worshipping the one, primary God full of grace, to the extent they possibly could. . . .[38]

This outraged exposure of the dark heart of Aryan religion and habits inverts not just Orientalist race theory but does so, ironically, by mirroring other colonial discourses of "savagism."[39] The Aryans, here, are the savages, entwined with a primitive nature, with the animals they hunt and eat, the intoxicants they drink, and the primitive gods they worship. This is nature, primitive and untamed, unlike the cultivated nature of the Velala. These Aryans who migrate to the Tamil lands find themselves at the lowest level of the class society, excluded from the religious traditions of the majority due to their meat-eating practices:

> All the old temples in the Tamil country have been established by the Tamil people and remain theirs by right. Since this is the case, none other than the Aticaivas, a community separated out and established as priests from among the Tamil Velalas, none of the Aryan Brahmins were permitted to touch the sacred images within these temples and perform worship. Note the persistence of this ancient custom even today. Since, in ancient times, the Aryan brahmans killed goats and buffaloes and ate their flesh, they were considered unfit to enter the temples of the Tamil country and unworthy of touching the sacred body of God and kept apart.[40]

Learning from this, wishing to elevate their status in this society, the Aryan Brahmins now voluntarily undergo what might be called a process of "Velala-zation" and extract their revenge with respect to the Velalas:

> The Aryan Brahmins, who had been degraded by the Velalas due to their practices of killing and dealing with meat gradually abandoned those practices, spoke highly of themselves, and aiming to degrade the very Velalas who had degraded them, started to call them *sudras*.

This intermeshing of race, religion, meat-eating, and vegetarianism in Maraimalai Adigal must not be dismissed as the foisting of a personal fad upon his historiography of ancient Tamil culture. Rather, it must be viewed in the light of a more general preoccupation with dietary issues closely linked to the ideology of Indian nationhood, in the context of colonialism, in figures as diverse as the socio-religious reformer Swami Vivekananda (1863–1902) or the Dalit ideologue Dr. B. R. Ambedkar (1891–1956), both contemporaries of Maraimalai Adigal. While the former espoused meat-eating as opposed to vegetarianism as part of a vision of engendering a masculine Hindu,[41] Ambedkar's reflections were concerned with the debunking of Hindu/brahminical self-representations. These latter reflections are particularly interesting for the links they establish between caste, status, and vegetarianism in the context of an anti-brahminical critique.[42] Ambedkar begins on the premise that the most significant dietary characteristic of Untouchables, which both defines them as well as makes them into the "Broken Men" of Hindu caste society, is their consumption of meat, specifically beef. He then unearths sufficient literary evidence from the sacred literature of the Brahmins, much as Maraimalai Adigal did, to show that Brahminical religion was once otherwise, and that Brahmins had once both slaughtered and eaten cows. He then goes on to address the question of why they abandoned the practice, converted it into a taboo, and then utilized this taboo to degrade one section of the populace. His answer to the question—that the Brahmins abandoned the practice to elevate themselves to a higher status than Buddhists—merits scrutiny in that it eerily parallels Maraimalai Adigal's explanation, based as it is on a view of Brahminical opportunism and strategizing to acquire and conserve power, accomplished in part by the erasure of an embarrassing past.[43]

Vegetarianism in Maraimalai Adigal, though, is much more ambivalent and fraught with contradictions than in Ambedkar; it is much more than a definer of caste status. Rather, in his understanding there is a coalescence and collision of both caste identity (and hence issues of commensality), and ethics, which would elevate vegetarianism beyond being merely a marker of caste identity to encompassing a broader sense of Tamil humanity.

The tension between these perspectives becomes obvious when we place two passages from *Velala Civilization* next to each other. In the one, Maraimalai Adigal speaks approvingly of the dietary conduct of Shaiva Velalas:

> From ancient times till today Shaiva Velalas worship Siva even while having rejected killing and meat-eating. Hence, they continue to live without eating together with any other community which eats meat or does not worship Siva. Generally, people from all castes will eat at the homes of Shaiva Velalas; the latter will not eat in the house of someone from any other caste.[44]

Yet, in another passage from the chapter titled "Only those who have grace and love are of High Caste," it is said:

> The Tamil way of elevating oneself is through conduct which is intelligent, loving and gracious. Only that conduct imbued with grace which does not harm any living being is the best among all kinds of conduct and gives status to those associated with one as well . . . Since the Aryans killed innumerable goats, cows and horses in the name of sacrificing them they do not have grace and hence they are also not superior people.[45]

The bio-morality of vegetarianism here is clear: It becomes the means to status elevation. The food-switching can become a code-switching, enabling one to both enter into a higher, civilized status and, simultaneously, through explicit dietary conduct, reveal one's ethical moorings.[46] In fact, this indeed is what Maraimalai Adigal suggests in the final chapter of his book: Theoretically, anybody can be accepted as a Velala who abjures meat-eating and adheres to the code of conduct outlined previously. Yet the palpable ambivalences in the book, whose very title speaks for its advocacy of a specific, caste identity and caste pride even while it attempts to dissolve this caste identity into a Tamil cultural identity, prevents any easy elision of the one into the other. In any case, the racial divide of Aryan, on one hand, and Tamil/Velala, on the other, cannot be elided through a common practice of vegetarianism since it actually camouflages another irreconcilable divide: that between fake vegetarianism adhered to for strategic reasons and true vegetarianism, born of grace and love.

CIVILIZATION AND THE COMMENSALITY

We have thus far seen how in *Velala Civilization* the qualities required for engaging in agricultural productivity are also the qualities required for the maintenance and nourishment of society. These include the ability to give (*ikai*), intellectual acuity (*nunnarivu*), and demonstrating compassion (*irakkam*) and hospitality (*viruttompal*).[47] In other words, only agricultural activity born out of strong attachment to the land makes possible a pragmatic altruism in a human being: With the Velala as the sole person in Tamil society who generates food, it is he alone who can give it away. His altruism can be vouched for and manifests itself in the giving of food, medicine, and other substances that he gives in order to enable others to live. The constant re-enactment of this original altruism within the context of the modern is, for Maraimalai Adigal, to reinstate both the lost and the ideal future pre-Aryan Tamil society.

In two long, contrastive passages which elaborate on this issue of hospitality and commensality, a vision which politicizes the domestic sphere as the arena of change is elaborated. The first passage is about the habits of Brahmin commensality:

> When Aryan Brahmins have a visitor to their house who is not from their caste but a friend, no matter how hungry the person is and how tired his face looks they will place him outside in the porch. Then, closing the front door, they and their kin will stay inside and eat softly till satiated after which they will serve the leftovers to the ravenous and half-alive guest, standing at door's length. After he has eaten those impure leftovers sorrowfully and hastily he will have to take the soiled leaf on which the food is served himself with his hands along the street [to fling it away] even as he will be followed in this by the daughter of the Brahmin who has served him food, carrying diluted cow dung and strewing it [on the path behind him to purify it]. We can see this even today.[48]

The second describes the Velalas thus:

> Now, as for Velalas, . . . they are not the types to leave a hungry guest outside and to close the door with themselves and their kin inside and eat. If they do not have the requisite Shaiva conduct to have the guest sit and eat with them they will first feed the guest and then eat later. Or else, they will place them on one side and themselves on the other and arrange for both of them to eat simultaneously. Further, Velalas are not remiss in eating together with those who are not of their caste and practice killing and meat-eating. It is all too true that some of those belonging to the Velala caste these days, seeing the Aryan Brahmins and wishing to emulate them, place guests from other castes outside and eat inside, offer the leftovers to them and, regarding falsely that if they were to offer the leftovers to the pariahs they would be polluted, they dig holes and bury it. Nevertheless, these people should reform themselves, realising that such heartless conduct is completely unworthy of the Velalas who are naturally, from ancient times, those with love, compassion and grace.[49]

I believe these two passages in *Velala Civilization* are significant for several reasons. They depart radically from the reconstruction of an ideal, lost past, reconstructed out of present grievances, in order to focus on the grievances themselves. History is dissolved here into a narrative mode which is immediate and resonates with immediately felt injustice. The emancipatory potential, and it is only a potentiality, of these passages lies precisely in this transformation of the discursive mode, even while this discursive mode has been led up to and made possible only through the construction of a Velala historiography which is set up as a parallel one and an inversion of an Aryan-centered historiography. In this context, let us take into account the biographical imperative in Maraimalai Adigal to repeatedly demonstrate a whole-hearted allegiance to a Velala identity. As Pandian has pointed out, both Maraimalai Adigal's mother as well as most of his mentors and teachers were not from a Velala background but from lower in the non-brahmin caste rankings. His mother, so to speak, "married up" into the elite Shaiva Velala group when she married his father. The implications of this for his own intellectual formation are clear: Maraimalai Adigal remained sympathetic to lower-caste aspirations even while maintaining as his caste ideal the Shaiva Velalas.[50] This would also account for why, in the passages cited previously, Maraimalai Adigal is able to transcend his own biographic and historiographic constraints and allow for the admission of the fallibility of contemporary Shaiva Velala identity, even while not radically repudiating it and seeing in it the potential for a reformed ideal. It can be argued that this is nothing but a resolution of caste inequality on the basis of a "romanticized Velala moral economy." Thus, Pandian argues:

> Adigal resolved the problem of power between Vellalars and others by means of a romanticized Vellalar moral economy: 'with the lowly

> submitting themselves to their superiors [the Vellalars] and the superiors protecting the lowly, the ancient Tamils led a beautiful life of peace and order.' Foregrounding a moral economy of paternalism without engaging with the question of power was quite evidently a move to salvage the Vellalars as representing an ideal.[51]

Yet, I would argue that the matter is not that simple. For one quotidian moment, to speak of the sharing of food means to speak of present shame as well as past pride. Thus, the second passage evidently appears to speak to those who would valorize a better Velala future on the basis of a Velala past, Nevertheless, in its acceptance of shame and "heartlessness," in its repudiation of aspects of contemporary Velala identity the passage makes an implicit appeal which transcends explicit limitations to refer to a potential future which might bring into question the very valorization of the Velala that is its goal—a future in which commensality is based on common humanity and universal ethical values.

NOTES

1. Most Tamil words have been translated in accordance with the Madras Tamil Lexicon with the exception of names of towns or that of Maraimalai Adigal himself, where I adhere to popular usage.
2. For the emergence of Dravidian nationalism in the late nineteenth to early twentieth century in Tamil Nadu, see C. J. Baker, *An Indian Rural Economy, 1880–1955: The Tamil Countryside* (Delhi: Oxford University Press, 1984); C. J. Baker and David Washbrook, *South India: Political Institutions and Social Change* (Delhi: Vikas, 1975); Nambi Arooran, *Tamil Renaissance and Dravidian Nationalism, 1905–1944* (Madurai: Koodal Publishers, 1980); Eugene F. Irschick, *Politics and Social Conflict in South India: The Non-Brahman Movement and Tamil Separatism, 1916–1929* (Berkeley: University of California Press, 1969); Eugene F. Irschick, *Tamil Revivalism in the 1930's* (Madras: Cre-A Publications, 1986); and R. Suntharalingam, *Politics and Nationalist Awakening in South India, 1852–1891* (Tuscon: University of Arizona Press, 1974), among others. For aspects of its cultural features, see Sumathi Ramaswamy, *Passions of the Tongue: Language Devotion in Tamil India, 1891–1970* (Berkeley: University of California Press, 1997) and V. Geetha and S. V. Rajadurai, *Towards a Non-Brahmin Millennium: From Iyothee Thass to Periyar* (Calcutta: Samya Press, 1998).
3. Geetha and Rajadurai, *Non-Brahmin*, 120–121: "Thus there came to exist in the Tamil cultural universe two sorts of history: a 'soft' history, where insight and imagination held sway in equal measure, and a 'hard' history that looked to the evidence of the epigraphs, coins, inscriptions, and the findings of archaeology."
4. For a concise biography of Maraimalai Adigal, see Ramaswamy, *Passions*, 215–219. For extensive studies, see M. Thirunavukkarasu, *Maraimalai Atikal Varalaru* (Chennai: South India Shaiva Siddhanta Works Publishing Society, 1959); T. S. Raghavan, *Makers of Modern Tamil* (Thirunelveli: The South India Shaiva Siddhanta Publishing Society, 1965); Arooran, *Tamil Renaissance,* and V. Ravindran Vaithesspara "Caste Hybritity and

the Construction of Cultural Identity in Colonial India: Maraimalai Adigal (1876–1950) and the Intellectual Genealogy of Dravidian Nationalism", 1999 (Ph.D. diss., University of Toronto).

5. On this, see the preface to the first edition of *Velala Civilization,* reproduced in the 1997 edition. Maramalai Adigal, *Velalar Nakarikam* (Velala Civilization) (Chennai: Manivacakar Patippakam, [1923] 1997).
6. Adigal, *Velalar Nakarikam*, 22. All translations from this text are mine.
7. Ibid., 20.
8. See Ramaswamy, *Passions*, 45. And further, "The consolidation of industrial modernity in the West has frequently sparked nostalgia for a life in nature, away from city lights and urban sprawls, amid fresh fields and rolling pastures. *Tamilparru*, I have insisted, is a discourse of modernity. But it was conducted in the milieu of a colonial culture whose own ideology of the civilizing mission deemed that the natives lacked 'culture' and 'civilization.' Tamil's modern devotees, therefore, yearn not for nature but for culture and for civilization." See also M. S. S. Pandian, *Brahmin and Non-Brahmin: Genealogies of the Tamil Political Present* (Delhi: Permanent Black, 2007): 129: "One needs to bear in mind that the husbandman as an ideal has a long presence in the pre-colonial Tamil region, as evident from literary representations. Further, colonialism had recovered husbandmen as the 'ideal citizenry' and tried, often violently, to 'settle' the itinerant."
9. Adigal, *Velalar Nakarikam*, 26.
10. The classical Tamil Cankam literature is considered the oldest literary evidence for Tamil life and society. With its earliest layers being composed in the early centuries of the turn of the first millennium, the literature became the object of re-discovery and was seen as the primary source for the early civilization of the Tamils, in modernity. On this literature, see A.K. Ramanujan, *The Interior Landscape; Love Poems From a Classical Tamil Anthology* (Bloomington: Indiana Universtiy Press, 1967); K. Kailasapathy, *Tamil Heroic Poetry* (Oxford: Clarendon Press, 1968); Kamil Zvelebil, *The Smile of Murugan: On Tamil Literature of South India* (Leiden: Brill, 1973); George L. Hart, *The Poems of Ancient Tamil, Their Milieu and Their Sanskrit Counterparts* (Berkeley: University of California Press, 1975); and Ganapathy Subbiah, *Roots of Tamil Religious Thought* (Pondicherry: Pondicherry Institute of Language and Culture, 1991), among others.
11. Nambi Arooran, *Tamil Renaissance*, 30; and Burton Stein, *Peasant State and Society in Medieval South India* (Delhi: Oxford University Press, 1980; 1994), 70–73.
12. See Kailasapathy, *Heroic Poetry*, 217: "It has also been seen that liberality or munificence was one of the cherished ideals in the Heroic Age and that 'the circulation of treasure was as essential a part of heroic life as its acquisition.'" In this context, Kailasapathy points to the use, in the Cankam poems, of phrases such as "foolish munificence" (*kotai malam*), "distributing gifts without caring for oneself" (*ompa ikai*), and "unfailing generosity" (*poyya ikai*)." Ibid., 217–219.
13. Subbiah, *Roots*, 136 quotes the Tamil grammar *Tolkappiyam* to show that the verbal root–*i* referred in particular to the kind of gift-giving where the suppliant is inferior to the giver, as opposed to *kotu*, where the suppliant is superior to the giver.
14. Adigal, *Velalar Nakarikam,* 27.
15. On this discovery and its impact, see Ramaswamy, *Passions*; and Norman Cutler, "Three Moments in the Genealogy of Tamil Literary Culture," in *Literary Cultures in History: Reonstructions from South Asia,* ed. Sheldon Pollack (New Delhi: Oxford Universtiy Press, 2003).

16. These include the writings of Sundaram Pillai, Kanakasabhai Pillai and Purnalingam Pillai, among others. For a broad survey of these literary histories, see Karthigesu Sivathamby, *Tamillil Ilakkiya Varalaru* (Chennai: New Century Book House, 1988). For a review of Sundaram Pillai's writings, see Geetha and Rajadurai, *Non-Brahmin*; on Kanakasabhai Pillai, see Ramaswamy, *Passions*, 34; on Purnalingam Pillai, see Cutler, "Three Moments."
17. Ramaswamy, *Passions*, 34.
18. M. S. Purnalingam Pillai, *Tamil Literature* (New Delhi: Asian Educational Series, 1904; 1994): 4. The book was first published in 1904 and later brought out in a new edition in 1929, now titled *Tamil Literature*. It is the latter work which is being quoted in this chapter.
19. Ibid., 5.
20. Thus T. R. Sesha Iyengar, *Dravidian India* (New Delhi: Asian Education Services, 1995), 176ff, even while referring to these divisions in terms of "classes" and "tribes" spoke of the high status of Velalas in this society. Kantaiyya Pillai, *Tamil Intiya*, 49–51, for his part, located the genius of ancient Tamil civilization—its art and literature—in the agricultural plains ruled by Velalas.
21. Adigal, *Velalar Nakarikam*, 26–30.
22. Pandian, *Brahmin*, 132.
23. Ibid., 31.
24. Ibid., 36–37.
25. See Thomas R. Trautmann, *Aryans and British India* (Berkeley: University of California Press, 1997); and Thomas R. Trautmann, "Die Entdeckung von 'arisch' und 'dravidisch' in Britisch-Indien. Eine Erzählung zweier Städte [The Story of "Aryans" and "Dravidians" in British India. A Tale of Two Cities]," in *"Arier" und "Draviden,"* eds. Michael Bergunder and Rahul Peter Das (Halle: Verlag der Franckeschen Stiftungen in Halle, 2002), 14–39. See also Andreas Nehring, " . . . Fur ein Halbbruder des griechischen Genius. Die Entdeckung des Dravidischen durch deutsche Missionare im 19. Jahrhundert," in *"Arier,"* eds. Bergunder and Das, on German Orientalism and missionary scholarship in the first half of the nineteenth century which, simultaneously and independently, came to identical conclusions, regarding the relationship between the South Indian languages.
26. Trautmann, "Die Entdeckung," 34–35.
27. See Nicholas B. Dirks, *Castes of Mind: Colonialism and the Making of Modern India* (New Delhi: Permanent Black, 2001), 142–143; and Trautmann, *Aryans*, and "Die Entdeckung."
28. On Caldwell's life, Ramaswamy, *Passions*, 192–193 remarks: Robert Caldwell, born in Ireland in 1814, arrived in Madras in 1838 as a missionary for the London Missionary Society. He spent most of his life in the small town of Idayankudi near Tirunelveli with the Society for the Propagation of the Gospel, and in 1877 he became bishop of Tinnevelly. A fellow devotee, R. P. Sethu Pillai, writes with affection that in the fifty-odd years he worked in Tamilnadu, Caldwell went home on furlough only three times. When he went back to England the third time, his friends there begged him to stay. But he refused. I have lived all these years for Indians. As long as I am alive, I will toil for them. I will give up my life in their land. And so he did, and when he died in 1891, he was buried in Idayankudi on the grounds of the church that he had himself built.
29. On Caldwell's writings, see Vaithesspara V. Ravindran, "The Unanticipated Legacy of Robert Caldwell and the Dravidian Movement," *South Indian Studies* 1 (1996): 83–110; Ramaswamy, *Passions*; and Geetha and Rajadurai, *Non-Brahmin*. For a recent incisive analysis of Caldwell's unforeseeable

and idiosyncratic impact on Dravidian nationalism, see Dirks, *Castes of Mind*, 134–148.
30. Geetha and Rajadurai, *Non-Brahmin*, 113.
31. Robert Caldwell, *A Comparative Grammar of the Dravidian or South Indian Family of Languages* (London: Harrison, 1856), 1–31.
32. Ibid., 77–79.
33. Quoted in Dirks, *Castes of Mind*, 140.
34. Ibid., 134–148.
35. A welcome addition to this research, which is still in its incipient stages, is Bergunder's recent article on the reception of Aryan race theory in Dravidian neo-Saivism, where he also particularly deals with Maraimalai Adigal: Michael Bergunder, "Contested Past: Anti-Brahmanical and Hindu Nationalist reconstructions of Indian prehistory," *Historiographica Linguistica* 31, no. 1 (2004): 59–104.
36. Adigal, *Velalar Nakarikam*, 23.
37. See Dirks, *Castes of Mind*, 142. "British writers frequently used the Aryan theory to justify a view of Dravidians as markedly inferior to the Aryans. In the 1860s and 1870s, Henry Maine and Meadows Taylor emphasized the barbarity and superstition of the early Dravidians, who "had infected ancient Hindu society and destroyed its pure Aryan features."
38. Adigal, *Velalar Nakarikam*, 63.
39. See Gananath Obeyesekere, *Cannibal Talk: The Man-Eating Myth and Human Sacrifice in the South Seas* (Berkeley, CA: University of California Press, 2005), 10, following Pearce, where "savagism" is defined as a discourse which regards the "savage" as standing in opposition to "the civilized values of rationality, progress, and the knowledge of the true religion. . . . The discourse of savagism deals with those who do not have these values and live in a state of nature, close to the very animals they hunted."
40. Adigal, *Velalar Nakarikam*, 27.
41. cf. Parama Roy, "Meat-Eating, Masculinity, and Renunciation in India: A Gandhian Grammar of Diet," *Gender and History* 14, no. 1 (2002): 65: "If the Macaulayan rhetoric of British colonialism had characterised the Bengali and paradigmatically the westernised, English-educated Hindu male as 'feeble even to effeminacy,' the object of derision had, ironically, made the stereotype of degeneracy his own. Vivekananda's prescription of 'beef, biceps, and Bhagavadgita' as the curative for such feebleness is perhaps only the best-known of the Indian responses to such a reproach."
42. Re: B. R. Ambedkar, *The Untouchables* (Balrampur: Jetavan Mahavihar, 1969).
43. Ibid., 146–149. Ambedkar noted, "To my mind it was strategy which made the Brahmins give up beef-eating and start worshipping the cow. The clue to the worship of the cow is to be found in the struggle between Buddhism and Brahmanism and the means adopted by Brahmanism to establish its supremacy over Buddhism. . . . In this connection it must be remembered that there was one aspect in which Brahmanism suffered in public esteem as compared to Buddhism. That was the practice of animal sacrifice which was the essence of Brahmanism and to which Buddhism was deadly opposed. That in an agricultural population there should be respect for Buddhism and revulsion against Brahmanism which involved slaughter of animals including cows and bullocks is only natural. What could the Brahmins do to recover the lost ground? To go one better than the Buddhist Bhikkus not only to give up meat-eating but to become vegetarians—which they did."
44. Adigal, *Velalar Nakarikam*, 32.
45. Ibid., 38.

46. Joseph Alter, in his study of Gandhi's bodily practices, has analyzed the "biomorality" which governs the latter's views on vegetarianism, pointing out that it is much more than simply a question of personal choice or a brahminocentric obsession with purity. Rather, Alter suggests that Gandhi's vegetarianism sets itself in opposition to a biology of race: "Confronted with racial prejudice in South Africa Gandhi set about converting meat-eating boorish school children into 'civilized' vegetarians whose subsequent reverence for life and compassion for living beings would break down racial prejudice." Joseph Alter, *Gandhi's Body: Sex, Diet, and the Politics of Nationalism* (Philadelphia: University of Pennsylvania Press, 2000), 10.
47. Adigal, *Velalar Nakarikam*, 20.
48. Ibid., 41.
49. Ibid., 42.
50. Pandian, *Brahmin*, 122–123.
51. Ibid., 135.

4 Can a Muslim Be an Indian and Not a Traitor or a Terrorist?

Huma Dar

Your history gets in the way of my memory.
I am everything you lost. You can't forgive me.
. . .
If only somehow you could have been mine,
What would not have been possible in this world?[1]
(Excerpt from "Farewell")

Agha Shahid 'Ali explains in a brief note, at the end of the collection of his poems, *The Country Without a Post Office,* that this particular poem, *Farewell,* "at one—but only one—level is a plaintive love letter from a Kashmiri Muslim to a Kashmiri Pandit."[2] Perhaps it is the special boon of poetry, and especially that crafted by Ali, that the meanings unfold and interweave like a set of Russian Babushka dolls, each doll hiding a multitude of dolls nestled within its womb. The powerful ambiguity of a love/hate relationship; the unrequited love reinventing itself into hate; the erstwhile lover and friend transmogrifying into the "perfect enemy"—the "Enemy" par excellence; the all too familiar entanglement of memories and histories; the overwhelming nostalgia of a recurring "what if;" the sense of irretrievable loss necessitating a need to acknowledge, understand and thus forgive, and yet an inability to do so—an attachment to that self-same pain, the Nietzschean *ressentiment;* the silencing of ineffable pain fragmented into defensive amnesia or obligatory muteness and yet spilling all over; all signify images that resonate hauntingly in the context of post-Partition South Asia.

Through a deconstructive reading of selected historical writings, literature, and autobiographical narratives, documentary and feature films produced in South Asia, I hesitatingly step into the arena of the passionate debates raging on the Partition, 1947, and its aftermath. My focus will necessarily be on the "western" segment of the Partition between India and the erstwhile "West" Pakistan, due to the limitation of time, and that of my linguistic range—Urdu, Hindi, English, and spoken Punjabi. In this chapter I argue that besides the immediate context of Kashmir, 'Ali's poem could very well describe not only the dialectics of the India–Pakistan relationship and the construction of the Muslim "Other" within India, but also that of some Indian Muslims' feelings of betrayal and disdain for the Pakistanis. The first is fraught with the unimaginable possibility of nuclear chaos between the two countries and thus deserves urgent study; the last is an incidental tragedy,[3] perhaps implicating the other two constructs, and although I will touch upon it here, it is the second—the construction of the Muslim "Other"—that I will focus my attention on, as it is this "tyrannical" discourse that is directly connected to the frequent anti-Muslim pogroms in India, and especially to the genocide carried out against the Muslims in Gujarat, in 2002. It is in this context that I will critique the "limits" of certain discourses of liberalism in India, as epitomized by the films *Mr & Mrs Iyer* (2003) and *Pinjar* (2003)—two films that won the Nargis Dutt Award for the Best Film on National Integration in India, in the years 2003 and 2004, respectively. Through this critique I endeavor to dis-entangle *some* memories from *some* histories—not to cast blame, but to protest the critical silences and the blame displacement which has been instrumental in the demonization of Indian Muslims; to propose a process that initiates acknowledgment, understanding, and thus mutual forgiveness; to bring an end to the state-imposed defensive amnesia, as that institutionalized in Pakistan, which means an endless repetition of the cycle, as tragically brought to the fore by the liberation war of Bangladesh and the ensuing genocide; and finally to "learn to learn from below"[4] in order to deal with the pain that is ineffable. About this blame displacement Paul Brass says:

> [W]hat is more important for India's present and future in all these respects is to escape from the self-perpetuating traps of blame displacement and the complementary traps of minimizing or maximizing [*sic*] the significance of horrific violence. In short, it is necessary to fix responsibility and penetrate the clouds of deception, rhetoric, mystification, obscurity, and indeterminacy to uncover what can be uncovered, knowing full well that the whole truth can never be known, but that the evident actions and inaction of the perpetrators and apologists of violence, of known persons, groups, organizations, political leaders, media, academics seeking causes, and patriots seeking comfort can be uncovered, exposed, and brought to book.[5]

Brass is talking here about "blame displacement" with regard to the Gujarat pogrom, and by the "maximizing" of the violence he is pointing out that statements of certain "leftist and secular writers" who claim that "the latest wave of riots is the worst since the Partition massacres of 1946–47" can actually backfire by "conjur[ing] up the retributive genocidal massacres of Partition in the Punjab [*sic*] in 1946–47, seeming to herald yet another monumental catastrophe, which will include the further weakening or disintegration of India or the obliteration of its Muslim population."[6] Instead of describing it as a "maximizing" discourse, I think that it would be more appropriate to think of it as the discourse of incorrect genesis or inaccurate reference. The "minimizing," of course, indicates the Hindutva (Hindu nationalist) position of "taking comfort in the fact that riots did not spread from Gujarat to other parts of India, as they did in the last great wave of 1992."[7] For Brass's first assertion regarding the Partition, an implicit assumption is that the public has a "received" knowledge of Muslim culpability, as if greater, in the Partition riots, which again plays into the hands of the Hindutva, and which predicates retributive violence against the Muslims until they are no longer in India. The usual Hindutva slogans at such riots regarding Partition or "amputation of Bharat Mata," the spectre of rapes of Hindu women, and their kidnappings to rouse the "masculinity" of Hindus are evidence of Hindutva's comfort with this paradigm; the difference between the two is that the left, or the secularists, are pessimistic about the situation while the Hindutva is not. The documentary film *Hey Ram*, made by Gopal Menon, depicting the plight of the Muslims in Gujarat and released in summer 2002, begins with some black-and-white footage of trains overflowing with the Partition refugees arriving at platforms as if conceding Partition as the "origin" of all Hindu-Muslim violence. Perhaps helped by a deconstruction of the "blame displacement" of Partition itself, it is here that the de-coupling of the discourses of the frequent pogroms from those of the Partition is essential, which otherwise unwittingly falls martyr to the "retribution" paradigm, an entanglement of history and memory that is eloquently mourned by 'Ali in "Farewell":

> *Your history gets in the way of my memory.*
> *I am everything you lost. You can't forgive me.*
> *I am everything you lost. Your perfect enemy.*
> Your memory gets in the way of my memory.

Gyanendra Pandey concludes his article "Can a Muslim Be an Indian?" with the following passage:

> No nation, no state is natural; no people as chosen or pure as they might pretend. This is true of Germany in the 1930s as it is of Germany today; as it is of Israel or Japan or any other modern nation-state. And it is—one might say fortunately—manifestly true in the Indian case. No citizen of India can avoid being Hindu/Muslim, Bangali/Kannadiga, shopkeeper/laborer, man/woman, father/mother, lower caste/upper caste, at the same time. It is tyrannical, in my view, to suggest that this is somehow traitorous.[8]

Many historians of the communal problems in India, and some Indian Muslims writers themselves, have tried to trace the origin of the "Muslim Problem"[9] in India and the all–too–many pogroms aimed at them, to the "difficult historical legacy of Pakistan: the [resultant] stigmatization of the Muslims in India,"[10] and "to persistent suspicion of their national loyalty [which] is seen as one of the gravest consequences of Partition. Deeply resentful of this mistrust, some [Muslim] authors challenge it by asserting their genuine commitment to India and emphasizing the Indian Muslim's right to his hereditary homeland"[11] while they recurringly confess an "irreligious outlook."[12] In her excellent article in *The Annual of Urdu Studies,* Professor Ulrike Stark gives the examples of Nafis Afridi, Badiuzzaman, 'Abdul Bismillah, Rahi Ma'asum Raza, and Manzur Ehtesham as amongst the first wave of Indian Muslim writers writing in Hindi, and confronting the generic post-Partition stigma of being Muslim. The period immediately after Partition in 1947 saw Hindu and Sikh refugees from West Pakistan arriving in U.P., East Punjab, and Delhi, as well as the leaders of the Hindu right wing, demanding that all Muslims from those regions should be sent to Pakistan, and that their properties be confiscated and handed over to Sikhs and Hindus.[13] As Pandey observed,

> Few people now cared to differentiate carefully among the Muslims of India. The regional, caste, and occupational markers by which generations of Muslims had been known . . . seemed to lose much of their significance. The Muslims were now, more and more—in official documents, in journalism, and in common conversation—simply "Muslims," and all of them were suspect as open or closet Pakistanis.[14]

This blanket category of the undifferentiated "Muslim" is by extension de-regionalized and de-Indianized. No surprise that in their writings the Indian Muslim writers portray a vividly detailed regional ambience, and write the justly famous "regional" Indian novels of that era. A common critique of the representation of Indian Muslims in Bollywood films is this exact same flattening of regional and class differences. The stereotype that emerged for the "Muslim" man was that of a decadent, rapacious, feudal *nawab,* or some version thereof, with an "army" of children in tow, replete with huqqah, *shaa'iri,*[15] and flowery Urdu, or the later even uglier trope of the underworld gangster-cum-terrorist. For a "Muslim" woman we have the two stock representations as either the hyper-sexualized *tawa'if*[16] or as the oppressed, *burqa*-clad, yet sensual, Muslim woman.[17] Wouldn't a Freudian reading of the aforementioned ever-present tropes yield an explanation of "lack" or castration anxiety projected by Hindutva onto the Muslim "Other," hinted at through the fetishization and the recurrent obligatory performance of the "loud confessional"?[18]

> *You needed me. You needed to perfect me*
> *In your absence you polished me into the Enemy.*

Pandey explores this "easy" formation of "Us" versus "Them" when he quotes Babu Sampurnanand, the Educational Minister in the Congress Government of U.P., from an article of the latter in *Vartman,* a newspaper published on 19 June 1947: "We are going to recover that [precious] thing that we lost a thousand years ago."[19] Pandey correctly reads "how easily, not to say naturally, the 'we' is constructed as 'Hindu': today 'we' (Hindu/Indians) are going to recover that freedom which we lost with the coming of the 'Muslim' power."[20] On 28 September 1947, *Hindustan Times*, the pro-Congress newspaper, published a demand to "liquidat[e] enemy pockets, and [build] a strong army on the Nazi model."[21] In this context of bristling hostility, the cultivation of an "irreligious outlook" by the Indian Muslim writers might be read as a defensive move to survive in India, or even as a genuine turning away from religion as a result of interpreting a cynical manipulation of religion to be the cause of the trauma of Partition. These writers are also representative of the Indian Muslims who express a sense of betrayal from the Pakistani Muslims as Rahi Ma'asum Raza does in his famous novel *Aadha Gaon*.

> "If Pakistan is not created, these eighty million Muslims will be transformed into Untouchables." The second [student from Aligarh Muslim University] spoke.
>
> "O Brother, I feel as if your reading and writing has all gone to waste. You guys don't even know that it is the *Bhangees* and *Chamaars* that are Untouchables. Are we *Bhangees* or *Chamaars*? Those that neither *are* nor *do* the Untouchable [work], how can they be made into Untouchables? You tell me, did you hear me [?]" [Kammo said.]
>
> "At this moment you might as well not understand this point, but it will indeed come to pass. Cows will be tethered in our mosques." [The Aligarh student spoke.]
>
> "Eh Sahib, if Muslims leave for Pakistan, then whether it is horses tethered in the mosques or cows, what difference does it make? Now all Hindus cannot be expected to go offer *namaaz*[25] in the mosques. What compulsion, we ourselves leave for Pakistan, and the Hindus should keep guard over our mosques!" [Kammo exclaimed.]
>
> . . . A lad [from Aligarh] got flustered. He said, "Very well, but when the Hindus run away with your mothers and sisters, then please do not complain." (My translation)[22]

Raza then describes how the inflammatory rhetoric of the students from Aligarh, punctuated with calls of "Allah-o Akbar," right inside the mosque, is able to sway a large section of traders and weavers to decide to vote for Muslim League as a "religious duty."[23] Raza also depicts the Aligarh students to be superficial, exemplified especially by an incident in the mosque at the Friday prayer, when one of the students nudges the Shi'a student to fold his hands in the Sunni way.[24] The gesture itself is open to interpretation: Are they both Shi'a and just being hypocritical by doing their *namaaz* the Sunni way, perhaps in a Sunni mosque, or is the writer trying to expose any "Sunnification" of the Muslim League discourse? In either case the Aligarh students—the exponents of Pakistan, and perhaps the future Pakistanis, come out painted as rather flat and one-dimensional characters through Raza's stroke of the pen, especially when compared to his very sensitive and vivid portrayals of the other Gangauli*wallahs*:

If only somehow you could have been mine, what wouldn't have happened in this world?
I'm everything you lost. You won't forgive me.

In Gopal Menon's film *Hey Ram* (2002), after the nefarious Hindutva slogan of "Baabar kee santaan, jaao Paakistaan, yaa jaao qabristaan [*sic*]"[26] resounds in the theater, the need for Indian Muslims to distance themselves from Pakistanis is immediately comprehensible. Embedded within the documentary is an interview with a young man who responds to the slogan by exclaiming, "Men Paakistaan kyoon jaaoon? men un par thookta hun![27]" or "Why should I go to Pakistan? I spit on them [Pakistanis]!"

At a certain point I lost track of you.
You needed me. You needed to perfect me:
In your absence you polished me into the Enemy.

Manzur Ehtesham, in his novel *Sookha Bargad* (1986), depicts this ambivalent relationship between Indian Muslims and Pakistanis with exquisite sensitivity, through the characters of Soheil and Rasheeda, their thoughts and debates, whispers and outpourings. An intriguing aspect of the thorough demonization of the Indian Muslim carried out at the behest of the Hindu right-wing parties[28] as well as that of the supposedly secular Congress[29] and the articulation of the "Muslim Problem" is the development of the "double consciousness" that Du Bois talks about in the context of African Americans.[30] This theme is also explored by Pandey in the current context.[31] At one point, infuriated by a discussion about the difficulties of Indian Muslims and the possibility of moving to Pakistan, Soheil exclaims:

> The one who hankers after fake upward mobility should indeed move to Pakistan, which needs [the immigration of] well educated Muslims from Hindustan for the sake of publicity to convince the world and people like you, that the Muslims here [in India] are in great suffering.
>
> Our father wasn't stupid when he decided to stay on [in India] in the year '47. Even if we just look at the matter of his earnings, for a person of his education there were greater opportunities in a new country. But he preferred to spend his life amongst similar Hindus, than live and die amongst Muslim strangers, whether they were Arabs or Pakistanis. (My translation)[32]

Hearing bits of the preceding debate, Rasheeda muses to herself about the dangers of critiquing Muslims and uncritically looking up at the Hindus all the time, and rightly relates it to another form of *katmullaayiat* or fundamentalism[33]:

> It is a historical truth [*sic*] that a country was divided into two on the basis of religion, and this happened against the wishes of millions of

people. However big a truth religion might be, the worldliness cannot be denied either. In his [*sic*] worldly manners the Muslim from U.P. will have greater rapport with the Hindu from U.P. rather than with a Muslim from Punjab. But for a layperson religion has no importance—that would be a lie as well. Our father chose worldliness over religion and as a matter of principle we have nothing to do with Pakistan or with Pakistanis, but can the truth of those instants be denied when we are forced to think about them even against our volition. These we can call our *"moments of weakness."*[34] (My translation; my emphasis)

Interestingly, in *Aadha Gaaon*, it is the common weavers and traders of U.P. who seem to be wiser than the "educated", or *parhe-likkhe,* young men from Aligarh University, putting up resistance to the discourse of the Muslim League, whereas in *Sookha Bargad*, Rasheeda confesses that unlike in the case of her father, who was a well-known lawyer, religion is of great importance in the lives of the *aam aadmee* of U.P.—the common people—thus implying their preference for the Muslim League. The franchised Muslims of the United Provinces of Agra and Awadh (U.P.), or U.P. *wallahs*, overwhelmingly voted for the Muslim League in early 1946[35], and this voting was taken as a default plebiscite for Pakistan, which points to a more nuanced situation, perhaps in between those posited by Raza and Ehtesham. The discourse of Partition appears explicitly and implicitly in many of the major works[36] produced by Indian Muslims, and even Pakistan puts in an appearance, albeit grudgingly, in one of the "moments of weakness":

If only somehow you could have been mine, what wouldn't have happened in this world?
I'm everything you lost. You won't forgive me.
My memory keeps getting in the way of your history.

In Shashi Tharoor's[37] novel *Riot: A Love Story,* an Indian Muslim character called Professor Mohammed Sarwar says in an interview given to Randy Diggs:

> Pakistanis will never understand the depth of the disservice that Jinnah did us, Indian Muslims as a whole, when he made some of us into non-Indians. There are still so many Indians who—out of ignorance as well as prejudice—think of us as somehow different from them, somehow foreign, "not like us." . . . [Someone on the train remarks:] "But you're not like *them* at all!"
>
> Not like them at all. I began to say something, but was suddenly overcome by the sheer futility of the attempt.[38]

At this point, I would like to briefly unpack the construct of "Partition of India and Pakistan in 1947 and its sole responsibility at the hands of separatist Muslims." The Muslim League passed the Pakistan Resolution as late as the

23rd of March, 1940, in Lahore, and three weeks later, on the 15th of April, 1940, Pandit Jawaharlal Nehru made a revealing statement:

> [Nehru was] "pleased, not because he liked [the Resolution]—on the contrary he considered it to be the most insane suggestion—but because it very much simplified the problem. They were now able to get rid of the demands about proportionate representation in legislature, services, cabinets etc. . . . [He] asserted that if people wanted such things as suggested by the Muslim League at Lahore . . . they and people like him[self] . . . could not live together in India."[39]

Maulana Abul Kalam Azad, the first Education Minister of India, and the president of Congress from 1939 to 1946, also exposes the myth of "the Congress for Unity, the League for Partition[40]" in his memoir *India Wins Freedom*, the complete version of which was published in 1988. The Urdu translation was done by Humayun Kabir and approved by Maulana Azad during his lifetime. It is the italicized text kept under lock and key until 1988 that provides a fuller picture of the events leading to the Partition.

> 16 August, 1946 was a dark day [or a day of ignominy] not just for Calcutta, but for all of India. Events had taken such a turn that the expectation of a peaceful compromise between the Congress and the Muslim League had become almost impossible—*this was amongst the greatest tragedies in the history of India, and with immense regret I have to confess that a major part of the responsibility of these events goes to Jawaharlal [Nehru]. His [pathetic] unfortunate statement that the Congress will be free to make amendments to the Cabinet Mission Plan, opened up the whole issue of political and sectarian compromise yet once again.*[41] (My translation)

Commenting on the political climate of U.P., Azad says that Nehru's shortsighted refusal to cooperate with the Muslim League while forming the goverment in U.P., after the latter's crushing electoral defeat in most other provinces, gave a new lease on life to the Muslim League in U.P.[42] *"Jawaharlaal ke is aml ne U.P. men Muslim Leeg ko ek nayee zindagee ataa kar dee."*[43] Contrary to the prevalent demonology of Jinnah in India,[44] Azad writes in these newly revealed thoughts that at a distance of ten years, he now appreciates that Jinnah's stand on various issues, including that of the Cabinet Mission Plan, and the entailed question of grouping, was a legitimate, correct, and forceful one.[45] According to Roy, Azad had warned Nehru in 1946 that "if we agreed to Partition [over the Cabinet Mission Plan] the verdict would be that India was not divided by the Muslim League but by the Congress."[46] Nehru himself, in 1960, made the revealing confession: "The truth is that . . . the plan for Partition offered a way out and we took it."[47] In spite of, or perhaps precisely because of, being handed the "moth-eaten" country, Pakistanis en masse indulged in amnesia, and celebrated the Independence as if it were an actual 'Eid.[48]

> History has often worked in such curious ways. In spite of the Muslim League's espousal of the two-nation theory and the Congress-Sikh-Mahasabha rejection of it, it was the latter's initiatives that seemed to call for a complete separation of the two communities, and not the former's. The consequences were far reaching.[49]

Although the history of Partition was a "subaltern one among Indian nationalist historiographies,"[50] as also confessed by Gyan Pandey in his essay, "The Prose of Otherness,"[51] it is no longer so. Nevertheless, when a historian of the "subaltern" Other of this Indian nationalist historiography speaks, such as Jalal initially spoke, she was quickly rejected as being concerned with "a very different set of heroes and villains."[52] And then we wonder, "Can the Subaltern Speak?" as enunciated by Gayatri Spivak, but who listens to the subaltern Muslim voice, unless it is of the "apologist" sort or the "avowedly irreligious variety"?

> *My memory keeps getting in the way of your history.*
> *There is nothing to forgive. You won't forgive me.*

The Hindustan Times, often called the mouthpiece of the Congress Party, and edited by a son of Gandhi, published the following on March 5th, 1947:

> Sikhs are much better organized and much better armed than the Muslims. For some time now they have seen a civil war coming and they have been preparing for it. High British officials of the Punjab Govt. told me that if they had to face a similar movement (like that of the Muslim League . . .) from the Sikhs, they would have four times more trouble. . . . Attempts are being made to organize the Sikh States in a federation led by the premier Sikh State of Patiala. This has met with encouraging response. So when the rival claims of communities in the Punjab are submitted to the arbitrament of force, the Sikhs will also have the powerful support of Rashtriya Swayamsevak Sangh which has also been preparing for [the] defence of the Hindu rights."[53]

The subsequent massacre of perhaps a million human beings (whose exact number we will never know) that followed the publication of the above editorial during the Partition riots, the migration of more than ten million across the newly formed borders, and the abductions and rapes of women is now a bloody part of South Asian history. Post-Partition, about 50,000 complaints of missing or abducted women were filed by "Pakistanis," and about 22,000 abducted Muslim women were recovered from India, re-patriated to Pakistan, and silently absorbed; almost 33,000 such complaints were filed by "Indians," and about 9,000 abducted Hindu women were recovered from Pakistan and were post-haste sent to *ashrams*. They were also separated from their children, who were sent to orphanages, causing a great debate in Indian Parliament about pollution, purity of race, and the religion of the poor children born out of rape.[54]

> A number of pamphlets were published which used the story of Sita's abduction by Ravana, showing how she remained pure despite her time away from her husband. From all accounts the 'purity' of women was of much more importance within India, to Hindus and Sikhs—perhaps because the Hindu religion places greater emphasis on purity and pollution. Apparently, abducted Muslim women were more easily accepted back into their families, and in Pakistan the All Pakistan Women's Association and other organizations worked hard at arranging marriages for many women who were recovered and returned. [. . .] So [Hindu and Sikh] women were given a choice: keep your children with you and stay—in all probability—in an ashram all your life, or give them up (such children were then kept in orphanages) and go back to your old family.[55]
>
> [. . .] Forcible evacuation was one thing. The women's acceptance into their families was another. Such was the reluctance of families to take these women back, that Gandhi and Nehru had to issue repeated appeals to people assuring them that abducted women still remained "pure."[56]

Dwivedi's film *Pinjar*, released in November 2003 and supposedly based on a story by the famous Punjabi writer Amrita Preetam, is a period film that portrays the travails of Hindu women abducted and raped around the moment of Partition, 1947. Nevertheless, if this were one's only introduction to that macabre moment and its accompanying horror, then it wouldn't be farfetched to come out of the theater believing,[57] or perhaps even being *reaffirmed* in one's belief, that only the Hindu women got abducted and violated by rapacious and barbarous Muslim men—the male protagonist, a Muslim man called Rasheed, being an aberration, an exception. On the other hand, the film did portray the *majboor*[58] and weak parents of the abducted woman, who refused to accept her back in order to safeguard the patriarchal construct of "family honor," yet their earlier representation as the doting and indulgent parents softens the blow. The only other negative portrayal of Hindus in the film involves a *panchaayat* (committee or Council) of hypocrites, but the negativity of these comic characters pales in front of the inhumanity of the Muslims, where men abduct and rape, *and even Muslim women become complicit in the hiding of these abductees.* Many voices are marginalized and muted to serve the cause of nationalism—the construction of "us" and "them." Coming one year after the Gujarat genocide, *Pinjar* becomes almost a post factum "explanation" or legitimization of the sexual violence visited upon the Gujarati Muslim women, men, and children.

> *I am everything you lost. Your perfect enemy.*
> *Your memory gets in the way of my memory.*

As a stark contrast, in a short story called "Khol Do," Sa'adat Hasan Manto explores the "small voice"[59] of literature through an abducted Muslim girl, Sakeena, who is violated twice over, on one side of the new border by the Hindu or Sikh "Other" and on the other side by the Muslim *razakaar* or volunteers [*sic*], although the perpetrators are never explicitly named. Manto also shows a great understanding of the madness of the Partition riots, by showing the woman as being violated not simply because of her religion or nationality, but because of her gender—she is subjugated on both sides of the border. Her father, Sirajuddin, has already seen his wife being murdered in Amritsar, and searches frantically for his lost daughter at the refugee camp in Lahore, until he finally follows the "dead" body of a girl into a hospital to see if it is indeed his daughter:

> The room was suddenly lit up. Sirajuddin saw the bright mole on the yellow face of the corpse and yelled, "Sakeena!"
> The doctor, who had turned the light on in the room, asked Sirajuddin, "What is it?"
> Sirajuddin's throat could only utter, "Ji–I, ji–I am her father."
> The doctor looked at the corpse on the stretcher, felt her pulse, and told Sirajuddin, "Open the window."
> Sakeena's dead body stirred, with lifeless hands she loosened her *azaarband* and slid her *shalwaar*[60] down.
> Old Sirajuddin silently screamed, "Alive! My daughter is alive!"
> From head to toe, the doctor got drenched with sweat.[61]
> (My translation)

The doctor of the short story and we, the readers, can read Sakeena's last gesture as an evidence of multiple sexual violations, yet her father, Sirajuddin, whose calling out of her name had failed to rouse Sakeena earlier, reads it as a sign that his daughter is alive. His scream expresses joy that his daughter is, and yet the "silence" of that same scream is an indication that he has read the violation at some level, though it is not foremost on his mind. It is this realization that drenches the doctor in perspiration. Read in conjunction with Butalia's, Menon's, and Bhasin's work, that seems a perfectly plausible explanation, especially given the "easier acceptance" of Muslim women by their families that Butalia's research indicates. Intriguingly, Veena Das analyzes this story of Manto's as "[the father] mistakes the movement in the body as a sign of life whereas it is the sign of her living death."[62] She describes this "living death" as "occupying a zone between two deaths, rather than between life and death,"[63] which she has traced to the rejection of raped women by their families due to an obsession with "purity" and "pollution." Is she reading the "small voice" of literature here, or is the small voice getting swept up in the dominant discourses? Is she not projecting the purity-and-pollution paradigm onto a frame where it does not perhaps belong?

> *I hid my pain even from myself; I revealed my pain only to myself.*
> *There is everything to forgive. You won't forgive me.*

This obsession with "purity" and "pollution" is an especial estate of *Rashtriya Swayamsevak Sangh*, or RSS as it is commonly called—the organization that is described by the Congress newspaper, *The Hindustan Times* of 5 March 1947, as "preparing for the defence of the Hindu rights," and which is the main militant Hindu nationalist organization in a group of parties united in their rabidly anti-Muslim, anti-Christian stance. Among them are the Vishwa Hindu Parishad or VHP, which spearheaded the movement to demolish the Babri Masjid mosque in Ayodhya and succeeded on Dec 6, 1992; the Shiv Sena, which organized the anti-Muslim pogrom that followed soon afterward in Bombay; and the current ruling party, Bharatiya Janata Party or BJP, which oversaw the murder, pillage, arson, and rape of thousands of Gujarati Muslims in 2002, while the state police at best stood by "with no orders of help," and offered active complicity in the tragedy at its worst.[64] One hundred fifty thousand people, overwhelmingly Muslims, were displaced and landed in makeshift refugee shelters including unkempt graveyards, where many of them are still miserably residing, awaiting an end of fear. Up to 500 mosques and shrines of Sufi saints were destroyed or desecrated, and in the instance of the shrine of Wali Gujarati, the pioneer Urdu poet and Sufi saint, a coal-tarred road appeared at the old site within a week.[65] A few months later, in Amritsar, Punjab, Ashok Singha, the President of VHP declared this to be a "successful experiment" in which many villages had been *purged* of the Muslims, the descendants of Babar, the quintessential invader, the Other.[66] In the militant Hindu nationalist discourse, Muslims are painted as the eternal foreigners, or the despicably weak "converts," who can never truly be Indian, as their sacred places lie outside the Subcontinent. As an aside, let me point out that although there is much anguish at the "violence of conversion" both to Islam and to Christianity, the putative "victim" is showered with disdain rather than sympathy.

In your absence you polished me into the Enemy.
Your history gets in the way of my memory.
I am everything you lost. You can't forgive me.
I am everything you lost. Your perfect enemy.
Your memory gets in the way of my memory.

It is in this context that I will put forward a critique of the limits of Indian liberalism as represented by the film *Mr. and Mrs. Iyer*, directed by Aparna Sen, released in 2002, and previewed at the Annual South Asian Conference at U.C. Berkeley in 2003. The protagonist is a Muslim from West Bengal by the name of Jehangir Choudhry, who passes as Raja Choudhry, a name that conveniently veils his religious identity. At the onset of the Gujarat pogrom he is shown taking a long bus drive, going out of his way to help a young mother traveling with her infant, the real Mrs. Iyer. When RSS people enter the bus seeking to slay Muslims, he is offered the refuge of hiding under the name "Mr. Iyer"—the slipperiness of his situation implicit in his many names. In an effort to represent Jehangir alias Raja alias Mr. Iyer as one of a "non-terrorist/non-traitorous" variety of Muslims, he is absolutely "un-marked" by Islam and yet, intriguingly enough, he is also un-marked by Bengal, and via this complete "de-regionalization" he is also made a stranger in his own country. Cast against the real Mrs. Iyer, with her carefully cultivated *Tam-Bram*[64] accent in English, this "flattening" of the Indian Bengali Muslim unwittingly plays into the construct of the Indian Muslims as "foreign." Not only does he speak English in a clipped accent, he asks Mrs. Iyer about the "significance" of her *bindi*—which he exoticizes and orientalizes as "the deep red dot on the forehead" that had always intrigued him even as a child, thus positing him as a foreigner in the land of his birth. Doesn't the Hindutva rhetoric claim the same for the Muslims? At a very obvious level the film is, of course, a story of the romance between Jehangir and Mrs. Iyer—a romance which is "forbidden" and therefore even more enticing—forbidden because the male protagonist is a Muslim and the female protagonist is a married Hindu woman, with a child no less.

> *If only somehow you could have been mine, what wouldn't have happened in this world?*
> *I'm everything you lost. You won't forgive me.*

The film shows two elderly passengers on the bus: a Muslim man, Iqbal Ahmed Khan, and his wife, Najma, getting killed at the hands of the RSS, and they are the ones represented as "traditional" Muslims—replete with the veil over the head, U.P. Urdu, *namaaz,* and *tasnbih.*[67] Does that mean that to pray in public is to invite murder, and to be safe one should be "studiedly irreligious?" When the silver-haired, bespectacled man, Iqbal, performs his *maghrib namaaz*[68] inside the narrow bus aisle,[69] making everyone else squeeze around him in discomfort, a fellow passenger says in a Bengali accent, "These people are something else: *bloody terrorists.*" At this point it is Mr. Cohen, a Jewish passenger, who rebukes the bigot and comments on Iqbal's frailty and age, and thus the impossibility of his being a terrorist. What if a younger and healthier man had been offering his *namaaz*? Would that have automatically made him a terrorist? It is this same Mr. Cohen, who surprisingly becomes the informant par excellence inside the bus and points out Iqbal as a Muslim man to the RSS murderers, but who soon relents and confesses his fears regarding his own circumcision and the possibility of being mis-recognized as a Muslim.[70] Considering the miniscule Jewish population in India, when I asked the filmmaker about this conundrum, she replied that "they do exist" and that she just wanted to "represent them in the film." Nonetheless, to show the "Jew" as taking the blame for the despicable act is tantamount to scapegoating yet another Other, especially given the outer context of post-9/11, and the continuing Palestinian–Israeli conflict, plentifully present in the film through the opening shots that show various news clippings of "terrorism" in New York, Israel, Palestine, Gujarat, and elsewhere.

While *Mr. & Mrs. Iyer* shows Jehangir talking with great emotion of the despicable anti-Sikh pogrom of 1984, which he witnessed as an eight-year-old, the film shows some selective amnesia by having him not allude at all to the post-Babri Masjid demolition pogrom unleashed against the Muslims when up to 3,000 Muslims were killed while the state simply watched—he would have been sixteen at that point.[71]

My memory keeps getting in the way of your history.
There is nothing to forgive. You won't forgive me.
I hid my pain even from myself; I revealed my pain only to myself.

In the narrative of the film *Mr. and Mrs. Iyer,* Sen tries to do a balancing act[72] by depicting the violence against Muslims as equal to the violence against Hindus, by juxtaposing the murder of the Muslim couple with scenes of a whole village burnt by the Muslim mob, outside of which a poor Hindu orphan girl is seen crying miserably. This so-called "balancing" rings false and resurrects the specter of the public demonstrations and protests against Mani Rathnam's film *Bombay* (1995), which showed such violence as being equally distributed in the 1992–1993 pogrom, and thus enraged some Muslims, while being upheld as "the real film of the Bombay riots" by Bal Thackeray, the architect of that particular anti-Muslim pogrom.[73]

So "can a Muslim be an Indian and not a terrorist or a traitor?" And, if kindly allowed to be one, does he or she have to be necessarily "irreligious" as posited by the liberals? I would like to end on a positive note by reminding us of the last three lines of Faiz's oft-cited poem *Subh-e Azaadi.* This is a poem that depicts the angst of Partition with its opening lines "*Yeh daagh daagh ujaalaa, yeh shabgazeedah sehr*" [This stained, tarnished light, this night-bitten dawn], but ends with a hesitating optimism—an end which is either never quoted or is quoted with a subtle mis-translation that clobbers the optimism:

Abhee garaaniye shab men kamee naheen aayee
Najaat-e deeda-o dil ke gharee naheen aayee
Chale chalo keh voh manzil abhee naheen ayee
The night's burden weighs heavy still.
Salvation for the eyes and the heart—the moment is yet to be.
Keep going—that the destined dawn is still ahead.[72]

NOTES

1. This last couplet from Agha Shahid 'Ali's poem "Farewell" in The Country Without a Post Office (New York: W.W. XXXX & Company, 1997, 22–23, repeated once before, is an intertextual reminder of a famous poem, "*Mujh Se pehli si muhabbat mere mehboob na maang*" ["Don't ask me, my beloved, for the love we once had"] by Faiz Ahmed Faiz, rendered memorably by Nurjahan and also translated by 'Ali in *The Rebel's Silhouette: Selected Poems of Faiz Ahmed Faiz* (Amherst: University of Massachusetts Press, 1991), 4–5. The corresponding verse in Faiz's poem reads "*Tu jo mil jaye to taqdeer nigoon ho jaye,*" which 'Ali translates as "If you'd fall into my arms, Fate would be

helpless" (Ibid.). The verse following this is: "*Yoon na tha, main ne faqt chaha tha yoon ho jaye,*" which 'Ali, in my opinion, mis-translates as "All this I'd thought, all this I'd believed," rather than the more appropriate "It wasn't thus, I had only yearned for it to be so." Intriguingly this next verse of Faiz wasn't thus, I have only yearned for it to be so," offers intertextual clues and helps decode Ali's "Farewell" as with the realization things were not the way they seemed and the confession of yearning for an idealized past and present remain silent yet in Ali's poem.

2. Agha Shahid 'Ali, *The Country without a Post Office: Poems* (New York: W.W. Norton & Co., 1997), 93.
3. How does one rank one tragedy above another? Perhaps because this particular dysfunctional relationship causes neither wars nor pogroms, I have ranked it last. As far as pain is concerned, the tragedy of families divided across the borders and lines of control (LOC's) is one that I am personally very aware of. With some family in Srinagar, Delhi, Chennai, and Bombay, it meant that my father could not attend my paternal grandfather's *janaaza* (funeral), and that my mother could not attend her paternal uncle's. It means that Daddy still weeps when he sees Srinagar in films, and that when my mother dreams of "home" it is only of the *Sheesh Mahal* (hall of mirrors) in Amritsar! It meant for us, the children, to be never totally "insiders" here or there.
4. Gayatri Chakravorty Spivak, "The New Subaltern: a Silent Interview," in *Mapping Subaltern Studies and the Postcolonial,* edited by. Vinayak Chaturvedi (Delhi: Oxford University Press, 2002), 333.
5. Paul Brass, "The Gujarat Pogrom of 2002," *Items & Issues* 4, no. 1 (Winter 2002–03): 8. This piece is part of Brass' subsequently published book, *The Production of Hindu–Muslim Violence in Contemporary India* (Seattle: University of Washington Press, 2003).
6. Ibid.
7. Ibid.
8. Gyanendra Pandey, "Can a Muslim Be an Indian?" *Comparative Studies in Society and History* 41, no. 4 (October 1999): 629.
9. To be a Muslim in India is to be constructed as a problem—perhaps even *the* problem. W. E. B. Du Bois writes about the question he was "repeatedly *not* asked" (see Gyanendra Pandey, *Routine Violence: Nations, Fragments, Histories* [Delhi: Permanent Black, 2006], 63): "How does it feel to be a problem?" He states: "It is a peculiar sensation, this double-consciousness, this sense of always looking at one's self through the eyes of others, of measuring one's soul by the tape of a world that looks on in amused contempt and pity. One ever feels (one's) twoness—an American, a Negro; two souls, two thoughts, two unreconciled strivings; two warring ideals in one dark body, whose dogged strength alone keeps it from being torn asunder." W. E. B. Du Bois, *The Souls of Black Folk* (New York: Signet Books, 1969), 45.
10. Ulrike Stark, "Tage der Unzufriedenheit: Identitat und Gesellschaftsbild in den Romanen muslimischer Hindischriftsteller (1965–1990) [Days of Dissatisfaction: Identity and Society in the Novels of Muslim Hindi Writers (1965–1990)]," *Annual of Urdu Studies* 11 (1996): 252–253.
11. Ibid.
12. Ibid.
13. Pandey, "Can a Muslim Be an Indian?", 614–615.
14. Ibid., 615. I will come back to this problematic "undifferentiated" and de-regionalized Muslim when analyzing Aparna Sen's film *Mr & Mrs Iyer.* It becomes a source of not just the de-regionalizing but also the de-Indianizing of Jahangir, alias Raja.

15. *Nawab:* A feudal landlord—the origin of the English word "nabob." *Shaa'iri:* Poetry, considered a classical component of the training of Muslim elite of North India.
16. *Tawa'if:* A courtesan.
17. "Mussalmans are more sensual, their womenfolk are trained differently; they have little faith in the other world" (from Pharichand Mitra's 1879 novel, quoted in Jasodhara Bagchi, "Female Sexuality and Community in Jyotirmoyee Devi's *Epar Ganga Opar Ganga*," in *Embodiment: Essays on Gender and Identity,* ed. Meenakshi Thapan (New Delhi: Oxford University Press, 1997), 84. The liminal nature of the *patibrata* (dutiful Hindu wife) can be maintained with the help of a potential rapist. Just as for the white American woman the potential rapist is a poor black man, similarly the *patibrata* preserves her chastity against "Ravana" the Muslim (Ibid).
18. Laura Mulvey, "Visual Pleasure and Narrative Cinema," in *Narrative, Apparatus, Ideology: A Film Theory Reader,* ed. Philip Rosen (New York: Columbia University Press, 1986), 208–209.
19. Pandey, "Can a Muslim Be an Indian?", 616.
20. Ibid.
21. Ibid.
22. *"Paakistaan na banaa to ye aath karor Musalmaan yahaan achhoot banaakar rakhe jaayange." Doosra [Aligarh ka student] bolaa. "E bhaayee, hammen ta aisaa lag rahaa ki aap logan kaa parhaa-likkhaa sab bekaar bhayaa. Kaahe maare, ki aap logan ko ta–eeho na maaloom, ki bhangee-chamaar achhoot hote hain. Ham kauno bhangee-chamaar hain? A jo achhoot hoibe naa kareehe, oko achoot kaise banaa deehe saahab? Aape bataaiye, tanee hamahoon sunen." [Kammo bolaa.] . . ."Is waqt aapkee samajh men yah baat bhale hee na aaye, lekin hogaa yahee. Hamaaree masjidon men gaayen baandhee jaayangee." [Aligrah ka student bolaa.] "E saahab, jab Musalmaan log Paakistaan chale jaiyahen, to phir masjid men ghora bandhe chaahe gaaye. Kaa pharak parihe? Ab Hindooaa sab omen jaake namaaz ta parhe se rahe. Achhee zabardastee hai ki ham ta jaayange Paakistaan, a Hindoo agoren hamaree masjid." [Kammo] . . . Ek [Aligarh ka] larkaa biphar gayaa. Bolaa, "Theek hai, lekin ja Hindoo aapkee maan-bahan ko nikaal le jaayan to faryaad na keejiyegaa."* Rahi Mas'am Raza, *Aadha Gaon* (Delhi: Hindi Press, 1966), 239–240.
23. Ibid., 243.
24. Ibid., 242.
25. *Namaaz:* The canonical Islamic prayer offered five times daily.
26. Babar's descendants—go to Pakistan or to the graveyard!
27. This is reminiscent of the film *Fiza,* where the eponymous character tells an anti-Muslim politician, albeit quite subtly, "Jinhon ne Paakistaan Jaanaa Thaa Woh Jaa Chuke Hen" [Whoever had to go to Pakistan has already gone]; Khalid, *Fiza,* DVD, directed by Khalid Mohammed, Fiza (Hindu/Urdu), 2000. (Iselin, NJ: VideoSound 2000).
28. Thomas Hansen, *The Saffron Wave* (Princeton, NJ: Princeton University Press, 1999), 177.
29. Pandey "Can a Muslim Be an Indian?," 616.
30. Du Bois, *Souls,* 45.
31. Pandey, "Can a Muslim Be an Indian?," 287.
32. *. . . Jise [jhooti taraqqiyon kaa laalach] ho vah beshak Paakistaan chalaa jaaye jise publisitee ke liye Hindustaan se bhaage parhe-likkhe Musalmaanon kee Zaroorat hai––duniyaa aur aap jaison ko yaqeen dilaane ke liye ki yahaan kaa Muslamaan baree taqleef men hai. . . . Hamaare baap bewaqoof naheen the jo san sentaalees men rahanaa tah kiyaa. Agar sirf kamaayee dekhee jaaye to un jitne parhe-likkhe logon ke liye ek naye mulk*

men kaheen zyaadaa sambhaavnaayen theen. Lekin ajnabi Musalmaanon ke beech--chaahe vah Arab ke hon chaahe Paakistaan ke--jeene aur marne se behatar apne-se Hinduon ke beech jeevan bitaanaa thaa. Manzur Ehtesham, *Sookha Bargad* [A Dying Banyan], Delhi: Hindi Press, 1986, 77.

33. Ibid., 78.
34. *Yah ek etihaasik sachchaaee hai ki ek mulk do tukron men, mazhab ke naam par baant diyaa gayaa aur laakhon logon ki marzee ke khilaaf aisaa huwaa. Mazhab chaahe jitnee baree sachaaee ho, sanskaar ko kaise nakaaraa jaa saktaa hai? U.P. kaa Musalmaan apne sanskaaron men U.P. ke Hindoo ke adhik nikat hogaa yaa Panjaab ke Musalmaan ke? Lekin ek aam aadmee ke liye dharm kaa mahattva naheen, yah bhee kahanaa jhoot hogaa. Hamaare Abbu ne dharm aur sanskaar men se sanskaar ko chunaa aur asoolan hamen Paakistaan yaa wahaan basne waalon se kuchh lenaa-denaa naheen, lekin un kshanon ki sachaaee se bhee kyaa inkaar kiyaa jaa saktaa hai, jab na chaahte hue bhee ham un logon ke baare men sochne par majboor ho jaate hain? Inhen ham apne kamzor kshan kah sakte hen.* (Ibid).
35. Ayesha Jalal, *The Sole Spokesman Jinnah, The Muslim League and the Demand for Pakistan.* (Cambridge, UK: Cambridge University Press, 1985).
36. Although Fredric Jameson's thesis that *all* texts coming out of the Third World are allegories of the nation has been critiqued, quite aptly I believe, by Aijaz Ahmed amongst others, the difference here, I think, is between *many* and *all.*
37. The author need not be Muslim, of course, to realize the pathology of the situation and reflect it sensitively in his or her work.
38. Shashi Tharoor, *Riot: A Love Story* (New York: Arcade Publishers, 2001), 111.
39. Asim Roy, "The High Politics of India's Partition: The Revisionist Perspective," in *India's Partition: Process, Strategy, and Perspective,* edited by Mushirul Hasan (New Delhi: Oxford University Press, 1993), 125.
40. This recurrent myth shows up in the works of the even the most perceptive and sensitive writers, as in the excerpts from Raza's *Aadha Gaaon,* Ehtesham's *Sookha Bargad,* and Shashi Tharoor's *Riots: A Love Story.* Such declamations are indeed most poignant and effective when enunciated by Indian Muslims.
41. *16 Agast 1946 sirf Kalkutte ke liye hee yom-e siyah naheen thaa, poore Hindustaan ke liye thaa. Waaqe'aat ne jo mor ikhtiaar kiyaa thaa, us ne Kaangress aur Muslim Leeg ke maabain kisee puraman hal ke tawaqa' ko taqreeban naa-mumkin banaa diya thaa*—yeh Hindustaanee taareekh ke 'azeem tareen almion men se ek thaa aur mujhe intihaa'ee afsos ke saath yeh kehna parh rahaa hai keh in waaqe'aat ki zimmedaaree kaa ek baraa hissa Jawaharlaal ke sar jaataa he. Un ke is badbakhtaanah byaan ne keh Kangress Kaibinet Mishan Plaan men tarmeem ke liye aazaad ho gee siyaasi aur firqawaaraanah samjhote ke poore sawaal ko phir se khol diyaa. (Abul Kalam Azad, Azadi-e Hind: Mukammal Matan—Tees Baras Ba'ad Ki Asha'at [Urdu translation of *India Wins Freedom*] [Lahore: Maktaba'i Jamaal, 1989]), 232. The italicized text is the one that had been kept from the public eye until 1988.
42. Ibid., 232–233.
43. Ibid., 234.
44. See the excerpt already quoted from Tharoor's novel on p. 102 as an understated example of such a vigorous demonology. Attenborough's film *Gandhi* (1982), Helene Cixous' play on Indian independence, and Rushdie's comments on *Gandhi* in an essay in his *Imaginary Homelands,* all re-enact this demonization of Jinnah in the hegemonic discourse of Indian historiography, which makes Azad's comments refreshing and touchingly courageous. Almost the only positive thing Rushdie says in his essay about the film is that it was "witty to portray Jinnah as Count Dracula" (London: Viking Penguin Books, 1991), 104.

45. Ibid., 250–252.
46. Roy, "High Politics," 104.
47. Jason Francisco, "In the Heat of Fratricide: The Literature of India's Partition Burning Freshly," review article in *Annual of Urdu Studies* 11, (1996): 237.
48. "Moth-eaten" is what Jinnah first called the contours of Pakistan, and Azad, among others, made the observation about the Eid-like atmosphere in Pakistan at the moment of Independence.
49. Gyanendra Pandey, *Remembering Partition: Violence, Nationalism and History in India* (Cambridge and New York: Cambridge University Press, 2001), 31–32.
50. Ayesha Jalal, "Secularists, Subalterns and the Stigma of 'Communalism': Partition Historiography Revisited," *Modern Asian Studies* 30, no. 3 (July 1996): 4.
51. Gyanendra Pandey, "The Prose of Otherness," in *Subaltern Studies VIII: Essays in Honor of Ranajit Guha* (Delhi: Oxford University Press, 1994), 204–205.
52. Jalal, "Secularists, Subalterns," 6.
53. As cited in S. M. Ikram, *Modern Muslim India and the Birth of Pakistan,* 2nd edition (Lahore: Sh. M. Ashraf Publishers, [1965] 1970), 381–382.
54. Veena Das, "Language and Body: Transactions in the Construction of Pain," in *Social Suffering,* ed. Arthur Kleinman, Veena Das, and Margaret Lock (Berkeley: University of California Press, 1997), xv; Ritu Menon and Kamla Bhasin, "Exchange of Women," *Outlook* (Special Issue: Partition) 3, no. 22 (28 May 1997): 55.
55. Urvashi Butalia, *The Other Side of Silence: Voices from the Partition of India* (Durham, NC: Duke University Press, 2000), 128.
56. Ibid., 127.
57. Ashis Nandy has succinctly described this particular position of Bollywood in the Indian psyche as "the slum's point of view of Indian politics and society, and for that matter, the world." Ashis Nandy, *The Secret Politics of Our Desires: Innocence, Culpability, and Indian Popular Cinema* (London: Zed Books, 1998), 2.
58. *Majboor:* Compelled or constrained.
59. "The 'small voice' of literature—like the "small voice" of history—is now in greater danger than ever before of being swept away by the forces of nationalism, of globalization, and of the attendant 'disciplines'", Pandey observes in "Can a Muslim Be an Indian?," 203. Pandey also cites Ranajit Guha's view,"If the small voice of history gets a hearing at all . . . it will do so only by interrupting the telling in the dominant version, breaking up its storyline and making a mess of its plot." Ranajit Guha, "The Small Voice of History," *Subaltern Studies* 9 (Delhi, 1996): 12.
60. *Shalwaar:* Loose pants with draw-strings, worn beneath the long tunic shirt, called *qameez; azaarband:* The draw-strings for the *shalwaar.*
61. *Kamre men dafa'tan roshnee huyee. Siraajuddeen ne laash ke zard chehre par chamaktaa huwaa til dekhaa aur chillaayaa, "Sakeena!" Daaktar ne, jisne kamre men roshnee kee thee, Siraajuddeen se poochhaa, "Kyaa hai?"*

    Siraajuddeen ke halq se sirf itnaa nikal sakaa, "Ji men—ji men iskaa baap hoon."

    Daaktar ne strecher par pari huwee laash ki tarf dekhaa aur uskee nabz tatolee aur Sirajuddeen se kahaa, "Khirkee khol do."

    Sakeena ke murdah jism mein jambish huwee, bejaan haathon se usne azaarband kholaa aur shalwaar neeche sirkaa dee. Boorhaa Siraajuddeen khaamoshee se chillaayaa, "Zindah hai. Meree betee zindah hai."

*Daaktar sar se pair tak paseene men gharq ho gyaa (*Zubair Rizvi, ed., *Fasaadaat Ke Afsaane* [Tajzion Ke Saath] [Delhi: Zehn-e Jadeed, 1995], 39).

62. Das, "Language and Body," 77.
63. Smita Narula, "We Have No Orders to Save You: State Participations Complicity in Communal Violence in Gujarat." *Human Rights Watch Report*, 14, no. 3 (April 2002).
64. Madhav Gokhale, "VHP's War-Cry: Secular India's Days Numbered." *Indian Express*. Dec. 29, 2002.
65. Ibid., 79.
66. This desecration occurring but a year after the much-mourned desecration of the Bamiyan Buddhas in Afghanistan went un-mourned and un-mentioned in the Western media.
67. *Tam-Bram*: Tamil Brahmin.
68. *Namaaz:* Islamic obligatory prayers, performed five times daily; tashbih: rosary beads.
69. *maghrib namaaz*: The Muslim evening prayer, offered a little after sunset.
70. Interestingly enough, no one told Ms. Sen that most Muslims can and do perform their *namaaz* while seated when traveling.
71. At the Berkeley screening of her film, Ms. Sen also pointed out that Cohen's remorse at that point is emphasized by the Sufi lyrics *"Kithe Mehr 'Ali, kithe teree sanaa, gustaakh akhiaan kithe jaa lariaan,"* ("who is [this] Mehr 'Ali that he [dares to] praise you, where have these insolent eyes dared to gaze") sung by Zakir Hussain in the background and showing up mis-translated in the subtitles. According to Sen at the Q & A, as well as in the subtitles, *"gustaakh akhiaan"* means "guilty eyes," though any Urdu speaker would easily tell you that *"gustaakh"* means audacious or impudent rather than "guilty," especially given the context of the Sufi lyrics of Mehr 'Ali.
72. Jehangir's initial reaction to the horrifying murder of Iqbal and Najma, where he distances himself from his own hair-breadth escape by taking out his camera and taking photographs of Iqbal's abandoned spectacles on the ground outside the bus, might be construed as defensive and as a survival strategy; but other than his private reminisces to Mrs. Iyer about the anti-Sikh pogrom in 1984, he hardly seems to reflect on his own impotence at being unable to rescue the elderly couple, rudely dragged to their deaths by the RSS goondas; the precariousness of his position and that of other Indian Muslims as well as of other religious minorities; and the political repercussions of the events. The return to normality of the rest of the passengers on the bus is even more frightening and ominous.
73. Many "progressive" narratives have been marred by this "balancing act," implicating writers like Krishan Chandar in "Peshawar Express" as well as movie makers like Mani Rathnam, in his film *Bombay* (1995)
74. Tejaswini Niranjana, "Banning *'Bombayi'*: Nationalism, Communalism, and Gender," *Economic and Political Weekly* (3 June 1995), 1291–1292.
75. My translation. Faiz Ahmed Faiz, from "Subh-e Aazaadi" (August 1947). Even Agha Shahid 'Ali, an otherwise gifted poet, mis-translates the last verses as: "friends, come away from this false light./ Come, we must search for that promised Dawn." Now, how 'Ali gets the "com[ing] away from the false light" is anybody's guess. I would venture that this translation was done prior to the Kashmir insurgency 1989–present. . . . The original "chale chalo" of Faiz seems to carry a promise of the dawn still ahead.

5 Variants of Cultural Nationalism in Pakistan

A Reading of Faiz Ahmad Faiz, Jamil Jalibi, and Fahmida Riaz[1]

Amina Yaqin

As a nation which legitimized the necessity for its existence on the behest of ideological belief, Pakistan's birth is different from that of an integrated "Imagined Community," as theorized by Benedict Anderson, coming together through a common language and the rise of a homogenizing print capitalism.[2] Since acquiring the status of a nation, its culture has been repeatedly mythologized.[3] Today, this cultural quest manifests itself most obviously in the discursive struggle of defining a unique Pakistani identity. In this chapter, I wish to critically review the commentary of selected Pakistani intellectuals on the idea of Pakistani culture post-1947.

The well-known literary critic Terry Eagleton has suggested that the crisis of nationalism has given a renewed sense of importance to culture in the twentieth century. He writes of culture comprising "a common language, inheritance, educational system, shared values and the like," as a guiding force for "social unity." In his view, once this culture acquires a dominant political identity it becomes a matter for urgent intellectual debate.[4] In the case of Pakistan, while it has been argued that its nationalism has been in crisis since its inception,[5] there are specific political occurrences, such as Pakistan's formal recognition as an Islamic Republic, the entrenchment of a bureaucratic-military oligarchy since the 1950s, its volatile foreign policy, and the emergence of religious parties, which have contributed to ideological clashes amongst its political elites. In order to sustain its territorial groupings in a modern postcolonial environment, the ruling elites have identified the religious community as one of the defining features of a uniform Pakistani nationalism.[6] This discursive reaffirmation has been critically received, bringing forth a range of intellectual viewpoints which both challenge and support this identification.

In order to trace the finer nuances of the debate on Pakistani cultural nationalism, I have selected to illustrate and analyze commentaries from three intellectuals who have participated in this discussion on culture. The selected writings of Faiz Ahmad Faiz, Jamil Jalibi, and Fahimda Riaz are representative of the changing definition of Pakistani identity from the 1960s to the 1980s. By participating in the ideological debate on national culture they have, I argue, subsequently become a part of the mythology of culture. Here, it should be emphasized that one of the cultural pieces under scrutiny by Jamil Jalibi was composed in the 1960s, before the break-up of East and West Pakistan and the formation of Bangladesh in 1971, while Faiz Ahmad Faiz's lectures followed in the immediate aftermath. Fahmida Riaz wrote her book in the latter half of the 1980s. Another point worthy of consideration is that, at the time of writing, Faiz was located in the central region of the Punjab, while Jalibi and Riaz were based in the off-center setting of Karachi.

I wish to examine the extent to which their textual productions mythologize and/or challenge the notion of a distinctive national identity. Myth can be understood in the sense that Roland Barthes has suggested: as "a system of communication," which manifests itself through a "mode of signification" and takes shape through forms of language.[7] Barthes' conceptualization of myth as a structure that is projected within already present linguistic forms provides a key focus toward an understanding of local and national trajectories of culture.[8] For example, it can be argued that, in Pakistan, Islam is already present as a "mythical" system identifying the nation, and national discourse shapes it further within the language of cultural belonging, gender, and class differences.[9]

In this environment, how do we understand the role of iconoclastic "unofficial" national poets such as the celebrated and internationally renowned Faiz Ahmad Faiz? His poems were imbued with the spirit of social revolution, and his poetic style was layered with the changing symbols of tradition and modernity.[10] He was also commissioned by the former Prime Minister of Pakistan and leader of the Pakistan People's Party, Zulfiqar 'Ali Bhutto, to participate in an "official" search for Pakistani culture and nationalism. His findings were aired on national television and have since been published as a series of lectures in Urdu entitled *Pakistani kalchar aur qaumi tashakus ki talash* [Pakistani culture and the search for national character].[11] In these lectures, Faiz references the Nehruvian ideal of "unity amongst diversity" as a desirable quality of *qaumi* (national) culture.[12] He argues,

> Pakistan was made not to escape cultural confusion but to be trapped in it. If you remember the two-nation theory—Muslims are a separate *qaum* (nation) and so need their *watan* (homeland) because their culture is separate . . . At that time nobody asked the *qaum* if our culture is separate then what is our culture?[13]

Faiz's ideas on culture followed on from the indefatigable Urdu scholar Jamil Jalibi's thesis on Pakistani cultural identity in post-Partition Pakistan. Jalibi's ruminations on culture were originally composed in the 1960s, before the Partition of West and East Pakistan (now Bangladesh). While he does not ponder the significations of *watan* or *qaum*, his search is punctuated by a psychoanalytic reading of Partition as a defining moment for cultural identity in Pakistan which is marked by the memory of an extremist culture of hatred and opposition. He writes: Our understanding of the past is governed by geographical restrictions imposed by passports and visas.[14] In Jalibi's view, cultural ambassadors who are associated with religious symbolism, such as the poets Altaf Husain Hali and Muhammad Iqbal, are often misunderstood in a national atmosphere which polices intellectualism and the freedom of thought. For him there are two strands of Islamic thinking in Pakistan, one which was perpetuated by Sayyid Ahmad Khan and the Aligarh school and the other by Maulana Maududi and the *Jama't-e Islami.* According to his reading, the most detrimental factor in the struggle toward national culture is the divisive force of regional nationalisms, which is unable to overcome differences in order to form a common law and moral conscience.

More recently, this discourse on culture and identity has engaged the feminist Urdu poet Fahmida Riaz, who circumvents the idea of a singular "imagined community" by focusing on the plural tradition of regional literatures. As a political activist she has suffered the excesses of the authoritarian state in Pakistan, which include the accusation of treason by General Zia-ul Haq's regime in the 1980s.[15] She exiled herself to India and wrote in her defense, "I am a poet, committed to my people."[16] During her stay in India she published a monograph entitled *Pakistan: Literature and Society*, in 1986.[17] This study, in English, focuses on the marginalized provincial literary traditions of Sindhi, Punjabi, Balochi, and Pashto, proposing the idea of a hybrid national literature, which is equally representative of the regional languages as it is of Urdu. She writes in the preface to her book, "The story of Pakistani literature is one of struggles between ideals and social forces operating at various levels under the specific cultural and political conditions of that country."[18] Riaz returned to Pakistan in 1988 and continues to oppose the hegemonic notion of a national community. Her dissenting voice in English can be read as what Pnina Werbner, in another context, describes as a "national subject's" representation of "ambivalences and the sheer efflorescence of cultural products, ethnicities and identities" in an authoritarian state.[19]

Overall, Faiz, Jalibi, and Riaz represent three different strands of the debate on Pakistani culture. Faiz was both a people's poet and a nationalist, Jalibi voices a *muhajir*'s (migrant's) perspective, while Riaz encapsulates the perspective of a resistance feminism. Before focusing on their writings, I will briefly outline two key features which operate as national trajectories of culture in Pakistan, namely, the national language and the political makeup of the nation.

URDU AS A LINGUISTIC SIGNIFIER OF THE PAKISTANI NATION

Variously known as the Persian *rekhta* (mixed), Turkish Urdu (camp), and Indo-Aryan Hindi, Urdu as it is known today is a hybrid language. Scholarly opinions vary on the origins of Urdu, ranging from its status as a language of "low culture," exemplified by its organic germination as a *lingua-franca* in North India during the period of the Delhi Sultanate, to its canonicity as a literary language of "high culture," traceable to the Deccan Muslim kingdom of Golconda in the late fourteenth century A.D.[20] Subsequently, it was utilized as a language of power complicit in the formation of a new service gentry loyal to the British and subservient to the British way of life in the nineteenth century. Thus Urdu gained its identity as a political language under the auspices of the British Raj. Under this new patronage, Urdu became a major signifier in the political development of Muslim separatism in India.[21]

Urdu writers and intellectuals in the nineteenth century were deeply divided over the advantages of a Western-style education and its potentially negative impact on a unique Muslim cultural tradition. A well-known reformer and early modernizer, Sayyid Ahmad Khan, founder of the Mohammadan Anglo-Oriental College (later Aligarh University), was extremely influential in instigating linguistic reform and advocating cultural change for the Muslims of India. He was the founder of the Aligarh movement which came to signify "modernist and rational thinking among the Muslim elite and, [was] ironically enough, also the harbinger of latter-day Muslim 'separatism' and 'communalism.'"[22]

Urdu exists at two levels within the nation: first as the discourse of the privileged elite, and second as a lingua-franca, it has become a mythologizing force in the new nation. As a national language used by the state, it conveys the ideological message of Islamic nationalism, and as a lingua-franca it reflects the everyday experiences of those who speak it. In turn, the intellectual proprietors of Urdu have begun to show signs of a "conscious intentional hybridity" in their literary creations.[23] Its linguistic hybridities permeate the surface of literary texts through a dialogic relationship between unconscious and conscious utterances. This can be detected in the works of writers such as Intizar Husain, Fahmida Riaz, and Kishwar Naheed, whose writings can be read as representative of "both subjectivity and communication."[24] The ambiguity emanates from their relationship to Urdu as the language of their pre-Partition homeland and its newfound status in their post-Partition home. Their writing is reflective of what Homi Bhabha has described as the "particular ambivalence that haunts the idea of the nation, the language of those who write it and the lives of those who live it."[25]

However, for the Urdu intellectual cultural vision to be in accord with the ideological nation, it ought to portray the Pakistani "self" as different, "Othering" the national self from its rival neighbor India and imagining a unique cultural heritage. But Pakistan's religious separatism is torn by the presence of a considerable Muslim minority in India. At the same time the language, being used for cultural expression, remains one that has a shared history across the Subcontinent. However, in this sameness lies the difference of Urdu's political association with the Muslims of India and later its identity as the national language of Pakistan. Thus, the intellectual debate on Pakistani national culture, aired through the medium of Urdu language, remains marked by ambivalence.

POLITICAL INSTABILITY AS A SIGNIFIER OF PAKISTANI CULTURE

Since political power has remained an enterprise of the elite in Pakistan, it is difficult to speak of democratic structures and representative politics. The monologue of Pakistan's governance has lain with the military or the bureaucracy. Between the two there has been a courting of Islam, either economically or ideologically, and in both cases it has led to the constitutional reaffirmation of an ideological Islamic state.[26] In writing about the nation, Urdu writers have been confronted with the nationalist appeal of political personas such as the founder Muhammad 'Ali Jinnah and the poet it honors as its poet-laureate, Muhammad Iqbal. Iqbal's poetry gives the Muslim his/her sense of *khudi* (selfhood) and the shift from a pan-Islamic *milli* identification to a region-specific *qaumiat* (homeland), while Jinnah's legendary leadership as the "sole spokesman" continues to inspire renewed faith in the two-nation theory.[27]

Yet, there are problems with both Jinnah and Iqbal as representatives of the cultural nation. While Jinnah's political equation of the two-nation formula emphasized a monolithic uniformity among the Indian Muslims, Iqbal did not fully endorse Jinnah's views because he advocated communitarian politics based on the Qur'anic ideals of an Islamic society. Iqbal's poetry encouraged an ambiguous *qaumiat* among Indian Muslims which rejected the ungodliness of secular nationalism but identified with the territorial nationalist struggle because it was anti-colonial. He also propagated the idea of an Islamic reformation through the utilization of *ijtihad* (independent reasoning)—a forum he wished to be independent of clerical hierarchies and the state, reviewing Islamic practices in modernity through debate and consensus.[28] After Partition, on the political front, Iqbal's religious point of view was selectively appropriated by Syed Abu'l-'Ala-Maududi (1903–1979), the founder of the Islamic political party the *Jam'at-e Islami*, appealing both to the Muslim reformists and the traditionalists, while the modern secularists struggled to find suitable governance for their newfound freedom.

In contrast to Iqbal's spiritually determined intellectual thought was the Marxist-led post-Partition poetry of Pakistan's Faiz Ahmad Faiz. Faiz's influences can be partly attributed to the Progressive Writers Movement of the 1930s, which nurtured the next generation of literary revolutionaries, including the well-known novelist Ahmad 'Ali. The Progressive Writers Association was formed in 1934, and its official political wing, the Communist Party of Pakistan (CPP), was set up in 1948 with Sajjad Zaheer at its helm as the Secretary-General. It came under close scrutiny by the Government and was officially banned in 1954. This restriction was imposed because two of its members, Faiz Ahmad Faiz and Sajjad Zaheer, were detained in 1951 under the charge of conspiracy to overthrow the government of Liaquat 'Ali Khan with the aid of the then military chief of staff, General Akbar Khan, who was also arrested. All were found guilty in the trial. According to Hafeez Malik, the overtly political policies of the Progressive Writers Association drew unwanted attention from the Government of Pakistan, who declared them to be a political party in 1951. Accused of collaboration with foreigners/outsiders by Field Marshal Ayub Khan in 1958, the Association suffered a similar fate to that of the Communist party and was shut down.[29] Ironically, Ayub's period of military dictatorship (1958–1969) was seen as a period of pro-Western alliance and is remembered for its progressivism and liberalism.

Under Ayub's auspices, a new writing association, called the Pakistan Writer's Guild, was set up in 1959. The Guild was devoted to the promotion of new Urdu writing, the giving of annual national prizes, and national recognition of new writing. Their mission statement acknowledged writers of the Guild as writers of Pakistani literatures dedicating themselves to the development of the nation and international peace, identifying with human rights standards set by the United Nations. But in the opinion of Altaf Husain Qureshi, the right-wing editor of the *Urdu Digest,* and Mashkur Husain Yad, a retired Urdu professor and left-leaning literary critic, the Writers Guild was a showcase for advocating governmental policy rather than nourishing genuine creative talent: "The writers had money in their pockets but it came at the price of censoring their own writing."[30] Ayub had succeeded in his challenge to curb the freedom of intellectual thought in Pakistan.

When Pakistan experienced a return to democracy during the decade of the 1970s under the leadership of Zulfiqar 'Ali Bhutto, whose party proclaimed, "Islam is our faith, democracy is our polity, socialism is our economy, all power to the people,"[31] his government commissioned literary treatises on Pakistani culture and heritage, to foster a new sense of national belonging and to regenerate the freedom of thought. Bhutto, with assistance from the intellectual elite, tried to forge a national identity which combined religious affiliation with cultural formations. For this purpose, Bhutto appointed the progressive and popular poet Faiz as the founder and Director of the Pakistan National Council of Arts, *Lok Virsa,* in 1971. As a civil servant, Faiz advised the government on cultural policy and represented Pakistan in international conferences. However, just as the discussion on culture was being aired for public consumption, the political map narrowed again as the social revolution Bhutto promised degenerated into a "bureaucratic-military oligarchy." Democracy was forsaken for military rule, and Bhutto was incarcerated and later hanged. In 1977, when General Zia came to power, Faiz resigned from his position and went to live in exile in Beirut, having previously experienced the excesses of an authoritarian state under Ayub's regime. In Faiz's view, his role as a poet, in a nation caught up in a web of growing uncertainty and insecurity, was to enable the Pakistani people to realize their responsibility to themselves and their country.

Thus, throughout the political periods of Ayub and Bhutto, conscious efforts were made toward the visible formation of national culture. In the authoritarian period it was imagined by the state leaders and governed by the laws of censorship. During the democratic interlude it was seemingly mediated through the structures of civil society. In the 1980s General Zia-ul Haq won the hearts and minds of the Muslim traditionalists and the reformists by proclaiming himself to be an honest spokesman for Islam. In his words, "Islam, unfortunately, is the most misunderstood religion in the West.'[32] He undertook an aggressive *Nizam-e Mustafa* (The Rule of Muhammad) campaign of Islamization in the country which targeted, in particular, the visibility of women in an Islamic state. Zia's Islamic renaissance was marked by the implementation of Shari'ah, or Islamic law, through the promulgation of the *Hudood* Ordinance in 1979 and the *Qanun-e shahadat* (The law of evidence) in 1984.[33] He also enforced a strict censorship policy in the national press.

Zia's policies had a direct effect on the life of the private individual. Fahmida Riaz, as editor of the Urdu magazine *Awaaz* published from Karachi, found herself under continual surveillance as a direct result of this strategy. She was served with regular notices culminating in the charge of sedition. This charge carried the threat of capital punishment and was instrumental in her decision to leave Pakistan.[34] Riaz's experience of censorship can be read as a microcosmic example of what was happening at a national level to the freedom of speech in the country.

Overall, the politics of Ayub, Bhutto, and Zia have had a lasting impact on the formation of culture in Pakistan. In order to appreciate their discursive positions, we also have to take into consideration the official documents of nation formation, such as the constitution. Pakistan's first constitution formally declaring it as an Islamic Republic was formed in 1956, nine years after independence. Those nine years were reflective of a nation in turmoil as it witnessed Jinnah's death in September 1948; Liaquat's assassination in 1951; the growing divisions between the Islamic parties and the secularists, and the rising discontent over language and empowerment between the East and the West wings.[35] The constitution of 1956 was thrown into disarray with the military challenge issued by Ayub, who promulgated a new constitution in 1962 and created his own political myth. This was amended in 1973 by the civil administration of Bhutto and again by General Zia in 1985.

There has thus been a constant battle over the authorial ownership of the constitution. With every change of power there was a symbolic challenge to the supremacy of the predecessor and his construction of national identity. In 2007–2008, under the dictatorship of General Pervez Musharraf, a political stalemate had presented itself over the question of when elections were to be held in Pakistan and which party leaders would be allowed back into the country to lead the campaigns for their respective parties. Eventually, it seemed as if a compromise had been reached between the Leader of the People's Party and former Prime Minister, Benazir Bhutto, and General Musharraf while Nawaz Sharif, Leader of the PML-N and former Prime Minister, was also given the go-ahead to contest the elections. Tragedy struck with Benazir Bhutto falling victim to a suicide bomb attack after an election rally in December 2007. The elections were postponed, and a state of emergency was declared. In the meantime, the General was also in dispute with the judiciary after dismissing the Chief Justice of the Supreme Court, Iftikhar Muhammad Chaudhry, an act which again destabilized the structures of civil society. Elections were successfully held in February 2008, with Musharraf's party experiencing an overwhelming loss of seats and positive results for both the PPP and the PML-N.

A recent outcome has been a coalition between the two parties, which can potentially create a problem for Musharraf's continued term as President of the country. However, this internal challenge has to face the continued affirmation of Pakistan's President by countries such as the United States and the United Kingdom, who have lauded his efforts in the "International War Against Terror," making national politics in Pakistan a matter of international concern. In the following section I offer a close analysis of some of the debates on national culture which took place in the 1960s, 1970s, and 1980s so that we can get a historical sense of the internal cultural response to the external national turmoil.

JAMIL JALIBI—THE FORMATION OF NATIONAL CULTURE

The search for a unique cultural identity is the central thesis of Jamil Jalibi's debate on Pakistani culture written in 1964. The first section of his book, entitled 'Freedom, tehzibi [cultural] problems and difference,' begins by critiquing Pakistan's independence as a poisoned chalice which brought in its wake the psychological trauma of hatred and difference. Additionally, he adds, Pakistan's newfound freedom was rapidly destabilized by the neo-colonial forces of American imperialism. Therefore, he views freedom from colonial rule as a relative term. In his opinion, the current nation does not reflect a true independence from its "colonial heritage" and, more importantly, "it does not echo our own moral universe." Associated with this loss, he argues, is the continued marginalization of indigenous cultural heritage in favor of modern European culture. "Our independence interlaced with the Partition of India has meant that we either look to Europe for modern culture or try to retrieve it from the archaeological remnants in Mohenjodaro, Taxila and Harrapa which were originally discovered by Mr Wheeler."[36] The major obstacle in Jalibi's vision of nationalism is the process of globalization, or what he refers to as "internationalism," which promotes Western values. For him there is a clear separation between Islamic and Western values. He says that this trend toward Western values is accentuated by a reliance on foreign aid and American dependency and is psychologically detrimental for the development of a sense of self and independent thinking. There is no sense of national pride.

Shifting from the general to the specific, his cultural journey stagnates because it cannot break free from the boundary of the Wagah border drawn with India in 1947. He asks the question, "Can we forget one thousand years of Indo-Muslim culture? Should we disregard everything that happened before 1947 in order to make it the starting point for our cultural memory?"[37] In order to get away from this downward spiral and to recover national pride, he suggests forging the spirit of unification between East and West Pakistan, as well as, making a conscious effort towards resolving cultural differences between provinces. He specifies the two cultural standards of moral conscience and rule of law which uplift a society. Pakistani society, he argues, has an inherited colonial system of law which has been hijacked by the ruling elite, and morality has disappeared from the equation altogether.[38] For him Pakistan is an unhealthy society which needs to define its culture. He is the self-proclaimed reformist who is initiating a return to the definition of culture itself. [39]

There are two major themes in his book, seen in chapters titled "The Problems of Qaumi Unity" and "Religion and Culture 1 and 2." In the former, the overwhelming problem he foresees is that "Pakistani culture is nameless and we have to identify it." Deeper than the quandary over Pakistani culture is the conceptualization of the nation, the "*qaum*," which does not come together at the national stage. The collectivity of this *qaum* is disrupted by the troublesome nature of "*ilaqai qaumiat*" (regional nationalism).[40] He argues that in order for the nation to succeed it must have an understanding of: "What were we? Where are we? Where do we go? And where do we want to go?" in order to succeed as a collectivity.[41] With this knowledge, he believes, there will come the understanding "which will bind us to our 1200 mile distant Bengali half and bring us together as a nation."[42]

The other issue, which emerges in his discussion on national integration, is that of migration, *muhajir* identity, and the Islamic history of the original migration of the Prophet and his followers from Mecca to Medina. The link with Prophetic migration is very important for Jalibi, because he argues that the Muhajirs perceived their struggle for Pakistan as a holy cause and their migration as a divine sanction. For the Muhajirs, Pakistan is a holy land and their migration has a higher purpose; it is a coming home. The failure of integration, he argues, is that the "*millat*" was unable to sustain "*qaumiat*." Jalibi argues that a more forward-thinking approach for settling the *muhajirin* (used in the Islamic sense of the word) would have been to initiate a dialogue between the settlers and the indigenous population, discussing and sharing their respective attitudes and preferences as well as hopes and expectations. If this had been done, then the migrating population's love for the new nation would have been in abundant evidence. He does, however, grudgingly admit that the migrating population also came with a sense of cultural superiority which did not endear them to the indigenous communities. This, he says, resulted in friction and enmity. He compares the Pakistani situation with what he understands to be the more successful Jewish model in Israel, bearing in mind that he first wrote this book in 1964.[43]

In his chapters titled "Religion and Culture" he initially puts forward his own understanding of religion, bemoaning the separation of matter and spirit in modernity. He quotes the examples of Imam Ghazali and Shah Waliullah as exemplary leaders in the development of Islamic thought. While he applauds the direction of Ghazali's thought, he seems to be arguing for the need to move away from a Sufistic sense of religiosity. But on the other hand, he is not very forthcoming about the hybridity of Iqbalian thought. He says, "We are misguided like Iqbal was when he put Bergson, Nietzche, Lenin and Rumi on the same platform. This happens when we separate our daily life from our Islamic faith and it is a foundational mistake. We can't imitate the West. Our spirituality is intertwined to our daily lives."[44] In his reading, Iqbal failed to negotiate the right balance between a Western idea of progress and a distinctive cultural heritage. Yet Jalibi agrees with Iqbal on the necessity of *ijtihad* (independent reasoning) for the successful formation of a modern Islamic society. In his view, it is only an *ijtihadi* council which can create a successful model of integration between religion and culture in Pakistan instead of the oppositional structure which exists between the two at present.[45]

Jalibi's own position becomes a bit clearer when he historicizes the picture of religion and culture for a Pakistani audience. The two individuals who figure most prominently in this historical survey are Sayyid Ahmad Khan and Maulana Maududi. Each had an important message of reform, but they were diametrically opposed to each other. The former instigated a more Westernized reform for nineteenth-century Indian Muslims, while the latter rallied twentieth-century Muslims toward a return to "pure Islam."

If we take into consideration the umbrella term of *reform* in nineteenth century Indian nationalism, then according to Partha Chatterjee, the reformist stance manifested itself in latter day nationalism through the material and spiritual distinctions of cultural life. In the field of literature, nationalist writers identified the material realm as one which was on the outside, "a mere external that influences us, conditions us, and forces us to adjust to it" and secondary to the primary spiritual sphere which was, intrinsic to the self and Indian morality: "it is that which is genuinely essential."[46] Thus, Chatterjee's conclusions accentuate the ambiguous material/spiritual dyad underlying the dream of the Muslim modernists, and it is this ambiguity which continues to haunt Jalibi in the early nationalist phase.[47]

In the concluding chapters on cultural nationalism he returns to the topic of regional nationalism, which has superseded all discussions on *qaumiat*. His proposed solution lies in the contentious area of language. He suggests the introduction of a two-language formula in the school curriculum, which would give recognition to one regional language and a national language. Thus the learning of two languages as a compulsory means of integration would, in his estimation, bring both East and West Pakistan away from a disruptive model of nationalism. For him, English is the crux of the problem as the state language because it symbolizes a colonization of the mind. He says because of English we have lost the concept of "meaning" and "free thinking."[48] Jalibi's model of Pakistani nationalism is, in his own words, based on the nineteenth-century ideal of the nation as one land, one political system, one history, one language.[49] His book is an attempt to define a mythical vision of the nation, and in it he laments the absence of a suitable model for national culture which would have led to the unification of Pakistan.

FAIZ AHMAD FAIZ—DEFINING PAKISTANI CULTURAL NATIONALISM

Faiz has many personae, foremost among which is his revered status as a revolutionary verse maker for which he has a loyal following in Pakistan. To understand his popularity in Pakistan it is useful to briefly summarize his career. He started off as a lecturer in the mid-1930s, joined the British Indian war publicity department in Delhi as a captain in 1942, and was made a lieutenant colonel in 1944. He returned to Lahore in 1947 and turned to a career in journalism as editor of the new national dailies, *The Pakistan Times* and *Imroz*. He was a member of the bourgeoisie and aligned himself to the political left. His political positioning was not viewed in a favorable light by the ruling establishment, who saw no room for the left in Pakistan.

Thus, it is difficult to separate Faiz the poet who questioned the myth of nationalism from Faiz the journalist who contributed toward the perpetuation of national myths. In Barthes' view, while modern poetic language is resistant to myth, the causality of newspaper journalism easily lends itself to mythmaking. He says, "Contemporary poetry is *a regressive semiological system*."[50] While myth attaches itself to a system of signification, poetry does otherwise; it seeks to be an "anti-language" outside the realm of reason and logic. Therefore, in modern poetry, meaning is not a tangible entity which connects itself directly to the sign, the signifier, or the signified. It conveys itself as an abstraction, and it is this quality which separates it from the factual, value-based understanding that is myth. So when Faiz writes as a poet, his verse has the potential to transcend the strictures of language, but his articulation on culture remains embedded in myth, exacerbated by the Prime Minister's public commission to search for national culture and a prominent post in the bureaucracy.

In his lectures on culture, Faiz (like Jalibi) reviews the etymology of the word *culture* and tries to find its equivalent in Urdu. In his opinion, at the time of his writing, the word *saqafat*, used in Urdu to refer to the English culture, is itself a borrowing from Arabic. Faiz, like Jalibi before him, prefers the word *tehzib*. However, unlike Jalibi, who used *tehzib* as a combined word incorporating the Perso-Arabic heritage of Urdu, Faiz justifies his appropriation of *tehzib* as a new word for culture in tandem with the modern English word. He also makes the point to dissociate *tehzib* from the older word of *civilization*. For him, *civilization* is a limited and closed word, as it is very exclusive in its meaning, whereas *culture* has equitable open-ended possibilities. Independent of his opinion, his translation presents an interesting choice for a "cultured Urdu-speaking" audience who would find the subtle nuances of *tehzib* resonating a civilizing impulse.[51] Rather ironically, Faiz's use of *tehzib* dredges up the very civilizational undertones that he wishes to undercut.

Faiz outlines three interdependent characteristics of culture, which he says come into focus in every nation—namely, personal character, the arts, and society. For his purpose, this adds the necessary depth for a comprehensive definition of culture and allows him to refine two further features, which are the apparent and the hidden, again points in common with Jalibi. He argues that sense is governed by the apparent, such as dress, language, eating habits, place of abode, tradition, and so on, while sensibility answers to the value system of a society. He reasons that in Pakistan the value system is underwritten by religion, and that in itself is the foundation of Pakistani culture. Thus, "nationalist doctrine" is subservient to religious ideology.[52] But he finds it problematic to interchange Pakistani *tehzib* for Islamic *tehzib,* because Islam extends beyond the territorial boundaries of the nation, while national culture is circumscribed by the geopolitical nation. According to him, Pakistani *qaumiat* incorporates both *Islamiat* and *Muslimiat*.[53] This *qaumiat* defines the morality and etiquette of Pakistan as advocated by Islam and is not a differential or oppositional energy. It connects Pakistan to other Muslim nations in the Middle East and takes on aspects of Arab "*wataniyya*," "which calls for political unity of all the Arab peoples."[54] Here, Faiz is careful to separate his search for national character from the patriotic idealism which came out of early twentieth-century Pan-Islamism, including the Khilafat movement (1919–1924) led by Mohammad Ali.[55] In his view, pan-Islamism confused the ideology of nationalism.[56]

His agenda is to refine a unique identity for Pakistani culture which includes its *din* (religion) and *wataniyat*. He suggests that *qaumiat* is best understood as religious self-recognition for the nation defined against its non-Muslim neighbors, and *wataniyat* as a difference from other Islamic nations drawing upon immediate surroundings. "The word (*wataniyya*) appeared at the end of the 19th century, in the context of the extension to the field of state politics of *watan* . . . 'homeland', hitherto applied to place of birth or of residence.[57] Faiz appears to be using it in this context of homeland. His difficulty lies in outlining a shared or common memory of the past in Pakistan. According to him, if Islamic countries such as Iran, Turan, Sudan, and Egypt can have their indigenous culture as well as their *qaumi* culture of Islam, then Pakistan too needs to define its Pakistaniat. He is adamant that Islamic culture cannot be made into national culture because the latter needs to account for everyday life, regional geography, and history. Expanding on this point, he juxtaposes the unifying forces of modern political history against primordial territorial ties. As a solution, he proposes an ambiguous compromise which marries a general Islamic religious nationalism with specific territorial affiliations, such as the ancient Indus valley civilization, as well as a Marxist understanding of the structures of society. In his view this combination of land, religion, and class addresses the differing issues of Islamiat, Pakistaniat, regionalism, and post-colonial societal underdevelopment.

The other concept of Pakistani nationalism he wishes to modify is that of the two-nation theory, which divided people on the basis of what he calls a "vertical division" between Muslims and non-Muslims. In his estimation this changed with the formation of the two new nations of Bharat and Pakistan, and the division occurred on a "horizontal" plane rather than the old Hindu–Muslim equation.[58] He reminds his listeners of Jinnah's vision for the new nation immortalized in his speech made to the Constituent Assembly on 11 August 1947:

> If you change your past and work together in a spirit that every one of you, no matter to what community he belongs, no matter what relations he had with you in the past, no matter what is his colour, caste, or creed, is first, second, and last a citizen of this State with equal rights, privileges and obligations, there will be no end to the progress you will make. [. . .] We should begin to work in that spirit and in course of time all these angularities of the majority and minority communities, the Hindu community and the Muslim community . . . will vanish.[59]

He also reiterates Jinnah's recommendation that, after independence, Muslims who remained on the other side of the border would have to adopt Indian nationalism out of necessity, and their identity as Muslims would be that of a "sub-nation." Thus, Faiz wishes to return to Jinnah's counsel, moving beyond the religious community after the attainment of a separate nation. In expressing a desire to "achieve the Nehruvian ideal of unity amongst diversity" he inadvertently compares the ideological Pakistani self with its secular "Other" Indian neighbor. But his musings on culture deal primarily with Pakistani Muslims and their sense of home and belonging separate from those of the Indian Muslim.

In Faiz's opinion, there needs to be something deeper which connects the individual to her/his homeland. He wants national identity to be shaped by "concentric circles" linking provinces, districts, and villages to their local legends, literature, tradition, and so on. At this juncture he brings in the theme of having an equitable society, without which there is little chance of success as a nation.[60] He compares the two definitions of culture, one defined by the elite metropolitan group and the other by local or ethnic groups, and recommends a clearing out of the dusty mental cobwebs which surround the conceptualization of Pakistani culture. He lists four problems which need to be addressed before the debate can go ahead: first, the idea that culture is self-indulgence; second, the notion of regional culture and national culture being on a collision course; third, culture being opposed to religion; and finally, the misconception that class culture is against national culture.[61]

On the theme of national language and Urdu, Faiz debunks the outlook which traces Urdu's origins from India's southern region of the Deccan to its northern homeland of Delhi. He presents an alternative scenario proposing that the Urdu used in Pakistan today is representative of the organic street language rather than the language of the former courts of Delhi. He argues that this everyday language was utilized by the Sufis, *'ulama* (religious scholars), and, historians, among many others who were born on the land that comprises Pakistan today. With regard to the conflict between East and West Pakistan over the issue of national language, he is noncommittal and argues for a resolution devoid of emotion and based on logic. Ultimately, for Faiz, culture is a factual occurrence rather than a theoretical premise. In order to have a representative culture of the nation, he promotes the practice of researching regional cultural traditions and underlines an agenda for finding similarities between regions rather than focusing on the differences. This particular comment is made with reference to former East Pakistan, where he feels that constant attention was drawn to its difference of language from West Pakistan, and because of the geographical distance separating the two regions there was no real attempt at cultural unification. On the question of combining Urdu and Bengali to make a third language, he opines that such projects should be done scientifically, with appropriate research looking into the wisdom of such an enterprise.[62] For him, Urdu is an essential language for Pakistani nationalism because it offers a canvas, independent from the emotive nature of regional languages, for the construction of new stories of the nation.

Eventually, Faiz shifts focus from rationalizing the religious framework to the presentation of a Marxist outlook. In his opinion, Pakistani society will only progress through education, factual learning, political stability, and equal opportunities. Throughout he presents a logical and fresh approach to the question of "what is Pakistani culture?" but he is unable to resolve the dilemma of a secular cultural nationalism with the ideological religious nation. He says, "Religion shapes your manners and morality not your clothes, food and living . . . It is a common misunderstanding to portray Islamic culture as national culture."[63] His argument is that religious culture cannot be *qaumi* culture, but the latter need not separate itself from the former. Thus his criticism of culture rejects an ideological nationalism which gives precedence to religious belief separating itself from Iqbalian thought, and arguing instead for a reformulation of nationalist thinking.

FAHMIDA RIAZ: REGIONAL CULTURES VERSUS NATIONAL CULTURE

It is quite significant that Fahmida Riaz has chosen the medium of English to disseminate her vision of *Pakistan: Literature and Society,* published in 1986. Also noteworthy is the fact that she composed this monograph while she was in exile in India. The identity of English in India as the language of secular nationalism is not so easily replicated across the border in Pakistan, and Riaz's choice of language certainly suggests a comparative framework for Pakistani nationalism.[64] Bhishsam Sahni writes in his foreword to Riaz's book:

> The book has many a lesson for us in India. Although we are fortunately placed and exercise greater personal freedom, yet linguistic chauvinism is very much present in our midst too, as also the tendency to join language with religion, and to use religion and language as tools of political aggrandisement. The need to strengthen our secular, democratic polity which alone can guarantee the growth and flowering of a multi-lingual, varied culture, is felt in all its urgency, as we read this book.[65]

At the heart of Riaz's argument lies the singular determination to break free from the "linguistic chauvinism" which colors any discussion on Pakistani literature and culture. In her preface she writes, "There is a Pakistani literature that exists in the perception of the people of North India, written only in Urdu, which, again in their imagination, was the language of the Indian Muslims."[66] Her book is an attempt to redress the balance of representation in a national framework, giving voice to the often marginalized regional literary traditions. She divides her book into four sections, similar to the provincial divisions of Pakistan, barring the disputed region of Kashmir. In these sections she focuses on the undermining of regional languages by the centripetal force of Urdu. She draws our attention to specific examples and resistance writings by regional writers in Sindhi, Punjabi, Baluchi, and Pashtu. Her chapters on Sindhi and Punjabi literature are forcefully argued and engage with the political period of the 1960s and 1970s. The chapters on Baluchi and Pashtu are very thin and only confirm literary trends in those languages as well as the presence of resistance literature. Therefore, in this section I will only discuss the first two chapters.

In her focus on Sindhi literature, Riaz airs the hostility between the migrant Urdu-speaking Muhajirs who settled in the urban city of Karachi, and the local population in Sindh. She demystifies the myth surrounding the Muhajir identity as represented by Jalibi. She argues that "The loaded word muhajir was never to be used by the Sindhis. Instead—perhaps more realistically—they called the immigrants panah-geer, which is the exact equivalent of the word 'refugee.'"[67] For the *muhajir*s:

> the local inhabitants had turned out to be only "so many ruffians" who dressed strangely, spoke some uncivilised tongue with most strange sounds, and to whom Islam was also highly suspect as many of them failed to lift the fore-finger at a particular point of namaz. They did not burst into raptures of joy at the mention of Mohammad bin Qasim and his conquest of Sindh. The defeat of Kafir Raja Dahar, too, left them cold and unconcerned. . . . The muhajirs decided to leave the people of Sindh alone. Their land, however, was another matter, a substantial part of which was soon to become their own property by virtue of the most unscrupulously filed claims of property, real or imaginary, left back in India as evacuee property.[68]

Furthermore, Riaz claims that during the Bhutto years 108 Sindhi newspapers and periodicals were banned. The ban effectively curtailed the spread of Sindhi nationalism through the print media, as these publications were seen to be unpatriotic and out of tune with Pakistani nationalism. Riaz is quick to point out that the Sindhi writers and publishers worked together and produced alternative publications which did not arouse suspicion from the authorities and in fact fostered the growth of resistance literature. She also reminds the reader that the decade of the 1970s was perceived as a period of political freedom as it marked the rise of Bhutto, the restoration of provincial status to Sindh, and the return of Sindhi language in educational institutions. So, while Sindhi nationalists were critical of the democratic structures in Bhutto's style of government, his effective mobilization of the class system in Sindh meant that there was little they could do to alter public opinion. Riaz takes great care to reassure the reader of the authenticity and urgency of the "resistance" in Sindh to a Punjabi-center-dominated national identity.

The other literary community in Sindh that Riaz pays attention to is the Urdu-writing *muhajir* group. Riaz finds a problematic absence in their writing of representations from the local population. For this, she blames a lack of foresight on the part of the government, which did not encourage interaction between the settlers and the local populace—a move, she argues in hindsight, that may have led to better integration amongst the two communities. The *muhajir* community's lack of integration with the Sindhi population is considered to be a missed opportunity by Riaz because they were also deliberately cast outside the central circle of the ruling elite during the Ayub era. The *muhajirs* found themselves taking second place to the

Punjabis and the Pathans. In opposing Ayub's rule they became the victims of state oppression. But as an elite group they were also on the margins of Bhutto's People's Party, which targeted the mobilization of the working and middle classes. Her message for the *muhajir* writers is to exchange their nostalgic sensibility for a more engaged tone of resistance to the center, and to foster new themes of cultural hybridity and integration.

Picking up on the theme of *muhajir* marginalization by Ayub in her chapter on Punjabi literature, Riaz regrets the shift of the capital city status from Karachi to Islamabad, which she contends was a major setback for the "*muhajir* psyche":

> The muhajirs were literally made to feel "left behind"; the real political power was now residing in Punjab. This gradual but very visible ousting of the muhajir from Pakistan's realpolitik will remain a regrettable development, because, whatever their weaknesses and illusions, it is undeniable that in Pakistan muhajirs were the only community without any feudal roots in the region. Being non-feudal, their natural aspirations came closer to the ideals of liberalism and democracy.[69]

Here, there is a myth of origins for the *muhajir* persona which disregards their problematic settler identity and focuses instead on an "intrinsic" civilized urbanity that sets them a cut above the rest. It is interesting to contrast the preceding statement with a piece she wrote as a foreword to her poetry collection, *Dhup* (Sunshine), celebrating the earthiness of Urdu:

> My language too is related to a land. That land where the bones of my ancestors lie deep in the earth. Even today this language is spoken in every village over there. This language's basic foundations, grammar, phraseology and the mannerisms of its structure erupted from this land. Tulsi and Kabir are folk poets of this language. This language is the language of the farmers of UP, CP and Bihar.[70]

In her discussion of Punjabi literature, Riaz is troubled by the imperialist power wielded by Punjab at a national level. She tends to mythologize the Punjabi identity as the antithesis of secular ideals, and to infantilize Punjabi mind. For instance, recounting the declaration of martial law in 1953, she criticizes the Punjabis for their lack of resistance: "During the years preceding martial law, the power scramble in the upper echelons of politicians and bureaucracy was too complex to be comprehended by them, besides, it had little relevance to their problems or aspirations."[71] One of the reasons cited for the Punjabis, ignorance is the censorship of the media, hence their lack of knowledge about the "complex situation" in East Pakistan and benign acceptance of the "One-Unit" scheme which did away with the federal structure of the state. In other words, the "politically immature" Punjabi welcomed an undemocratic government.

The other main criticism of literature in the Punjab is its preoccupation with anti-India sentiment, especially after the Indo–Pakistan war in 1965. Here, Riaz makes the ridiculous assertion that the war's "sudden termination disappointed the people," which smacks of anti-Punjabism more than anything. She finds the post-1965 literature with its hatred of India stifling and lacking in intellectual progression. For Riaz, the most distressing casualties of this war were the Urdu literary heavyweights such as Ashfaq Ahmed and Ahmed Nadeem Qasimi, whose writing diminished in stature because both writers fell prey to the bureaucratic hatred of India which permeated the atmosphere in the Punjab. In Riaz's estimation, Urdu literature in the Punjab experienced a creative surge in the early 1960s, but the progress was short-lived because of the war of 1965 when literature was compromised in the name of a "stifling" Pakistani nationalism. Commenting on a lack of similar jingoism among writers in Sindh, Riaz does not take into account the relatively close and long geographical border shared by the Indian and Pakistani halves of Punjab and the fairly recent trauma of Partition as it was experienced in that region. She concedes that although martial law did not help the freedom of thought in Punjab, the literary intelligentsia did make feeble efforts to resist the bureaucratic supremacy. But their resistance was touched by conformity because of the heavy price which came with free speech.

Another sharp criticism of the Punjabi intelligentsia is their lethargic reaction to the secession of East Pakistan and the creation of Bangladesh. She blames this on their complacency and naïve faith in Pakistani nationalism. She reminds the reader that when Bhutto put the wheels in motion to recognize the state of Bangladesh, it was the *muhajirs* who put up the strongest resistance "because of their fraternal ties with Biharis" and not the Punjabis.[72] She claims that the *muhajirs*' concern for the plight of the Biharis was misappropriated as anti-Bangladesh sentiment, and again this was because they

> had never the moral strength to stand up, and speak as muhajirs, to face their real situation of a displacement community which had been rendered most vulnerable to social and political changes in Pakistan. Forever they had to speak as the creators and champions of Pakistan.'[73]

Here, Riaz comes full circle with her defense of the *muhajirs* as well as her discussion of Urdu literature. In Riaz's opinion, literature in the Punjab truly flourished during the Bhutto years when the regional Punjabi writers really came into their own. She appreciates the refreshing lack of patriotic chauvinism in Punjabi literature, a welcome change from the anti-India sentiment saturating the Urdu writing in the region. She also gives space to Siraiki literature as an important, yet often sidelined, linguistic culture in the Punjab. Her reading of Pakistani society through the lens of literature presents an interesting and varied contrast to the more didactic approach toward culture adopted by Faiz and Jalibi. In engaging with literary texts and regional writers, she presents an alternative model for the study of national culture in Pakistan.

CONCLUSION

If we understand ideology in the Althusserian sense of a system of social practices which are articulated in the religious, educational, familial, and legal procedures, then the two representations by Jalibi and Faiz fall in different ideological camps. Faiz's search for Pakistani culture manifests itself in those ideological state apparatuses by which subjects (of the nation) become part of an ideological framework. His vision for national identity stems from the liberal arts perspective, while Jalibi's sensibility is shaped by the ideal of a predestined collectivity. Riaz, on the other hand, works against the principle of what Michel de Certeau has described as a "culture in the singular" which imposes itself from the center and is empowered by a dominant system of law and order.[74] Her analytical review of regional literary traditions attempts to unravel the intricate web of power between the center and periphery and eventually points us toward a more pluralistic practice of culture in Pakistan.

Underwriting both Jalibi and Faiz's reading of Pakistani culture, its inclusions, and exclusions is the religious identity of the nation as an Islamic Republic. Jalibi remains caught between religion and language in his answer to the dilemma. For Faiz, the religious state is a foregone conclusion and a necessary one. His definition of culture seems to be informed by Matthew Arnold's nineteenth-century idea of "sweetness and light [. . .] our *best self*."[75] Yet he remains trapped in a dialectic of Islamiat, Muslimiat, and Pakistaniat in his overarching attempt to define a unique concept of *qaumiat* which is different from Iqbal's territorial identification. One of the problems with his approach is that he seems to be projecting religious identity in Pakistan as a uniformly shared experience. He is also keen to deploy scientific rationalism as a strategy of understanding religion and culture, visualizing them outside their emotive appeal. Faiz's views on these two ideas are different to those of his predecessor, Iqbal, and are contained within the boundaries of Enlightenment philosophy and his left-wing radicalism. His reflections on culture aim to cohere a sense of national unity and operate within the structure of a predetermined mythology of the nation. His overall view is closer to a secular nationalism than a religious one, but he seems to be combining the two in order to make sense of Pakistan's cultural heritage.

Jamil Jalibi's search for national culture is punctuated by the act of remembering the past. Underlying his emphasis on the significance of the retrieval of a pre-Partition memory is a question mark over the birth of the nation in 1947. He also finds the idea of Pakistan as an independent nation a problematic one because of the continuing relationship with America through foreign aid and foreign policy. For him Pakistani culture cannot be free while the country remains subservient to a neo-imperial state. He also opens up the mythology of a shared religious culture within the nation by noting that the *qaum* has not managed to absorb the *millat*. In addition, the two problems which he feels must be overcome in order to be a successful nation are those of regional nationalism and ethnic difference. In discussing the East and West Pakistan divide at the time of writing, his suggested resolution was a two-language formula for national integration. It is interesting to note the contrast here with Faiz, who felt that too much was made of the linguistic difference between the two regions and not enough attention was paid toward emphasizing common cultural traditions. Faiz's understanding of a unified cultural nationalism relies on a shared common language across the nation, while Jalibi feels that the national language has to co-exist alongside regional variations in order to make the nation viable. Jalibi has an additional agenda, which is to critique the position of English as a state language in Pakistan, which he feels further undermines national culture. Overall, Jalibi is critical of the mythology of national culture and is unconvinced of Pakistan's status as a nation.

In contrast to both Jalibi and Faiz, Riaz's outlook represents an interesting counterpoint. She again takes the discussion to the regional margins. Her focus on the diversity of linguistic and literary traditions brings to the forefront the debate on the hegemonic role of Urdu in Pakistan. Like Jalibi, she is interested in the question of *muhajir* identity and their struggle as a group to integrate with the Sindhis. Although she is in agreement with Jalibi about the *muhajir*'s sense of superiority over the Sindhis in civilizational terms, she blames the impasse between the two communities on the central government and its policies. She also feels that there was a deliberate marginalization of the Muhajirs during the Ayub era in the 1960s, which pushed them outside the circle of the ruling elite. According to Riaz, the *muhajirs* have been repeatedly scapegoated by the Punjabis in state affairs that have gone horribly wrong, such as the secession of East Pakistan in 1971. With regard to literary cultural traditions, she is skeptical of writing from the Punjab as a model of resistance against oppressive national structures because she remains convinced that writers settled in the region have been unwilling to challenge the status quo. She finds Sindhi literature to incorporate a better model of resistance, and her ideal national community seems to be the *muhajirs* who have "non-feudal" aspirations and are hence closer to "ideals of liberalism and democracy." In fact, one of her aims in the book seems to be a retrieval of *muhajir* identity from its state-led mythologization in order to identify a marginal "Other" pitted against the dominant Punjabi "self" of the nation. However, the overall argument of resistance literature as a model of cultural expression doesn't sustain itself in her book, as she is unable to offer an equivalent analysis for Pashtu and Baluchi as she does for Sindhi and Punjabi.

Overall, in reviewing the various writings on Pakistani culture, my aim has been to critique these opinions as forms of "mythical speech" which are marked by ambivalence. I argue that Faiz and Jalibi are overtaken by the myth of nationalism while formulating their own representation of a unique national culture. Riaz, on the other hand, situates herself outside the collective national consciousness and argues for a continued cultural resistance through the medium of multiple regional languages against dominant national forms. These selected writings have shown that culture is a much debated topic in Pakistan and continues to be so. There seems to be a consensus in all the discussions that there is no essential national identity to be found. In the current political climate, where Pakistan is a key player in the international War on Terror, it can be argued that for the state, the task of defining a national culture has become more urgent than ever. Intellectual contributions such as these will no doubt help to historicize current and future dialogue.

NOTES

1. Parts of this chapter were given as conference papers at the "New Perspectives on Pakistan: Contexts, Realities, and Visions for the Future" conference held at Columbia University, New York, in April 2003, and at the "Contemporary South Asia Seminar" held at Queen Elizabeth House, Oxford, in October 2003. Thanks are also due to Kelly Pemberton for the references she provided on religious identity and cultural formations.
2. See Benedict Anderson, *Imagined Communities: Reflections on the Origin and Spread of Nationalism*, rev. ed. (London: Verso, 1991), and also Homi K. Bhabha, ed., *Nation and Narration* (London: Routledge, 1990).
3. Timothy Brennan, in his influential essay, "The National Longing for Form," refers to the ambiguity of the phrase "the myths of the nation," which can be taken to represent both the mythical occurrence of the nation and the invention of tradition by governments to "give permanence and solidity to a transient political form." In Bhabha, ed., *Nation and Narration*, p. 47. For the full text of Brennan's essay, see pp. 44–70 of that work.
4. Terry Eagleton, *The Idea of Culture* (London: Blackwell 2000), 25.
5. See Muneer Ahmad, "Failure of Nation-Building in Pakistan," *Pakistan Forum* 2, no. 3, (December 1971): 7–14.
6. Here, I am aware of the problematic nature of the term "postcolonial" and am not using it as a theoretical complexity but more as a reference to the political and historical transition from colonial rule to independence.
7. Roland Barthes, *Mythologies*, ed. and trans. Annette Lavers (London: Vintage, 2000), 109.
8. Here, I find it useful to refer to a specific example of "mythical speech" given by Barthes in order to convey his understanding of two semiological systems in myth: "a linguistic system," or what he calls the "*language-object*," and "myth itself," which he refers to as "*metalanguage*." The example is as follows:
   "I am at the barber's, and a copy of *Paris-Match* is offered to me. On the cover, a young Negro in a French uniform is saluting, with his eyes uplifted, probably fixed on a fold of the tricolour. All this is the *meaning* of the picture.

But, whether naively or not, I see very well what it signifies to me: that France is a great Empire, that all her sons, without any colour discrimination, faithfully serve under her flag, and that there is no better answer to the detractors of an alleged colonialism than the zeal shown by this Negro in serving his so-called oppressors. I am therefore again faced with a greater semiological system: there is a signifier itself already formed with a previous system (a black soldier is giving the French salute); there is a signified (it is here a purposeful mixture of Frenchness and militariness); finally, there is a presence of the signified through the signifier." (Barthes, *Mythologies*, 116).

9. Ibid., *Mythologies*, 115.
10. Gopi Chand Narang, "Tradition and Innovation in Urdu Poetry," in *Poetry and Renaissance: Kumara Asan Birth Centenary Volume,* ed. M. Govindan (Madras: Sameeksha, 1974), 415–434.
11. Faiz Ahmad Faiz, *Pakistani kalchar aur qaumi tashakhus ki talash* [Pakistani culture and the search for national character], ed. Sheema Majeed (Lahore: Ferozsons Ltd., 1988).
12. Jawaharlal Nehru (1889–1964) was the first Prime Minister of India from 1947–1964.
13. Faiz, *Pakistani kalchar*, 39 (my translation). There are many academic debates on the significance and meaning of the words *watan*, *qaum*, *wataniyat,* and *qaumiat.* In this chapter, I am translating them in the context they have been used in by Faiz. More generally, on *watan* see Bernard Lewis, *The Middle East and the West* (Bloomington: Indiana University Press, 1964), 75–77. On *qaum* see Bruce B. Lawrence, *Shattering the Myth: Islam Beyond Violence* (Princeton, NJ: Princeton University Press, 2000), 23–24.
14. Jamil Jalibi, *Pakistani kalchar: qaumi culture ki tashkil ka masala* [The problem of the formation of national culture] (Islamabad: National Book Foundation, 1995), 21.
15. See Amina Yaqin, "The Intertextuality of Women in Urdu literature: A Study of Fahmida Riaz and Kishwar Naheed" (Ph.D. diss., University of London, SOAS, 2001), 118–121.
16. Fahmida Riaz, "A Letter to the Prime Minister of Pakistan," *Mainstream* (11 July 1987): 30.
17. Fahmida Riaz, *Pakistan: Literature and Society* (New Delhi: Patriot Publishers, 1986).
18. Ibid., 11.
19. Pnina Werbner and Tariq Modood, eds., *Debating Cultural Hybridity: Multi-Cultural Identities and the Politics of Anti-Racism* (London and New Jersey: Zed Books, 1983), 2.
20. For a useful and concise survey, see Christopher Shackle's entry, "Urdu," in the *Encyclopaedia of Islam* (Leiden: E. J. Brill, 2000): 873–881, and C. M. Naim's entry, "North and Center: Urdu," in the *Encyclopaedia of India, Pakistan, Bangladesh, Sri Lanka, Nepal, Bhutan and the Maldives,* ed. F. Robinson (Cambridge: Cambridge University Press, 1989), 424–427. For a lively account of Urdu from the nineteenth century to the present, see Christopher Shackle and Rupert Snell, *Hindi and Urdu Since 1800: a Common Reader* (London: University of London, SOAS, 1990). On the theme of canonization in Urdu literature, see David Lelyveld, "The Fate of Hindustani: Colonial Knowledge and the Project of a National Language," in *Orientalism and the Postcolonial Predicament: Perspectives on South Asia,* eds. Carol A. Breckenridge and Peter van der Veer (Philadelphia: University of Pennsylvania Press, 1993), 189–214. For a historical account of the period of Turkish rule from Delhi known as the Delhi Sultanate (1211–1399 A.D.), see Romila Thapar, *A History of India, volume 1* (New Delhi: Penguin Books,

1966; 1990), 266–288; on Urdu, see p. 313. The timeline of this period has been taken from the chronology of Indian history given in Ainslie T. Embree et al., eds., *Sources of Indian Tradition, Volume One: From the Beginning to 1800*, 2nd ed. (New York: Columbia University Press, 1988).

21. See Ayesha Jalal, *Self and Sovereignty: Individual and Community in South Asian Islam Since 1850* (Lahore: Sang-e Meel, 2001), 102–138; Sugata Bose and Ayesha Jalal, *Modern South Asia: History, Culture, Political Economy* (London and New York: Routledge), 84–85; Francis Robinson, *Separatism among Indian Muslims: The Politics of the United Provinces' Muslims 1860–1923* (Cambridge: Cambridge University Press, 1974; 2008), 133–174; Lelyveld, "The Fate of Hindustani."
22. Jalal, *Self and Sovereignty*, 77.
23. See Bakhtinian hybridity as referred to in the introduction to Werbner and Modood, *Debating Cultural Hybridity,* 4.
24. Kristeva refers to this ambiguity as Bakhtinian intertextuality. See Julia Kristeva, *Desire in Language: A Semiotic Approach to Literature and Art*, ed. Leon S. Roudiez, trans. Thomas Gora, Alice Jardine, and Leon S. Roudiez (New York: Columbia University Press), 68.
25. Bhabha, *Nation and Narration*, 1.
26. Nausheen Ahmad, "The Superior Judiciary: Implementation of Law and Impact on Women," in *Shaping Women's Lives: Laws, Practices and Strategies in Pakistan,* eds. Farida Shaheed, Sohail Akbar Warraich, Cassandra Balchin, and Aisha Gazdar (Lahore: Shirkat Gah, 1998), 4.
27. The phrase "sole spokesman" is borrowed from Ayesha Jalal's monograph entitled *The Sole Spokesman: Jinnah, the Muslim League and the Demand for Pakistan* (Lahore: Sang-e Meel, 1985; 1995). For an informative debate on the "two-nation" theory, see the chapter "The Partition of India and the Creation of Pakistan," in *Modern South Asia*, eds. Sugata Bose and Ayesha Jalal, pp. 165–189. Also see C. M. Naim, ed., *Iqbal, Jinnah and Pakistan: The Vision and the Reality* (Syracuse: University of Syracuse Press, 1979). On Iqbal, see Annemarie Schimmel, *Gabriel's Wing: A Study into the Religious Ideas of Sir Muhammad Iqbal* (Leiden: E. J. Brill, 1963) and Iqbal Singh, *The Ardent Pilgrim: An Introduction to the Life and Work of Mohammed Iqbal* (Delhi: Oxford University Press, 1997).
28. Stephen Hay, ed., *Sources of Indian Tradition, volume 2: Modern India and Pakistan*, 2nd ed. (Delhi: Penguin, India, 1988; 1992), 205–218; Shaheen Sardar 'Ali, "Misogynistic Trends in Islamic Jurisprudence—A Feminist Perspective," in Kishwar Naheed, ed. *Women: Myth and Realities* (Lahore: Sang-e Meel, 1993), 154–155.
29. Hafeez Malik, "The Marxist Literary Movement in India and Pakistan," *The Journal of Asian Studies* 26, no. 4 (1967): 649–664.
30. Altaf Husain Qureshi and Mashkur Husain Yad, personal communication, April 9, 2000.
31. Quoted in Ayesha Jalal, "The Convenience of Subservience: Women and the State of Pakistan," in *Women, Islam and the State,* ed. Deniz Kandiyoti (Basingstoke: MacMillan, 1991), 313.
32. "From Coup to Coup," *East,* BBC Pebble Mill Productions, 2000.
33. See F. Gardezi, "Islam, Feminism and the Women's Movement in Pakistan: 1981–91," in *Against All Odds: Essays on Women, Religion and Development from India and Pakistan,* eds. K. Bhasin, Ritu Menon, and Nighat Said Khan (Delhi: Kali for Women, 1998), 51–58.
34. See Fahmida Riaz, "Letter to the Prime Minister of Pakistan," *Annual of Urdu Studies* 6 (1987), 131–2. Reproduced from *Mainstream* (11 July 1987): 30.

35. See Hay, *Sources*, 379–411.
36. Jamil Jalibi, *Pakistani kalchar*, 21.
37. Ibid., 22.
38. Ibid., 34–36.
39. Ibid., 39–58.
40. Ibid., 59–105.
41. Ibid., 71.
42. Ibid.
43. Ibid., 96–103. Despite a second reprint in 1966 and a third in 1973 and a fourth in 1981, he has not amended this particular argument in the wake of the continuing Middle East crisis.
44. Ibid., 24.
45. Ibid., 110, 134.
46. Partha Chatterjee, *The Nation and Its Fragments: Colonial and Postcolonial Histories* (Princeton, NJ: Princeton University Press, 1993), 120.
47. This ambiguous relationship between modernity and religious beliefs continues to occupy both the religious leaders and the secularists in Pakistan. See Ainslee T. Embree, "Pakistan: Defining an Islamic State," in *Sources of Indian Tradition: Modern India and Pakistan*, vol. 2, ed. Stephen Hay, 2nd ed. (New York: Columbia University Press, 1988), 379–411.
48. Jalibi, *Pakistani kalchar*, 84–9. See Ernest Renan's nineteenth-century idea of the nation in his article, "What is a Nation?" derived from a lecture delivered at the Sorbonne, 11 March 1882 and reprinted in Bhabha, *Nation and Narration*, 8–22 (trans. Martin Thom).
49. Ibid., 96.
50. Barthes, *Mythologies*, 133.
51. Faiz, *Pakistani kalchar*, 15–26.
52. Brennan in Bhabha, *Nation and Narration*, 59.
53. Faiz, *Pakistani kalchar*, 28.
54. *Encyclopaedia of the Modern Middle East*, volume 3 (New York: MacMillan, 1996), 1322.
55. See Aziz Ahmad, *Studies in Islamic Culture in the Indian Environment* (Delhi: Oxford University Press, 1999); Robinson, *Separatism among Indian Muslims*, and Gail Minault, *The Khilafat Movement: Religious Symbolism and Political Mobilization in India* (New York: Columbia University Press, 1982).
56. Faiz, *Pakistani kalchar*, 80.
57. *The Encyclopaedia of Islam*, volume 11 (W–Z) (Brill: Leiden, 2002), 175.
58. Faiz, *Pakistani kalchar*, 81.
59. Hay, *Sources*, 386.
60. Faiz, *Pakistani kalchar*, 79–84.
61. Ibid., 56.
62. Ibid., 48.
63. Ibid., 36.
64. While there are well-known Pakistani writers and poets in English, as evidenced in Muneeza Shamsie's anthologies *Dragonfly in the Sun* and *Leaving Home,* the theme of nationalism remains a minor concern among these writers.
65. Riaz, *Pakistan: Literature and Society*, 8–9.
66. Ibid., 10.
67. Ibid., 16.
68. Ibid., 17.
69. Ibid., 68–69.

70. Riaz, *Main mitti ki murat hun* [I am an icon of the earth] (Lahore: Sang-e meel 1988), 220. (My translation).
71. Ibid., 79.
72. Ibid., 89.
73. Ibid.
74. In Michel de Certeau, *Culture in the Plural,* trans. Luce Girard (Minneapolis: University of Minnesota Press, 1998), 100.
75. Matthew Arnold, *Culture and Anarchy,* ed. J. Dover Wilson (Cambridge: Cambridge University Press, 1960), 72, 95.

Part II

Landscapes of Ritual Performance

Ritual, Agency, and Memory in Focus

6 Ambivalent Encounters

The Making of Dhadi as a Sikh Performative Practice[1]

Michael Nijhawan

This chapter examines the relationship between a popular Punjabi folk genre called *dhadi* and practices of Sikh self-representation. The *dhadi* genre is just one of a number of popular Punjabi musical forms, yet it is particularly suited to address the relationship between popular culture and religious practices because of its rather ambiguous place in the contemporary landscape of religious politics in Punjab. While today, the genre is closely affiliated with the Khalsa Sikhs, and most *dhadi* singers have taken *amrit* (baptism), *dhadi* aesthetics and narrative repertoires reflect a broader spectrum of religious and cultural practices of saint veneration in Punjab. Indeed, *dhadi* singers have a reputation of being *mirasi* bards from the lower social strata and "carriers" of a pluralistic Punjabi vernacular oral tradition. More recently this particular form has become associated with a rather exclusivist project of a militant Sikh separatist movement. This connection is very explicit in songs staged at Sikh *gurdwaras*, today more frequently in diaspora settings than in Punjab itself. The "militant link" is also manifest in some of the newly arranged videos and songs that are currently circulating on the Internet. As *dhadi* goes YouTube, and people in chat rooms comment on explicitly militant *dhadi* videos with "they rock" or "damn Khalsa is awesome," the contexts of *dhadi* musical production and reception have obviously changed fundamentally compared to what used to be locally and regionally defined notions of aesthetic receptivity. Before I get into a discussion of the linkages between *dhadi* performative practice, Sikh religiosity and modern Sikh identity politics, let me begin with a few remarks on this particular circulation of *dhadi* sounds today.

Interestingly, many of the new video clips bear the signature of an exclusivist ideology that propounds Sikh nationalism; sometimes the songs justify the use of violence in a rather blunt fashion. This can, for instance, be seen in a video that depicts two young turban-wearing boys in front of a large Sikh gathering, in which they praise the two Sikh militants known for the assassination of a Punjabi newspaper editor.[2] On another video clip from YouTube that promotes a British-Asian music label (Immortal Productions), we find very explicit militant symbols in the form of an AK-47 rifle and references to former militant leader Jarnail S. Bhindrawale. Noticeably, enticing *dhadi* vocals and sound patterns are now built into a popular, urban-cosmopolitan drum'n bass music, which in itself is a topic worth of study.[3] What I am concerned with here is the normative rendering of *dhadi* based on an exclusively Khalsa vision of Sikh identity with strong undertones of the Khalistan movement. At a first glimpse, this is may be not so surprising.[4] In fact, *dhadi* song performance has served as a popular mode of producing a Sikh martyr history and thus was linked to the Sikh martial tradition since the seventeenth and eighteenth centuries. The frequent use of martyr narratives and their aesthetization through musical idioms of *bir rasa* (heroic mood) might explain why this folk genre has been open to the political message that is now being conveyed in the new diasporic media outlets.[5] But from a different perspective, it seems more than ironic that *dhadi* practice is now almost exclusively seen in this framework, for unlike in other scenarios of cultural translation and diasporic travel, where the hybridity of new cultural forms is celebrated for its capacity to disrupt existing boundaries of social and religious identities, the *dhadi* productions mentioned previously flatten out such potentials. It seems the *dhadi* form is reduced here to its most simple ideological and exclusivist message, almost completely shorn of the complex social and performative contexts in which it has been historically situated.[6] Hybridity at the musical level is met with a narrowing of discursive possibilities, to say the least.

The dissemination and re-sampling of *dhadi* sounds and images is part of a broader trend in the cultural industry. The particular linkage between new/urban *dhadi* sounds and Khalistan narratives, however, must also be seen as one of the discursive and aesthetic effects of political violence that came about during the 1980s Punjab crisis. The events of 1984 (Operation Blue Star and the anti-Sikh riots in Delhi that followed the assassination of Prime Minister Indira Gandhi) were certainly felt as an atrocity that concerned the community as a whole. In this aspect, post-1984 sentiments were foundational for a new Sikh diasporic imaginary to emerge.[7] It is in the same historical context that *dhadi* music traveled from the local scene in Punjab to diasporic sites in Birmingham, London, Vancouver, and elsewhere. People still remember the passionate voices of the Nabhevale Bibiam, who performed the *dhadi var* (a musical genre typically associated with *dhadi*) in the vicinity of the Golden Temple in 1984. *Dhadi* music resurfaced at the height of the conflict between the Indian army and the Sikh militants that culminated in the Operation Bluestar. In the course of these events, *dhadi* music acquired public recognition as the musical voice of Sikh militancy. In the years to follow, when the staging of *dhadi* songs was censored by the state, *dhadi* tapes circulated undercover and subsequently reached the diasporic context. It is precisely in the diaspora context where *dhadi* sounds kept their ties to the political project of Sikh nationalism. I shall come back to this point at the end of this chapter.

While the events of 1984 had a lasting influence on the self-understanding of many ordinary Sikhs and implicitly on the public image of Sikh *dhadi*, it also led to changes within the dhadi performative community.These events had the unforeseen effect of unsettling and rearranging the patron–client relationship that had historically posed *dhadi* performers as socially inferior. These effects, I would argue, point in sharply different directions and expose the relationship between *dhadi* and a particular normative rendering in terms of a militant Sikh ideology as deeply ambivalent. At a closer look, the issue of social stratification and the gendered image of the *dhadi* performer in fact challenge the story of heroic masculinity and self-sacrifice that characterize the Khalistani rhetoric. Indeed, *dhadi* musicians were for a long time branded as low- or outcaste *mirasi*, and social conduct was delimiting to such an extent that selected groups were not allowed to perform or participate in Sikh religious settings.[8] At the same time, some of the *dhadi* performers that I have encountered during my fieldwork continued to pay reverence to saintly figures outside the established boundaries of Sikh institutionalized religion, such as the Sufi *pir*s (holy men) that are still popular in the Punjabi countryside. This is perfectly in line with what we know historically. Nonetheless, in official discourse this has become a suppressed site to the same extent that grievances by *dhadi* performers against their patrons have hardly opened into public debate, too marginal it seems their specific concerns are for the Sikh *panth* (community) as a whole.

This chapter examines some of the junctions and disjunctions inherent in contemporary *dhadi* performances. First, I want to delineate how common knowledge about the shared idioms of cultural and religious engagement that was once so characteristic for the *dhadi* form has been recast in the post-1984 discourses. For this purpose I will focus on conversations and selected public performances that I have witnessed within the *dhadi* scene during my research work in 1999 and 2000. Second, I want to demonstrate that the reconfiguration of Sikh *dhadi* does not translate into a subaltern resistance narrative. One would assume that the move from a broader cultural framing to an exclusively religious framing of Sikh *dhadi* has pushed the agenda in the direction of what then, in Western liberal discourse, is translated into "fundamentalism." However, the straightforward linkage between religion and fundamentalism is problematic in its own terms, and it fails to acknowledge the differentiated employment of religious discourses in the context of the *dhadi* musical culture. I will show instead how, in the post-1984 context, the idioms of Sikh religiosity have again shifted from a dominant concern over guarding the boundaries of Sikh sacred symbols (crucial to the mobilization of collective identity during the Punjab crisis), to a more lucid interpretation of Sikh ethical idioms that *the dhadi* performers acknowledge in their emancipatory potential. This shift in signification is not audible in the voice of "collective resistance," but in a change in aesthetics and ethics in relation to the everyday life worlds in which *dhadi* performers see themselves to belong. This move does pose a challenge to the institutional framework of Sikh religion, but only implicitly and from a viewpoint that sees religion itself as a field of social transformation rather than just metaphysical orientation.[9]

SHARED IDIOMS, EMBODIED DIFFERENCE

Historically, *dhadi* performers have been part of a loosely defined segment of Punjabi service castes (*mirasi*), a name that only during colonial times acquired the negative tinge it still has today. *Dhadi* performers were not bound geographically to a particular region in Punjab, but it seems that they had close social ties with the Jats, a demographically and politically influential group in Punjab that, since the seventeenth century, constituted a majority within the Sikh community. Long held in high esteem by Sikh patrons and audiences, *dhadi* performers have in this context been identified with bards specializing in the delivery of Sikh heroic history. Performers themselves did not necessarily (and formally) adopt the Sikh faith. This did not seem to be problematic in the context of a pre-modern *dhadi* idiom to the extent that Sikhi as a religious philosophy was traditionally open to followers of other faiths, provided certain basic tenets of Sikhi were accepted.

Nonetheless, considering the dominant image of Sikh *dhadi* today, it is noteworthy that historical records trace *dhadi* performers with Muslim names and indicate a close affiliation with Sufi *pir*s. Even today, in a cultural landscape dotted with major shrines and minor monuments of Sufi commemoration, there is indeed no shortage of opportunities *for dhadi* performers to participate in song and narrative related to these sites of ritual commemoration. *Dhadi* performers have routinely traversed the boundaries of these different sites and affiliated communities, and have been cited as archetypal figures for the cultural and religious pluralism of the region. Participating in the heterodox universe of Punjabi vernacular culture, *dhadi* performers were also known as singer-composers of the famous Punjabi *qisse* (stories) of Hir Ranjha, Soni Mahiwal, and others, tracing the signature by some of the best-known Punjabi poets, such as Varis Shah or Bullhe Shah. This literature, both oral and written, continues to be held in high esteem across communal boundaries and in the public writ large.

The turn to Sikh *dhadi* with a more or less exclusive repertoire of martyr stories is the result of changes introduced in the late colonial period, the consequences of which are still felt today.[10] Clearly, the politicization of religious identities at the time of India's partition (1947), the hardening of communal boundaries in the years following that event, and more generally the long-term effect of a re-scripting of *dhadi* songs by Sikh reformists all contributed to changes in the production and reception of *dhadi* music.[11] It was the Partition of 1947 that had the most significant impact on *dhadi*, however. As it is now well known, the Partition event was accompanied by mass-scale migration and violence between members of the different religious groups, which, consequently, almost entirely disrupted the established patron–client system that had enabled *dhadi* to flourish as a medium of expression with broad-based appeal across boundaries of religious identity. After Partition, we witness a general decline of the *mirasi* performers, which were firmly tied to local Sufi and Sikh shrines and their inheritors.[12] At the same time, Sikh institutions such as the Shiromani Gurdwara Prabhandak Committee (SGPC) that administers Sikh *gurdware*, were successful in providing a religious framework for Sikh *dhadi* performance by officially sanctioning *dhadi* practice as a standardized part of weekly gurdwara congregations and by recruiting old and new *dhadi* performers through their institutional ranks. Despite the fact that *dhadi* performers were embraced by dominant institutions, there is still evidence that the repositioning of *dhadi* within the Sikh panth was not as smooth a process as such a narrative would make one believe.

As a way to engage in this discussion, I want to briefly discuss an incident that occurred in November 1999, when I was invited to attend a meeting of a local *dhadi sabha* (association of traditional Sikh orators and bards). The gathering took place in the vicinity of Ludhiana, where I conducted a major part of my ethnographic fieldwork in 1999 and 2000. Listening to the conversations at this meeting was particularly instructive to get an idea of how *dhadi* singers organize their everyday affairs and situate themselves as a distinctive group within the wider society. There was a deliberate effort in bringing together the scattered groups of *dhadi* performers in a *sabha* or association. This, it was upheld by the participants, would give them more power to negotiate claims with the Sikh institutions and other patrons. The meeting can be described as truly democratic, as people elected their spokespersons and engaged in open debate and discussion. In this regard, communicative practices were also set apart from other, highly formalized modes of public performance. Thus, these practices opened a discursive space that was at once couched in the language of Sikh ethics and yet remained less constrained by the normative regulations and audience expectations that typically frame public events in Sikh religious settings.

Apparently, all participants within the *sabha* appeared in the full gear of baptized Sikhs, wearing the turban and the *kirpan*, the ceremonial dagger, visibly on top of their white *kurta pajama* dress. While I listened to these conversations, however, it became clear that this symbolically marked body entered language in twisted ways; that is, hidden meanings of Otherness and alternative imaginations of social belonging were given expression in the different speeches. Sant Singh, for instance, who is a renowned performer in the region, was among those to address the gathering with some opening remarks. In his speech, he reprimanded Sikh patrons and institutions for having failed to fulfill their duties toward the *dhadi* community. He said:

> Am I not telling the truth if I say that the Shiromani Committee and the Shiromani Akali Dal expect that we commit ourselves to their cause?

That we would prepare their ground? We crunch the stones on the ground! We mould bricks from earth! We do everything! But with their cowardice they do not even recognize how clear this ground has in fact been made. They also know that we are upright people, but tell me, up to today what kind of help did we receive from the Shiromani Akali Dal and the Shiromani Committee people?[13]

Idioms of labor such as were used that day by Sant Singh are surely well chosen. A majority of those present at the meeting used to work in agriculture or construction, or continue to provide cheap labor in menial jobs. Interestingly, the rhetoric of labor here also includes what *dhadi* musicians and orators produce on the stage; thus the language of "molding bricks" indexes a process of narrativization and oral persuasion through which the common man's mind is "prepared" for accepting Sikh religious beliefs. Sant Singh portrays the bodily labor of oratory and bardic music as a "sweatshop" of cultural and religious production that is erased from official memory. For the majority of performers I have worked with, the economy of signs that pertains to *dhadi* performative language is framed in a similar fashion as a suppressed site of productivity–politically censored by the state in the years after 1984 and marginalized by other social and political forces in the contemporary context. Yet, as it became increasingly clear to me, it was exactly through this economy of signs that the process of social reproduction in the performative community was sustained.

The way in which a stigmatized body becomes the surface for a discourse of social improvement to be staked out is further illustrated in the words by another performer, Gurbaksh Singh, who argued in turn:

We restless people, we *dhadi*, I say that we have become orphans, washing someone else's underwear. Do you understand? We wash them for the Sikhs, and still nobody would appreciate our deeds [. . .] With our limited means of serving others, have we ever refused to serve the master tea and milk? Did we ever attempt to change our affiliation? . . . There has been a need for us to find a place in this world [society]. In whatever way we can achieve this, with the help of our new president . . . we must be aware that they will just add a tail to it and name it their own.[14]

Not only was there a clear distinguishing line between "us" and "them," *dhadi* performers and "the Sikhs," it was once more in the notion of a serving and laboring body, manifest here in metaphors of washing the underwear for the Sikh patrons, that the social condition and identity of the dhadi performer was problematized. Thus, the speaker drew on a popular idiom that names *dhadi* singers as those "with the worn out underwear," using the term *kachera* ("shorts") that is one of the symbols for the baptized Sikh body. To say someone has worn out *kachera* is a demeaning remark on his presumed immorality and fallen status. Appropriated as a signature of social orphanage, however, the stigma of washing the patron's underwear is invested with a self-reflexive twist that carves out the performer's body as a site for intervention and change.

The kind of subjectivity of the *dhadi* performer produced in such discourse is cast in the traditional idiom of patron–client relationships, rather than in idioms of subaltern resistance. Note the idiom of serving tea and milk, which alludes to intimacies of social interaction and which must be considered basic forms of politeness in everyday conduct in Punjab. *Dhadi* public speech, even in its critical reformulation, operates within the framework of a cultural habitus through which both patron and client recognize each other's role and identity. The cultural specificity of this language of servitude notwithstanding, it should be noticed that the *dhadi* orators here do stake a claim upon the patron—the absence of specific gestures on the part of the patron is read as a double negligence: a lack of social recognition and a deficiency in terms of economic and cultural reciprocity. It is significant, therefore, to pay attention to the work of language through which a notion of the *dhadi* subject is produced. At the same time, the speeches I have discussed are, in a particular way, oriented to the practicing body of the *dhadi* performer. In fact, as I shall demonstrate in the following section, the body itself becomes the site in which a new religious sentiment can be produced. I want to first discuss *dhadi* oratory during a staged event that I recorded and subsequently return to the *dhadi* sabha discussions. It was in these discussions in which notions of everyday conduct, bodily practices, and virtuous behavior were targeted as key sites through which the stigmatized *dhadi* body could potentially be undone.

DHADI ORATORY: WHY WORDS OF PRAISE ARE DOUBLE-EDGED

The common perception of *dhadi* performers in contemporary Punjab is that they do not articulate their individual concerns and ideas but rather put their voices into the service of a larger collective interest or representation of an event. While hypocrites say they do whatever you pay them for, people knowledgeable of the tradition would argue that the very purpose of *dhadi* singers as "the people's historians" is to give voice to collective ideas and values. This might be true and resonate in *dhadi* performers' self-description in public contexts; however, it misses the point of creativity, reflexivity, and voice-production in a *dhadi* performative event entirely. In the following I want to discuss how within a context of public performance that is clearly framed in terms of a collective event of commemorating a local writer, poet, and patron of the arts, Mohan Singh, staged *dhadi* oratory and song has multiple registers and can be seen to be strategically employed for a variety of purposes, not all of which fall under the commemoration part. I think this discussion is relevant, for there has been a long debate in the broader framework of South Asian studies of how to conceptualize forms of subaltern agency under explicit forms of political domination or cultural hegemony.

One such example I want to briefly comment on is Gyan Prakash's essay on the oral traditions of the outcaste Bhuinya in highland Orissa. In this text, Prakash describes how storytelling rituals help to mimetically re-enact the Bhuinya subordinate position and by doing so create room for social transformation. Noticeably, in Prakash's words, it appears that even though storytelling rituals "incorporate the principles of caste hierarchy and dependent ties . . . [the Bhuinya storytellers] did not simply replicate an 'original' scheme of hierarchy and dependence; rather, they fissured and pried open the Bhuinya position as outcaste and dependent laborers for reformulation and reconstitution."[15] As he continues to argue, song performers ascribe supernatural powers to Bhuinya culture heroes (*birs*—heroic warriors) were that to some extent mimetic of high-caste attributes: Their own hero was "malik-like . . . but he was still a Bhuinya."[16]

Prakash's concept of agency avoids a simple dichotomy between (local) elite and subaltern folks. He also questions that ritual practices of storytelling simply operate to sustain hegemonic relations. Even though the context of ritual performance relates to a normative framework through which upper-caste groups legitimize structures on inequality, it is also within the domain of the religious that such structures can become unsettled. Prakash argues that storytelling rituals have a transformative potential that is not restricted to a temporary act of "embodiment" (singular event of transgressing the everyday by means of the citation of authoritative voices) but, due to its repetitive forms of bodily enactment, is continuously working to destabilize the dominant cultural narrative. This, argues Prakash, is significant for the very understanding of Bhuinya identity. I want to take up this idea for my discussion of *dhadi* performance here. Similar to the Bhuinya example, *dhadi* storytelling performances are ritualized events insofar as they employ formalized speech, are based on particular bodily techniques, and make use of a religious symbolism in a way in which it distinguishes them from everyday forms of conduct and social interaction. Heroic plots and aesthetics play a similarly important role.

Let me now elaborate on a particular incident of a *mela* performance in October 1999 in the city of Ludhiana, which staged some of the performers, who were present at the *dhadi sabha* meeting.[17] During the two-day gathering of the Professor Mohan Singh Mela, the "*dhadi darbar*" was staged as the opening event along with other Punjabi and Rajasthani folk performances. An audience of about 150 mostly elderly men was assembled on the ground. A number of performers sitting on the stage waited for their turn to take the microphone. One of those was Kamal Singh's *dhadi jatha*, a group of one orator and two musicians. The piece they chose to deliver was a legendary tale of the Anglo-Sikh war in 1846. Their selection of songs and oratory focused on the story of Sham Singh Attari, a well-known General, who served under Maharaja Ranjit Singh and who played a significant role in this war. Sikh memory enshrines Sham Singh as a self-sacrificing soldier who lost his life fighting the British. The *dhadi* orator dramatized how Sham Singh was called to the battlefield by two of his Sikh companions, known as Teja Singh and Lal Singh, who would "treacherously" leave the battlefield by tricking Sham Singh into a hopeless situation, as he was left cornered by a superior British force.[18]

The story is significant at different levels: First, it amounts to Sikh heroism and discourses of martyrdom. Second, it engenders the issue of betrayal within the in-group of the Sikh *panth*, which is metaphorically mapped on the present situation of post-1984 politics in Punjab. Take, for instance, the first song verses in which the singers could be heard: "There is injustice on the Earth, as it happened in Punjab," "friends turn into enemies, inciting injustice," or "the fatherland is threatened by slavery." Although these verses relate to the historical narrative on Sham Singh Attari, the idiom of betrayal clearly had a contemporary feel. Third, the performers raised a moral concern that was discussed frequently in their day-to-day conversations: political corruption and a general sense of moral decay of publicly known figures. Politics, in particular, is regarded as a field in which ruthless motives of accumulating wealth and power are pursued at the expense of any concern for the staggering conditions of the common farmers and workers, who have suffered major economic setbacks since the Green Revolution.

By taking Sham Singh as an exemplary model, the *dhadi* orator succeeded in staking out an ideal character of Sikh moral virtues as it is implied in his martyrdom, and thus evoked an image that was diametrically opposed to this idea of moral decay. At one point in the presentation the orator could be heard saying:

> Since hundreds of years, millions of people would come and leave this world every day, but rare are those sons on earth whose name, bravery and deeds get written down in the golden letters on the pages of history. Thus, a poet's life endures; it does not get extinct from this world. And the martyrs have become immortal; the world will never forget them.[19]

By associating the poet (*sha'ir*) with the martyr (*shahid*), the orator drew an interesting allegory: A timeless truth is incorporated in the poem, in the manner that Sikh martyrs are seen to incorporate a universal truth. The heroes have left their names "in golden letters on the pages of history." What can be inferred from such instances is how a modern concept of historical consciousness is constructed in a given *dhadi* oratory. And this is, indeed, a very common facet of Sikh *dhadi* song performances. Furthermore, through the allegory between *sha'ir* and *shahid*, the narrative plot was contextually anchored in the *mela* occasion that honors the local poet. The orator demonstrated eloquence in praising the life of Mohan Singh when he quoted from the latter's popular poems to elaborate on the ethos of martyrdom. It must be said that within this performance setting, the language of martyrdom bears an ideological tinge that is clearly in line with a Khalsa narrative of Sikh history. But note how, toward the end of the performance, the orator evokes the idea of the immortality of the *sha'ir*:

> And, while presenting two lines of Sardar Mohan Singh, I want the audience (*sangat*) to draw attention to the eminent patrons of Punjabi culture, Jagdev Singh, to Sardar Parman Singh and Sardar Gurbhajan Singh. They have selflessly promised to broadcast the heritage of Punjab's favored poet, for whom since twenty-one years this *mela* is being held. And Professor Mohan Singh has written two marvelous lines in his poem "Nurjahan". And, according to "Nurjahan", Professor Mohan Singh heard a voice in a dream: "The way you have valued my poetry and dropped on my grave a few tears // The same way people will weep in your memory and drop countless tears" [*Meri shai'ri di jis tarah qadar kar ke, meri qabar te gire ne car hanju // Aiwain rona tainu wi yad kar ke, lok giran ke beshumar hanju".*] Today, Punjabis are dropping their tears in memory of their favorite poet.[20]

Speaking in such words of praise, the audience was not only reminded about the continuous need to remember the poet Mohan Singh (people might forget), the *dhadi* singers also project an image of their own group as socially significant. Eventually, the orator expresses his gratitude to patrons and audience, reminding them to honor Mohan Singh as an arbiter of a particular moral commitment expressed in his poetic verses.

The form of bardic speech as it was enacted during this event certainly accounts for the de-authorization of individual voice that seems to be characteristic for bardic discourses throughout North India. In the context of the *dhadi* performance, however, this surrender to the collective has also a force in staking historical truth claims and the moral accountability of the contemporary patrons. The praise of the patrons in the last paragraph follows the social conventions and can be seen as a fully appropriate statement to the liking of the patron. Yet, in a nuanced reading, I would argue, a distinct voice can be heard. Thus, the speaker issues an implicit critique of the organizing committee in reminding them about what he considered to be Mohan Singh's legacy.[21] It is a legacy of the "heroism" of Punjabis reframed in terms of religious concepts of self-sacrifice and moral virtue. Obviously, this issue has become secondary to the political and social agenda of the folk festival that was organized around local election campaigns. We can say with some plausibility that the *dhadi* group's evocation of Sikh normative language was also directed against what they considered moral failures within the Sikh community as they materialized in the present context of folk patronage. This is something that was not missed on the part of the festival organizers, as I was reassured in later conversations.

Thus, similar to Prakash's example, *dhadi* cultural performance rests on a storytelling ritual that is based on a "malik-like" version of history, voiced from the perspective of a dominant historical narrative, but reappropriated by a particular speaking subject that claims his own voice in the process. This is not to suggest that all comparative levels would hold together here. As argued previously, Sikh *dhadi* performers, though sharing a history of subalternity, are meanwhile recognized officially as a segment of the Sikh institutional landscape. Ambivalence in the encounter between *dhadi* and normative Sikhism, it could be argued however, is still perceptible. In the public event discussed herein, the reenactment of conventionalized forms of speech and the submission to particular forms of social authority is not simply mimetic of dominant structures but alludes to a reflexive position toward those forms, and a kind of agency that in Judith Butler's words "exceeds the power by which it is enabled."[22] In the previous example—the speeches given at the *dhadi sabha*—this ambivalence was much more explicit, for the enabling aspect resulted from a linguistic mediation of two different sets of bodily metaphors, each signifying a different subject and social memory, which was not openly articulated during the stage performance. It was only during the group's conversations that the visible body of Sikh religious identity markers would intersect with a hidden, laboring, and recognizably low-caste body that, is also a body of Otherness through which the *dhadi* singers become marked as marginalized and subjugated. In both discourses, however, voices of dissent are cast in idioms of Sikh ethical conduct, not in a disjunction between *dhadi* as a form of cultural practice and Sikh patronage as its institutional framework of an organized religion.

By drawing attention to these issues, my aim is not to suspend notions of "misrecognition" of the "what" of what ritual practice does beyond peoples' strategies and intentions. It would nonetheless be a mistake to think that there is no space for a conscious and deliberate intervention in the way *dhadi* performance is publicly practiced, based on shifting forms of cultivating Sikh pious bodies in particular aesthetic form—in the *dhadi* way. I will now further discuss this issue by returning to some of the conversations that I observed during the *dhadi sabha* meeting.

FROM THE ORPHANED BODY TO ETHICAL SPEECH

During their conversations, members of the *dhadi sabha* repeatedly evoked notions of proper speech and conduct as intrinsic to the Sikh gurus' words and teachings (*gurmat*). The purpose of such discourse was not simply that of putting on a public face that suited collective interests of social recognition. While questions of social improvement and social recognition were at the top of the agenda for the members of the *dhadi sabha*, the evocation of Sikh *gurmat* had far deeper implications.

First, and linking this up with what I have referred to before, the speakers at the *sabha* issued a general grievance about a lack of morals and a widespread sense of corruption. The word "politics" here bears all the negative connotations of economic inequality, rampant individualism, and favoritism. These issues did not stop short before an assessment of issues pertaining to the established religious institutions, but were also aimed at ordinary Sikhs and their inner attitudes toward religious teachings. The *dhadi* performers were not the only ones issuing such concerns. Over the years in which I conducted fieldwork in Punjab, and more recently within the Sikh diaspora in Europe, I heard such narratives repeatedly. Often enough, individuals who have distanced themselves from Sikh political organizations issue such concerns. Take, for instance, the words by Gurwinder Singh, who spent time in Indian prisons during the Punjab crisis and later claimed an asylum case in Germany. This is how he assessed the situation in regards to principles of *Sikhi*:

> (Q): In Punjab you were called a Sikh, even now you say you are a Sikh. At that time you were engaged in politics, demanding freedom (for Punjab). Now you are in Germany, because you had problems there. How do you assess the difference between then and now? You say you are a Sikh now, and you were a Sikh then, but I feel there is a difference. What difference do you think it is and why?
>
> (A): The difference is that before we used to think of ourselves as Sikhs, but in fact we were not. *Sikhi* was given to us; it was simply part of our culture. However, how little knowledge did we have of our religion and *gurbani*? *Gurbani*, at that time, meant behavior; it was not inside us. We did not have the religious background. This is why I say we were not Sikhs. I actually still do not call myself a full Sikh. Because we still do not have acquired enough knowledge of *Sikhi*. It is only now that I feel I learn something, since I make an effort to read and understand *gurbani*.
>
> (Q): What do you think Sikhism consisted of there, at that time? What was the meaning of being a Sikh?
>
> (A): Then, we used to think that, well, we are *amritshak* (baptized), wear the five K's, and can read *gurbani*, so we called ourselves Sikhs. But in truth, it was a misunderstanding.
>
> (Q): And now, by developing your knowledge further, what do you think is the meaning of being a Sikh, I mean what is the "real" meaning?
>
> (A): The true meaning of being Sikh is revealed in the path described in *gurbani*. The gurus have told us how to live our life in truthfulness, which means we do not say one thing and do another.

> (Q): What other main points does the *gurbani* say? What are the major points that tell us what a good life should be?
>
> (A): A good way of life is one that, in my understanding, is based on truthfulness. Nothing such as anger or rage against someone else is justified by it. Everyone is equal. "*Abal Allah Noor Upaiah, Kudrat ke Sab Bandeh*" (All beings are of God). We should understand this and not do any bad deeds toward anyone; do not lie. Tell the person the truth. Avoid gossip or talking bad about others.
>
> [. . .]
>
> I also said earlier that because we have *Sikhi* in our culture, we do not know its true value. It is like if you receive a present, you do not necessarily recognize its value. In the same way, because we have *Sikhi* [inherited] in our culture, we do not know its value. And we are just losing our life. We are proud that we are Sikh, but there is nothing inside us.[23]

Although Gurwinder is not a trained performer or *gurbani* expert, he clearly shares the cultural horizon and the prior engagement in Sikh political life that some of the other actors that I have referred to here also participated in. The brief excerpt condenses very well what I have heard from many other baptized Sikhs, including the members of *the dhadi sabha*. So, within the broader religious framework, there are strong currents of internal criticism that result from an interpretation of the Guru Granth Sahib and ensuing ideas on Sikh ethics. This is not surprising as such, for the Sikh institutional and organizational framework is far less hierarchically structured than that of, say, Roman Catholicism. It accordingly becomes more difficult to mark out dominant and counter-currents.

But it is interesting that *dhadi* bards, who for considerable time were not seen as fit to participate in such a discourse, now play an active role in it. Staking out an ethical position as Sikh *dhadi* performers becomes a core feature of constituting a *dhadi* performative community in the contemporary situation.[24] Contemporary here means specifically post-1984—a situation, as I remarked initially, that drew *dhadi* performers into the arena of Sikh militancy and confronted them with state counter-insurgency, one of the effects being a de-facto censorship of politically loaded *dhadi* song and oratory, arrests, and sometimes torture. While this is not the place to enter a detailed discussion of the former political alliance and the role *dhadi* performers played for the Khalistan movement, it needs to be mentioned that for most of the performers I worked with, the Punjab crisis and the political violence that has shaped it had long-term demoralizing effects. To this extent, the public image of the *dhadi sabha* was of course a key concern, which is why many conversations focused on how *dhadi* singers were seen in the public. But, as I have indicated, the target was not simply a "wrong perception" in the public, but rather a focus on the self-improvement of the performers.

In this context, the fissures between spoken words (on the stage) and publicly ascribed notions of speakers' sincerity came to be seen as crucial. According to one of the speakers at the *sabha*, it was by means of improving the self according to the principles of the Sikh *rahit maryada* (code of conduct) that *dhadi* performers would be recognized as morally accountable and respectable speaking subjects in the wider public. Precisely because the notion of a new or reformed speaking subject necessitated an active engagement of self-improvement and discipline—that is what the performers said—it is necessary to look more closely at the actual processes of debate and persuasion characterizing the group meetings that I could observe. For the Sikh *dhadi* singers, quotations from *gurbani* as well as references to *gurmat* would provide the argumentative structure through which social change and new social visions are aspired and materialize in the social world. For them, the question is not solely how to couch a social and political agenda in religious language or ideology, but to consider ethical principles as an end in itself and only secondarily as an implicit challenge of the status quo of power relations and social stratification. Let me illustrate this with words of Charan Singh, former spokesperson of the association.

Far too long, argued Charan Singh in the first part of his speech at the meeting, have quarrel and suspicion prevailed in the community, partly because of the entanglement with "politics" and partly because of the envy people held against individual members, who could achieve a better social position when compared to the large majority of *dhadi* performers present at the meeting. Charan Singh carefully elaborated on notions of group solidarity that were historically undermined by the structure of patron–client relations. The solution for him consisted not so much in demands for better salaries or other material gains (an issue that was still considered significant for many of those present) but quite the opposite, in a gesture of abstention. Thus, he said that *dhadi* performers would only accomplish their goals once they were widely recognized as pious selves, based on a lifestyle characterized by chastity, honesty, and what could be called a puritan lifestyle—precisely the opposite of the public image that associates rural dhadi groups with a witty character, promiscuity, and widespread drug abuse (consumption of liqueur and opium).

Charan Singh's speech was interesting to listen to, as he succeeded in several argumentative shifts to evoke the idea of a social body of *dhadi* performers, produced through and authenticated by an idiom of Sikh religiosity. This was to be based on a deliberate choice on the part of those gathered in the meeting, not on the basis of a utilitarian interest, but grounded in an understanding of self in "willful obedience" to divine authority:[25]

> Maharaj has given orders, and we should follow these. And with the Guru's blessings [I shall say]: 'if you improve yourself, then you will be able to reach me. And after you accomplished this task, you have the

> whole world at your disposal. If you continue following the Guru, then the whole world will belong to you.'[26]

There is no talk here of a separate Sikh Raj or retributions against suffered injustice, but of an ethical regime based on the observation of core principles of Sikh conduct as expressed in Sikh *gurmat*. These ethical principles hinge upon everyday bodily practices and on a principle of pure and truthful speech. This shift in emphasis in the Sikh *dhadi* context is by no means circumstantial. Considering the difficult socio-economic conditions under which *dhadi* performers accomplish their profession, the reconfirmation of ethical principles that transcend the practical necessities of life and the reciprocal logics of patronage are sincerely held to be the way of change. The pronunciation of such issues by a leading spokesperson is of course meant to have a binding effect on everybody in the *dhadi sabha*. But from what I have observed, it in fact confirms the general attitude among participants of making ethical choices within the particular socio-political framework in which they currently found themselves. Social improvement in this reading should depend on a process of self-improvement to be initiated by each individual member of the *dhadi* community as his or her own individual "duty." Does this rule out that various performers would consider such ideas as moral imperatives to be passively followed rather than ethical choices to be actively made? Maybe not. Nonetheless, the focus on Sikh *gurmat* in the *dhadi* performative scene appears as something novel and radically changing the character of how *dhadi* performers would position themselves publicly. Kamal Singh, the orator who delivered the piece on Sham Singh Attari (see "Dhadi Oratory," earlier in this chapter), also emphasized this notion of gurmat when he talked about the reasoning behind *dhadi* public performance:

> Whether it is in honor of Guru Maharaja or not, wherever we *dhadi* singers appear, our talk will be about Sikh history, about the principles of Sikhism. We talk about *gurmat*. We present *gurmat*. We will deliver what the Gurus prescribed as "duty" and taught as religious truths. . . . Rather than speaking about those who disregard the principles of the faith, our presentation is about the ethos of being Sikh (*Sikhi*), about the history of Guru Maharaja, the history of the Singhs, about the principles/doctrines of *Sikhi*. Whatever place, as long as there is an assembly of listeners (*sangat*), we shall give voice to *dhadi vars*.[27]

He comments here on how the actual process of *dhadi* performance ought to be grounded in notions of religious duty through which the transformative character of a performance is then channeled. It is at the same time a comment on how the performer's agency is extended through an incorporation of particular linguistic gestures in concrete ritual practices.

I am not intending here to confuse an analysis of performative processes with their discursive framing within and beyond the Sikh *panth*. The exploration of ritual performance as scenes of encounter can only make sense in a properly contextualized ethnography that takes into account many situational and historical factors that I cannot investigate further at this point. The argument I would like to pursue here is a step removed from an anthropological performance analysis. In other words, when a performer such as Kamal Singh talks about the "duty to perform *gurmat*," it is of course not equivalent with seeing his own action before an audience entirely through this frame. Audience responses are mediated by a notion of aesthetic receptivity, as well as the appraisal of narrative content.

What I want to demonstrate in this section, however, is the relationship between a performers' subjectivity and the actual performative act. So this is about the move by *dhadi* singers—in recognition of the dominant perception of their art—to make the aesthetic and discursive form itself subject to scrutiny. This move occurs in a fieldwork situation in which there has grown an empathic and mutual understanding of the complex conditions and entailed risks taken on the *dhadi* stage. In the case described here, the performers know about the relatively stable set of expectations and evaluations held by particular audiences, specifically if this occurs in the context of a folk festival. But this is precisely the point: While the members of the *dhadi sabha* recognize the institutional effects of folk discourses on their art (which is usually seen by Sikh *dhadi* singers as a negative one), they now also recognize the possibility to change this set of expectations and audience perceptions to the extent that they can and do respond to it in actual performative practices in different social situations.

THE RASA OF DHADI

Participants of the *dhadi sabha* operate in a space of public deliberation that, in a comparable manner to what Charles Hirschkind has shown for new religious movements in modern Egypt, is a space that ties together, rather than separates, disciplinary and deliberative aspects of religious reasoning.[28] In his work, in which he focuses on the role of Islamic cassette sermons and the kind of citizen-subject produced by the practices of listening to these sermons, Hirschkind argues that the fashioning of a pious Muslim body essentially hinges on an aesthetic process of cultivating "the ethical and therapeutic virtues of the ear" of the pious listener.[29] The "honing of an ethically responsive sensorium" of the ear (and the responsive "heart"), Hirschkind further agues, has helped the listeners to cassette sermons in Egypt to form a self through a particular aural aesthetics that "recruits the body in its entirety" and produces the conditions for an ethical-political reasoning. This idea is distinctively set apart from a prevalent notion among secularists that the Muslim low-class fellows on street would fall prey to the persuasive rhetoric of the religious orators' passionate discourse.[30]

In this final section of the chapter, I want to engage with Hirschkind's emphasis on the aesthetics of listening which, he argues, are as instrumental to the production of forms of religiosity and pious subjects as social organizational aspects or political mobilizations of religious identities. To the extent that the core idioms of *dhadi* voice production and music are similarly based on notions of aesthetic effect and listeners' receptivity to *dhadi* sounds, the connections are not random at all.

Before I discuss this any further, let me first point out that while in Hirschkind's work the linkage between religious discourse and the aesthetics of listening are constructively tied to each other within a broader project of Islamic revivalism, there is something distinctive about how *dhadi* aesthetics relate to prevalent notions of a reformist Sikh religiosity.[31] In the preceding sections, I have emphasized the ambivalences that situate the *dhadi* subject within the parameters of a Sikh normative context. In these final remarks, I want to point out that the very form of *dhadi* musicality and voice production is part and yet set apart from the spiritual registers of Sikh religious musicality, which itself finds common expression in the practice of devotional Sikh *kirtan*. Genres associated with *dhadi* music are actually embedded in the musical lyrics of the Guru Granth Sahib. Nonetheless, as a part of the historical reconfiguration of Sikh patronage of *dhadi* singers, there has been a discernible move to forms of bardic music that were cogent to the broader North Indian musical culture, but not necessarily in tune with the musical aesthetics of the Sikh religious text.[32]

This is obviously something that is reckoned with by the *dhadi* performers themselves. It is clear that when they speak about the undoing of inherited habitual lifestyles, a radical undoing of the recognized differences between musical aesthetics that distinguishes processes of listening to *kirtan* from processes of listening to *dhadi* is not even aimed at. There might be several reasons for this. For instance, the framing of *dhadi* as a practice of bardic storytelling guarantees access to a religious public sphere for social actors, who would otherwise be shorn off these resources. The social milieus *dhadi* singers are traditionally are recruited from are more likely to choose these bardic genres than the more "elevated" forms of practicing Sikh *kirtan*. This is not to say that the distinctions between these genres mirrors caste or class distinctions—there are *kirtan* singers who come from a low-class background as there are *dhadi* performers who do well economically and socially. Nonetheless, a certain pattern of social affiliation is still discernible. But, more importantly, there is something specific to the idea of *rasa* (aesthetic pleasure) and the politics of affect that relate the heroic form of *rasa* with notions of violence and martyrdom. All of this further complicates the discourse on ethics within the *dhadi* performative community.

Let me explain this in some more detail. Common to the perception of *dhadi* performance is the idea that there must be *rasa*. This is something that is shared by performers across social and religious boundaries and thus is something that is clearly tied into what we might call the shared cultural idioms of *dhadi* performance in Punjab. The notion of *rasa* is crucial for understanding the emotional energy of *dhadi*. *Rasa* is a key concept within the Indian dramaturgic and musical traditions and focuses on the aesthetic production of an inner affect. In the case of *dhadi*, the most common aesthetic idioms are those of sorrow/sadness (*dukh*) and the heroic (*bir*). These moods are variously described in terms of bodily effects on the listener—experiencing "heat" and the eruption of inner energies. Performers have a clear understanding of how to practice voice, sound patterns, and sarangi tunes to produce the desired effect. When, for instance, the genre of a *var* is performed, the voice is of very high pitch and is intense (*tez*) on the vocal cords; whereas in a *baimt*, the voice is sweet, prolonged, and vibrating on the vowels—fashioned in a way to express a degree of mourning or lament. Good performers are masters of these differently nuanced musical-poetical forms of voice production.

Now, the issue I want to raise here concerns the transformation of such notions of *rasa* due to what could be called the changing conditions of listening to Sikh *dhadi*. As I outlined in the beginning, these changing conditions are the product of a politicization of the musical scene, and they are also subject to changing modes of musical production and transmission through new technologies. In the 1984 context, processes of listening to *dhadi* staged performances as well as *dhadi* tapes that circulated along with tapes containing the political speeches by Jarnail Singh Bhindrawale (who was killed during Operation Bluestar) were clearly tied to a process of political mobilization and the arousal of strong passions. Within the specific temporality and experiences of suffering triggered by the events of 1984 and after, the politics of affect were, in fact, tied to an aural aesthetics of violence. Listening to passionate performances of the *dhadi* voice was not only increasingly popular again, it also opened up the male-dominated scene to women performers, as it was the female voice in particular that was seen to produce the desired effect in the listener during those years.

The point that interests me here is how this public re-orientation toward *rasa* produced in the *dhadi* voice relates to what years later performers would argue are their own specific orientations to *dhadi* aural aesthetics. Apparently, for some of the emerging *dhadi* musicians and orators, the orientation towards rasa in *dhadi* works on a much deeper level.[33] It is through the embodiment of aesthetic idioms in *dhadi* music, these performers argue, that they "complete" a personal journey of spiritual uplift, which is also often a "conversion" story to the Sikh faith. But how does this aesthetic orientation fit into the discursive orientation which, as I have demonstrated, is organized around Sikh ethical idioms, when the sounds of Sikh *dhadi* are publicly perceived for their political undertones rather than a deeper religious engagement as would be the case with Sikh *kirtan* music?

As indicated before, unlike Sikh *kirtan* music, the musical and narrative repertoires of *dhadi* songs are renderings of folk tunes and motifs that are not based on *gurbani*.[34] In that sense, it is crucial to understand the current dividing line between *kirtan* and *dhadi*, which becomes clear in the different organization and placement of *dhadi* performance in the religious setting, even though historically this is a questionable divide. So there are external constraints, but there are also internal attachments that must be reckoned with. In fact, it seems to me that the very attachment to the performative aesthetics of *dhadi*, despite providing a differentiating access to Sikh religious spaces (dhadi singers do not perform sitting next to the Guru Granth Sahib, but in a standing position and usually also in a different setting within the *gurdwara* complex), also works as a deterrent from achieving full recognition in the same way than *kirtan ragis* would normally do. However, it appears to me that precisely because *dhadi* performance (unlike Sikh *kirtan*) has been anchored in different sites of saint veneration in Punjab (thus by definition breaking the boundaries between different sacred sites and symbols) it has remained attractive to people in rural Punjab who are still tuned in with these different sites of veneration.

Access to the world of Sikh *gurmat*, therefore, occurs through a particular lens; or, differently stated, it is made possible through an implicit knowledge of a much more complex and diverse universe of spirituality expressed in *dhadi* performative contexts. This is something I need to further explore in another essay, but let me indicate here by way of concluding this chapter how some of the female performers and members of the *dhadi sabha* have indeed articulated their assessment of *rasa* in *dhadi* in those regards. Thus, for the female performers, the mood instilled through *dhadi* music was experienced to cause stillness and contemplation, which is quite exactly in line with a widely shared understanding of the bodily effects of listening to gurbani hymns. *Dhadi* singers would certainly not confuse the different idioms and realms of practice, but they deliberately linked the idioms of *dhadi* music with an idea of Sikh religious piety. One might say that is consonant with what we heard in the discussions of the *dhadi sabha*. *Rasa* in that sense has also changed its meaning: The meditative idiom and mood of Sikh *kirtan* now contains the passionate-interpretive form ("bringing the blood to boil"), which is still upheld as a rationale for "what *dhadi* singers do." Yet, the inner affect experienced by the musicians is discursively construed as something quite different than just the "arousal of the passions."

Is it a co-incidence that this occurs in the aftermath of political violence in Punjab? And what does it tell us about how the actual *dhadi* performative scene responds to the ill effects of those events? I think that the careful elaboration of the complex realities surrounding the *dhadi* genre that I have endeavored, demonstrates how social actors work within a given normative framework to keep the boundaries open rather than subsuming to an all too simple equation with political or religious ideology.

Finally, to link this up with my introductory examples on urban *dhadi*, it now can be argued that the diasporic shifts in political ideology intersect with a shift in the practices of listening to and producing *rasa* through dhadi music. There are many traveling *dhadi* groups that reach *gurdwara* audiences, and some of the female performers I have mentioned are part of this circulation of religious professionals. But, more interestingly, there is a new, disembodied, and hybrid format of *dhadi* urban music that draws on the very notion of the energy of *rasa*. It seems that this music has had some success in reaching out to audiences that would otherwise shy away from a more "traditional" *dhadi* performance in the *gurdwara* setting. But it is also within this new hybrid, electronic format that the actual link between a broader project of reconstituting ethics in *dhadi* aesthetics is being interrupted. Let me quote a few passages from the recently co-authored contribution with Virinder Kalra to further elaborate on this point:

> The musical-lyrical mapping of violence and victimization that is taking place in urban dhadi thus departs from the times of the insurgency movement in the 1980s, where it is in mass congregations that the dhadi voice was seen as particularly suited. The sonic connection between dhadi voice and the Khalistani movement is so important, as it is precisely this connection that is captured in urban dhadi, otherwise shorn of any of the performative contexts which are so central to its generation of *rasa*. [. . .] But it is precisely by means of musical entertainment (sonic pleasure) that urban dhadi reaches the young diasporic listener. Through such a displacement urban dhadi retains a notion of *rasa* and further acquires a global motif, linking it up with the oppressed from Brazil, to West Africa, to France, Germany and Britain. It achieves this goal precisely by filling a void created by the more traditional kind of dhadi. Reaching diasporic lands first through the *gurdwara*, then through cassette culture and finally audio archives on the internet, dhadi largely failed to attract the swathe of young folks who have been into Bhangra-pop. Hence, it is precisely this group who is the target of the new dhadi urban music, by using tunes that borrow extensively from contemporary hip hop tunes which in turn have also borrowed and mixed in *tabla* and Hindi film songs, this way creating sonic pleasure that is tuned into these popular forms.[35]

In other words, urban *dhadi* music that is currently produced and consumed outside of the typical performative context of *dhadi* singing has succeeded in creating links between an exclusivist political ideology (still current among certain diasporic groups) and a broader cosmopolitan culture that is open as far as social and other registers are concerned. Thus, at least from the perspective of those behind these musical outlets, it is through the disembodiment of *dhadi* sounds and lyrics that the linkage to political ideology can be sustained most convincingly. What happens at the same time is that the complex social and political environments in which performers in Punjab have reworked their agenda is now out of the radar of the politically engaged diasporic listener. How this will affect the politics of identification within the global Sikh community and, more broadly, a process of recovering the more inclusive, shared idioms of *dhadi* practice is an open question to be further investigated in the future.

NOTES

1. Some parts of this chapter were initially published in my *Dhadi Darbar: Religion, Violence, and the Performance of Sikh History* (Delhi: Oxford University Press, 2006), chapter 6. This chapter is both a revision and an expansion of the theoretical framework employed in that monograph.
2. See http://www.youtube.com/watch?v=b4KhByIaKKo, last accessed June 07, 2007.
3. See http://www.youtube.com/watch?v=xEC7wcdn6yU, last accessed June 08, 2007.
4. "Khalistan" (tr. "land of the pure") is a term used by Sikh sovereigntists to pursue claims for an independent Sikh homeland in Punjab. During the 1980s, when the Khalistan movement received significant support from the Sikh population, many Sikh *dhadi* performers were affiliated with its main propagators. For a detailed discussion of urban *dhadi* music and how it fits into this political context, see Virinder Kalra and Michael Nijhawan, "Cultural, Linguistic and Political Translations: Dhadi Urban Music," *Sikh Formations* 3, no. 1 (2007): 67–81.
5. For a discussion of diasporic *dhadi* songs that represent the ideology of the Khalistan movement, see also Joyce Pettigrew, "Songs of the Sikh Resistance Movement," *Asian Music* (Fall/Winter 1992): 85–118.
6. Nonetheless, Kalra and Nijhawan argue that interpreting these forms simply as the expression of xenophobic diasporic cultures would be misguided, for the requirements for translation are often not met at the listeners' end. Furthermore, in the digital age there is little potential for controlling how these sounds might be used.
7. See in particular Brian K. Axel, *The Nation's Tortured Body: Violence, Representation, and the Formation of a Sikh "Diaspora"* (Durham and London: Duke University Press, 2001).
8. For a discussion of the role of *mirasi* in Punjab's musical culture, see Adam Nayyar, "Musical Regions: Punjab," in *The Garland Encyclopedia of World Music*, ed. Alison Arnold (New York and London: Garland Publishing, 2000), 762–772.
9. For this point, see Martin Fuchs, "Articulating the World: Social Movements, The Self-Transcendence of Society and the Question of Culture," *Thesis Eleven* 61 (2000): 65–85.
10. Sikh teachings do not encourage religious conversion in the strict sense of the term, but rather invite followers of other faiths to be guided by the revelatory teachings of the Guru Granth Sahib. Historically, however, conversion has played an important role in Punjabi politics. Because Sikhs were a demographic minority, it became vital during the colonial period to react to the conversion campaigns by other religious groups, specifically the Arya Samaj that through its *shuddi* campaigns openly denied Sikhs a separate status by aggressively converting ordinary Punjabis who were more loosely tied to Sikhi.

11. See Nijhawan, *Dhadi Darbar*, chapter 3. The late nineteenth and early twentieth centuries witnessed a larger effort on the part of Sikh reformist and performers to introduce changes into the performative and narrative idiom of dhadi and other genres.
12. Two well-known performers to be mentioned here are Idu Shareef in Chandigarh, India, and Muhammad Shareef Ragi in Faisalabad, Pakistan. Both are among the few *mirasi* performers who have managed to make a living in the folk sector of the music industry. I have interviewed both performers, video-taped Idu Shareef's Hir-Ranjha rendition, and collected a number of Shareef Ragi's taped recordings at Rahmat Grammophones. A discussion of the differences between Sikh and Sufi *dhadi* can be found in Michael Nijhawan, "Shared Melodies, Partitioned Narratives: An Ethnography of Sikh and Sufi Dhadi Performance in Contemporary Punjab," *International Journal of Punjab Studies* 10, nos. 1–2 (2004): 57–77.
13. Public speech by Sant Singh; *Dhadi* Sabha meeting at Mulanpur, Punjab, October 1999, my translation.
14. Public speech by Gurbaksh Singh; *Dhadi* Sabha meeting at Mulanpur, Punjab, October 1999, my translation.
15. Gyan Prakash, "Becoming a Bhuinya: Oral Traditions of and Contested Domination in Eastern India," in *Contesting Power: Resistance and Everyday Social Relations in South Asia*, ed. Douglas Haynes and Gyan Prakash (Berkeley: University of California Press, 1991), 146.
16. Ibid., 163.
17. A *mela* is a cultural festival and provides one of the traditional spaces for dhadi performance in Punjab. A *mela* gives occasion to a large gathering of listeners from different strata of the society. Earlier in Punjab, a *mela* was patronized by rulers, landlords, and religious authorities like the Sufi *pir*s and their successors. A *mela* forms a space of remembering religious figures and culture heroes. Following the religious calendar of such fairs, the *dhadi* bards change their stories and melodies, adopting performative styles according to the local tastes and commemorative frameworks set by the localities and patrons. At the Professor Mohan Singh Mela, there was a high percentage of lower class and rural audience members and an almost complete absence of the urban middle class. Interestingly, however, local politicians and honorable guests were present to attend the festival.
18. Note that the Anglo-Sikh war terminated Sikh sovereignty in the Punjab under the reign of Maharaja Ranjit Singh.
19. *Dhadi* oratory Kamal Singh; Ludhiana, Punjab November 1999, my translation.
20. Ibid., my translation.
21. I have had long discussions with the performers about their opinions on folk festivals and their organizers. My argument is based on these conversations and on my own observance of the festival in 1999.
22. Judith Butler, *The Psychic Life of Power* (Stanford University Press, 1997), 15.
23. This is part of a longer interview that my colleague, Khushwant Singh, and I conducted for the documentary film "Musafer: Sikhi is Traveling" (2008).
24. It should be evident from what I have argued so far that the term "community" cannot mean a "natural" bounded-ness or mode of belonging that is self-evident. This is generally the case if one evokes collective formations such as "the Sikh community" but it is even more problematic for a loosely bound association of musical performers who today come from different social backgrounds.

25. For the notion of "willful obedience," see Talal Asad, *Genealogies of Religion* (Baltimore, MD: Johns Hopkins University Press, 1993).
26. Public speech by Charan Singh; *Dhadi* Sabha meeting at Mulanpur, Punjab, October 1999, my translation.
27. Interview with Kamal Singh; Ludhiana/Punjab November 1999, my translation.
28. Charles Hirschkind, *The Ethical Soundscape* (New York: Columbia University Press, 2006).
29. Ibid., 9.
30. Ibid., 10, 25.
31. See Arvind Mandair's chapter in this volume for a discussion of the reconstitution of basic tenets of Sikh religiosity in the course of the Singh Sabha reform movement.
32. Today, only few Sikh musicians know that there are a few particular *raga*s in the Guru Granth Sahib that are associated with the *dhadi* genre. It can be argued that during the times of the gurus, *dhadi* was an intrinsic part of the *kirtan* tradition. Thanks to Bhai Baldeep Singh for sharing his views on this particular issue. He is one of the few performers who can claim competence in playing those tunes.
33. For a longer discussion on the gender dynamics in this genre, see Nijhawan, *Dhadi Darbar*. Interestingly, women performers appeared on the scene during the Punjab crisis, after a group known as Nabhewale Bibiam became famous for their high-pitched performance of *dhadi* songs. This induced changes within the performative tradition and had a lasting impact on the post-1984 emergence of women *dhadi* groups in the formerly male-dominated tradition.
34. The recitation, singing, and listening to the hymns of the Adi Granth are central elements of Sikh liturgy. More than that, *kirtan* is seen as a mindful and spiritual engagement with the text. The repeated and repetitive practice of kirtan ideally leads to an undoing of self-centeredness. For a discussion of Sikh *kirtan* and other ceremonial practices, see Kristina Myrvold, "Inside the Guru's Gate: Ritual Uses of Texts Among the Sikhs in Varanasi," Ph.D. diss., Lund Universtity, 2007.
35. Virinder Kalra and Michael Nijhawan, "Cultural, Linguistic, and Political Translations," 77.

7 Ritual, Reform, and Economies of Meaning at a South Asian Sufi Shrine

Kelly Pemberton

As one of the most popular and widely patronized Sufi shrines in India,[1] the burial shrine, or *dargah*, of the Chishti saint Khwaja Mu'in ud-din Chishti, located in Ajmer Sharif (a city found in the Northwest state of Rajasthan), evokes a number of associations that suggest that a desire for harmonious communal relationships lies at the heart of ritual exchanges between the Muslim servants of the shrine and their clients. The shrine is regularly touted in the mainstream English-language press as a symbol of Hindu-Muslim unity. Until the bomb blasts of October 2007 that took place within the shrine complex, it was widely perceived to be a place untouched by both communal strife and the threat of terrorism. It is frequently described as an example of cultural fusion and "national integrity," shorthand for the Government of India's purported efforts to bring about the national integration of India's various communities.[2] It is a sacred realm where pilgrims seek to tap into the spiritual power that resides within the shrine and its saint, regardless of caste, class, creed, national origin, political affiliation, or secular or religious mindset; all who come are believed to have been "called" by Khwaja Mu'in ud-din, or Gharib Nawaz (Reliever of the Poor), as he is affectionately known.[3]

This study of ritual life at the shrine of Mu'in ud-din Chishti suggests a nexus of contradictions surrounding the veneration of deceased Sufis. Some of these contradictions illustrate the limitations of shrines and their servants in overcoming communal tensions—and their underlying economic, political, or social causes—that undergird the surface of everyday relations among religiously defined groups in India. Other contradictions suggest a tension between competing discourses of "authenticity," exemplified by debates about the propriety, from the standpoint of Islamic Sharia,[4] of ritual exchanges between the "servants" of the shrine and their clients. These latter often pivot on the question of whether Sufi shrine culture is properly "Islamic" or an amalgam of local pious traditions coated with an Islamic veneer.[5] Narratives of authenticity are used by Muslims who are openly critical of Sufis, such as the reformist Tablighi Jamaat and Ahl-i Hadis groups, so-called Wahhabi traditionalists operating in India,[6] and non-Muslims who are critical of Indian Islam or, alternatively, who are critical of Sufi practices as well as their relationships with pilgrims from a wide variety of cultural, religious, and social backgrounds.

Questions of authenticity are notoriously difficult to evaluate and often open more lines of inquiry than they are able to answer. The term "vernacular Islam," recently used to great effect in a study by Joyce Flueckiger to describe the kind of healing practices that take place at a shrine in Hyderabad, in which a Muslim female healer (*piranima*) shares the spotlight with her husband, a *pir* (both are now deceased), suggests a more insightful alternative to understanding how identity narratives are articulated with respect to local cultural practices. As Flueckiger's study demonstrates, boundaries of ethnic, religious, and cultural identity tend to become muted among the disciples and clients of the *pir* and *piranima* within the space of the healing room, or alternatively, they (discursively and/or ritually) disappear. However, outside of this ritual space and context, more exclusivist narratives of identity may well reassert themselves.[7] In trying to account for the different forces that index articulations of the sacred within the space of the shrine, I operate from the assumption that shrines like the Gharib Nawaz *dargah* at Ajmer sit at the crossroads of multiple forces—religious, social, historical, economic, and political among them—that are essential to understanding how the production of narratives of identity unfolds.[8] Thus, while not ignoring the salience of a palpable tension between dominant narratives of Islam seeking to articulate a "universal" form of the faith that is applicable to all believers, and local "micronarratives" that are able to mobilize discourses of exclusivity and exclusion (e.g., in belonging to a spiritual elite, or in the perception, frequently articulated by shrine "servants and their Sufi "guests" alike, that Muslims—or Sufis—suffer as a persecuted minority in India), the major concern of this study is with the production of such narratives. In other words, this study investigates how discursive and ritual acts of identification and naming—particularly as carried out by the servants of the shrine, as its representatives to the wider world—operate as rhetorical strategies that seek to build relationships of sacred exchange.

This study relies heavily on ethnographic data, using a participant-observation approach to assess how the articulation of narratives about identity is shaped by the ritual contexts of devotion I have observed over years (1996–2003) of visits to the shrine, and participation in ritual ceremonies as an "associate" of the Gudri Shah Chishti order, whose *khanaqah* (lodge) is adjacent to the *dargah*. Since my study also seeks to index the impact of institutional, historical, and other structuring forces on the shape of these identity narratives, I draw upon classical Islamic formulations of prayer, sanctity, religious authority, and the Islamic "religious sciences" (*'ulum ud-din*) as evoked in the writing of Sufi *shaikh*s and their disciples, particularly as they pertain to the sources of Sufism frequently indicated by the servants of the shrine and their disciples. These begin, of course, with the Qur'an and *sunna* of the Prophet Muhammad, but also include the literary output of well-known Sufi *shaikh*s, philosophers, and their followers. At times, the narratives of Islamic identity conveyed within the pages of these classical sources appear to contradict the more personalized narratives of faith and piety I have encountered among servants of the shrine. Rather than seeing in these apparent contradictions evidence of "un-Islamic" (or extra-Islamic) beliefs and ritual practices as mediated by the shrine's servants, I consider these as evidence of an ongoing dialectic of collectivity on one hand, and on the other, a self-reflexive self-fashioning. This latter is a prerequisite of the work of "servanthood," and a reflection of the ability of the actor to strategically adapt language and action to particularized contexts. The dialectic between narratives of collective belonging and individual self-fashioning is further captured by the character of the Ajmer shrine itself, which embodies, channels, and evokes sometimes complementary, sometimes contradictory aspects of its own identity as an institution that serves as both an integrator of diverse groups and a symbol of the success of Islam in the Subcontinent.[9]

Ritual events at the Mu'in ud-din shrine are framed by Islamic discursive traditions that draw from rather more individualized concepts of the sacred even as they speak to a shared grammar of religious experience. In the everyday experience of those who seek the saint's blessings, the boundaries of the "Islamic" and "not Islamic"[10] are equivocal, framed as they are by both personal and collective understandings of spiritual authority. These index subjectivities that are shaped by prior experiences that are themselves embodied in ritual performance, and a shared grammar of the sacred that is discursively modified by adaptations geared toward the faith community with which the pilgrim is identified by the servants of the shrine. My characterization of ritual exchanges at the shrine of Mu'in ud-din Chishti suggests a "ritual stance," in the view of Humphrey and Laidlaw,[11] in which intentional ritual action is often performed "un-intentionally," that is to say, as a re-enactment of established forms of praxis guided by a mediator (the servant of the shrine), which are then given meaning by the ritual performer (the pilgrim himself or herself). But I would stop short of seeing a prescribed ritual act as entirely devoid of meaning until the pilgrim infuses it with such, nor would I assign such autonomy to the ritual actor. The question becomes one of agency, and with respect to the understanding of the shrine servants themselves, ritual performances at the shrine follow a format that is itself predicated upon a "prior text" of faith in the efficacy of prayer to Mu'in ud-din Chishti. It is the saint himself, in the multiple spaces he occupies as healer of hearts, mediator between the divine and human realms, exemplar of perfect faith in Islam, and spiritual guide for the sincere pilgrim, who acts as a catalyst for the transformation of the pilgrim, and the servant of the shrine as mediator of the saint's message as well as his power. And it is the belief in, and experience of, the power of the saint that serves as the basis for pilgrims' belonging to a community of faith.[12] The ritual practices enacted at the shrine of

Mu'in ud-din, I propose, ultimately serve as a script for constructing new internal configurations that enable the believer to self-identify on a number of different levels. The least implication of this process is that the believer is not restricted to boundaries of religious community, but rather, becomes more open to a number of multiple designations of personhood.

Much has been written about the generally accommodating atmosphere of Sufi shrines: on the whole, they have operated as cultural integrators, drawing pilgrims from near and far in a shared community of faith centered on the person of a deceased saint, on his or her living representatives, or on the shrine itself as a locus of *baraka* (spiritual power). Functionaries attached to the shrine, which include living *shaikh*s, mediate this *baraka* on behalf of pilgrims, but also operate as mediators between members of the surrounding community and local government authorities. In so doing, the social services provided by the shrines and their functionaries also help to fill a need for the poor, since government and non-government relief agencies are in many cases unable to comprehensively provide for the basic necessities—food, shelter, etc.—that the most depressed elements of the population may lack. Since the establishment of institutions of Sufism in the Subcontinent, Sufi *pir*s and *shaikh*s have drawn the faithful to them through their use of vernacular languages and their widespread use of indigenous cultural, literary, and religious traditions, idioms, and tropes (such as the *virahini*, or maiden longing for her lover, especially noteworthy in Krishna-centered devotion).[13] Through these media, they have disseminated their teachings on the human–divine relationship, whether wittingly or unwittingly, and have deepened their own mystical experiences of the divine. In these respects, the shrine at Ajmer shares much in common with the many other Sufi shrines that dot the landscape of the Subcontinent. Yet its history, and the place that it holds today as a representative of Sufism in the Subcontinent, also distinguishes it among other shrines.

Indeed, the history of the Ajmer shrine suggests that a number of structural and historical forces have contributed to the character of its contemporary inclusivist ritual and ceremonial culture. The historical importance of Ajmer and its environs as a site sacred for Hindus, Jains, and others even before the arrival of Mu'in ud-din towards the end of the twelfth century has also been an important factor in the shrine's ability to draw a diverse pool of pilgrims. The twelfth-century ARhai-din-ki Jhonpra functioned as a Jain temple before being converted to a mosque by Sultan Qutb ud-din Aibak toward the end of that century. The epic tales *Mahabharata* and *Ramayana* also name the adjacent town of Pushkar as an important pilgrimage site, thus helping to facilitate its evolution (as well as that of Ajmer) as an important sacred venue for Hindu devotees. In medieval India, Ajmer was situated along the main trade route that linked Delhi with Gujarat, and this geographic location played an influential part in the shrine's attraction to ruling elites and those jockeying for power in the region, such as the Rajputs, Marathas, and others who patronized the shrine.[14] According to the biographical source *Siyar ul-'arifin,* the successors of Mu'in ud-din established a tradition of pilgrimage to the shrine as early as the fourteenth century, drawing Sufis from various parts of India. Jamali, a Sufi of the Suhrawardi order and author of the *Siyar ul-'arifin,* refers to an established practice of gifts being made to the shrine by Hindus and Muslims alike. Despite the existence of these early pilgrimage traditions, it was the repeated pilgrimages made and generous endowments bestowed by the Mughal emperor Akbar in the sixteenth century that significantly changed the shrine's fortunes. In part because of its historical patronage links with the court at Delhi, the shrine's servants integrated Mughal court rituals into some of the daily prayer services, investiture ceremonies, and other ritual performances. Over time, these regularly occurring events have provided an effective framework for creating an atmosphere of cooperation, tolerance, and mutual understanding among the shrine's diverse pool of pilgrims and client-patrons.[15] Notwithstanding the influence of these historical and institutional forces upon the contemporary character of devotional life the Ajmer shrine, the role of the shrine as a social, cultural, and religious institution continues to evolve, reflecting the changing needs and worldviews of its pilgrims. Yet the spirit spirit of openness, accommodation, and devotion to the saint that still prevails at the shrine—and indeed, has become even more pronounced over time—has attracted considerable criticism of contemporary shrine-based practices from many of their detractors.

CONTEMPORARY SHRINE-BASED SUFI PRAXIS AS DUBIOUS "OTHER"

While the act of praying to, or in the name of, Mu'in ud-din[16] suggests that there can be, for Muslims and non-Muslims alike, a "privileged form of piety . . . associated with saint veneration,"[17] popular devotion to Sufi saints has often been characterized as "dubious," "un-Islamic,"[18] "syncretic," or "Hindu-influenced." These kinds of ascriptions are especially striking in the Orientalist literature that emerged from the British Raj beginning in the early nineteenth century, when land surveys revealed the pervasiveness of belief in pilgrimage to Muslim saints' shrines in the Subcontinent. Far from being mere descriptions of commonly observed cultural and religious practices, Orientalist narratives overwhelmingly served the purpose of colonial dominance by discursively producing the "subject(s)" of observation. In most, though not all, Orientalist narratives, contemporary Sufism comprised ignorant, low-class pilgrims, women (seen as generally more prone than men to "superstitious" beliefs), and charlatans who claimed to mediate the power of the saint. These narratives worked both to erase the heterogeneity of the "subject(s)" and to justify the colonial enterprise of exercising pervasive control over the bodies, hearts, and minds of the colonized.[19] As the anthropologist Katherine Ewing has observed, Orientalist scholars also effectively bifurcated contemporary Sufis from Islam, seeing in the former the degeneration of a "pure" religion.[20] This binary view dominated studies of contemporary Sufism in South Asia until the work of Annemarie Schimmel, Richard Eaton, Carl Ernst, Marc Gaborieau, Bruce Lawrence, and others in the late 1970s and 1980s effectively challenged it.

Criticisms also appeared within the ranks of Sufis themselves, particularly those belonging to the historically "mainstream" orders, from the beginning of Sufism's institutional history in the Subcontinent. For their part, Sufis distinguished between actions not merely on the basis of whether they were forbidden or permitted in Islam, but in consideration of the disposition, intention, and station of the adept. This is particularly true of those Sufis who lived prior to the nineteenth century. Writing from Lahore (in today's Pakistan) during the latter part of the eleventh century, Shaikh 'Ali Hujwiri said of *sama,* or listening to music:

> You must know that each Sufi has a particular grade in audition and that the feelings which he gains therefrom are proportionate to his grade. Thus, whatever is heard by penitents augments their contrition and remorse; whatever is heard by longing lovers increases their longing for vision; whatever is heard by those who have certain faith confirms their certainty; whatever is heard by novices verifies their elucidation (of matters which perplex them); whatever is heard by lovers impels them to cut off all worldly connexions; and whatever is heard by the spiritually poor forms a foundation for hopelessness. Audition is like the sun, which shines on all things but affects them differently according to their degree: it burns or illumines or dissolves or nurtures.[21]

While such observations are commonly found in works of literature composed by Sufis and their disciples, the dissemination of views about the permissibility or forbidden nature of Sufi practices substantially increased from the late nineteenth century, with the development of innovations in communication, transportation, and print, and the increased accessibility of these technologies to a large segment of the population. These kinds of innovations facilitated the publication of debates over the constitution, conception, and reformulation of Islam, Sufism, and the South Asian Muslim community at large in ways that had not been previously possible. Some of the demotic, reform-minded Sufi texts that appeared from the late nineteenth century appropriated the pejorative language of Orientalist and reformist scholarship, while many others (particularly texts composed by Barelwis and members of the Chishti, Qadiri, and Suhrawardi orders) sought to defend shrine-based Sufism against charges of being "un-Islamic." One method of so doing was to delineate acceptable methods of some of the less controversial practices observed at Sufi shrines (such as reading the *fatiha* prayers in the name of the saints) by providing "proof" (*dalil*) from the Qur'an, Hadis, or works of Islamic jurisprudence.

Although reforming the popular devotional practices of Indian Muslims occupied the minds of Sufis and non-Sufis alike,[22] the Deobandi and Barelwi movements, both with close ties to the institutions of Sufism, rose to prominence within the landscape of reform. Generally, both movements are characterized as seeking to recast the role of the Sufi *shaikh* as an exemplar of the kind of Islam practiced by the Prophet Muhammad (with emphasis on the *fard* (religious obligations) and the Prophet's practice, or *sunna* as "normative"). This can also be said of the majority of reform-minded movements of the period, which ultimately succeeded in reorienting Muslims toward the scriptural sources of Islam, as historian Barbara Metcalf has observed.[23] However, Deobandis are commonly described as being opposed to the devotional practices associated with rural, shrine-based Sufism, while the Barelwis are understood to support these practices. This perception persists today, and one need only examine the popular literature being sold at Sufi shrines to see how pervasive these associations have become. As the Barelwi author of *Jannati Zewar* (a work structurally modeled on the hugely popular Deobandi manual *Bihishti Zewar*) wrote:

> There are Wahhabi and Deobandi sects which have bled the Islamic community in the name of reform. These people have committed such wrongs as declaring all customs (in terms of their lawfulness and unlawfulness) forbidden (*haram*) and innovations (*bid'at*); moreover, they have [sought to] establish [these things as being] infidelity (*kufr*) and polytheism (*shirk*). . . . They have [also] declared other quite lawful things like placing a cloth over the Qur'an, offering the *fatihah* prayer in the name of the deceased (*buzurg*), and the commemorations held on the third and fortieth day after death, as innovation and forbidden [practices]. They have written that the assemblies held on the Prophet's birthday (*milad sharif*) are forbidden [practices] and innovations and are, moreover, worse than [the celebration of] Krishna's birthday. . . . They have written that the death-day anniversary celebrations (*'urs*) for the saints (*buzurgan-i din*) are unlawful and forbidden; that during Muharram, the recollections (*zikr*) of martyrdom and the distribution of sherbet (as a pious act) are forbidden.[24]

However, consensus was rare, even within the early generations of these two movements, about what constituted "correct" practice, let alone which practices could be interpreted as truly Islamic, sanctioned by the sources of the tradition, and which should be condemned as unlawful "innovation" (*bid'a*).[25]

PRAYER AND THE VENERATION OF SAINTS: ACTS OF PIETY, NARRATIVES OF FAITH AS SYMBOLIC CAPITAL

For Muslims, prayer serves as a marker of group boundedness, or belonging to a global faith collective (*umma*). The physical act of prayer at five prescribed times of each day is a symbolic statement of unity: the world over, Muslims perform the same series of mental, physical, and discursive acts as part of the daily *salat* (*namaz* in Urdu). Many Muslims also perform supererogatory prayers (*nafl namaz*, *du'a*) above and beyond the five, and the classical texts of Sufism are replete with examples of extended, extraordinary acts of prayer performed by believers. In these classical texts, prayer is understood to symbolize the unity of Muslims, but it also carries much more symbolic capital as a measure of the believer's journey towards (knowledge of) the Divine. For Sufis and their followers, each act of prayer can produce a physical consequence (as in the case of prayers performed to produce a tangible result, such as rain after a long drought, or the avoidance of harm). Prayer has psychological and metaphysical effects that bring about changes within the individual believer and that can potentially affect whole groups (as in the case of collectively performed prayers, particularly when in the presence of a spiritual master). It encompasses outward and inward aspects that guide the believer to a more comprehensive and elevated understanding of his or her own self (*nafs*), brings the believer nearer to God, and at the final stages of spiritual development, helps the believer experience Divine Unity. When performed with purity of intention and mindfulness, it produces humility, sincerity, obedience to God's will, detachment from the material world and its vagaries, purity of the heart, and elevated states (*ahwal*).[26] These effects are experienced as a matter of faith in the Divine rather than as a mark of belonging to the Muslim *umma*.

While the Qur'anic prescriptions for prayer address both daily, obligatory (*fard*) acts (*salat/namaz*) that include formulaic recitations and gestures, and supererogatory acts (*nafl namaz, du'a*) that comprise personal, informal prayers, a much broader repertoire of ritual and contemplative acts comprising prayer have developed within Sufi circles.[27] In Sufism, prayer comprises both the obligatory acts; other formulaic prayers (e.g., *istikhara*); more personalized acts of addressing or "conversing" with God, or with one of God's "mediators" (e.g., a deceased spiritual guide [*shaykh* or *pir*], or other divinely gifted being); and a range of other acts (ritual and otherwise) designed to appeal to the munificence of God or one of his mediators. These include the performance of Qawwali (particularly when such a performance is dedicated to the Prophet Muhammad or to one or more Sufi guides); the repetition of a name or God, or any other kind of prayer formula (*zikr*) whose repetition is directed by a *shaikh* or one of his representatives; the recitation of the *fatiha*;[28] *muraqqaba*, or meditation on the *shaikh* as a spiritual discipline; the offering of cloth coverings (*chadar*) to the saint, most often performed in procession; and the act of sanctifying water and/or food in the name of the saints (which often include an extended *fatiha*). It can also include the daily acts of service to the saint and shrine when performed with mindfulness by the *khadims*[29] at the shrine of Mu'in ud-din Chishti.[30] Closely connected to these acts of prayer, as deeds that work externally to produce the proper ritual atmosphere, and internally to cultivate the dispositions necessary to experience the *baraka* of the saint and shrine, are narratives of faith (about the shrine, the saint, and the pilgrims who come to pay their respects to both). These narratives also testify to the ability of the shrine's servants to accommodate the worldviews and spiritual proclivities of pilgrims. Such questions of praxis—and, more pointedly, the connections between praxis, Islamic Shari'a, and the identities (read: spiritual and familial genealogy) of the shrine's servants—have become a focal point for debates about the nature of shrine culture as "Islamic" or something other.

The heterogeneity of opinions about such matters suggests that the different ways of understanding (and facilitating) prayer rituals and other matters of shrine-based praxis are strongly informed by, but not coextensive with, Islamic (i.e., Qur'anic and Prophetic *sunna*) and Sufi explications of the self. For instance, belonging to a community of faith defined by a common belief in, and devotion to, Mu'in ud-din Chishti and his representatives is described by the *khadim*s as a fulfillment of Shari'a (in the broader sense, rather than in strictly legalistic terms). While the existence of numerous classical Islamic theological treatments of *shari'a* as a code of moral and ethical guidance that is not unique to Islam (thus, one reads of the *shari'a* of the Jews and the *shari'a* of the Christians) may well be within the awareness of the *khadim*s, they do not, collectively, draw on such distinctions. Rather, their emphasis is increasingly on values that may be articulated within an Islamic discursive framework of faith in God and the necessity of submission to his will, but that also speak to more "universal" humanitarian values: compassion, patience, charity, and selflessness.[31] More pointedly, ritual actions within the shrine setting are guided by the objective of producing, through bodily (physical, mental, and discursive) practices, a "purified" self: one that is cleansed of sins, in whose heart God dwells, that has overcome the limitations of the lower soul (*nafs*), that desires constant communion with God and his saints, and that serves others before himself (or herself) and strives to bring peace and understanding to the afflicted souls of the world, irrespective of caste, creed, or religion.[32] These constitute some of the major spiritual benefits of prayer as articulated by the servants of the Mu'in ud-din shrine.

The forms that discursive and bodily praxis (i.e., the different forms of prayer) assume are further mediated by the charismatic authority of the saint and the moral and ethical values he is believed to represent. According to the majority of *khadim*s I interviewed at the shrine, these values are timeless, and speak equally to the concerns of twelfth- and thirteenth-century spiritual seekers in Mu'in ud-din's time as they do to seekers today. An emphasis on the relevance of Mu'in ud-din's message today is also apparent in ritual performances of Qawwali music, and in particular in those performances that mention the accomplishments of the *shaikh*. Overwhelmingly, he is memorialized in song as a saint who brought mercy, faith, moral guidance, and hope to the hearts of those in need. The night of September 17, 2002, on the occasion of the *mahfil-i rindan* (Assembly of Love Songs), a musical assembly hosted by the Gudri Shah Chishti order in their *khanaqah,* or lodge (adjacent to the Mu'in ud-din shrine), female Qawwali singers praised Ajmer and its saint thus:

> Don't look for the pain of love in the places where rich people search;
> Because you'll find the cry of the [spiritually] impoverished [only] in the alleyways of Ajmer . . .
>
> The sea of mercy and kindness resides [here in Ajmer] day and night . . . Look after [us] Khwaja Mu'in ud-din Ajmeri . . .

Such characterization of the saint is echoed within the "official" websites that have been launched by several of the *khadim*s of the shrine, which not only emphasize his concern for the welfare of all living beings, but his desire to bring believers together in a shared community of faith:

> Gharib Nawaz loved humanity in general and the Indians in particular. Indeed he had a mission to bring a social and spiritual revolution.
>
> He ruled over [*sic*] hearts. The concepts of national integration, composite culture (Ganga-Jamni Tehzeeb) originated from his life style and teachings and thereafter were spread by his representative disciples.
>
> Perhaps in no other country were the effects of this social and cultural revolution so marked and so far-reaching as in India. Sufism (Islamic mysticism) reached India when it had entered the last and the most important phase of its history, the organization of Sufistic structure of Islam having various denominations, especially Chishtiya, Qadriya, Naqshbandia, and Suharwardia. Among these denominations the Chishtiya order has been supremely successful on all levels of pluralistic society of India based on cultural, religious, and social differences.[33]

This aspect of Mu'in ud-din's mission is a major theme in the "tour" that each pilgrim receives on his or her first visit to the *dargah* at Ajmer. When a pilgrim enters the shrine for the first time through its main gate, the *Bihishti Darwaza*, he or she is accosted by several *khadim*s who are seeking clients. Once a *khadim* and client have been matched up, it is the job of the former to take the pilgrim on a tour of the main circuit of tombs in the shrine complex, beginning with Mu'in ud-din's and including those of several members of his family, all popularly considered saints. At each tomb, the pilgrim is asked to place his or her head at the feet of the saint (*qadam bosi*) and under the cloth covering the tomb, which is embroidered with Qur'anic verses, names, or numerals written in Arabic. This act symbolizes recognition of the charismatic authority (*baraka*) of the saint and the humbleness of the pilgrim before him or her. The pilgrim is also asked to say a prayer and give *nazrana* (pious offering to a superior) to the attendant *khadim* seated at the foot of the tomb. Although this act of gift-giving appears to function as little more than a way for *khadim*s to supplement their (increasingly prosperous) incomes, symbolically it also implies recognition of the authority of the *khadim* to mediate the power of the saint. Sometimes, the *khadim* will suggest which prayer to recite; if the pilgrim is a Muslim, the *khadim* will direct him or her to recite the *fatiha* or the *durud* prayer[34]; otherwise, the pilgrim is asked to recite a prayer from his or her own tradition (such as the Lord's Prayer for Christians), or an impromptu prayer of his or her own choosing.

Thus, while the framework of pious devotion to Khwaja Sahib follows established patterns of ritual praxis, patterns that are couched within an Islamic (or Islamicate[35]) idiom of faith (meaning they draw upon Islamic discursive traditions and ritual praxis), they are also individually tailored to accommodate pilgrims' particular worldviews. This is especially the case with repeat visits from pilgrims who have established, or seek to establish, long-term relationships with the *khadim*s at the shrine. A good and effective *khadim* is familiar with the existence, and some of the teachings of, the Christian Gospels, the *Guru Granth Sahib*, the stories of the major Hindu deities, and so on.[36] He will be able to suggest prayers from these traditions, or at least engage in a low-level discussion of some of their theological points. If the pilgrim speaks Panjabi, or some other language that is neither Hindi nor Urdu, the *khadim* may also speak to the pilgrim in this language (or at least use a few key words), if he knows it, all in an endeavor to establish connections that will be meaningful within the exchange relationship between *khadim* and pilgrim. At several of the tombs, the performance of prayers is followed by a blessing. Inside Mu'in ud-din's tomb, a *khadim* is on hand to hand out, as *tabarruk* (sacred substance imbued with *barakat*, or spiritual power), some of the fresh flowers that have been placed on the grave that day. The flowers are kept on the person, or a portion of them is eaten. The giving and ingestion of *tabarruk* is a common sight at Sufi shrines. Yet it also shares much in common with the practice of giving and eating *prasad* at a Hindu shrine or Sikh *gurdwara*. In all three cases, the material is believed to be transformed by its physical contact with the sacred site or entity, imbued with an intangible substance that not only conveys blessings, but has the potential to transform the heart, mind, and soul of the believer. These acts also work to transform monikers of collectivity into "mobile collective" identities that transcend definitions of the self, whether self-imposed or ascribed.

Such productions of subjectivity may appropriate the language of a more dominant group, philosophy, or worldview. Thus, aside from the early textual sources of Islam themselves,[37] Chishti ethics at the shrine of Mu'in ud-din are shaped by as much by the life example provided by the saint (evidenced in textual sources as well as the oral recollections of the *khadims*) as by a sense of Islam as a "religion of peace" founded upon the idea of submission to the will of a single God.[38] What this suggests is that a decision to emphasize the complementary over the conflictual aspects of saint veneration, or an appeal to the unifying mission of Mu'in ud-din Chishti over his Islamic "credentials" or miracle-working abilities, operates as a kind of "rhetorical strategy" which facilitates building relationships of sacred exchange. Among the *khadim*s and their "inner circles" of disciples, perceptions of Mu'in ud-din's life story are framed as much by his purported adherence to Islamic (viz. *Shari'atic*) norms of ethical moral behavior as by his reputed miracle-working abilities or interest in promoting exchanges across boundaries of culture, class, and religion. For these disciples, the discourse of Islam becomes much more pronounced, in part because the spiritual path to God begins in earnest with a more perfect understanding of Islam. This stance is encapsulated by a turn toward the foundational sources and models of Islamic praxis, which has become more visible within the Sufi orders today.

REFLECTIONS OF THE SELF: POWER, PRESTIGE, AND HIERARCHY IN THE SERVICE OF SANCTIFICATION

Many studies of contemporary Sufi praxis in the Subcontinent have noted the development of what Fazlur Rahman has dubbed "neo-Sufism," that is to say, a Sufism that has been influenced by traditions of reform and revival as they unfolded throughout the Muslim world in the late nineteenth and early twentieth centuries. Though such traditions have remained heterogeneous, making it difficult to classify them, or their adherents, according to any definite set of criteria, they have all generally emphasized the need for centering practice on Islamic Shari'a. Research by Katy Gardner on *pir*s in Sylhet, by Arthur Buehler on the Naqshbandi order, and by Carl Ernst and Bruce Lawrence, among others, has all noted that particularly today, generations of reformist efforts to Islamicize Muslims have resulted in a greater correlation between the foundational symbols of Islam (Qur'an, Shari'a, and the Prophet Muhammad) and the perceived legitimacy of Sufi religious authorities.

Power differentials between *khadim*s competing for clients (or recognition as legitimate claimants to the legacy of the saint and his descendants) also reflect the effect of reformist movements (and discourses) that seek to orient Muslims toward the scriptural tradition of Islam. This becomes a basis for articulating authenticity within *khadim* and Sufi circles, and it can also become a factor in the relationships between *khadims* and their non-Muslim pilgrims. This is not to suggest that the *khadims* try to convert their clients to Islam. Debates over Islamic "propriety" remain largely internal, among Muslims. Rather, it indicates the importance that Islam holds in the *khadims*' articulation of their own spiritual authority as representatives of the saint. For *khadims*, as for many pilgrims, Islam can come to represent a shared sense of the authoritative that weighs heavily upon how a *khadim* is perceived as mediator of the saint's *baraka*.

The pilgrim–guide relationship is shaped not only by hierarchical notions of expert–novice, but also by perceptions of access to particular types of authority, whether spiritual (as it pertains to divinely gifted beings) or divine (as it pertains to Allah). The *khadim*, thus, represents as much a link to these kinds of authority as protector and guide of the pilgrim or disciple. His work at the shrine serves as a catalyst for the meeting of individual pilgrim and God, through a journey in which the seeker encounters a host of pious and saintly figures. These include the Prophet Muhammad and Mu'in-ud-din Chishti, and may also include a supporting cast of other figures such as the *panj-i pak*,[39] Sufi figures connected through spiritual lineage to Mu'in ud-din (such as 'Abdul Qadir al-Jilani, whose death-day anniversary is also celebrated at the Mu'in ud-din shrine), other Chishti *shaikhs*, and that others whose mediation may be invoked on behalf of the pilgrim. As representative of Mu'in ud-din and of the spiritual lineage(s) radiate through him, the authority of the *khadim* to act as guide to others rests on several criteria.

First, the *khadim* is often sought out by pilgrims as much for his ability to demonstrate a connection with certain of the key foundational symbols associated with Islam as for his familiarity with what is often regarded as "true" (*sahih*) Sufi practice (limited here to a discussion of prayer, but what is important to note is that in all Sufi settings, prayer is tied up in notions of reciprocal love—not only the *khadim*'s love for the saint and for the Prophet Muhammad, but also of their love for him). Much of the impetus behind these kinds of associations is functional. In other words, those who guide pilgrims (facilitating the prayers of others, praying on behalf of clients, conducting the many ritual ceremonies held at the shrine) must be familiar with certain kinds of prayers (such as the *fatiha* or the *durud*). These prayers may be conceived of as Islamic insofar as they are derived from the Qur'an and insofar as they have referents in the Hadis and in the *sunna* of the Prophet, and they are Sufi insofar as they are regarded as prayers that are particularly effective and guaranteed to achieve results when performed with the help of someone who is a perfected Sufi master or is connected to one through blood or spiritual lineage, and who understands their "inner" meanings. Further, the efficacy of prayers, at least in the Sufi setting, and among the *khadims*, is closely tied up with notions of being endowed with a special mark of favor by God and the saints, that which is passed down through heredity and which is spoken of as the *bij* or *barakat* of spiritual masters before him.[40]

The nature of what might be referred to as "Sufi practice" is also informed by notions of descent, both spiritual and hereditary. Most of the *khadims* who live and work in and around the shrine claim hereditary (blood ties) and spiritual (through designation as spiritual "deputies") descent from Mu'in ud-din through his children. In Sufi belief, spiritual descent from a Sufi master conveys not only the authority to pass on the teachings of the master and the order he represents, but also something called the *bij*, or seed, which is akin to a kind of spiritual power manifest in the person of the saint. The term *barakat* is also sometimes used interchangeably with *bij*; *barakat* connotes the charismatic power that Sufi saints possess and can pass on, which in one sense is a direct line to Allah, and in another sense can be manipulated to achieve whatever material effects are desired. Those who possess the seed or the *barakat* are also popularly seen as having proximity, and thus access, to the saint and to God in a way that ordinary people do not. Descent from the Prophet through the progeny of his son-in-law 'Ali and his favorite daughter Fatima is also regarded as a privileged status. In the Sufi conception of piety, this is translated as an inherent "nobility" of character (*sharafat*) but is often conflated with the sense of *barakat* insofar as the Prophet, 'Ali, Fatima, and their sons, Hasan and Husain (the *panj-i pak)* are conceived of as powerful intercessors with God. It is through their connections, then, with both Mu'in ud-din and the family of the Prophet, that the *khadims* and *shaikhs* of the *dargah* are able to provide the link between pilgrim and saint, and ultimately Allah. This link becomes manifest not only in the performance of ritual acts like prayer, however, but also in the *khadim*'s knowledge about Mu'in ud-din, and his ability to effectively pass on the relevant aspects of this knowledge to pilgrims as each particular encounter demands.

Most of the information for Mu'in ud-din's Chishti's life that is available to us today comes from the *tazkira*, or biographical literature, and oral stories. The saint himself seems to have left behind no written works, although many believe that he wrote letters to his disciple and successor, Qutb ud-din Bakhtiyar Kaki (d. 1236).[41] The *khadim*'s job, besides taking pilgrims on a circuit of the tombs within the shrine complex, is to tell the pilgrim about Khwaja Sahib's life story. In my own initial encounters with the *khadims* at the shrine, the aspects of Mu'in ud-din's life that were most highlighted emphasized his Islamic credentials in several ways. First, the saint was presented to me as someone who had brought Islam to a land where it did not exist. This was, according to the *khadims* I interviewed, because his spiritual master, 'Usman Haruni, had instructed him to do so. Second, much was made of Khwaja Sahib's travels, early in his spiritual journeys and prior to his arrival in Ajmer; these travels were, as in many of the hagiographies of the Sufi saints, through some of the major centers of Islamic scholarship at the time. Mu'in ud-din is said to have traveled to Samarqand and Bukhara, Baghdad, and then to Harun (in present-day Afghanistan), where he met his master. In both the hagiographical sources for the *shaikh*'s life and the oral retellings of-the *khadims*, Mu'in ud-din traveled to these places in order to study Hadis or traditions, jurisprudence, law, philosophy, logic, and exegesis of the Qur'an. Although there are many discrepancies about the exact trajectory of his early travels, in effect, those hagiographic accounts that locate Mu'in ud-din in the centers of Islamic learning, before his first meeting with the man who would become his spiritual guide, emphasize his grounding in these "external" Islamic sciences. The British scholar Simon Digby points out that learning in the Islamic sciences (as well as a reputation for adherence to the Shari'a, Islamic law) often functions, at the level of popular conceptions, as an indication that a Sufi *shaikh* was the recipient of Divine grace. This concept is in part traceable to the belief, particularly in Sufism, that Divine Truths are revealed in the Law; thus one who has a command of this can more readily aspire to the highest goal of Sufism: union with the Divine.[42] The tone of narratives Mu'in ud-din's practice of Islam suggest a kind of ambivalence about these two aspects of his identity: exemplar of Islam, and unifier of different groups in the name of forging a common humanity. While the grace of the saint, his mercy and respect for humanity "for all irrespective of caste, race, creed, faith, or colour," is emphasized in numerous places on these websites, and religions are presented in comparative perspective, Islam is ultimately characterized as the superlative faith. A *khadim*'s website that is now defunct once claimed that:

> The true purpose of religion is that human beings should follow the right path according to divine teachings. But before asking people to follow these teachings, it is first necessary to explain the teachings and whose they are; secondly, about the one who is preaching them, and finally, the great religious benefit that will be derived by following them. These are the fundamentals on which religions are formed. To have a comparative study of Islam in the light of the teachings found in other sacred books, is to know what a comprehensive world religion Islam is, pointing out also how the author of such a religion was decidedly the last great Prophet, there being consequently no further necessity at all for another Prophet to rise. Quran is the final revealed Book of Allah and Mohammad is the last Prophet.[43]

Another *khadim*'s website, still functioning, describes Islam in similar terms, but with greater emphasis on Islam's role as unifier:

> Allah has sent Hazrat Muhammad (S.A.W.) (peace be upon him), the last prophet of Islam, as Rahmatul-lil-Alamin (Mercy for the entire creation) and not for any specific community."

Dr. Bhagwan Das rightly points out that the word Islam is indeed, by itself, the very essence of religion. Derived from Salam (peace, shanti) it means peaceful acceptance of God. Extolling the unity of man since the beginning of creation, the Quran explains "Mankind" were one community, then they differed among themselves, so Allah sent prophets to announce good tidings and warn them (2: 213). Prophet Muhammad (S.A.W.) does not claim to be the founder of Islam, but he holds that all prophets preached and practised the truth and they prophesed only one religion for which the Arabic word is Islam.

Prophet Muhammad (S.A.W.) preached the unity of God, which culminates into the unity of man exploding all the myths of caste, creed, colour, race, rank and region. The principle of human equality propounded by prophet Muhammad (S.A.W.) as revealed by the Holy Quran naturally follows from the principle of the unity of human origin revolutionized social relations. It contrasted sharply with the laws governing the class-ridden and caste-stricken societies of the Roman, Byzantine, Iranian and, later on, of the Indian empires.[44]

The tone of many of the *khadims*' websites demonstrates a similar ambivalence: While emphasizing the universally benevolent qualities of Mu'in ud-din's good will to others; service to humanity at large, especially the helpless, weak, and infirm; and the cultivation of love for God, the importance of certain foundational symbols of Islam are emphasized. For instance, in the first website just cited, the importance of performing the daily obligatory *namaz* prayers appears among the reputed sacred sayings of the saint (here the statement seems to be specifically directed at Muslims, as the next line stresses the importance of orthopraxy). In the section entitled "Life of a Sufi," the importance of conformity to "Islamic theology and traditions" is juxtaposed with a more general description of the qualities of detachment, a desire to realize Divine Truths, and the rigorous spiritual training that is the path of holy men and women everywhere. In the second website quoted previously, Mu'in ud-din's close connection with the Prophet Muhammad is emphasized.[45] And yet, if there is one simple and universal message to be gleaned from all of the narratives of the saint presented by *khadims*, and reflected in their websites, it is that the best approach to him is through love and sincerity of purpose. Indeed, the story of Mu'in ud-din's life, the centuries-long tradition of pilgrimage to his burial site by pilgrims from all walks of life, the history of endowments to the shrine by a diverse group a patrons, the availability of one of the *dargah's* administrative posts to non-Muslims, and the everyday ritual life there all suggest a long history of sharing among the different communities in the Subcontinent. In the hearts of pilgrims as well as the opinions of even those inclined to skepticism when it comes to the value of venerating saints, the Ajmer shrine is a place in which one may transcend essentialized monikers of religious identity, even if only temporarily.

NARRATIVES, PRAXIS, AND THE CREATION OF SUBJECTIVITIES

Narratives of collectivity, as played out in the field of ritual activity at the shrine of the Sufi saint Mu'in ud-din Chishti, emerge as the staging grounds for the articulation of identity. While this methodological stance apparently consigns the subject to the role of actor engaged in a process of production and performance, it also suggests one of the mechanisms by which subjects are assigned positions that place them within a community of faith defined not by belonging to a particular religion, class, caste, or ethnic group, but by participation in a shared community of faith centered on the person—and deeds—of a thirteenth-century Chishti saint. In the case of the *khadims* at the Ajmer shrine, the overarching framework of an implied "normative" Islam is closely connected by them with the idea of the "true" form of Sufism they represent, one based on the idea of the fundamental unity of humankind. This message of unity is undergirded by an outward manifestation of conformity to *Shari'a* law, which the *khadims* also demonstrate ritually, and which is closely connected to their ability to act as representatives of the saint, as men who are capable of wielding his *baraka* for the benefit of pilgrims (and for the purpose of actualizing the message of unity through selfless service to other sincere seekers and supplicants).

For some, the appeal of the Sufi is as something "other," even antithetical to an Islam that is increasingly identified with exclusivity, intolerance, and rigidity. Though the *khadims* themselves may at times buy into a vision of Islam that suggests rather more exclusivist markers of faith, in the ritual space they are subordinate to values that are more broadly and universally identifiable as humanitarian. These values—love for all humankind; the sublimation of personal, individual identity to the will of the Divine; respect for all the saints and signs of God, regardless of their outer manifestations; and an ability to tune into the needs and desires of others, among others—stand as identifiable indicators of "the Sufi spirit" for *khadims* and pilgrims alike. They are Islamic values in their connection with key ideas found in the Qur'an, in the traditions of the Prophet Muhammad (*sunna*), and in the stories of the saints and pious ones of Islam, and inasmuch as they exemplify "exterior" ritual practices and articles of faith in Islam. For pilgrims, though, a disassociation of Sufi *khadims* from mainstream Islam can serve the purpose exemplified by the mission of the saint: Sufis may indeed be Muslims, but they are Muslims of a different sort, because they respect and value the contributions of non-Muslims, and seek the betterment of all humankind. Moreover, they make a conscious effort to incorporate and accommodate elements of the non-Islamic: this is nowhere more apparent than in ritual performances. Thus, Islam can become, in this line of thinking, the "Other" in the sense of an Islamic framework modified by its local environment, and something that, at least for some believers, stands outside the pale of mainstream Islam as it is often conceived. For *khadims* themselves, however, this position remains problematic, and they are, at the level of everyday practice, constantly engaged in the task of modifying both what it means to be Islamic and what it means to be Sufi; for one, they run the risk of being accused of "un-Islamic" behavior, and in consequently Sufism itself becomes tainted as such.

I have tried to look at the interstices of discourse and practice at the Mu'in ud-din Chishti shrine as evidence of a fluidity that is both germane and indispensable to the notion of language as unlimited in its presupposition of given, continuous, temporal, or atemporal unities (as in the laws of the *Shari'a* or the teachings of the Qur'an). As a statement or set of statements seeking to conceptualize and constitute its object, discourse must be considered in light of the speaking subject's intention, the outside constraints (or frameworks of knowledge) that operate upon him or her in particular circumstances, and the relationship of discourse to the subject's self-perception or awareness of others' perceptions of the subject. While discourse as a prescriptive mode often seems to suggest a normative system of values, beliefs, and practices, the precariousness of such a system comes to light in the field of practice, wherein what constitutes the normative itself may shift or be "explained away." Yet the idea of Islam as a critical, normative framework of reference for self-identification, and action, a framework that exercises persuasive force on the belief of many Muslims that it is an unequivocal category with an essential reality, should not be dismissed.[46] The *khadims* are unable to exercise absolute autonomy in their articulations of the sacred, bound as they are by the "prior texts" of Islam and Sufism that informs their worldviews, and the ritual actions they mediate exert a precarious effect upon the self-identification of believer. These ritual performances, as with other types of performances, can produce ambiguities in identity, which I have investigated in light some of the processes by which they are produced.

NOTES

1. The other is the *dargah* of Hazrat Nizam ud-din Auliya' in Delhi. Nizam ud-din was fourth in the line of succession of Chishti *shaikhs* that began with Mu'in ud-din Chishti's arrival in India at the end of the twelfth century.
2. National integration in India is defined by Paul Brass as an endeavor beginning with the nation or state and seeking to develop loyalties to it that transcend attachments to primary groups (e.g., religious, caste, class). Paul Brass, *Language, Religion and Politics in North India* (London: Cambridge University Press, 1974), 4.
3. See, for instance, "India—Faith Is All; One's Religion Does Not Count Here," *The Hindu*, 17 April, 1999; "India—Ajmer 'urs begins on a grand

note," *The Hindu*, 2 April, 2000; "India—Pilgrim Country," *Business Line*, January 31, 2000.

4. There are two commonly understood definitions of Shari'a. One refers to the body of legal pronouncements that govern religious praxis and social relations (which is, more precisely, *fiqh*), while the other refers to what anthropologist Brinkley Messick has called "total discourse" representing the "core of Islamic knowledge" for Muslims of the "social mainstream." See Brinkley Messick, *The Calligraphic State* (Berkeley: University of California Press, 1993), 3.
5. The problems with this kind of center-periphery model—as applied to theories of conflict and "syncretism"—are outlined in an article by Tony K. Stewart, "In Search of Equivalence: Conceiving Muslim-Hindu Encounter through Translation Theory," *History of Religions* 40, no. 3 (2001): 260–287.
6. The term "Wahhabi" is difficult to pin down, and often does not refer to individuals or groups who have ideological or logistical ties with the eighteenth-century reform movement in Saudi Arabia. While in the Subcontinent the term has historically been used to refer to the Tariqa-i Muhammadiyya movement launched by Sayyid Ahmed Bareilly in the early part of the nineteenth century, it is also frequently lobbed at those who are considered to be literalist, narrow interpreters of the faith, and openly hostile to the institutions of Sufism.
7. Joyce Burkhalter Flueckiger, *In Amma's Healing Room: Gender and Vernacular Islam in South India* (Boomington; Indianapolis; Indiana University Press, 2006).
8. See Peter Gottschalk, *Beyond Hindu and Muslim: Multiple Identity in Narratives from Village India* (New York: Oxford University Press, 2000), 22.
9. For more on this character of Sufi shrines, see Pnina Werbner and Helene Basu, *Embodying Charisma: Modernity, Locality, and the Performance of Emotion in Sufi Cults* (London: Routledge, 1998), 3–5. The authors also point to the Sufi shrine's role in "organizing the sacred" for pilgrims.
10. In the sense I use it here, "not Islamic" implies difference from, but not necessarily opposition to, normative Islamic belief and practice as it was articulated in the narratives of my interviewees.
11. Caroline Humphrey and James Laidlaw, *The Archetypal Actions of Ritual* (New York: Oxford University Press, 1994).
12. With this stance, my views are much more in line with those of Klaus-Peter Köpping, Bernhard Leistle, and Michael Rudolph. See the introduction to their volume, *Ritual and Identity: Performative Practices as Effective Transformations of Social Reality* (Berlin: LIT-Verlag, 2006).
13. This has been the case with many, but certainly not all, Sufis. Indeed, some have openly demonstrated hostility to Hindus, or to what they saw as the "Hinduization" of Sufism or Islam. These kinds of attitudes are discernible among some of the "warrior" Sufis described by Richard Eaton in *Sufis of Bijapur 1300–1700* (Delhi: Munshiram Manoharlal, 1978) and in the writing of Shaikh Ahmad Sirhindi, whose Sufi leanings have been largely ignored by scholars in Europe and America until fairly recently.
14. Bruce B. Lawrence, "Islam in India: the Function of Sufism in the Islamization of Rajasthan, Gujarat, and Kashmir," *Contributions to Asian Studies* 17 (1982): 36–37.
15. Syed Liyaqat Hussain Moini, "Rituals and Customary Practices at the Dargah of Ajmer," in *Muslim Shrines in India: Their Character, History, and Significance,* ed. Christian W. Troll (Delhi: Oxford University Press, 1989): 61–63.
16. The distinction between these two types of activity is often lost on the critics of Sufi shrine cults. The differences are both semantic and theological. While praying *to* connotes an acknowledgment of primary authority and power (which, from an Islamic theological standpoint, is reserved solely for Allah),

praying *in the name of* (or its concomitant sense, through the medium of) allows the practitioner to simultaneously acknowledge the primacy of the omnipotent power of Allah and the efficacy of the charismatic power of the saint (*barakat*). The latter is often accomplished through a series of ritual acts, such as prefacing prayers with Qur'anic verses, or signs, such as the use of phrases like "X ke zariye mein."

17. Farina Mir, "Alternative Imaginings: Shared Piety in Panjabi Popular Narrative, c.1850–1900" (paper presented at the annual meeting of the Association for Asian Studies, Washington, DC, 2002).
18. In the sense I use it here, the "un-Islamic" implies willful opposition to the guidelines applicable to all Muslim believers.
19. The feminist scholar Chandra Mohanty outlines the contemporary parameters of this discursively constituted "colonization" in ways that resonate far beyond her immediate critique of feminist scholarship. See her chapter, "Under Western Eyes: Feminist Scholarship and Colonial Discourses," in *Feminism Without Borders: Decolonizing Theory, Practicing Solidarity* (Durham, NC: Duke University Press, 2003).
20. As Ewing points out, these kinds of discourses are not unique to Orientalist scholarship, and in fact may be found in today's Pakistan, where debates about the national character of the country often pivot on the question of the contemporary roles played by *pir*s and Sufis. Katherine Pratt Ewing, *Arguing Sainthood: Modernity, Psychoanalysis and Islam* (Durham and London: Duke University Press, 1997).
21. Shaikh 'Ali Hujwiri, *Kashf al-mahjub,* translated by Reynold A. Nicholson as *Revelation of the Mystery* (Accord, NY: Pir Publications, 1999), 406–407.
22. For further discussion of reform movements in Islam, and in particular within the Sufi orders, in the nineteenth and twentieth centuries, see Fazlur Rahman, *Revival and Reform in Islam: A Study of Islamic Fundamentalism* (London: Oneworld: 1999); Elizabeth Sirriyeh, *Sufis and Anti-Sufis: The Defense, Rethinking, and Rejection of Sufism in the Modern World* (New York: Routledge, 1999); and Usha Sanyal, *Devotional Islam and Politics in British India* (Delhi: Oxford University Press, 1996).
23. Barbara Metcalf, "Islam and Custom in Nineteenth-Century India: The Reformist Standard of Maulana Thanawi's *Bihishti Zewar,*" *Contributions to Asian Studies* 17 (1982): 64.
24. Allama 'Abd ul-Mustafa A'zimi, *Jannati Zewar* (Lahore: Ziya ul-Qur'an Publications, 1979), 112–113.
25. See Qeyamuddin Ahmad, *The Wahhabi Movement in Islam* (Delhi: Manohar, 1994).
26. Some of the more detailed Sufi expositions on the effects of prayer are found in al-Hujwiri's *Kashf al-Mahjub* (see Chapter 19 of R. A. Nicholson's translation) and Abu Hamid al-Ghazali's *Ihya 'Ulum ad din* (Revival of the Religious Sciences), esp. Book IV: *Mysteries of Worship.* There are several extant translations of parts of the *Ihya* available, among them Edwin Elliot Calverley's translation of Book IV, published as *The Mysteries of Worship in Islam* (New Delhi: Kitab Bhavan, 1992).
27. A fairly comprehensive taxonomy of prayers in Islam, not restricted to the Sufi milieu, can be found in Constance E. Padwick's *Muslim Devotions: A Study of Prayer-Manuals in Common Use* (Oxford: Oneworld, 1993).
28. Within the Sufi context, several types of *fatiha*s exist, such as the *fatiha* that is the first chapter (*sura*) of the Qur'an, and *fatiha* prayers recited in the name of, for the blessing (by God) of, or to commemorate a saint, holy person, the Prophets, or some other person who has died, which involve the recitation of the first chapter and several other recitations. The *fatiha* prayer as it is

recited over food and ritual implements contains several elements which may vary. One example of a *fatiha* recitation follows: (a) the *durud*, a prayer calling blessings upon the Prophet Muhammad and his family, is recited three times, (b) the first verse of the Qur'an, the *sura-i fatiha*, is recited three times, (c) verse one hundred and twelve of the Qur'an, the *sura-i akhlas*, is recited twelve times, and (d) the *durud* prayer is again recited three times.

29. The *khadim*s and pilgrims to the shrine often use the terms *khadim*s (when speaking English) or *khadim log* when referring to the servants of the shrine. Rarely, I also heard the term *khuddam*, the Arabic plural for *khadim*. Some of the *khadim*s are also Sufi *pir*s or *shaikh*s, terms which are often used synonymously in the vernacular, and which, generally speaking, connote "spiritual guide." For the sake of consistency, I will use the terms *khadim*s to refer to the servants of the shrine.
30. Some scholars, such as Saba Mahmood, have indexed a range of these types of acts as deeds intended to produce certain dispositions within the believer that help him or her to cultivate piety. Thus, Mahmood maintains something of a separation between prayer, other pious acts, and ordinary deeds intended to produce dispositions in believers that are conducive to the correct and sincere performance of the obligatory prayers. See her book, *Politics of Piety: The Islamic Revival and the Feminist Subject* (Princeton, NJ: Princeton University Press, 2005). By contrast, there are a number of discourses within Sufi circles that characterize such acts and deeds as themselves comprising forms of prayer.
31 This argument shares much in common with a similar one made by Carl W. Ernst and Bruce B. Lawrence, which connects a cognitive shift among Sufi spiritual authorities toward a more "broad-based spiritual aesthetic that is neither specifically Sufi nor generically Muslim" with the increasing use of modernizing technologies (print, Internet, "Bollywood" Qawwali music, etc.). See their book, *Sufi Martyrs of Love: The Chishti Order in South Asia and Beyond* (New York: Palgrave MacMillan, 2002), 138.
32. This methodological approach is informed by the work of Saba Mahmood on the "piety movement" she observed among women in Cairo today. Mahmood's approach underscores the importance of articulating the "architecture of the self" through physical praxis; in other words, her work seeks to understand how bodily practices operate to produce the (morally disciplined) self. See Mahmood, *Politics of Piety*, 118–126. Her approach, and perhaps more so my own, with its emphasis on *strategic* acts, also resonates with a theory developed by Catherine Bell, who argues that ritual works to infuse the body with the values of the ritual, which themselves index relations of dominance. As applied to the ritual activities I observed at the shrine of Mu'in ud-din Chishti, one might say that praxis as mediated by the *khadim*s operates in such a way as to infuse believers with the moral and spiritual values epitomized by Mu'in ud-din's life and (spiritual) work, or articulations of these as offered by the *khadim*s. See Catherine Bell, *Ritual Theory, Ritual Practice* (New York; Oxford: Oxford University Press, 1992).
33. See Moallim Syed Abdul Wasey Chishty, "Haj and Prophet's Command," at http://khwajagharibnawaz.com/khwajagharibnawaz.htm (accessed April 11, 2008).
34. Cf. footnote 28.
35. The historian Marshall Hodgson's explanation of "Islamicate" culture seeks to explain the inclusion of non-Muslims, and/or that which cannot be exclusively traced to the sources of Islam.
36. In fact, the *khadim*s have sought to emphasize the essential unity of these traditions, in part by recalling the divine truths embodied in the deeds and words of pivotal figures in these different religions. As one *khadim*'s website

notes: "Again and again through all successive ages, the apostles of God have successfully fought and defeated the forces of evil. Prophet David succeeded in overthrowing Goliath. Prophet Abraham survived the torture of a huge fire made by Namrood to destroy him but it turned into a garden of fragrant flowers and Namrood himself was destroyed by a gnat. Shree Ramchandra, the exiled but dutiful son of Raja Dashratha secured a mighty victory over Ravana the demon king of Ceylon, in righteous cause. In spite of all torture, the Holy Christ and his religion did survive even after his crucifixion and the Holy Prophet gave noble lessons of Christianity to the world. Prophet Mohammed was tormented by Abu Jehal and Abu Lehab with superior forces but he succeeded triumphantly in the end with his grand religious mission. The whole history of the world is replete with such illuminating and noble examples of the success of 'Truth' against evil and repeats itself again and again." Haji Syed Mohammed Sayeed Chishty, "Truth Always Prevails," http://www.dargahajmer.com/g_arrival.htm (accessed April 11, 2008).

37. In the case of the *Hadis* literature, consensus on what constitutes Prophetic tradition and what constitutes the "un-Islamic" is rare, as this body of literature is heterogeneous in itself. Even within the confines of those collections considered "authentic" (*sahih*), there is disagreement on the idea of custom and innovation in terms of both definition and permissibility in light of the *Shari'a.*
38. This definition of "true Islam" is found on several of the *khadims*' websites.
39. The *panj-i pak* are the Prophet Muhammad, his cousin and son-in-law 'Ali, his daughter Fatima, and their sons, Hasan, and Husain. In Shi'ah Islam and Sufi practice alike they are considered powerful intercessors with God.
40. As Sayyids, a social class that indicates blood descent from the Prophet Muhammad through his grandchildren Hasan and Hussain, some *khadims* are also believed to possess *sharafat*, or inherent quality of noble character, although this quality is no longer automatically associated with Sayyid status.
41. Excerpts from two of these letters are reprinted in the fourth appendix of Zahurul Hassan Sharib, *The Culture of the Sufis* (Southampton, UK: Sharib Press, 1999), 187–193. While a critical examination of these collected letters has yet to be produced, it is noteworthy that such an eminent and meticulous scholar and Sufi *shaikh* as the thirteenth-century Firdausi, Sharaf ud-din Maneri of Bihar, accepted them as real.
42. See Simon Digby, "The Sufi Shaikh as a Source of Authority in Mediaeval India," in *Islam et Société en Asie du Sud* [Islam and Society in South Asia], ed. Marc Gaborieau (Paris: Colléctions Purusartha, 1986), 60–61. Sharaf ud-din Maneri also considered adherence to and understanding of the Law as a prerequisite for becoming a truly superior Sufi master, and he dealt with this idea in many of his written works.
43. http://www.chistyshrineajmercom/kh_religion. html. (accessed January 10, 2002).
44. Moullim Syed Abdul Wasey Chishty, "Islam: Introduction" http://khwajagharibnawaz.com/islam.htm (accessed March 2, 2008).
45. In this narrative, it is the Prophet who is cast as the one who commanded the saint to travel to India to show people the "path of Truth," instead of 'Usman Haruni, as is the case in most hagiographic narratives. See Haji Syed Mohammed Sayeed Chishty, "Khwaja Gharib Nawaz," http://khwajagharibnawaz.com/khwajagharibnawaz.htm (accessed April 11, 2008).
46. See, for example, Mohammad Arkoun, *Rethinking Islam: Common Questions, Uncommon Answers* (Boulder, CO: Westview Press, 1994); Bassam Tibi, *Islam and the Cultural Accommodation of Social Change,* (Boulder, CO: Westview Press, 1990), 59–75; and Riaz Hassan, *Faithlines: Muslim Conceptions of Islam and Society* (Oxford, UK: Oxford University Press, 2002).

8 Gendered Ritual and the Shaping of Shi'ah Identity

Diane D'Souza

The city of Hyderabad in South India is home to one of the country's largest and most vibrant Shi'i communities: roughly 35 percent of the city's five and a half million people are Muslims, of which approximately two hundred thousand people[1]—somewhere near 10 percent of that population—are Shi'i.[2] This chapter examines the gendered contribution of ritual to the shaping of Shi'i identity within this community,[3] and looks in particular at the popular religious gathering known as the *majlis*, or mourning assembly.[4] I argue that implicit in the *majlis* is a powerful gendered message: namely, the strength and importance of women's actions and leadership. Men and women organize and attend these events throughout the calendar year (especially during the Muslim months of Muharram and Safar) to remember the suffering and death of beloved members of the family of the Prophet Muhammad (the *Ahl-e bayt* [Arabic: *Ahl al-bayt*]). When women participate in a *majlis* with men, ritual leadership is in male hands and women tend to follow the dictates of *purdah* (seclusion).[5] However, women also organize and participate in female-only assemblies in which they lead the recitations, ritual activities, and discourses. I contend that men and women experience and perceive the *majlis* differently, albeit with significant areas of commonality. To more closely examine these spheres of difference and overlap, I focus on the role of the *zakira*[6] (female orator) who fulfills—as does her male counterpart (the *zakir*)—the important religious responsibility of keeping alive the community's founding stories. I discuss the origin and growth of this role, and examine its impact on women's self-understanding, and on questions of identity among Shi'is. I begin, however, with a look at the complexities of religious and social identity for Shi'i women in Hyderabad.

MULTIPLE IDENTITIES: MUSLIM AND SHI' SELVES

A Shi'i woman in Hyderabad has multiple "belongings." She is a Muslim, a Shi'ah, an Indian, a woman, and has various regional, ethnic, class, and economic linkages. She also has family and sometimes professional identities based on life circumstances and roles (e.g., mother, daughter-in-law, teacher, lawyer). These are some of the frames of personal reference and group belonging which contribute to a woman's multi-layered sense of self. As Kelly Pemberton and Michael Nijhawan note in their introduction to this volume, the process whereby a sense of "community" or "groupness" is forged sometimes indexes transgressive moments in which essentialized, bounded symbols of group belonging are mobilized into action. Articulations of group identity, (like identity itself as an analytical tool) are not static, but rather are affected by particular interactions or events which can strengthen, weaken, or otherwise shape one's sense of self or group affiliation. In Hyderabad, sectarian affiliations, historical and political events, and economic change are some of the factors which contribute to Shi'i women's perceptions of self and community. Before looking at the contribution of religious rituals and leadership to Shi'i identity,[7] we would do well to examine more closely what it means to be Muslim and to be Shi'ah—not only generally, but also in the specific contexts of Hyderabad and India.

As a member of the Muslim *ummah* or community of believers, most Shi'i women identify themselves as part of a group which stretches back to the time of Prophet Muhammad—a divinely appointed messenger whom God chose to bring people back to the "right path." The theme of struggle found in the narrative of the Prophet's efforts to spread God's message resonates on several levels within Shi'i circles, as an index of the persecution and vilification Muslims confront daily, and as a marker of the persecution faced by the historical leaders of the Shi'i Muslims (the Imams, but more generally, the *Ahl-e bait*, or "People of the House" of the Prophet Muhammad) and their Shi'i supporters, through time. For many Muslims in India today, to identify oneself as an Indian Muslim is to have a sense that one is part of a distrusted, misunderstood, and persecuted minority. The experience of being a target of suspicion is one to which a majority of contemporary Indian Muslims can relate. It is possible, however, as we will see herein, that Shi'ahs have resources from religious tradition and history that help them put these experiences into a larger context.

While a Shi'ah has religious affiliations with the wider Muslim community that are brought into relief by a common sense of being under suspicion as disloyal (and potentially dangerous) members of the Indian citizenry, a Shi'ah also identifies herself as part of a group differing from the majority Sunnis in several ways. She firmly believes that the Messenger of God intended his cousin and son-in-law 'Ali to be his successor, but that political maneuvering prevented the Prophet's will from being followed.[8] This, according to Shi'i understanding, began a cycle of injustice and oppression which led people away from the path of God, splintered the Muslim community, brought about the assassination of Ali, and culminated in the martyrdom of the Prophet's own family at the hands of other Muslims. Coming to the fore during this difficult period was a line of infallible male leaders known as Imams (the first of whom is 'Ali), who are the temporal and spiritual guides of the community. Chosen by God but spurned by those who coveted worldly power, the Imams were persecuted and martyred one after another until the twelfth Imam vanished to a higher, invisible plane. From this elevated position he continues to guide his followers, and will do so until he returns at the end of the world, signaling the advent of the Day of Judgment.

In addition to a shared sense of meta-history, Hyderabad Shi'i Muslim narratives of selfhood are also shaped by more than four centuries of local history, including that of two Muslim dynasties: the Qutb Shah (1518–1687 CE) and the 'Asaf Jah (1724–1948 CE). The Qutb Shah rulers were among the first in India to adopt the Shi'i faith as a "state religion." They modeled devout behavior, patronized public devotional ceremonies, and built and supported religious structures.[9] Most Hyderabad Shi'ahs take pride in this Qutb Shah legacy. Many outstanding buildings and monuments—some of which continue to be in active use—were built under the patronage of these monarchs. Of particular relevance for Shi'i religious life are the centuries-old structures which were constructed for ritual and gathering purposes (*'ashurkhane;* sing *'ashurkhanah*[10]) and which are dotted throughout the old city. These well-used and well-loved sites are an ever-present reminder of the culture and power of the Shi'i community in Hyderabad.

It is within this specific context of a local Shi'i religious life that we need to understand the specific ties to other religious communities, Sunni Muslim and Hindu. When it comes to the Hindu majority, although there have been tensions and several incidences of "Hindu–Muslim" rioting in Hyderabad, Shi'ahs most commonly describe these events as politically motivated rather than reflective of a deep divide between the two. Many men and women are aware and proud of the fact that Hindus and other non-Shi'ahs participate in rituals like the highly visible Muharram procession that annually winds its way through the city streets. A Shi'ah generally sees this participation as testifying to the "rightness" of the Shi'i path. There is, thus, a strong attraction to the image of Hyderabad as a composite and harmonious culture. At the same time, Shi'ahs—like other Muslims—have tended to distrust certain Hindu political movements, including those that emerged during the buildup to, and in the wake of, Indian independence, and those associated with the more recent rise of "communal" tensions and Hindu nationalism.

Shi'i women's identities also have been influenced by economic changes and a shifting sense of place. Two hundred years ago there was no "old city" area in Hyderabad; rather, the region was the splendid center of the capital city: a place of palaces, fine shops, and markets, and the site of political and social power.[11] Today, however, it has been eclipsed by the explosive growth of the "new city" across the Musi River, where Hyderabad's current centers of economic, political, and social power reside. The old city is run-down and crowded in comparison, with a higher density of low-income families than most other parts of the city. It is also the region of Hyderabad which has the highest percentage of Muslims and Shi'ahs. Yet despite the social and political changes in the post-Partition period that witnessed the decline of the Shi'i community and a withering of Muslim political hegemony, the crowded Old City streets continue to have special meaning. Many of the area's religious shrines have been part of community life for generations, and although new shrines have come up in Shi'i neighborhoods in the new city, the most cherished and popular sites remain inextricably tied to Muslim heritage and culture as embodied in the Old City. Closely connected to this sense of heritage for Shi'ahs is one of the most visible markers of their identity: the religious ritual known as the *majlis*.

THE MAJLIS AND THE SHI'I RITUAL CONTEXT

Shi'ahs worldwide count the martyrdom of Imam Husayn and his followers on a desolate Iraqi plain nearly fourteen hundred years ago as a defining moment for the community.[12] For Shi'ahs, what took place at Karbala was not simply a historical massacre, but the ultimate struggle of justice and truth against falsehood and oppression. At the heart of the Karbala story is the fact that Husayn, whom Shi'ahs see as the legitimate leader of the Muslim community, refused to pledge his loyalty to the caliph, Yazid ibn Muawiyah (r. 680–683 CE), the dissolute second ruler of the Umayyad dynasty. Shi'ahs understand that Husayn yielded his life in order to uphold the "right path" as set out by God and transmitted through the Prophet, and that God transformed Husayn's brave death into a cosmic and redeeming sacrifice for the whole community. The community marks this central defining event by a cycle of special annual days, as well as through prayers and rituals which accompany the life-changing events of birth, sickness, marriage, and death. Shi'ahs observe the most important anniversaries during the first ten to twelve days of Muharram, when they commemorate the Karbala martyrdom of Husayn, his family and followers. The chief act of communal remembering is the *majalis* (pl. *majalis*), of which hundreds are held in Hyderabad during the first ten days of Muharram. After the climax on the tenth of the month, the number declines, although these assemblies continue to be held in Hyderabad homes and public *ishurkhane* throughout the full mourning period of two months and eight days.[13]

While in Urdu the word *majlis* can mean "assembly," "meeting," "congregation," or "party," among Hyderabad Shi'ahs the term refers specifically to a gathering to remember and mourn the suffering of members of the *Ahl-e bayt*. Shi'ahs in other parts of the world, including Iran, know these gatherings as *ta'ziyah majlis* ("consolation" gathering), or *majlis-rawzah-khwani* (or its shortened form, *rawzah-khwani*) after the first and most famous compilation of martyrdom stories, *Rawzat al-shuhada* (*Garden of the Martyrs*), written in Persian in 1502 CE (908 AH) by Kamal al-Din Husayn Sabzawari.

A *majlis* can contain a variety of ritual components. Almost all include an oration and the melodic recitation of remembrance poetry, both of which tend to focus on some aspect of the trials and sufferings of the *Ahl-e bayt* and their followers. In addition to these major performance elements, the *majlis* involves the shedding of tears by participants. This is central, for the purpose of the gathering is the sorrowful remembrance of the terrible losses suffered by the Prophet's family. The mourning usually reaches its climax with the performance of *matam*, the rhythmic—often impassioned—beating of one's chest in time to a melodious dirge (*nawha*). Other common *majlis* elements in Hyderabad include the display and honoring of revered icons, the formal offering of prayers, the calling down of blessings, and the closing distribution of an item which is specially blessed (*tabarrukh*)—usually food.

Each *majlis* has its own form, whether simple or complex. The style varies from gathering to gathering and from place to place. Variations generally reflect differences in local practices, the ritual history of a given family or shrine, the organizers' personal preferences, the number of people present, the holy personalities being honored, the time available for performance, and other factors. Variations encompass the chosen focus or theme (usually linked to the lives or incidents being commemorated); the balance between poetry and discourse, including the length of the oration (or even if there is one at all); the icons displayed or processed; and the inclusion (or not) of faith-based elements such as metaphorical re-enactments of certain elements of Shiʿah faith history.

The *majlis* is a blessed occasion, for it is popularly believed that Fatimah, the mother of the martyred Husayn and the daughter of Prophet Muhammad, visits each home or *ʿashurkhanah* where people gather to weep for the martyrs. Comforted and reassured in her personal loss by the passionate love and devotion which she witnesses, she (like Husayn) is believed to intercede with God on behalf of the faithful. Thus, every tear which a mourner sheds out of love of the Prophet's family brings the believer closer to the mercy of God and ultimate salvation. As the eighth Imam, ʿAlī ibn Musa al-Rida, reportedly said:

> Whoever remembers our sufferings and weeps for the crimes which have been committed against us, will be within our rank on the Day of Resurrection. Whoever remembers our suffering and weeps and makes others weep, his eyes will not weep on the Day when many eyes will weep. Whoever attends gatherings where our situation is kept alive, his heart will not die on the day when many hearts will die.[14]

Although weeping holds out a promise of eternal salvation, it would be a mistake to see this as the main motivation behind Shiʿahs' participation in the *majlis*. Much more immediate is the testimony to people's loyalty to the beloved family of the Prophet. Weeping for their suffering is a way to demonstrate love for and solidarity with these blessed souls.

GENDER DYNAMICS AND THE MALE-LED MAJLIS

Shi'i women participate in both mixed *majalis,* attended by both sexes, and *majalis* conducted and attended solely by women. There are explicit and subtle differences between these two events, although they share the common purpose of commemoration and the expression of love and loyalty to the family of the Prophet. We will analyze the dynamics of both types of gathering, starting with the male-led *majlis,* and will look at ties with religious history which help explain some aspects of their difference.

When women attend a *majlis* led by men, they most often sit in an area sectioned off by a screen or curtain, or in a separate room, veranda, or hall, sometimes with an audio connection to the main proceedings. In this setting they can be seen as the sidelined spectators to men's active participation. In a brief excerpt from my field notes, I give a sense of this dynamic in a typical Hyderabad *majlis*, which was held at an important *'ashurkhanah* in the city.

The melodic chanting, "Husayn! Husayn!" reverberates through the room. I am sitting cross-legged on the floor with about sixty other women, all dressed in black. The woman next to me cradles an infant across her folded legs. Tears glisten on her cheeks. A slatted bamboo screen separates this elongated alcove from the main hall where nearly two hundred men are getting to their feet. They too are dressed in black, a few in white or some combination of black and white. The oration has just finished and the haunting refrain of a *nawha* rings out over the crowd, achingly sad yet melodious. The words paint a picture of isolation, of pain and bravery as the martyrs embrace their tragic fate. Some of the women have now risen to their feet, others remain sitting. A few are talking among themselves, one woman summoning a child, drawing her to her lap. From the men's side of the screen the beat of the nawha pulses stronger, the crowd keeping the rhythm with blows to their chests. Between the slats and through the bodies I catch a glimpse of those leading the recitation. A group of teenaged boys and young men cluster around two men near the microphone. Many are beating their chests with stunning force, chanting the chorus in ringing voices. Around me most of the women are now on their feet. Many have joined in the chorus, their hands marking time on their bodies. I notice that a few of the women have adjusted their modest shawl (***dupatta***) so that they can slap their chests with little intervening cushion. Others keep the beat with a less vigorous but steady rhythm. Slowly, the recitation reaches a crescendo. I move slightly as a girl of about eight squeezes by, weaving her way through the crowd with a toddler on her hip. Next to me the woman who had been holding the baby is now standing, her child nestled against a shoulder. Her hand gently taps out the rhythm on the baby's back. The child sleeps on. Lips moving silently the woman mouths the chorus, tears streaming down her face. As the hall echoes with rhythmic grieving, her hand keeps a steady rhythm on the back of her child, pulsing like a heartbeat.

Dressed in the colors of mourning, men and women together participate in a male-led *majlis*. Both groups listen to the poetry, oration, and responsive dirges, although women and girls watch the male performance leaders from gaps in a bamboo screen which separates the male and female spaces. This sidelining of women is common not only in the *majlis*, but in other male-organized events, including the ritual processions which wind through the city streets on a few key anniversary days each year. On these latter occasions, women form the veiled piping along the streets through which men and boys process, occupying doorways, balconies, windows, and walkways. As the preceding example demonstrates, however, women are not simply silent spectators. In the *majlis*, many embrace the rhythm as do the men, weeping with the graphic accounts of the suffering of the *Ahl-e bayt*, rising when the oration concludes, and marking the beat of the melodious dirges on their bodies. A few join in the repetitive chorus of poetic lament, although their voices are relatively muted. In some sense, then, the custom of gender separation means that women are both "inside" and "outside" the male-led event. Moreover, amidst the cadence of mournful remembrance and the connection with the main performers in the ritual, there runs a very lively thread of ongoing life behind the screen. Alongside ritual activity, women and girls are engaged in the practical activities of caring for children, and in social interactions with relatives and friends. Women's ritual activity thus has not one center—the main performance area which establishes the rhythm of the event—but two: the central performance and the area of women's practical and social activities. In other words, participating in a *majlis* means giving energy and attention to a religious ritual with which there is connection, while also having the opportunity to meet extra-ritual needs for activity, communication, and exchange.

Men are aware of women's existence on the margins—whether they are visible or invisible. In a mourning gathering such as the one just described, men cannot see individual women, but their presence is audible via the sound of weeping, the cries which occasionally float above the loud lament, and the pulse of the *matam*—the rhythmic chest beating—which echoes from behind the screen. Mohammed Fazel[15] gives us a sense of the male perception of this presence as he recalls his regular participation as a young man in the ritual re-enactment of the Karbala tragedy. The *ta'ziyah,* or "passion play," which he describes is different from the *majlis* but shares some of the same elements, including the main purpose of remembrance and mourning. Unlike the *majlis*, the *ta'ziyah* uses reenactment as its primary means of recalling the Karbala event. Although the setting is somewhat different from that of the *majlis*, there is a close link between the gendered spaces of ritual mourning. As the male believer moves deeper into the self-inflicted pain which testifies to his willingness to stand beside the remembered and mourned Husayn, he connects not only with the hero, but also with the female voice which testifies to his sacrifice. The dynamics are much the same during the *majlis*. In fact, one could say that the female role is essential to it. Women are the witnesses to men's sacrificial action, a fact that is enacted through their presence on the margins of the male-led *majlis*.

The performed role of female witness mirrors and re-creates religious history. During the events of Karbala, as Husayn and his male family and followers battled the army of Yazid, the women were on the margins, keeping to the tents. In fact, when one woman grasped a tent pole to join her husband on the battlefield and die with him protecting the offspring of Muhammad, Husayn insisted that she return to sit with the women, for "it is not for women to fight."[16] The shedding of blood is a male, not a female, role—a fact which is mirrored in ritual performance today by restricting to men the performance of *matam* with swords, blades, and flails. Women did, however, have a role in the Karbala drama as it is popularly presented. In faith-based portrayals, each of the male descendents of the Prophet took to the battlefield after first taking leave of Husayn's sister Zaynab or other key females in the entourage. It was also to the women that men's lifeless bodies returned. Poetry and oration detail how women gathered, weeping over their dead, and had to be dragged away by their captors.[17] In some accounts, women embraced the still-warm remains to offer the final blessing, "May you enjoin heaven!"[18] As male actors participate in the rituals of the *majlis*, showing through passionate and often bloody acts of self flagellation their loyalty to Husayn and the family of the Prophet, they mirror and recreate a history in which women testify to and mourn male sacrifice. In this setting, women's main role is as a foil to the central narrative: bewailing the fall of the heroes. Once the men of the Prophet's family are dead (with one exception), the sisters, wives, and daughters of the dead martyrs assume their place as the defenseless prisoners of an unjust, cruel, and impious ruler. According to male accounts, the women's main suffering after the central loss of their loved ones is brought about by the shame of being exposed in public without veils.

We see this kind of portrayal in the recounting of the events of Karbala by the Shi' philosopher and theologian Allamah Tabataba'i. Tabataba'i notes that, following the martyrdom of Husayn and his followers, the soldiers of Yazid "plundered the *haram* [lit. the "forbidden" or "prohibited"; i.e., the women's quarters] of the Imam and burned his tents."[18] The soldiers then "moved the members of the *haram*, all of whom were helpless women and girls, along with the heads of the martyrs to Kufa." Tabataba'i notes that three men were captured along with the women, and gives their names, details about their ages and how they escaped the fate of the other men. He does not provide similar information about the lives and circumstances of the women captives. For this respected Shi'i leader, then, it is men who are the active figures in the Karbala story. His references to women and children are framed first in terms of possessions of Imam Husayn (*his haram* is plundered, *his* tents are burned), then as being helpless, passive objects to be moved to Kufa along with the martyrs' heads. A single exception is Tabataba'i's brief mention of Zaynab:

> The event of Karbala, the capture of the women and children of the Household of the Prophet, their being taken as prisoners from town to town and the speeches made by the daughter to 'Ali, Zaynab, and the fourth Imam who were among the prisoners, disgraced the Umayyads.[20]

Although Tabataba'i names Zaynab, he limits his comment to the shame her speech brought upon the Umayyads. Like his earlier reference to women as helpless victims, the purpose in mentioning her is to demonstrate the inhumanity and injustice of the enemy.

It is interesting to note that we could see Husayn and the other Karbala martyrs in the same light as Tabataba'i presents the women: as victims, helpless in the face of tyranny. Yet, the Shi'i community does not choose to cultivate such an image. Although ideas about male superiority are part of the reason for portraying women as peripheral to male-centered events, there are additional dynamics. Heightening the emotions and increasing the empathy of the audience are essential requirements of a successful *majlis*. Using remembrance poetry or discourse to portray Zaynab or others as a helpless sister or mother in need of protection furthers the call for male sacrificial warriors and encourages a greater degree of impassioned pain from a male audience longing to stand in solidarity beside the martyrs. Characterizing women as passive stimulates men's participation in ritual (or political action, like war) and helps explain the popularity of this traditional gender stereotype.[21]

The popular understanding of Karbala as demonstrated in the male-led *majlis*, then, is one of seventy-two martyrs actively embracing their fate, being faithful believers committed to the cause of justice.[22] When we frame the story of Karbala as a tale of martyrdom—defining bravery as the choice to give one's life on the battlefield—women automatically fall on the periphery. However, if we shift the frame of the story and move women's actions and perceptions from the periphery to the center, we begin to notice that, like the men, the women accompanying Husayn had key roles to play in events connected with the Karbala tragedy. These roles are mirrored in the female-led *majlis*.

FEMALE LEADERSHIP AND THE MAJLIS

Majalis which are led by women have the same basic structure as those led by men, although it is women who give the orations, lead the recitations and *matam,* and organize other ritual elements. Women in Hyderabad usually arrange their events in one of three venues: in homes (where the vast majority take place); in Yadgar Husayni, a popular, women-only *'ashurkhanah*; or during specific allocated times in other *'ashurkhane* which are under the direction and control of men (some or all of the shrine being closed to male visitors during such events). The clearest and most obvious difference between male- and female-led gatherings is the absence of men in female events, with men tending to be represented only through symbols and the stories told about the actions of the religio-historical figures. [23] Interestingly, the absence of men and the leadership of women mirrors a particular point in the Karbala story.

Shi'ahs know that the first organized remembrance gathering was held by Zaynab and the surviving members of the family of the Prophet in 61 AH, while they were still in the court of Yazid in Damascus.[24] Hind, the wife of Yazid, and her companions from the court were present at this *majlis* which, according to some faith-based accounts, lasted for seven days.[25] The women narrated the tragic events which took place at Karbala, focused on the gallant lives lost, and voiced their pain and grief. According to Lebanese scholar Shaykh Muhammad Mehdi Shams al-Din, the highly emotional accounts of the battle and the eulogizing of the martyrs was accompanied by a wailing kind of poetry and self-inflicted pain—the beating of face and breast.[26]

The powerful expressions of grief enacted during that first *majlis* were part of an already existing female mourning tradition (which continues to some extent today[27]). In fact, in Arabic society women were so known for their passionate and emotional responses to death that the grieving female became a powerful icon of bereavement. For example, in reporting on the return of Zaynab and her party to Madinah, historian Ibn Tawus noted that "They [men loyal to the family of the Prophet] grieve for them with the grief of bereaved women."[28] Women in Arab society also were known for composing vivid, poignant verses of mourning and praise for their dead; indeed, it was widely accepted that a hero's mother and sisters played a special role in offering poetic eulogies.[29] For example, history records the poetic response to Husayn's death offered by his wife, al-Rabab:

> Behold him who was a light shining in the darkness is now in Karbala slain and unburied . . .
>
> You were for me a fast mountain to lean upon, and you were a true friend in kinship and faith.
>
> Who is left for the orphans and the needy after him who used to provide for the destitute, and to whom every poor person would run for refuge. . . . [30]

Here al-Rabab offers an eloquent tribute to a beloved and fallen husband and hero, expressing the pain of a world made poorer by this loss. Women capitalized on the poetic tradition to powerfully express their love and bereavement, eulogizing the departed. It is clear, then, that the first *majalis* were shaped by traditional female practices—lamentation and wailing, the physical demonstration of pain and suffering at one's loss, and poetic eulogy. All these elements remain key in ways the Shi'i community remember and mourn the martyrs of Karbala today. In fact, one might even say that Shi'i practices of remembrance and mourning have been adapted from female initiatives and rituals.

THE *ZAKIRA* ROLE

To better understand the dynamics of the female-led *majlis*, I have chosen to focus on the central role of the orator, or *zakira*.[31] The retelling of the stories of the martyrs—through narration or poetry—is arguably the single most important aspect of a *majlis*. It is through this recounting that a collective memory is kept alive of the events which unfolded in and around Karbala. Here, too, the personalities of the key actors—Husayn, his sister Zaynab, and other members of the *Ahl-e-bayt*—are given shape and substance, with different aspects of their character being highlighted through oration or poetry. The role of the *zakira* is thus of central importance, and offers the most visible female leadership role in religious practice within the community. The word *zakira* comes from the Arabic word *zikr* which means "remembrance," "recitation," or "narration"; thus, a *zakira* is "a reciter" or "one who remembers." In the Shi'i context, a *zakira* (or a male *zakir*) narrates the incidents connected to early Shi'i history, particularly the events surrounding the Karbala massacre and its aftermath. In Iran and parts of the Indian Subcontinent, this person is known as a *razah khwan*, a "reciter of the *Rawzat*."

Shi'i women with whom I've spoken estimate that there are anywhere from twenty-five to one hundred *zakiras* in Hyderabad's Shi'ah community today. Yet, as one young graduate told me, "Each of us should have at least one woman in our own family who can lead if someone from outside is unable to come."[32] This means that the total number of women who actually deliver a *zikr* is much higher than the prior estimate. In Hyderabad, a popular *zakir* or *zakira* might speak at four, five, or even six *majalis* each day during the main mourning period, addressing anywhere from a dozen to several hundred men and women on each occasion. In an average *majlis* of an hour and a half in length, the oration (*zikr*) will often take forty-five minutes or more. On most occasions, the *zikr* is divided into two parts: a more reflective portion (*faz a'il*) which elaborates on a topic which the speaker sees as important for the community's knowledge and growth, and a portion (*masa'ib*) in which some aspect of the tragedy endured by the

Prophet's family is passionately related. A skilled orator makes the transition between the two seamless, the lesson first related finding its climax in the heart-rending martyrdom account.

A successful *zakira* must have a number of qualities pertaining to rhetorical skills. One is presence of mind and confidence, for a *zakira* develops her ideas and relates her stories before an audience without the use of notes. A *zakira* needs to know how to pace her delivery, to reach her listeners, and to assess the needs of the crowd. Finally, and most importantly, she must be able to arouse the emotional pitch of her listeners. Although she may touch upon a broad range of religious issues in the discursive portion of her *zikr*, her role in the *majlis* is not successful unless she helps to lead her audience back to the plains of Karbala, where the pathos and tragedy is so great that faithful believers are overcome by grief. The following narrative I recorded during an experience of participation in a *majlis* offers an example of this process.

I visit [Yadgar Husayni] on the morning of 'Arba in (the fortieth day following the tenth of Muharram). Yadgar Husayni's cavernous hall is filled with women: slim young girls, stooped worn figures, mothers with small children, whole families—but no men. Nearly two thousand women will gather for the *majlis* which is to start at 9.30. Gone is the fresh white cloth which has covered the floor since the beginning of Muharram; today women stand or sit on the bare stone floor. Two silver tomb replicas (*zarian*) enclosed in glass cases—one of Husayn, the other of Zaynab—have been pulled out from their usual alcove and stand alone in the very center of the hall. The central icons are a reminder of the partnership of Husayn and Zaynab. Visitors sprinkle flower petals or place garlands on the zarian, others lie sobbing across them, still others kiss the fragrant flowers or press their cheeks against them tenderly. Many of the women are weeping, all are solemn and dressed in black, the color of Muharram. After a while a small group sits down cross-legged before a microphone and begins to recite the *marsiyahs*. One mournful elegy after another fills the hall; today many focus on Zaynab: her grief, her courage. The crowd sighs and weeps and moans. More women fill the hall.

Twenty minutes later Zakia, the *zakira* for this *majlis*, steps to a microphone at the head of the hall. The room is quiet except for the sound of shuddering sobs. Beneath the veil of the delicate black sari which covers Zakia's hair, her face is lined with grief. Today she gives no reasoned sermon; the *minbar* (pulpit) has been pushed aside, and Zakia stands alone before the microphone, facing the women and the two tomb replicas which stand at the center of the hall in unadorned simplicity. She begins with a prayer—a short surah from the Qur'an—and then cries: "It is a day of cruel parting." Weeping, sweating, she laments the death of the martyrs, the loss which leaves Zaynab to carry on alone. There is no intellectualizing, no carefully reasoned sermon, only deep emotion. I notice that more people than usual are avidly attending to the *zakira*'s words; fewer are hiding their faces, immersed in their own private grief. Overhead, the fans slow to a halt as the electrical supply is cut, a common occurrence in summertime Hyderabad. The microphone, however, is hooked up to a battery-powered generator, so the oration is not interrupted. For twenty minutes Zakia stands, describing the cruelties of a family torn apart by tragic violence. At times she can hardly speak through her tears. Finally she wails, "They are going!" Choking with emotion, she re-creates the loss of the captives being taken off to Kufa. The women in the hall are with her, responding fervently: wailing, weeping, many slapping their thighs in self-inflicted pain. Zakia continues to call out amidst the breaking crescendo, her voice cracking with emotion. Finally, she brings her oration to a close with a sobbing call for blessing on Husayn, 'Abbas, 'Ali Asghar, Zaynab and others of the suffering family of the Prophet.

As the *zakira*'s voice dies away, the hall resounds with the wailing of the crowd. Then a gray-haired woman with a pure, strong voice begins the nawha, the sharp slapping beat of the *matam* keeping the rhythm. A group fanned out around her sings the verses with feeling but the chorus is picked up by all in a growing crescendo of voices, "Zaynab, I am coming!" The words hang in the air, conveying infinite sadness as the women promise that they too will be at Zaynab's side as she is forced to part with all those she has loved best in this world. The dozen women leading the chorus are pounding their chests with resounding force, many doing the difficult double-handed *matam*. An older woman next to me is weeping loudly, her face buried in her handkerchief, her shoulders shaking in grief. As the *nawha* draws to a close, the hall resounds with the passionate cry, "Husayn! Husayn! Husayn! Husayn!" Then, in a sound more poignant than any words, the haunting echo of thousands of hands striking sharp blows to the chest, the rhythm pulsing like a heart beat, powerful, driving and intensely moving.[33]

The success of a *zakira* is generally gauged by the finesse of her communication, demonstrated most tangibly by their ability to move the audience to tears. In this, a good *zakira* is much like a talented actor whose portrayal of a character is so nuanced and true that one is swept into the emotions of the drama, forgetting, at least temporarily, the medium of the film or play. As in the preceding example, the *majlis* orator takes her or his audience back to Karbala, where the pathos and tragedy of the scene is so great that one is completely overcome by grief. Unlike an actor, however, the *zakir* or *zakira* is not just putting on a show; he or she becomes the voice of the community's collective memory. By the end of a successful oration, the audience is beside itself in pain at the suffering of the *Ahl-e-bayt*, the *zakira's* voice finally being stilled by her own choked sobs.[34]

When I asked women in Hyderabad, "What makes a good *zakira*?" I received many responses. "Knowledge," replied one young mother who proudly identifies her family as a very orthodox one, observing all the commemorative days of the family of the Prophet. "The *zakira* should know the gist of the whole Islam: the history, the Qur'an, the *hadis*.[35] And the *zikr* [oration] of 'Ali should embellish her whole talk."[36] In other words, a good *zakira* is one who draws deeply on a wealth of tradition from respected sources, intricately weaving into the oration the sayings and stories of the revered first Imam, honored by Shi'ahs for his goodness, his leadership, and his loyalty to the Prophet.

"Confidence," answered a university graduate, who recently completed a course in fashion design. "She should be able to speak in front of an audience with ease." She took another bite of the food we shared. "And knowledge. She should be familiar with the whole of Islam."[37]

"See, anyone can read the traditions," explained one young teacher. "We've grown up with these stories our whole lives. We hear them every year. Even I can relate them." She pauses to give me an earnest look. "But a *zakira* has something more. When she relates the *masa'ib* [the emotional latter part of the oration] . . . she should be crying." She stops for a moment, thinking. "Another thing. She must practice what she preaches. That is very important."[34]

"A *zakira* must be religious," answered a grandmother who is the respected mother-in-law in a traditional joint family home. "She must do her *namaz* (ritual prayers), *roza* (fasting), all that. She must have knowledge, right from the time of the Prophet onwards. The whole Islamic history. She must be able to explain why a thing is, how a thing is. There should never be any doubt when people ask her . . . She must teach what Islam means . . . what it *really* means." She pause, searching, then to narrate a well-known story from the life of the Prophet. Each day, as the Prophet passed along a particular way, an old woman used to throw garbage on his head from her window. The Prophet never said a word, even when curses were hurled down as well. One day he passed along the street but was not assaulted. The second and the third day was the same, so the Prophet stopped and, making concerned enquiries, found out that the woman was ill. The mother-in-law paused to see if I had gotten the point. "Islam teaches us to be kind. A *zakira* must teach us Islam."

"The most important thing is a person's interest. Her enthusiasm. Without strong will power, she will not have the strength to become a *zakira*." The woman talking was a mother in her thirties, who worked for a Shi' social service organization:

> You see, none of this is taught in schools or colleges, so she must learn on her own. When she is a child, her parents and elders teach her. But at a certain time the child must decide to learn for herself. It's a question of interest. A child may be good in school but have no opportunity to really express herself. Or she may already be a leader in school and this quality of leadership carries over.[39]

A successful *zakira*, then, is one who confidently and knowledgeably teaches the intricacies of Shi'i faith, tradition, and history. A religious woman known to "practice what she preaches," she is a dedicated and successful communicator whose emotional recounting of the tragedies of the family of the Prophet not only demonstrates her own grief but moves her listeners to tears as well. In fact, her success is generally measured by her ability to arouse the emotional pitch of her listeners.

Like the *majlis* rituals themselves, however, the idea of what makes a good *zakira* has changed over time. A number of women with whom I spoke noted that modern generations have a different attitude to religion. "Blind faith still exists," said one sixty-year-old, "but education is changing the whole way we think and learn. The way we were taught twenty or thirty years ago is impossible today. We have to be able to give satisfactory answers to the questions young people ask." This means that the techniques a *zakira* used to capture and hold the attention of an audience fifty or sixty years ago may not be successful today. "People are less willing to accept the simple description and emotionalism of earlier days," said one popular *zakira*. She stresses that an analytical approach is essential, as well as an organized presentation of the topic. She thus sees her role as university professor and religious orator as closely linked, drawing on the same skills.[40]

CONTINUITY, CHANGE, AND THE MODERN ZAKIRA

Elderly *zakiras* in Hyderabad are clearly aware of how the *zakira's* role developed over the centuries.[41] They relate how women of the upper classes organized *majalis* at which they and their guests heard or recited poetry, practiced *matam*, and listened to written narratives which retold the stories of Karbala. Professional female performers were commonly invited to recite the mourning poetry while the guests reclined on bolsters, often with a bowl of roasted anise seeds circulating among the crowd. Someone would then read from a written account of the martyrdom event using "Muharram books" or "*majalis* books" containing separate readings for each day.[42] Some of the women who remember these affairs commented that the ladies who gathered were more spectators at an event than participants in it.

Without going into a detailed historical discussion at this point, I would like to make several observations about the development of the *zakira's* role in the *majlis*. First, we note that at times this religious leader had responsibility for reciting poetry and for narrating or reading martyrdom accounts—a mixture which probably echoes the original mourning practices of Zaynab and other women of the Prophet's family. This stands in apparent contrast to the male tradition where poetry and prose reportedly have been more distinct streams of performance.[43] We also observe that at least from the eighteenth century (and probably earlier), the *zakira* commonly played a larger religious leadership role in the female community: being invited to help women formulate prayers for supplication, to oversee rituals, and to teach the Qur'an. During these centuries she was often among a relatively small number of literate, educated women having facility in language, including the sacred language of the Qur'an (Arabic), and the language of poetry and religious commentary (Persian, Urdu). Finally, we see that the goals of the first *zakiras*—to tell the stories; to extol the courage and bravery of the martyrs; to express one's grief and pain; and to inspire empathy, loyalty, and sorrow in one's listeners—have remained fairly consistent throughout the development of the orator's role. As we will see, in the modern period the *zakira* takes on an additional goal of educating her listeners on religious themes wider than the Karbala story. This is in keeping with the growth of Shi' theology and the general expansion of the subject of narration from an initial focus on the immediate tragedy to an inclusion of stories about the Prophet, his family, the Imams, and other prophets who suffered in the service of God.

The biggest difference between the pre-modern orator and the contemporary *zakira* is that the latter generally supplements her stories about Karbala with an extempore religious discourse known as a *bayan* or *taqrir*.[44] Oral accounts of women in their seventies and eighties suggest that it was perhaps at the very beginning of the twentieth century that this style of oration began to emerge, although the exact dates and details are still somewhat unclear. Toby Howarth, basing his work on interviews with women in Hyderabad and Lucknow, argues that it was in the 1930s and 1940s that women first began their extempore preaching. In delineating this change, however, he is precise to distinguish discourses on the events of Karbala from talks having a focus on wider issues—the latter, he feels, are the true innovation of recent years. Howarth draws his conclusion about the uniqueness of the modern *zikr* knowing that male extempore oration about Karbala already existed from a much earlier date (he cites a *zikr* delivered in Bombay in the 1820s, for example). In other words, the new step was about a broadening of subject, not extempore oration per se.[45] Yet, the early preaching which Howarth makes note of was mainly delivered by trained and accredited religious scholars (the *ulama*), a group in which women were not represented. Unlike men, women did not have an established and legitimate religious platform for public address. Although Zaynab appears to have combined the force of extempore oration with poetry in her leadership at the earliest mourning gatherings, and later "professional" female poets and storytellers no doubt preceded or followed their recitations with some words of extempore introduction, there was not a distinct category of female extempore preachers as there was among men. By the nineteenth century, women's roles in the female-led *majlis* seem to have been largely ones of performing already written compositions—both poetry and prose (although women-authored works, especially of poetry, were among those recited). For *zakiras* in the earliest part of the twentieth century, the biggest step forward was to free themselves from this tie to established texts and offer thoughtful orations of their own. Thus, to deliver an extempore *zikr*—no matter the subject—was the big innovation of the modern era for women, even though it was in fact reclaiming a space Zaynab seems to have occupied fourteen hundred years earlier. As with men, and no doubt influenced by them, the scope of the *zakira's* address gradually widened to include a broad range of subjects.

This change to extempore oration seems to have been catalyzed by a number of factors, including reformist movements to recognize women's rights and abilities,[46] the push for women's education, the rising number of literate women who could make use of written materials, and the increase in discursive sermons at male-led gatherings. Interestingly, this last major transition in the development of the *zakira* tradition witnessed a brief time during which male orators addressed female gatherings. This trend seems to have been short-lived, and perhaps even hastened the rise of female extempore orators. One reason it did not persist was practical: many women did not feel comfortable removing their outer veil or cloak in the presence of an unrelated male. Thus, they remained in *pardah* for the whole gathering—something they never did in meetings involving only females. Secondly, some *zakirs* seemed to assume that women knew very little and therefore gave talks which a number of women found patronizing. As a group, women in Hyderabad did not seem to have encouraged male leadership in female gatherings. Rather, a handful of women used their own skills and abilities, capitalized on existing opportunities, and, within a relatively short period, became strong preachers of the faith.

GENDER, RITUAL, AND AGENCY

If we look at the initiative and energy with which Shi'i women organize, lead, and participate in regular devotional rituals, we can note that there exists a powerful model for women's leadership embodied in the role of the *zakira*. This fact is generally overlooked amidst dominant stereotypes about the oppression and passivity of Muslim women. I would argue that the *zakira's* central, visible role model helps to inspire women to be outspoken, articulate, and active leaders. Mary Hegland reaches a similar conclusion in her study of the "energizing ritual performances" of Shi'i women in Pakistan, where she notes that leadership in the various rituals of the *majlis* encourages confidence, competence, and self-determination.[47] In patriarchal societies, these qualities and abilities receive particular nurturance in female-only settings, as Erica Friedl observed in her analysis of the Iranian government's decision to enforce sex-segregation in schools:

> In such [female-only] environments women can express themselves freely, they have more opportunity to practice leadership and intellectual skills than they would have if men were present, and they can

> develop confidence even in such subjects . . . which in some societies are said to be the domain of men.[42]

Do we find that the self-confidence gained in all-women religious gatherings makes a difference in women's lives? I suggest that it does, as exhibited in the freedom with which so many women organize religious events, travel to and from the various gatherings they have arranged, and the frank confidence displayed by so many *zakiras*. To give one brief example, I was stopped one evening just outside the house of an Old City friend by a confident young woman whose long, patterned shawl identified her as a Shi'ah. She and the five veiled women whom she smilingly introduced as her mother, her aunt, and her sisters had seen me from a distance earlier, while calling upon a common friend. After enquiring my name, the young woman asked why I was studying the history of the community, and was delighted to learn that a "foreigner" was interested in researching her faith. Eighteen-year-old Miryam explained that the next day she, her sister, and her mother would be traveling to Karbala for the *ziyarat* (pilgrimage). She was visibly excited at the prospect of her first visit to Iraq. For her mother, she explained, it was the second trip, and her aunt had already been there five times. We talked for some time, and I was struck by the self-confidence with which this young woman spoke of her choice to be a *zakira* and what helped her to be a good one—not to mention her initiative to approach me, an unknown stranger about whom she was curious, on the street.

It was also interesting that she, along with her mother and other female relatives, had planned for and arranged a trip to see the holy shrines of members of the *Ahl-e-bayt*. As with a growing number of women (and men) in economically stable families in Hyderabad, they had arranged their travel through aShi'i tour operator who specialized in pilgrimages to holy shrines in Syria, Iran, and Iraq. The women went with the support and approval of the men in their family, but without their accompaniment. This independent travel stands in contrast to Muslim pilgrimage to Makkah, where a woman is required to be accompanied by a male relative. Not only are women traveling internationally to visit pilgrimage sites, they are also assuming leadership roles among mixed groups of men and women pilgrims.[49]

Modern transportation and high emigration rates mean that many women in the middle and upper classes also have opportunities to travel abroad to visit family. A woman visiting relatives and friends in foreign countries will usually participate in the local religious rituals there. Indeed, if the woman is a *zakira*, the host often takes advantage of her visiting guest by inviting her to address the women locally. Muharram is a particularly popular time for such visits; and often several of Hyderabad's *zakiras* are abroad during the mourning season. These international experiences further increase women's skill and confidence, as well as contributing to a transnational spread of stories, practices, and trends among the worldwide Shi'i diaspora.

Finally, women's confidence and leadership is powerfully displayed in the fascinating local history of the construction fifty years ago of Yadgar Husayni, Hyderabad's all-women's *'ashurkhanah*.[44] This major shrine was completed successfully in spite of initial lack of support from men, and today is a central place for the performance of women-led rituals. The idea originated with the *Markazi Anjuman Niswan Barkat-i 'Aza* ("central women's association for the blessings of mourning"), a Shi'i women's religious association founded in the late 1930s by devout women from mainly upper middle-class families in Hyderabad. Although the *Anjuman* gave its initial priority to assisting the faithful in the performance of the *majlis*, the female leadership soon expressed their desire to have a sacred space reserved specifically for the use of women. They rallied together and, with hard work and the charismatic leadership of the *Anjuman's* President, a highly respected local *zakira*, they involved the activity of a wide cross-section of Shi' women, using creative methods to raise the necessary funds. Today Yadgar Husayni is a large and thriving center for women's religious and social interaction, as well as a site which offers religious instruction to girls and economic support to women and families in need. Women from the Shi' community annually organize anywhere from three to five hundred *majalis* there in its spacious main hall, paying a membership fee and a modest contribution to the shrine for their use of the space.[51]

The stories of women's actions in the traditions of the religious past, nourished by visible female leadership in rituals like the *majlis*, offer example and encouragement to women's actions in the present—actions like the building of an all-women shrine. "Shi'ah women started a revolution," one middle-aged woman explained to me one day as we made our way out from a crowded *majlis* at Yadgar Husayni. She went on to say that it was Zaynab's crying in the prison of Damascus which had made women in that town aware of the massacre of the family of the Prophet. Up until then, many people did not know the identity of those whom Yazid's army had slain. "They [the women] went on strike [when they learned this]," this faithful believer continued, "The women refused to do any housework until their men questioned Yazid about the whole thing. When the unrest grew and men started to ask Yazid difficult questions, he was forced to let the women go." Later, as we stopped to reclaim our shoes at the steps to the shrine's inner hall, I told her about my research on the history of how women succeeded in building this female-only *ashurkhanah*, expressing my admiration at women accomplishing such a major undertaking. She laughed in reply, put her arm around me and said, "We're Shi'ah women. What do you expect?"[52]

CONCLUSION

The *majlis* communicates a number of important messages among believers. One is the expression of loyalty to and love for the family of the

Prophet, most notably demonstrated by sharing in their sufferings and trials. Another is a belief in standing for what is right against persecution and overwhelming odds—including the indifference or attacks of a non-Shi'ah majority. The powerful message of women's strength, action, and leadership that is also found in the *majlis* is conveyed not only through the historical actions of female figures like Zaynab, the granddaughter of the Prophet, but through the ongoing action of women ritual leaders like the *zakira*. Although men do acknowledge the important role played by Zaynab, the male portrayal of events tends to emphasize women as the witnesses of male sacrifice, and the helpless victims of violence against the community. Such emphases strengthen male identity and resolve, but do not necessarily resonate with women's aspirations and experiences. Women have made use of the practice of gender segregation to engage in women-led rituals which, although substantially similar to male-led events, have women at the center as leaders and shapers of the gathering, with the noticeable absence of sidelined witnesses.

Do these gendered differences in perspective threaten Shi' boundaries of identity? Do they shift the identity of the community in any substantial way? I would suggest that within the Shi' community there exists a paradigm for female strength and leadership which nurtures women's confidence, and also provides a space for male perceptions of powerful women actors. Thus, for example, a pilgrimage tour to Shi' shrines can be led by a woman, and a women's religious association can build and run an impressive shrine. At the same time, there is a sense that men stand above women in an overall hierarchy of power, demonstrated in part by the all-male clerical establishment. When women choose to participate in spheres shaped by male power structures—for example, in public male-led religious gatherings, or even conferences organized by the local Iranian Consulate—they tend to conform to male-specified requirements, such as keeping to the sidelines, following male leadership, and wearing approved forms of modest dress. As with social and religious identities in general, then, women's senses of themselves as female Shi'ahs are complex and shifting, with different emphases coming to the fore depending on the particular situation or circumstance. One cannot overlook, however, that an important part of women's religious identity is as competent, powerful leaders who contribute to the strength of the religious community. Women have been able to shape this empowering space within the religious mainstream by making use of traditions upholding female leadership, and the socially accepted practice of gender segregation.

NOTES

1. The exact number is notoriously hard to confirm, since government census figures do not require one to specify one's religious sect. Also, Shi'i faith incorporates the belief that one can deny one's religious (Shi'i) affiliation if to

claim it presents a significant risk to life or livelihood (a doctrine known as *taqiyya* or dissimulation); see Sayyid Muhammad Husayn Tabataba'i, *Shi'ite Islam*, trans. and ed. Seyyed Hossein Nasr (Albany: State University of New York Press, 1975), 223–225.

2. In this chapter, "Shi'ah" refers to Ithna' Ashari, or "Twelver" Shi'ahs: those who believe in the twelve imams—the divinely designated leaders and sinless successors to the Prophet. They are the majority among Shi'i groups in India and worldwide.
3. Interesting discussions of the nexus between ritual, identity, and gender can be found in a number of recent books, including: Saba Mahmood, *Politics of Piety: The Islamic Revival and the Feminist Subject* (Princeton, NJ: Princeton University Press, 2005); Salma Ahmad Nageeb, *New Spaces and Old Frontiers: Women, Social Space, and Islamization in Sudan* (Lanham, MD: Lexington Books, 2004); Lara Deeb, *An Enchanted Modern: Gender and Public Piety in Shi'i Lebanon* (Princeton, NJ: Princeton University Press, 2006); and chapters in the collection edited by Pamela J. Stewart and Andrew Strathern, *Contesting Rituals: Islam and Practices of Identity-Making* (Durham, NC: Carolina Academic Press, 2005).
4. Relatively little has been written on women and the rituals of the *majlis*, and still less on the role of the *zakira*. Consequently, I have relied heavily on personal interaction and conversation with local Shi'ahs, as well as my own observation of and participation in Shi'i rituals in Hyderabad, where I lived for nearly twenty years. In addition to my own work in the Indian context, "In the Presence of the Martyrs: The 'Alam in Popular Shi'i Piety," *The Muslim World* 88, no.1 (1998): 67–80; "Devotional Practices Among Shi'a Women in South India," in *Lived Islam in South Asia: Adaptation, Accommodation and Conflict*, eds. Imtiaz Ahmad and Helmut Reifeld (New Delhi: Social Science Press, 2003); Mary Elaine Hegland, "Flagellation and Fundamentalism: (Trans)Forming Meaning, Identity, and Gender Through Pakistani Women's Rituals of Mourning," *American Ethnologist* 25, no. 2 (1998): 240–266; "A Mixed Blessing—The Majles: Shi'a Women's Rituals in Northwest Pakistan and the Politics of Religion, Ethnicity and Gender," in *Mixed Blessings: Religious Fundamentalism and Gender Cross-Culturally*, eds. Judy Brink and Joan Mencher (New York: Routledge, 1995); "Shi'a Women of Northwest Pakistan and Agency Through Practice: Ritual, Resistance, Resilience," *Political and Legal Anthropology Review* 18, no. 2 (1995): 65–79; and Ursula Sagaster, "Observations Made During the Month of Muharram, 1989, in Baltistan," in *Proceedings of the International Seminar on the Anthropology of Tibet and the Himalaya*, Sept. 21–28, 1990, at the Ethnographic Museum of the University of Zurich, eds. Charles Ramble and Martin Brauen (Zurich: Völkerkundemuseum der Universität Zürich, 1990), have chronicled women's participation in private mourning gatherings in Pakistan. Mrs. Meer Hasan 'Ali, *Observations of the Mussulmans of India: Descriptive of their Manners, Customs, Habits and Religious Opinions*, second ed., notes and introduction by W. Crooke (London: Oxford University Press, 1917) has provided thick ethnographic description of Shi'i women's practices in nineteenth-century North India. And Toby Howarth, *The Pulpit of Tears: Shi'i Muslim Preaching in India* (Amsterdam: Vrije Universiteit, 2001) records and discusses the orations of several women preachers in contemporary Hyderabad. A number of studies have also shed light on women and mourning assemblies in Iran: see Anne Betteridge (1989); Elizabeth W. Fernea (1965); Robert A. Fernea and Elizabeth W. Fernea (1972), Azam Torab (1998), and Zahra Kamalkhani (1993), all in the bibliography at the end of this volume.

5. *Purdah* can be used to indicate physical seclusion, the separation of women from men, or an outer covering or veil with which a woman covers part or all of her body.
6. In writing Urdu vocabulary in English, I have followed a transliteration system developed at the Henry Martyn Institute in India. Thus "*zakira*" replaces the more traditional form "*dhakira*," and makes pronunciation less opaque for non-specialists. I have tended to use the English convention of making plurals by adding "s" to the singular form of the Urdu word.
7. For an excellent discussion of Muslim ritual and its contribution to group and individual identity, see Stewart and Strathern, eds., *Contesting Rituals*.
8. Sunnis, of course, have another story, and maintain that the Prophet did not leave clear instructions about who his successor would be.
9. The Shi'ah faith first achieved prominence in the southern part of India in the fifteenth century under the reign of the Bahmani kings (1347–1526). For a good summation of its spread during this period, see Howarth, *The Pulpit of Tears*, 37–39. According to Saiyid Athar Abbas Rizvi, *A Socio-Intellectual History of the Isna 'Ashari Shi'ahs in India*, 2 vols. (Canberra: Ma'rifat Publishing House, 1986), 292, public expressions of Shi'i belief, although without formal state affiliations or sponsorship, were found as early as the thirteenth century in North India.
10. Literally, "the house of *'ashura*," *'ashura* being the tenth of Muharram and the day on which Husayn was martyred. Other names for these structures include *bargah, yadgar, alava*, or *dargah*. In North India the more common term is *imambarah* (lit. "enclosure of the Imam"). For a general discussion of (*ashurkhane* focusing primarily on the Iranian context, see Gustav Thaiss, "Rawzah Khvani" in *The Oxford Encyclopaedia* 4 (1995): 412–413; for a discussion of the *'alam* in the context of Hyderabad *ashurkhane*, see D'Souza, "In the Presence of the Martyrs."
11. The city of Hyderabad was founded just over four hundred years ago when the Golconda fort grew too small for the expanded court of the Qutb Shah regents. Although historians disagree on how the city got its name, it seems most likely that it was named in honor of 'Ali, the first Imam, whose popular name (among others) is "*hydar*," or "lion." For a solid assessment of the sociological development of the old city, see Ratna Naidu, *Old Cities, New Predicaments: A Study of Hyderabad* (New Delhi: Sage Publications, 1990).
12. Nearly every Shi'i religious text has some reference to the Karbala event. A basic primary source is *Maqtal al-Husayn*, written by Abu Mikhnaf Lu ibn Yaya (died 157/774). I. K. A. Howard notes that this is the basis for much of what the classic historian Abu Ja'far Muhammad ibn Jarir al-Tabari relates in *Ta'rikh al-rusul wa'l muluk*; see *The History of al-Ṭabari: An Annotated Translation*, vol. 19, "The Caliphate of Yazid B. Mu'awiyah," trans. and annotated by I. K. A. Howard (Albany: State University of New York Press, 1997).
13. Although Shi'ahs all over the world organize various ritual activities to commemorate the martyrdom tragedy during the main period of mourning, the length of that time varies from place to place. In some places the mourning period is composed solely of the first ten days of Muharram; in other localities it concludes with Arba'in, the fortieth day after the martyrdom. The longest mourning period seems to be in the South Indian Deccan (of which Hyderabad is a part). For greater detail about the development of the *majlis* and other Shi'i rituals of mourning, see Shaykh Muhammad Mehdi Shams al-Din, *The Rising of al-Husayn: its Impact on the Consciousness of Muslim Society*, trans. I. K. A. Howard (London: The Muhammadi Trust, 1985), and Yitzhak Nakash "An Attempt to Trace the Origin of the Rituals of 'Ashura," *Die Welt des Islam* 33 (1993): 161–181.

14. Quoted in Shams al-Din, *Rising*, 156. For more details on the intercessory benefits of crying for the martyrs see 80–82, 115–119, and passim; and Mahmoud Ayoub, "Redemptive Suffering in Islam: A Study of the Devotional Aspects of 'Ashura in Twelver Shi 'ism" (The Hague, Netherlands: Mouton Publications, 1978), 142–144, 198–216.
15. Mohammed K. Fazel. "The Politics of Passion: Growing up Shia," *Iranian Studies*, 21, nos. 3–4 (1988): 46.
16. Al-Tabari, *History*, 131. This fascinating story is part of a gendered history which I explore in my upcoming book on Shi'i devotional practices.
17. See al-Tabari on faith-based accounts like that of Shams al-Din.
18. Al-Tabari, *History*, 131.
19. Tabataba'i, *Shi'ite Islam*, 199.
20. Tabatabi 'i, *Shi 'ite Islam*, 200.
21. For a glimpse of efforts to refashion the way in which the faithful think about Zaynab and Fatimah, see the writings of the Iranian reformist 'Ali Shariati. Marcia K. Hermansen, "Fatimeh as a Role Model in the Works of Ali Shari'ati," in *Women and Revolution in Iran*, ed. Guity Nashat (Boulder, CO: Westview Press, 1983), 87–96; and Farah Azari, ed., *Women of Iran: The Conflict with Fundamentalist Islam* (London: Ithaca Press, 1983), 30ff offer some commentary on this.
22. See, for example, Tabataba'i's description: "Imam Husayn was determined not to give his allegiance to Yazid and knew full well that he would be killed. He was aware that his death was inevitable in the face of the awesome military power of the Umayyads. . . . Some of the outstanding people of Mecca stood in the way of Imam Husayn and warned him of the danger of the move he was making. But he answered that he refused to pay allegiance and give his approval to a government of injustice and tyranny. He added that he knew that wherever he turned or went he would be killed" (Tabataba'i, *Shi'ite Islam*, 198).
23. In a few events organized in women's homes, women arrange for an audio system to transmit the proceedings to male family members and friends sitting in a separate room. Men listen and respond to the poetry, prayers, and oration through the very same system men sometimes set up to allow women in *purdah* to follow a *majlis* organized by men.
24. A number of authors point out that spontaneous expressions of mourning also occurred as the women and children grieved over the bodies of their loved ones following the battle at Karbala, and as people heard the account of what had happened from the captives as they were taken to Kufa and then Damascus.
25. As cited by Ayoub, *Redemptive Suffering*, 152.
26. Shaykh Muhammad Mahdi Shams al-Din, *The Rising of al-Husayn: its Impact on the Consciousness of Muslim Society*, trans. I.K.A. Howard (London: The Muhammadi Trust), 1985.
27. See Lila Abu-Lughod's description of her 1987 visit to an Awlad 'Ali bedouin community in Egypt in "Islam and the Gendered Discourses of Death," *International Journal of Middle East Studies* 25 (1993): 187–205.
28. Ibn Nama, *Muthir al-Ahzan*, 41; quoted in Shams al-Din, *Rising*, 184.
29. Reynold A. Nicholson, *A Literary History of the Arabs* (London: T. Fisher Unwin, Ltd., 1907).
30. Ayoub, "Redemptive Suffering," 164–165.
31. Zaynab, the granddaughter of Prophet Muhammad, functioned as the very first *zakira* when, as leader of the group of captured survivors, she called for and led a mourning gathering with the women of Yazid's court in Damascus. From the beginning, the main function of the *zakira* was to relay the story of what took place at Karbala, to testify to the courage and bravery of those who were martyred, to express her grief and pain at the loss, and

to inspire empathy, loyalty, and sorrow in her listeners. These goals have guided orators throughout the centuries and continue to offer direction and inspiration to today's *zakiras*.

32. Interview with Zaynab, Dar al-Shifa', Hyderabad, 26 June 1997. My translation.
33. This event took place on Arba'in; 19 July (20 Safar) 1995.
34. This quality is the same for both male and female orators; the aim is to help the assembly to re-experience the tragedy of the martyrdom and be moved to grief and tears.
35. In the Shi'i context, the *hadi,s* or "traditions," are a record of things said or done by the Prophet, the Imams, or the Ahl-e-Bayt. For Sunnis, it is limited to the sayings and doings of Prophet Muhammad.
36. Interview, Dar al-Shifa', Hyderabad, 17 June 1997. My translation.
37. Interview, Dar al-Shifa', Hyderabad, 26 June 1997. My translation.
38. Ibid.
39. Ibid.
40. Ibid.
41. I have relied primarily on the recollections of local women in trying to reconstruct this portion of history, for written resources are scanty.
42. The women with whom I spoke with did not give the names of titles, although it appears that the Dah *majlis* was popular, as were other Urdu translations of the text.
43. See Howarth's history of *majlis* preaching, *The Pulpit of Tears*, 19–64.
44. In the Deccan region formally trained male religious scholars (*'ulama*) had been giving sermons in conjunction with mourning commemorations for at least as far back as the Qutb Shah period. See Howarth, *The Pulpit of Tears*, for the fullest documentation of this.
45. Howarth, *The Pulpit of Tears*, 50–56.
46. For the possible influence of Muslim reformers, one might look more deeply into the activities of Sayyid Chiragh 'Ali, for example.
47. Hegland, "Flagellation and Fundamentalism," "A Mixed Blessing," and "Shi' Women of Northwest Pakistan."
48. Erika Friedl, "Sources of Female Power in Iran, "in *In the Eye of the Storm*, eds. Mahnaz Afkhami and Erika Friedl (Syracuse, NY: Syracuse University Press, 1994), 166. Friedl's observation receives support from Gloria Steinem, *Revolution from Within* (Boston: Little, Brown and Co. 1992; 1993), 123, who notes that going to an all-women's college may offer North American women greater chances of developing their intellectual and emotional skills—including self-esteem.
49. For example, Syeda Zainab Fatima was the group leader of the Indian men and women on a Shi'i pilgrimage tour when eighteen of the Indian and Pakistani male pilgrims were abducted and killed by terrorists in Iraq; see the report "Families of Terrorist Victims Shocked" in the daily newspaper *The Hindu*, Sept. 3, 2006, p. 1.
50. Diane D'Souza, "Yadgar Husayni: an All-women 'Ashurkhana in Hyderabad," in *Islamic Ideologies and Women's Realities: Muslim Women in India*, ed. Imtiaz Ahmed (New Delhi: Rainbow Press, 2005)."
51. I have based these numbers on figures taken from the Anjuman's Annual Report of a representative year, and confirmation with Anjuman representatives; see Anjuman Niswan Barkat-I Aza, *Qawa'id-o-Dawabit* (Hyderabad: Markazi Anjuman Niswan Barkat-e-Aza, 1981), 2ff. I will be publishing a more complete history of the shrine and its development in the coming year in my book on Shi' women's devotional practices.
52. This interaction took place in Hyderabad on 26 June 1997. My translation.

9 History, Memory, and Other Matters of Life and Death[1]

Christian Lee Novetzke

In the Census of India conducted in 1911, we have a record of a killing in a Punjabi village that may have turned murder into historiography. The passage tells us Afridi Pathans of Tirah[2] had no holy shrine within their precincts to serve as a site of worship, thus they had no *dargah* honoring a *pir* to whom they could apply for assistance in their daily lives. The Census recorded the story this way:

> Smarting under a sense of incompleteness they induced by generous offers a saint of the most notorious piety to take up his abode amongst them. Then they made quite sure of his staying with them by cutting his throat; they buried him honourably; they built over his bones a splendid shrine at which they might worship him and implore his aid and intercession in their behalf, and thus they purged themselves of their reproach.[3]

Perhaps the Afridi understood that the power of history lies in the quality of one's monuments and the degree to which a monument generates a perpetual interest among people that is both social and economic. Villages around the Afridi could mark time by their *dargah*s, by the date when their *pir* passed on, and by the years clicked off by annual rituals enacted and through bygone wishes granted. We might view the actions of the Afridi as a metaphor for the work of modern historiographers (in what Hayden White might call the "trope of irony"), but perhaps with a level of subjective self-awareness that has only fully entered our scholarly epistemology with the advent of feminism and postmodernism. Consider that a *dargah*, as opposed to a living *pir*, is a permanent site of worship, attracting votaries to the *pir*'s monument who bring with them more than wishes and pleas, but also money and the mobile economy of religious pilgrimages. Consider also that such monuments under the Islamic rule of the Sultans and Moghuls, preserved to a large degree under the British, and current in contemporary India and Pakistan, were provided for by a *waqf* or stipend for the maintenance of a *dargah*. This generous gift of state was bestowed not to memorialize a living teacher of the faith, but rather, to immortalize (in stone) the mortal *pir*.[4] The death of a Muslim saint, the creation of an enduring memorial, and the commencement of an economy of ritual around the site—these things bring the Afridi into the realm of the state as well as into its official history. It is here, in the world of religion, economics, historiography, and social structure—rather than in any psychological sense of incompleteness—that we find the reason for the killing of a *pir.*

Modern historians should find in this incident the familiar motif of the centrality of death. Like the strange boy in M. Night Shyamalan's film, *The Sixth Sense*, the modern historian sees dead people. They haunt historical texts. Michel de Certeau describes history as something which "aims at calming the dead who still haunt the present, and at offering them scriptural tombs."[5] At the center of the modern Western "scriptural tomb" is the nation if we follow the thinking of Ernest Gellner, Benedict Anderson, and Eric Hobsbawm. The late Columbia Professor of History and Politics, Carlton Hayes, called nationalism a religion and asserted that the regard Western cultures had for prophets, messiahs, and martyrs they likewise held for presidents, revolutionaries, and fallen soldiers.[6] Indeed, how could the history of Europe exist without its numerous graves, dug after the French Revolution or the two World Wars? How could America know its past without Plymouth Rock or the Alamo? Nations may exist in the imagination of social groups, but they also require physical evidence, mnemonic devices like towering obelisks, stoic statues, and carved mountsides. The texts of history require physical sites as well, what Pierre Nora has called "les lieux de mémoire," and this is especially true when a history purports to represent communities of identity, such as nations, ethnicities, families, and particularly religions.[7]

This chapter is likewise situated in a land of the deceased, the literal and figurative remains of thousands of religious figures in South Asia whose physical absence is repeated in the presence of places, performances, and stories that recount their extraordinary lives, and whose sites of memory become shared objects in the formation of identity, particularly through identification with the past. One finds the *dargah*s of Sufi *pir*s throughout the Subcontinent, along with the *smritsthalas* ("memorial site") and *mandir*s ("temple") maintained in memory of Hindu saints. We have what are said to be the literal remains of the Prophet Muhammad—beard hairs for the most part—in various areas of northern and northwestern South Asia. And any picture book on South Asian architecture will disclose to the reader those early marvels of remembrance, the Buddhist *stupas*, enclosing the "relics" of Gautam Buddha himself, and surrounded by "gates" engraved with his biography in pictorial form.

In this chapter, I investigate a "scriptural tomb" associated with a thirteenth-century Marathi Varkari "saint" (*sant*) named Jnandev or Jnaneshwar. In memoriam of this saint and his actions is a confluence of text and place united by the unlikely historiographic devices of a dream and a tree. Through this phantasmal medium, a shared idiom of remembrance is developed that weaves the present with the past eight centuries, not in a haphazard, semi-lucid way that might exemplify the dream-state, but in a way that takes as a priority the rational assessment of evidence and the rectification of textual material, linked to the ecstatic ritualism that characterizes memorialization in the Marathi Varkari religious tradition. I will argue that this congeries of memorial devices—site, text, and ritual—provides both a sense of history and a system of historicizing evident among the Varkaris and helps constitute this important feature of Varkari identity as a historical reality.

The story of Jnaneshwar's memorial is one for the history books. As a young man, in a small town called Alandi in what is today the Indian state of Maharashtra,[8] Jnaneshwar underwent a ritual called "taking *samadhi*," which is the act of reaching the deepest levels of meditation or, in some instances, committing a rather peaceful ritual suicide, in order to cease the cycle of rebirth. In Jnaneshwar's case, he had himself interred in a special tomb, also called a *samadhi*, where he entered a meditative state resembling death, which is how he remains today, Varkaris believe, peacefully meditating at the very threshold between life and death. Gathered around him were his principal friends and colleagues, his fellow Varkari saints, and one companion in particular, the saint Namdev (thirteenth to fourteenth centuries). Namdev is remembered to have engineered the celebrations and eulogies surrounding Jnaneshwar's exceedingly ascetical decision. After the entombment, he is also said to have composed (though never written down) a threnody in memory of his friend, which he appropriately called "Jnaneshwar's Samadhi" [JS]. Thus the word *samadhi* maintains multiple meanings. It indicates a ritual act, a memorial place, and a text that memorializes both the act and the place. It is important to note here a hierarchy of dependence among these three meanings. The primary level is of the act itself, of Jnaneshwar's voluntary entombment, because this is the core historical moment that bears up the latter two meanings: the memorial place commemorates the act, as does the text that recounts the act in narrative form. The moment when Jnaneshwar "takes *samadhi*" is therefore the historical *subject* (the act) of the historiographic *objects* that follow (text and place). One key concern that will play out in the pages that follow is how these three elements are linked (historical act and its historiographic representation) in a way that suggests the historical veracity of the *samadhi* story, the "provability" of the truth of the events, at least within the cognitive spheres shared by many Varkaris.

Varkari lore recalls that all three associations of *samadhi* with Jnaneshwar—the act, the place, and the text—would have been forgotten but for the efforts of a sixteenth-century Brahmin scholar-saint named Eknath. And here is where the dream provides a linchpin in our story. Jnaneshwar appeared to the somnial scholar-saint one night, and the details of this dream led Eknath to that small town where Jnaneshwar had entombed himself three hundred years earlier. Eknath is remembered as having rediscovered the site of the *samadhi*, reinstated the ritual remembrance of the event of Jnaneshwar "taking *samadhi*," and perhaps edited at least one textual record attributed to Namdev that describes Jnaneshwar's last moments, *Jnaneshwar's Samadhi*. The key piece of evidence that allowed Eknath to conduct these acts of archaeology, textual editing, and rememorialization was the appearance in Eknath's dream of a tree, called an *ajanavriksha*, or a "sui generic tree," one like no other, that stood as indisputable, direct evidence. The tree was said to have grown from a staff planted in the ground by Jnaneshwar at the time of his death, a story we know since it was recounted by Namdev in his narrative about Jnaneshwar's act. The tree then appeared to Eknath in a dream, and stands today just outside the entrance to the complex of temples and memorials at the site of Jnaneshwar's *samadhi* in Alandi.

Text and place were drawn together in the sixteenth century to form a yearly ritual that endures to this day and that forms an idiom of historical memory shared for at least four centuries around Alandi. To understand this shared idiom of historical memory, we will first review the Varkari religion and the three principal figures in this tale of a tree. We will then move to an examination of the text attributed to Namdev called *Jnaneshwar's Samadhi*. From there, we will shift to place and observe how the two are linked in a way that positions the collection of phenomena surrounding Jnaneshwar's entombment somewhere between the modern descriptive spheres of memory and history. South Asia evinces many examples of narratives that accompany pilgrimage places, memorials, and physical sites—both natural and fabricated—and we have excellent scholarship that explores the connection between text and place. This article enters the same scholarly discourse, but seeks to align the meeting point of narration and site with larger questions about the interaction of historiography and religious practice. In doing so, I argue that while scholarly thinking about the relationship between memory and history provides important insights into how to understand the texts and practices that surround Jnaneshwar's *samadhi*, it still fails to adequately comprehend the idiom of historical memory shared over centuries among the Varkaris.

JNANESHWAR, NAMDEV, AND EKNATH

The Varkari community is one of the largest devotional (*bhakti*) traditions in Maharashtra, and one of the oldest as well. The Varkaris form a loosely organized religious, cultural, social, economic, and literary community in modern-day Maharashtra that trace their history back at least eight hundred years, if not more. They worship Vitthal, a deity associated with Krishna and his mythology, whose main temple is in the southern Maharashtrian town of Pandharpur. Yearly pilgrimages to Pandharpur are a central feature of Varkari practice. The most famous of these occurs on the eleventh day (*ekadashi*) of the month of Ashadh during the monsoon, usually in early July. Varkari practice is often called "syncretistic" in that it has absorbed elements of Shaiva Natha[9] practice, Buddhism, Jainism, Islam, and Christianity over the last one thousand years, though its expressions of belief have always espoused an explicit association with the worship of Vishnu, or Vaisnava practice. The Varkaris have emphasized the principles of egalitarian access to religious practice, open temple worship, regular pilgrimage, and other aspects of devotionalism. As with almost all devotional traditions in South Asia, this ethos of egalitarianism has not always transferred to practice however (hence, e.g., Sane Guruji's fast-unto-death to open temple doors to Dalits in 1947).

The Varkari tradition recalls a number of figures who lived exemplary lives, attained great wisdom, and embodied the ideals of the tradition, thus earning the designation *sant*, loosely approximate to the English word "saint." Of the numerous saints whom the Varkaris revere, Jnaneshwar, Namdev, Eknath, and Tukaram (seventeenth century) are the most important. For our purposes in this chapter, we will concentrate on the first three. Jnaneshwar is remembered as having been born into a Brahmin family in the late thirteenth century. Jnaneshwar's parents had renounced the world and had therefore become "outcaste" as Brahmins. However, when Jnaneshwar and his siblings—two brothers, Nvrittinath and Sopan; one sister, Muktabai—were born, their parents reinstated their Brahminical status with a petition to a religious council in the city of Paithan. As part of the agreement, Jnaneshwar's parents pledged to commit ritual suicide by drowning themselves in the Ganga River (an act called *jalasamadhi* ["*samadhi* by water (*jala*)"]) in Benares, which tradition recalls they did. Thus, though Jnaneshwar's parents were outcaste, Jnaneshwar and his siblings were, by caste (*jati*) and culture, Brahmins. All four were highly literature, well educated, and indoctrinated into esoteric religious practices, such as the Natha yogi sect. Still, the songs attributed to them, and the legends that surround their names, recall them to have been egalitarian in many social and cultural respects. Jnaneshwar's most renowned work is a commentary and translation in Marathi of the famous Sanskrit text, the *Bhagavad Gita*. This act of devout and scholarly work earned Jnaneshwar the honorific title "Lord of Knowledge."

Said to have been a contemporary of Jnaneshwar and his siblings, Namdev is remembered by the Varkari tradition as having been born into a low-caste family of tailors (*shimpi*) in the latter part of the thirteenth century. Unlike Jnaneshwar, Namdev is quite explicitly remembered to have been illiterate—or rather, Namdev is remembered to have shunned writing and reading as appropriate modes of expressing and preserving his thoughts. Instead, Namdev is attributed with having taken an older form of ritually chanting God's name, called *kirtan*, and transforming the practice into a complex performance art that contains moral and philosophical exposition, cultural critique, and historical narrative in the context of music, dance, and audience participation. A Marathi *kirtan* is a multifarious performance art that ranges from a simple line of devotees dancing and singing a song under the direction of a *kirtan* leader, or *kirtankar*, to scholarly treatises, to social and political commentary, to a linguistic exposition on the meaning of a term.[10] As a performance art, Marathi *kirtan* relies upon artful narrative techniques such as allegory, pathos, and humor, all in the service of imparting a moral or ethical thesis to an audience. Namdev's ascribed distance from literacy is attributed to this commitment to the practice of *kirtan* as the most appropriate means to express his devotional and social sentiments and to address a *bhakti* public, a general audience that coheres around the various principles associated with *bhakti*.

Namdev also represents the advent of the Varkari biographical tradition as its first biographer. He is said to have composed biographies of many of his companions, the most famous of which is a narrative triptych that recalls three aspects of Jnaneshwar's life. The first, called the *Adi* (or "Beginning"), is an account of the life of Jnaneshwar's grandparents, parents, and siblings, giving particular attention to the resolution of Jnaneshwar's family's caste designation and the petition at Paithan. The second narrative, the *Tirthavali* (or "Travelogue"), recounts a journey by Namdev and Jnaneshwar to a handful of sacred sites in northern India. However, a majority of the story takes place in Pandharpur, and not in traveling elsewhere. Instead, we have a narrative that insists upon the supremacy of Pandharpur as a pilgrimage site, in the first third of the story, and a morality tale against the evils of "caste-ism" (*shudrati*) in the latter two-thirds.[11] The last narrative is the one that will receive our attention in this chapter, a piece called *Jnaneshwar's Samadhi*, which has a companion narrative called the "The Glory of Jnaneshwar's Samadhi," in Marathi, *Sri Jnaneshwarsamadhi Mahima*. In the former text, Namdev recounts for us the final moments of his friend Jnaneshwar's life, the hours before Jnaneshwar voluntarily entered a tomb (also called a *samadhi*) in Alandi to attain a meditative state that essentially holds the body in stasis, not quite dead but not animate (*sanjivan samadhi*). The latter text expounds the glories of the former, as a story, and details the place of Jnaneshwar's entombment and the enactment of ritual remembrance that surrounds the event.

The stories of Eknath's life recall that he was born and educated as a Brahmin, like Jnaneshwar was, in the sixteenth century in the town of Paithan, the same place where Jnaneshwar's parents, three hundred years earlier, had brought their petition for the re-instatement of the Brahminical status of their four children. Like Namdev, Eknath is remembered as having been an excellent practitioner of *kirtan*, who would thrill audiences with his great performances. And like Jnaneshwar, Eknath is remembered as having been extremely well educated in Sanskrit and its rhetorical arts. Eknath also had a guru in Sanskrit and philosophy named Janardan, who, legend recalls, encouraged him to produce written texts on various philosophical and moral subjects. In addition to this authorial role, Eknath is remembered to have been concerned with the conservation and preservation of texts and memorials. The two subjects that received his curatorial attentions were Jnaneshwar's *Jnaneshwari* and the memorial to Jnaneshwar, his *samadhi*; and perhaps a third, the *Jnaneshwar Samadhi* attributed to Namdev.

THE TEXT: "JNANESHWAR'S SAMADHI"

As already mentioned, Namdev is considered the archetypical Marathi *kirtan* performer who inaugurated a kind of performance art unique among the host of arts called *kirtan* in South Asia.[12] Namdev is also considered the first Marathi saint to mention other *kirtan* performances in his songs. The most common references to *kirtan* in such songs appear in accounts of the deaths and burials of Namdev's friends and fellow authors from the fourteenth century. These threnodies eulogize Jnaneshwar, Muktabai, Sopan, Nivritti, Chokhamela, and other contemporaries. These compositions also form a distinct layer of preserved textual sources for the various written compilations of Namdev's literary corpus, represented in manuscripts from the seventeenth century onwards. Several of these "*Samadhi*" songs are ritually recited during the death anniversaries of the various saints. The most famous ritual recitation of a threnody attributed to Namdev is the *samadhi* celebration for Jnaneshwar in Alandi in the month of Kartik (usually November). During this "memorial service," Namdev's *palkhi*—a palanquin that holds "memorabilia" of the saint, such as images, busts, and sandals—is brought by his followers on foot to Alandi from Pandharpur.

The JS attributed to Namdev recalls Jnaneshwar's announcement of his desire to enter *sanjivan samadhi*, a state in which many Varkaris believe Jnaneshwar still lives. No other saint within Varkari lore has the distinction of having entered, through yogic skill, a state of "still living" *samadhi*. In contrast, Jnaneshwar's siblings and contemporaries, including Namdev, are thought to have lived and died more or less as mortals normally do.

The JS attributed to Namdev is as much about celebration as it is about lament. The composition tells us how Namdev and his group enacted a kind of before-and-after wake, filled with music, song, and tears during a procession from the local river to the site where Jnaneshwar would "take *samadhi*." A huge audience gathered around the place, and the crowd began to perform *kirtans*. Namdev's children prepared the site of the *samadhi*, cleaned it, and laid out a straw mat on the floor. At this point, we hear the voice of the deity Vitthal asking Jnaneshwar if he has any last wishes. Jnaneshwar requests that every year a celebration be held in Alandi to recount the greatness of Vitthal and, hence, to remember Jnaneshwar's *samadhi*. Vitthal is happy to oblige and says that the river and site where Jnaneshwar sits will forever be a place to receive the blessings of Vitthal.

A blueprint for the yearly ritual that commemorates Jnaneshwar's *samadhi* is then enacted in the text of the JS (and has been re-imagined in films such as *Sant Jnaneshwar* by the directors Damle and Fattelal in 1940). In a procession, Jnaneshwar, along with Namdev, Jnaneshwar's siblings, and other contemporary saints, walk to the river, called the Indrayani, in Alandi and bathe. They proceed to the Siddheshwar temple (which is now partly submerged in the Indrayani River), worship there, then proceed to the site of the *samadhi*. They ritually circumambulate the site, then sit outside the entry to the tomb and begin a series of *kirtans* that last throughout the night. For several days the group fasts and stays awake, performing songs and remembering stories. The *kirtan*s involve recalling moments from Jnaneshwar's life and parsing out from them life-lessons—a kind of didactic eulogy. The *kirtan*s are suspended only for Jnaneshwar to deliver a philosophical discourse (*pravacana*). On the tenth day when Jnaneshwar is to enter his *samadhi*, the group breaks their fast with a communal meal. They return to performing *kirtan*s and celebrating throughout the rest of the day and night. When the *kirtan*s have gone on for too long, Namdev expresses his fear that Jnaneshwar will be too tired to carry out his own demise:

> They ate until the late afternoon.
> When the meal was finished, the *kirtan* started up.
> The vibrant performance enthralled Govinda [Vitthal],
> [Yet he thought,] 'It's time for Jnaneshwar's *samadhi*.'

Nama says,

> 'Dear Lord, if this goes on much longer,
> Jnaneshwar will be too fainthearted to leave us.'

Jnaneshwar is then led to the *samadhi* site, where he plants his staff in the ground, thus marking by the *ajanavriksha*[13] the site of the *samadhi*. He sits inside the tomb, and his older brother and guru, Nivritti, places the text of the *Jnaneshwari* in front of him, so his brother will have his prized work with him for eternity. Nivritti rolls the stone that seals the tomb into place, and Jnaneshwar's *samadhi*—spiritual, physical, and textual—is completed. Namdev concludes the threnody by telling us that all gathered went home, in multiple directions, speaking of the experience they had just shared and vowing to return to Alandi every year to remember. Thus, this passage contains the event and person to be remembered, the injunction to remember, and the very process by which this memory can be maintained. Immortality is also importantly present here. It is explicitly the subject of the story (Jnaneshwar's eternal *sanjivan samadhi*) and implicitly the metaphor of it, the perpetuity of the memory through reenactment and re-construction. This text is very clearly challenging death (or near death) with memory.

The presence of emotionally ambivalent "celebrations" to commemorate the death of a famous figure at the site of that figure's death or burial is so common in the Varkari tradition that the *kirtan* itself bears a distinct relationship to death. *Kirtan* is described as a cure for death, because "*kirtan* . . . can save everyone . . . [can] break the yoke of death . . . and cut the rope of the body."[14] Namdev's songs suggest that *kirtan* can "banish the ravages of time"[15] and in the act of performance, "Time and Death are trampled under the rhythm of the dancing feet, stamped out in the ringing of the ankle bells,"[16] an illustration that evokes an image of Shiva as the Dancing Lord, Nataraja. The *kirtan* thus shares with modern historiography the sense of a performative immortalization, a way of accurately remembering across the generations that come and go for the bodies that remember and forget, especially if we follow de Certeau's idea that history and religion share a preoccupation with the cultural management of death.

The physical, literary remnant of Namdev's JS poses several problems to the text critic. It is the least represented of Namdev's other two biographies involving Jnaneshwar. The other two are found in Marathi manuscripts (*bada*) with colophons marking their date of composition as 1581 CE. In contrast, we find no written record of the JS until the eighteenth century. However, we do find as early as 1581 CE records of the companion narrative to JS, as noted, the "The Glory of Jnaneshwar's Samadhi," or the *Sri Jnaneshwarsamadhi Mahima* [JSM].[17] This text appears to be a performative expansion of "Jnaneshwar's Samadhi," as if it were a transcript or recording of a performance of the JS itself. Recall that Namdev, the purported author of both texts, is remembered to have been an expert performance artist and someone who put no faith in writing. In this light, we can view the better-documented text JSM as a record of the JS in performance, like a sound recording of a famous musical work. Furthermore, the very existence of JSM implies the contemporaneous presence of the unwritten JS. But the question arises: Why would we have manuscriptival records of the performance of a text, but not the text itself?

The answer to this question might be found in the yearly memorial service of Jnaneshwar's death anniversary, his *samadhi* in Alandi, which is celebrated, in part, by a recital/performance of Namdev's JS. I recently asked P. D. Nikte, the director of the Namdev Temple in Pandharpur, about the JS and its absence from manuscript sources. He suggested that because the composition was used in a particular ritual—the pilgrimage from Pandharpur to Alandi made every year to remember the *samadhi* of Jnaneshwar—it was considered "sacred" and preserved only orally.[18] Nikte's assertion implies an understanding within the Varkari tradition that this particular text was not to be written down, perhaps reflecting a view that in the particular case of this text the medium of literacy was inauspicious and inappropriate (which is also a traditional attribute of other sacred texts within Hinduism, most notably the Vedas, said to be preserved appropriately only in oral form). Thus, while a secondary text recounting the glory of its primary source was acceptable, the commitment to writing of this primary source, intertwined with a yearly ritual, was not acceptable. Resistance to writing down sacred materials in Sanskrit and other languages has a long history, and Nikte's observation points in this direction of practice. There is still a pervasive belief, especially with Sanskrit, that the written text is inferior to the "human" one (the text committed to the mind and heart—committed to memory). Curiously, the first anthology of Namdev's songs, which appeared in 1849, took the form of a lithograph of the JS, perhaps auguring the shift in epistemological perspective that some scholars have attributed to the advent of the printing press in the modern world. What had largely elided literacy in handwritten media could not escape the printing press in the colonial period.

THE PLACE: JNANESHWAR'S SAMADHI IN ALANDI

The complex of temples and courtyards that now surrounds the purported site of Jnaneshwar's *samadhi* quite overshadows the small structure that is said to hold Jnaneshwar's still-conscious body. The "tomb," housed inside a modest edifice, is marked by a marble slab, usually strewn with flowers. Atop the slab is a bust of Jnaneshwar, itself usually garlanded, and behind the bust, a small niche with the icons of Vitthal and his "consort" Rukmini. The Indrayani River runs just near the *samadhi* complex. Behind the *samadhi* sits the *ajanavriksha*, which figures prominently in the story of the preservation of the site of Jnaneshwar's *samadhi* by Eknath in the sixteenth century.

The Varkari tradition and scholars of the history and literature of Old Marathi seem unequivocal regarding Eknath's hand in conserving and preserving the text of Jnaneshwar's *Jnaneshwari* through compiling all available manuscripts and critically editing the work in the latter part of the sixteenth century.[19] What receives less attention from scholars, but remains nonetheless essential to Varkari history, is the idea that Eknath also discovered, refurbished, and set in motion the perpetual preservation of the site of Jnaneshwar's *samadhi* in Alandi. The story of Eknath's conservation efforts with regard to the site of the *samadhi* is a common story to hear in Alandi, among Varkaris, and in Marathi devotional scholarship about the Varkari saints.

As we have seen, the link between Eknath of the sixteenth century and the sacred site of Jnaneshwar's Samadhi in the thirteenth century is made by reference to a dream. In a song attributed to Eknath we hear the reason for the saint's interest in a *samadhi* forgotten through the centuries:

> Jnaneshwar appeared in a dream
> And told me something bewildering.

'Divine One, radiant as the sun,
One who speaks only of the Highest Brahman,
The root of the Ajana tree has ensnared my throat.
Come to Alandi and loosen it.'
This was the dream, so I went to Alandi,
Where I found a door submerged in the river.
[Eknath] received his grand reward;
I met the great teacher Jnaneshwar.[20]

The language of the poem does not speak of a *samadhi* or any structure other than "a door" in the river. The Indrayani River runs quite close to the site of the *samadhi* in present-day Alandi, and the temple that figures in the JS attributed to Namdev is indeed partially submerged in the river. Though dreams are a fairly regular means for Varkari and other saints to communicate with one another across the planes of mortality, they are rarely symbolic in a Freudian sense. Instead, these dreams are literal moments of communication between saints, however one-way the communication may be.

In this case, Jnaneshwar gives a "clue" to Eknath, a thing that becomes a *sign* of Jnaneshwar and his *samadhi*: the *ajanavriksha*, the roots of which ensnare Jnaneshwar's throat in the song. In retellings of the story, particularly in Alandi, the *ajanavriksha* becomes the very reason Eknath could find the site of the *samadhi*. First, it was the tree's roots that instigated the dreamscape complaint by Jnaneshwar. Second, it was the site of the tree that must have guided Eknath to the proper spot. Today, in Alandi, a tree stands near the site of the *samadhi*, and it is considered the self-same *ajanavriksha*, referenced in Namdev's songs and to which people offer garlands and pay homage.[21] Being a "unique" or sui generis tree, it unmistakably marks the site of Jnaneshwar's tomb because it is inimitable by its very nature, as its name implies. Furthermore, it is living, still believed to be growing near the site of the *samadhi*, and thus linking Jnaneshwar in the thirteenth century with Eknath in the sixteenth century and current visitors to Alandi in the twenty-first century as a kind of synecdoche for cultural, living memory—though people (other than Jnaneshwar) could not live to link these centuries in living memory, the tree could. The tree is a device of remembrance in this song and in the Varkari narratives that one hears in Alandi. It is also the key to understanding how this memorial practice approximates a historiography. The tree, I want to argue, stands as the link between figures or moments of living memory as a means of preserving, objectively, a historically true narrative about the past.

This is what history does, it links the memory forged in a moment (usually traced through the remnant of the archive) to the cultural memory of the present, usually presented in the form of the modern historical narrative. Oddly, perhaps, the tree serves some role in this intermediary space and hence also articulates a link between memory and history. But before we examine the tree as a device of history, let me explain what I mean by memory and history in general.

HISTORY, MEMORY, AND A TREE

In the humanities over the last thirty years we have seen the rise of the key word "memory" as a significant historical, social, and cultural category in scholarly inquiry. We have "memory" studies, as well as a "memory industry."[22] And sometimes this work is even conducted by "memoriologists."[23] We find memory configured as proto-history, pre-modern history, and post-modern history. Memory is a thing richly present in our contemporary world, or it is a thing crushed under the successive waves of modernity, the industrial revolution, the professionalizing of historiography, and the decline of religious lifeworlds. We have it and/or it has us. Individuals practice it, but they do so "collectively" and socially. Memory is both myth and the most real assessment of the actuality of past events that humans can hope to accomplish.

Despite what seems a morass of memories, some thematic unities emerge over the long discourse of memory in human life. Memory is associated with modernity as an antithetical, anachronistic way of recalling the past. This means for some scholars, memory exists in the world today as an artifact of a pre-modern era or an alternative historiography in the post-modern one, as if archeologists had discovered an ancient tool, and rather than put it behind glass in a museum, they put it to use in the contemporary world.[24] For other thinkers, such as Pierre Nora, memory is a victim of modernity, obliterated by the historical consciousness of modern historiography. In a pithy line germane to French academic writing, one reads, "We speak so much of memory because there is so little of it left."[25] For Nora and others, memory went the way of "peasant culture," as well as "so-called primitive or archaic societies," foreclosed in the world by "colonial violation."[26] This location of memory regularly carries with it an association with "religious" thought, so often used to characterize "peasant" culture worldwide. Such arguments situate memory outside the scope of modernity, either before its advent or in the present condition of its (perhaps exaggerated) demise. A further illustration of memory's antagonism with modernity is the common codification of nonliterate recollections within the realm of memory. Thus we find memory articulated in places, physical sites, and structures, or recalled through testimony, and witnessed by the body. With the exception of the modern memoir, memory usually enters writing as evidence adjudged by the historian and composed in the authorized historical narrative form.

Underwriting memory studies is an understanding of historical consciousness that is tightly bound to Hegel, Marx, Freud, and Weber—our celestial doyens of modernity and history. We can identify two relevant strands of thought that ought to be highlighted in the context of this chapter. The first is the relationship between Hegel's "people without history," that is, those who remember rather than historicize, and those who perceive history, the moderns. This debate cannot be heard apart from arguments about orality and literacy made famous by Walter Ong and Jack Goody, among others.[27] The second strand involves the imbrications of memory in religious life, a world apart from the modern in Hegel, Marx, and Freud, but one deeply intertwined with the modern in Weber's work.

Famously illustrated by a long lineage of authors (especially postcolonial historians) is Hegel's idea the world can be divided into those "with history" and those without; the fault lines here generally fell between the "Oriental World" and the Greek, Roman, and German ones. Furthermore, one must not forget Hegel's physical-anthropological-historical assessment of "The Geographical Basis of History," an evaluation that concludes "[t]he true theatre of history is therefore the temperate zone," that is, in Europe.[28] Though Hegel does not use the language of memory, he uses several of its partners, "myth" and "dream" primarily.[29] India becomes the least hospitable terrain for the "Spirit" of History to reside because India, mostly among the "Hindoos," is the land of caste, the social tendency toward inequality.[30] So for Hegel "Dreams" and "Dream-state" become characteristic of Indian remembrance.[31] And the "Dreams" of Indian pasts fall short of history because:

> History requires Understanding—the power of looking at an object in an independent objective light, and comprehending it in its rational connection with other objects. Those peoples therefore are alone capable of History, and of prose generally, who have arrived at that period of development (and can make that their starting point) at which individuals comprehend their own existence as independent, i.e. possess self-consciousness.[32]

While many students of South Asian history dismiss Hegel's presumptions about colonial India, they often take more seriously an allied set of assumptions about historical consciousness and memory imbedded in the discourse of orality and literacy. In their famous article "The Consequences of Literacy," Jack Goody and Ian Watt contend that literacy is required for history to emerge as a category of knowledge distinct from myth or fable. Without literacy there is "no enduring record" of the past and "no historical sensibility" in the present; in short, "faced with permanently recorded versions of the past and its beliefs . . . historical enquiry becomes possible."[33] Therefore, the consequence of literacy is history; the consequence of illiteracy is to be mired in myth (read as memory). In non-literate societies—Goody and Watt choose indigenous groups in Ghana and Nigeria as models—there is no distinction between history and myth.[34] In literate societies—the authors choose ancient Greece as their model—we can see the clear dichotomy between the "mythical" thought of primitives (Ghana and Nigeria) and the "'logico-empirical' thought of civilized man" (ancient Greece).[35] Literacy leads inevitably to science, progress, individuality, and other hallmarks of modernity. Illiteracy creates inertia and stunts the growth of civilizations, which, without history, have no marker of their collective successes and failures; they are cognitively incapable of history.

Goody and Watt conclude that in studying these cultures, from the point of view of their histories, the skills of the anthropologist are required for illiterate societies, whereas the history of literate societies is the purview of the sociologist.[36] This parceling of subjects is common: anthropologists study culture, and sociologists study societies; all societies have culture, but not all cultures of the world, and of world history, have developed societies. While Goody has emended and softened this position in subsequent writings,[37] he has never shied from the essential formula that language which leads to writing then leads to history and science; whereas language that remains oral leads nowhere, that is, remains within the domain of the oral, the world of myth and memory.[38]

The opposition between literacy, science, and history, on one side, and its variously construed antitheses, on the other, raises a question too often ignored in memory studies: Could the opposition between memory and history be predicated on an understanding of memory as allied to religious, mythic, and "traditional" (as in "oral") thinking? While Hegel may have had his Spirit, with a complex, but readily apparent, relationship to religion, or rather, "Providence," the Rankean scientific approach to religion has certainly come to dominate the discipline. On the other hand, memory is awash in the language of religion.[39] And as a student of Durkheim, it is no surprise to see in Halbwachs a pre-occupation with religion.[40] He chose early Christian religion as his first subject for the application of his ideas about collective memory. Halbwachs argued that early pilgrims and other Christian travelers set in collective memory the locales of the Gospels, wedding memory, and place in a shared remembrance of the sacred geography attached to the life of Jesus.[41] Halbwachs does not argue that religion is the exclusive domain of memory, nor that memory is the only mode of recalling the past available to religion. But his choice of subjects presages the deep connections between memory and religion that would be a standard feature in the theoretical work of the 1980s and later. Pierre Nora states, "Memory installs remembrance within the sacred; history, always prosaic, releases it again."[42] Other, more recent explorations of memory and history, such as the exemplary article "On the Emergence of *Memory* in Historical Discourse" by Kerwin Lee Klein, make plain memory literatures' "associations" with the "sacred," ranging from "cultural religiosity" and "spirituality," containing "quasi-religious gestures," to the "semireligious" and "explicit religiosity."[43] Klein's take on Hegel is instructive: "Divine presence and structural memory converge upon the people without history."[44]

Certainly, part of the association between religion and memory is a result of the strong presence of the Holocaust as a site of memory in modernity, and Judaic traditions of remembrance as a practice of memory. However, the greater gyres of association involve memory not as a solution to crises in modern history, but rather as indicative of a cornucopia of anti-/pre-/non-/post-modern responses to positivist, objectivist, gendered, nation-centric historiography. And this line of reasoning, I have argued, is aligned with debates about orality and literacy, which are themselves reinstatements, along different lines of inquiry, of the Euro-centric world model Hegel provided for modern history. By the time we arrive at the work of Western philosophers of history like Croce, Dilthey, and Collingwood in the first half of the twentieth century, memory is clearly understood to be history's opposite in the field of recollection.[45] As Collingwood said in his lectures on the philosophy of history in 1926, "history and memory are wholly different things . . . memory [is] *subjective* [and] *immediate* . . . history on the other hand is *objective* [and] *mediate*." [46] Collingwood's point is that memory stands regardless of proof or rationale, while history must always rest upon some ground of evidence, proof, and rationality. The underlying assumption is that memory requires belief, while history requires proof.

The shape of this dialectic would largely remain intact, despite several brave postmodern interventions. Many of these interventions in the field of memory pivoted around the challenge of the Holocaust to the modern Western conceit within historiography of European progress and humanistic superiority. The difference between memory and history is so keenly entrenched that even premiere scholars of memory, like Nora, agree that history is a wholly other thing. For example, another contemporary doyen of memory studies, Jan Assmann, wrote in 2006, "the major difference between history and memory [is that] the distinction between fact and fiction is of no importance [in the context of memory]."[47] Jacques Le Goff, another star of memory studies, states plainly that "there is no such thing as history without *scholarship*," while, on the other hand, we are to understand that memory does not require the discipline of the Academy.[48] Instead, Le Goff calls memory "the raw material of history," its archive and source of substance, but memory cannot replace the historian's rational, adjudicatory charge.[49]

What does this have to do with Jnaneshwar, Namdev, and Eknath? The site of Jnaneshwar's *samadhi* is certainly a "memorial," a place people visit to experience and retell memories of Jnaneshwar's life and accomplishments, invoking his sacrality as a saint. It is also a place where Namdev's composition about Jnaneshwar's entombment is invoked. It is done so in order to reiterate an event understood to be "historical," which is different than the re-enactment of the event *at the site* every year to commemorate Jnaneshwar's "taking *samadhi*," an event that I would call memorial, mimetic, and intended to evoke a bodily "memory" of the event in those who actually have no direct memory of it. So we have here two orders of activity that span the discourse associated with sites in the language of memory: the centrality of the site and the centrality of a narrative about the site—its "event" narrative. And as mentioned earlier, it is perhaps even more interesting that our narrative about the event, the "Jnaneshwar *Samadhi*," remained "unwritten" for centuries, transmitted orally through performance primarily and repeatedly performed at Alandi before its subject, the site of the *samadhi*. Simultaneously, we have a text that glorifies both a narrative and a place, the second work associated with Namdev about Jnaneshwar's entombment, and one with a very early written legacy, called "The Glory of Jnaneshwar's Samadhi." The presence of these two texts speaks to a complex relationship with literacy and orality, historical memory and experiential or ritualized memory. It would be hard to speak of these activities as "historical" in any modern sense of the word; the mnemonic activities of the Varkaris in Alandi sit better within the sphere of memory than history.

Literacy, however, is not absent here, but rather it is made secondary, servile to oral performance and enacted ritual, a common feature of "religions" that are construed as slavishly devoted to ritual. Hence, we have the kind of preservation of narrative vital to configurations of literacy—and likewise essential to a historical sense—yet we have this act of preservation embedded in performance, eluding writing. We also see that it was a dream (recall Hegel) that caused a textual editor, Eknath, to preserve, in the present, things of the past. He refurbished the site of the *samadhi*, and in scholarship about the event proposes that Eknath thus found inspiration for his critical editing work on the *Jnaneshwari*, another thoroughly modern practice buttressed by modern historiography's belief in the recoverability of the past via the acquisition of "good data." Eknath may also have edited or standardized the two texts attributed to Namdev—one oral and one written—that recall the Jnaneshwar's *samadhi*.

So where's the history? This question brings us back to the tree. In order to understand why I am suggesting the approximation of a historiography here, we might think about the reasons Varkaris emphasize the uniqueness of the Ajana tree. The tree is not sacred, necessarily, or even supernatural; indeed, there is no religious association with the Ajana tree in any Indian literature that I know. I wish to emphasize here that the tree serves no religious purpose. Its nature is to stand as proof because it as an entirely unique physical object, recounted in text and substantiated, as it is claimed, in real life in the tree that is outside the *samadhi* in Alandi. But proof of what? Proof of the historical accuracy of the texts and practices that surround the tomb in Alandi, proof because it is so entirely unique. If you find the tree, since there's only one, you've found the site—you have proof. As a piece of historical evidence, it is ideal, inimitable, and indisputably singular. It may serve as a sign, but its nature is its uniqueness, not its power to signify. The tree is the sign for the physical truth of the place.

Nora, I believe, would also see the tree as a device of history. He defines history as "[a thing that] belongs to everyone and to no one, whence its claim to universal authority [that] binds itself strictly to temporal continuities, to progression and to relations between things."[50] The Ajana tree, as a wholly unique tree, without precedent or progeny, can thus be an *object*, that is, an objective artifact, a statement about a historical truth that does not require (in theory) any belief. It is meant to be the thing upon which the historicity of the statements of Namdev's text or of Eknath's refurbishment must hang.

The fact that I, as an ethnographer and historian, may not accept the uniqueness of this tree is on par with whatever doubt I might have with any other historical evidence, according to Varkaris. Indeed, the tree in Alandi, from my point of view, does not look unique, and one can find hundreds like it in the area; I am confident a botanist would not find this tree to be "unique" in any scientific way. But my interest here is in the claim made, or more precisely, the reason for the claim, which, I argue, is to present as objective fact some narrative about a past event, and to buttress that claim with "proof," which is the function of the tree. In other words, if, as with many memorial practices, the view were intrinsic, aimed toward the faithful, to those who already believed in the place, why would there have ever been felt the need to insert some object that would stand independent of the ritualistic, theological, or soteriological importance of the place? As a location for the attachment of affective memory, the very site of the *samadhi* is certainly sufficient, so why this tree? The answer, I believe, points toward an extrinsic interest in an understanding of the past that seeks toward objective evaluation and hence "historical truth" in addition to what we might call theological-memorial truth. Still, as with almost all narrative histories, one cannot separate proof from the telling of the story that is the object of proof; the narrative and the "science" remain interconnected.

Finally, the *ajanavriksha* does more than lead Eknath to the site of the *samadhi*, and continue to point people to that site today. It also serves to articulate, to join memory and history, text and practice, the past and present. It points toward Namdev's text that recalls Jnaneshwar's voluntary entombment, the JS. The *ajanavriksha* appears in the text and reappears in Eknath's dream as it ensnares Jnaneshwar's throat, and is said to stand today as a marker of the very spot as a unique memorial. A coincidence of time, the apparent fact that the first written records of Namdev's recollection of Jnaneshwar's *samadhi* occurred in Eknath's life, suggest that in the sixteenth century text and place required each other to substantiate their historical authenticity. Is it anachronistic, or culturally out of place, to attribute a historicist's intention to Eknath and his period, or to the Varkaris today? Is the rectification of text and place with reference to evidence—in this case the *ajanavriksha*—simply the revitalization of memory, the reinstatement of a memorial and commemoratory narrative? Can a dream constitute a historiographic method? Can a tree constitute historical proof?

These sites of memory and history form a shared idiom of recollection that crosses many temporal boundaries. As L. P. Hartley famously wrote, the past is another country, and such locations of recollection link continents of possible pasts.[51] Time and memory are shared in a vertically integrated measure of the past, a diachronic frame that extends from the purported moment of recollection to the present, linked by a consistent reference to a place, object, or localized ritual. In this case, the shared idiom of recollection is the *samadhi*, articulated in a physical form and place (the site of Jnaneshwar's entombment and the structures that exist there), a text (the JS attributed to Namdev), and the object of commemoration itself, Jnaneshwar's self-enacted entombment (*samadhi*). The shared symbol of this tripartite idiom of remembrance is the *ajanavriksha*, a symbol of the "objective" facticity of the past events recounted and ensconced in the structures of narrative that I have mentioned herein. This interconnected association of place, text, and object offers some approximation to a historiographic enterprise, a Varkari historical mnemonic, if you will. This enterprise centers on the way the tree is shared by the past and the present as a marker of veracity in the narratives pertaining to the *samadhi* (such as the text by Namdev, as well as the dream narrative of Eknath) and a physical device of corroboration located in the *lieu de mémoire* of the *samadhi* in Alandi.

Nora described historiography in France as "running a knife between the tree of memory and the bark of history," an act that leaves both bark and tree dead.[52] He has argued that memory and history are symbiotic, and their separation debilitates both endeavors. However, as Michel de Certeau has argued, the split between memory and history is made concrete by the configuration of historiography as a kind of autopsy performed upon the lifeless body of the past: memory resists death while history, like the story of the Afridi that opened this article, waits upon its subject to die in order for it to "be history" as the colloquial expression for death suggests. In contrast, the Varkari system of remembrance that surrounds the *samadhi* in Alandi operates in several idioms at once, of both memory and history. That at the very center of this set of mnemonic activities is said to sit a man, deep in meditation, still living after more than three-quarters of a millennium, may speak to some of the irrational beliefs of religions, but it may also speak metaphorically of the delicate balance between memory and history that marks so many memorial practices associated with religious traditions throughout the world. The investigation of comparative historiographies is an endeavor that must make us reconsider the constituent parts of historical narratives and practices and see historical consciousness as an idiom of remembrance shared by many in multifarious forms, a new template to lay over the old Hegelian global grid of World History and its Others.

NOTES

1. I would like to thank the Penn Humanities Forum at the University of Pennsylvania, which supported research for this project, and the members of the Religious Studies Colloquium at the University of Pennsylvania, who heard an early version of this chapter and gave valuable feedback. My thanks to Kelly Pemberton and Michael Nijhawan for their excellent editorial work. I would also like to thank several people who commented on earlier drafts of this chapter: Aditya Behl, James Caron, Whitney Cox, Shaman Hatley, Ayesha Irani, Naomi Janowitz, Devesh Kapur, Lisa Mitchell, Ramnarayan Rawat, and Jeffrey Witsoe. I am especially thankful to Sunila S. Kale for careful editorial and intellectual advice.
2. In 1911, the Afridi were a Pathan tribe inhabiting the mountains on the Peshawar border of the Northwest Frontier province of India. The area of Tirah lies between the Khyber Pass and the Khanki Valley. The Afridi are still an important community in Pakistan, Afghanistan, and elsewhere.
3. Quoted in Annemarie Schimmel, *Islam in the Indian Subcontinent* (Leiden: E. J. Brill, 1988), 127.
4. For more on the institution and distribution of *waqf* in South Asia, see G. Kozlowski, *Muslim Endowments and Society in British India* (New York: Cambridge University Press, 1985) and Irfan Habib, *The Agrarian System of Mughal India 1556–1707* (New Delhi: Oxford University Press, 1999).
5. M. de Certeau, *The Writing of History,* trans. T. Conley (New York: Columbia University Press, 1988), 2.
6. C. Hayes, *Nationalism: A Religion* (New York: The Macmillan Company, 1960).
7. Pierre Nora, "Between Memory and History: Les Lieux de Mémoire." *Representations* 26 (1989), 7–24.
8. For the sake of simplicity, I will refer to the Marathi-speaking area of India that today comprises the state of Maharashtra as "Maharashtra," though this reference is anachronistic before 1960 and 1947.
9. Shaiva Nathism is a form of Tantrism focused on devotion to the god Shiva. The Naths had a significant impact on the development and spread of hatha yoga.
10. Marathi *kirtan* is more similar to the various *katha* or "story" arts of devotional Hinduism than to *kirtan* in most other parts of India, which usually takes of the form of simple chanting and group singing (with the exception of Bengali *kirtan*, which is, like Marathi *kirtan*, more narrative and expository as well as musical and performative).
11. See Christian Lee Novetzke, "A Family Affair: Krishna Comes to Pandharpur and Makes Himself at Home," in *Alternative Krishna,s* ed. G. Beck (Albany: State University of New York Press, 2005), 113–138.
12. For more on *kirtan*, see Gobind Singh Mansukhani, *Indian Classical Music and Sikh Kirtan* (New Delhi: Oxford University Press, 1982) and S. Slawek, "The Definition of Kirtan: An Historical and Geographical Perspective," *Journal of Vaisnava Studies* 4 (1996), 57–113.
13. S. Barber et al. Sri Namder Gatha (Bombay: Maharashtra State Government Printing Press, 1970), 451 [1088.3].
14. Ibid., 595 [1466.1–2].
15. Ibid., 144 [369.3].
16. Ibid., 165 [408.4].
17. The text is also attributed to Namdev, but several Marathi scholars feel the composition ought to be attributed to Vishnudas Nama, a different figure, whose floruit is of the late sixteenth and early seventeenth centuries.

18. Oral information, Pandharpur, July, 2000. My translation.
19. See R. Ranade, *Mysticism in Maharashtra* (Pune: Aryabhushan Press, 1982[1933]); G. A. Deleury, *The Cult of Vithoba* (Pune: Deccan Colleg, 1960); G. Khanolkar, ed., *Marathi Vagmaya Kosh* (Mumbai: Maharashtra Rajya Sahitya Samskriti Mandal, 1977); and S. Tulpule, *Classical Marathi Literature: From the Beginning to AD 1818* (Wiesbaden: Otto Harrassowitz, 1979).
20. N. Sakhare, ed., *Sri Namdev Gatha* [*Sakala Santa Gatha*] (Pune: Varda Books, 1990), 664 [3527].
21. S. Babar et al., *Sri Namdev Gatha* (Bombay: Maharashtra State Government Printing Press, 1970), 451 [1088.3].
22. W. Kansteiner, "Finding Meaning in Memory: A Methodological Critique of Collective Memory Studies," *History and Theory*, 41 (2002): 179.
23. N. Gedi and Y. Elam, "Collective Memory: What Is It?" *History and Memory* 8, no. 1 (1996): 35.
24. M. Sturken, *Tangled Memories: The Vietnam War, the AIDS Epidemic, and the Politics of Remembering* (Berkeley: University of California Press, 1997).
25. Pierre Nora, "Between Memory and History: Les Lieux de Mémoire." *Representations* 26 (1989): 7.
26. Ibid., 7–8 and M. Matsuda, *The Memory of the Modern* (New York: Oxford University Press, 1996).
27. See Jack Goody, *The Domestication of the Savage Mind* (Cambridge: Cambridge University Press, 1977); *The Logic of Writing and the Organization of Society* (Cambridge: Cambridge University Press, 1986); *The Interface Between the Written and the Oral* (Cambridge: Cambridge University Press, 1987); Jack Goody and Ian Watt, "The Consequences of Literacy," *Comparative Studies in Society and History* 5, 3 (1963), 304–345; Walter Ong, *Orality and Literacy: The Technologizing of the Word* (New York: Methuen, 1982).
28. G. Hegel, *The Philosophy of History,* trans. J. Sibree (New York: Dover Publications [1837] 1956), 80.
29. Gedi and Elam, in their article, "Collective Memory—What Is It?," conclude that collective memory "is but a myth;" see p. 47.
30. Hegel, *Philosophy of History*, 162.
31. Ibid., 140, 167.
32. Ibid., 162.
33. Goody and Watt, "The Consequences of Literacy," 311, 344.
34. Ibid., 325.
35. Ibid., 320.
36. Ibid., 343.
37. Even in "The Consequences of Literacy," Goody and Watt add the caveat, "But, of course, we must reckon with the fact that in our civilization [the literate, modern "West"], writing is clearly an addition, not an alternative, to oral transmission"; see p. 345.
38. Goody, *Power.*
39. Hegel, *Philosophy of History*, 12–13.
40. Halbwachs was a Catholic who married a Jewish woman; politically, Halbwachs was a communist. His personal sentiments about religion are not speculated upon here.
41. For a superior study in the tradition of this line of investigation, see E. Castelli, *Martyrdom and Memory* (New York: Columbia University Press, 2004).
42. Nora, "Between Memory and History," 9.
43. Kerwin Lee Klein, "On Emergence of Memory in Historyical Discourse, *Representations* 69 (2000): 129, 130, 136, and 141.

44. Ibid., 134.
45. For example, see Robin Collingwood, *The Idea of History* (New York: Oxford University Press, 1994), 56, 221–225, 293–294.
46. Ibid., 365–367.
47. Jan Assmann, *Religion and Cultural Memory* (Stanford, Stanford University Press, 2006), 179.
48. Jacques Le Goff, *History and Memory* (New York: Columbia University Press, 1996), xvii.
49. Ibid., xi.
50. Nora, "Between History and Memory," 9.
51. From L. P. Hartley, *The Go-Between* (London: Hamish Hamilton, 1953; reprint New York: Penguin Books, 2004).
52. Nora, "Between Memory and History," 10.

Selected Bibliography

PRIMARY SOURCES

Adigal, Maramalai. *Vellalar Nakarikam*. Chennai: Manivacakar Patippakam, 1923; 1997.

al-Tabari, Abu Ja'far Muhammad ibn Jarir. *The History of al-Tabari: An Annotated Translation*. Vol. 19, "The Caliphate of Yazid B. Mu'awiyah," translated and annotated by I. K. A. Howard. Albany: State University of New York Press, 1997.

Anis, Mir Babar Ali. "Daulat Koi Duniya men Pisar se Nahin Behtar." In *Anis ke Marsiye*, edited by Salihah 'Abid Husain. New Delhi: Taraqqi Urdu Bureau, 1990.

Anjuman Niswan Barkat-e-'Aza. *Qawa'id-o-Dawabit*. Hyderabad: Markazi Anjuman Niswan Barkat-e-'Aza, 1981.

Azad, Abul Kalam. *Azadi-e Hind: Mukammal Matan—Tees Baras Ba'ad ki Asha'at*. Urdu translation of *India Wins Freedom*. Lahore: Maktaba'i Jamaal, 1989.

Babar, Sarojini, et al. *Sri Namdev Gatha*. Bombay: Maharashtra State Government Printing Press, 1970.

Bismillah, Abdul. *Jhini, Jhini Bini Chadariya*. New Delhi: Hindi Press, 1986.

Bismillah, Abdul. *The Song of the Loom*. Translated from *Jhini Jhini Bini Chadariya* by Rashmi Govind. Madras: Macmillan India Ltd., 1996.

Ehtesham, Manzur. *Sookha Bargad*. Delhi: Hindi Press, 1986.

Faiz, Faiz Ahmad. *Pakistani Kalchar aur Qaumi Tashakhus ki Talash*, edited by Sheema Majeed. Lahore: Ferozsons Ltd., 1988.

Faiz, Faiz Ahmed. *Nuskhaha-e Wafa*. Lahore: Maktaba'i Kaaravaan, 1998.

Gupta, Maithilisaran. *Bharat-Bharati 1912–14*. 37th ed. Jhansi: Sahitya-Sadan, 1991.

Hariaudh (Ayodhyasinh Upadhyay). *Premprapanc Arthat Premsambandhi Kavitavali*. Mumbai: Khemaraj Srikrsnadas, Srivenkatesvar Steam Press, 1900.

Hariaudh (Ayodhyasinh Upadhyay). *Bolcal*. Bankipore: Khadgavilas Press, 1927.

Hariaudh (Ayodhyasinh Upadhyay). "Dasaratha Vilap." *Vidya-vinod*, Asin, 1876, reprinted in Ayodhya Prasad Khatri, comp. *Khari Boli ka Padya: The Poetical Reader of Khari Boli*, edited by F. Pincott. London: W. H. Allen, 1888.

Hariaudh (Ayodhyasinh Upadhyay). *Priyapravas: Khari-Boli ka Sarvasresth Mahakavya*. 1914; revised 1941; 23rd printing. Varanasi: Hindi Sahitya Kutir, 1996.

Hariaudh (Ayodhyasinh Upadhyay). *Upades Kusum Arthat Ashtam Bab Gulistan ka Bhasanuvad*. Allahabad: Indian Press, 1901.

Hariaudh (Ayodhyasinh Upadhyay). *Venis ka Banka*. Kolkata: Aryavarta Press, 1889; 2nd ed. Varanasi: Pathak and Son Bhasha Bhandar Pustakalay, 1928.

Hay, Stephen, ed. *Sources of Indian Tradition*. Vol. 2, *Modern India and Pakistan*. 2nd ed. Delhi: Penguin, India, 1988; 1992.
Hujwiri, Shaikh 'Ali. *Kashf al-Mahjub*. Translated by Reynold A. Nicholson as *Revelation of the Mystery*. Accord, NY: Pir Publications, 1999.
Husam, Shaikh Hakim Abul Qasim, ed. *Hilal-e Muharram*. Vol. 2. Hyderabad: Kutabkhanah Haidari, 1990.
Iqbal, Muhammad. *Tulip in the Desert*, edited and translated by Mustansir Mir. London: Hurst and Co., 2000.
Khanolkar, Gangadhar, ed. *Marathi Vagmaya Kosh*. Mumbai: Maharashtra Rajya Sahitya Samskriti Mandal, 1977.
Khattri, Devakinandan. *Candrakanta*. 1892; Delhi: Navacintan Sahitya, 2004.
Manto, Sa'adat Hasan. *Manto ke Numaindah Afsane*, compiled by Athar Parvez. Aligarh: Urdu Ghar, 1981.
Mukhopadhyay, Pratap, ed. *Bangla Sokakabya Samgrah*. 3 vols. Kolkata: Praiti Prakasan, Paribesak, Pustak Bipani, 2001.
Nabha, Kahn Singh. *Gurshabad Ratnakar* (*Mahan Kosh*). Patiala: Bhasha Vibhag, 1931; reprint 1981.
Nu'mani, Muhammad Shibli. *Muwazanah-e Anis o Dabir*. Lahore: Maktabah-e Din o Duniya 1907; 1964.
Pillai, Kantaiyya. *Tamil Intiya*. Chennai: South India Shaiva Siddhanta Works Publishing Society, 1945; 1995.
Prasad, Vasudevanandan, et al., eds. *Magadh Bharati Sodh Granthmala*. Allahabad: Abhinav Bharati, 1977.
Qidwai, Begum Anees. *Azadi ki Chhaon Mein*. Delhi: National Book Trust, 1980.
Raza, Rahi Masoom. *Adha Gaon*. Delhi: Hindi Press, 1966.
Riaz, Fahmida. "Letter to the Prime Minister of Pakistan." Reproduced from *Mainstream* 30 (11 July 1987), *Annual of Urdu Studies* 6 (1987): 131–132.
Riaz, Fahmida. *Main Mitti ki Murat Hun*. Lahore: Sang-e meel, 1988.
Rizvi, Zubair, ed. *Fasadat ke Afsane (Tajzion Ke Saath)*. Delhi: Zehn-e Jadeed, 1995; Berkeley: University of California Press, 1998.
Rushdie, Salman. *Imaginary Homeland*. London: Viking Penguin Books, 1991.
Sakhare, Nanamaharaj, ed. *Sri Namdev Gatha* (*Sakala Santa Gatha*). Pune: Varda Books, 1990.
Savarkar, V. D. *Hindutva*. Bombay: Savarkar Sadan, 1929; 1989.
Singh, Bhai Vir. *Panj Granthi Satik*, Vols. 1–2. Amritsar, India: Shiromani Gurdwara Pravandhak Committee, 1942.
Singh, Bhai Vir. *Santhya Sri Guru Granth Sahib*. New Delhi: Bhai Vir Singh Sahitya Sadan, 1958; 1997.
Singh, Jodh. *Gurmat Nirnai*. 9th ed. Ludhiana, Punjab: Academy Press, 1932.
Singh, Sahib. *Sri Guru Granth Sahib Darpan*, Vol. 1. Jalandhar, Punjab: Raj Publishers, 1962.
Singh, Taran. *Gurubani Dian Viakhia Parnalian*. Patiala: Punjabi University, 1980.
Srivastav, Ramanuj Lal, ed. *Pratinidhi Sokgit*. Jabalpur: Lokcetana Prakasan, 1965.
Sur Das. *Sursagar: golokvasi Jagannath Das 'Ratnakar' dvara samgrhit aur sabha ko pradatt samagri ke adhar par sampadit*. 5th ed., edited by N. D. Vajpeyi. Varanasi: Nagaripracarini Sabha, 1978.
Tabataba'i, Allamah Sayyid Muhammad Husayn. *Shi'ite Islam*, translated and edited by Seyyed Hossein Nasr. Albany: State University of New York Press, 1975.
Teja Singh, *Shabadarth Sri Guru Granth Sahib*. Vol. 1, 8th ed. Amritsar: Shiromani Gurudwara Parbhandhak Committee, 1996.

Tharoor, Shashi. *Riot: A Love Story*. New York: Arcade Publishers, 2001.
Trumpp, Ernest. *The Adi Granth: Or the Holy Scriptures of the Sikhs*. 4th ed. New Delhi: Munshiram Manoharlal, 1877; reprint 1989.

SECONDARY SOURCES

Ahmad, Aziz. *Studies in Islamic Culture in the Indian Environment*. Delhi: Oxford University Press, 1999.
Ahmad, Nausheen. "The Superior Judiciary: Implementation of Law and Impact on Women." In *Shaping Women's Lives: Laws, Practices and Strategies in Pakistan*, edited by Farida Shaheed, Sohail Akbar Warraich, Cassandra Balchin, and Aisha Gazdar. Lahore: Shirkat Gah, 1998.
Ahmad, Qeyamuddin. *The Wahhabi Movement in Islam*. Delhi: Manohar, 1994.
Alter, Joseph. *Gandhi's Body: Sex, Diet, and the Politics of Nationalism*. Philadelphia: University of Pennsylvania Press, 2000.
Ambedkar, B. R. *The Untouchables*. Balrampur: Jetavan Mahavihar, 1969.
Anderson, Benedict. *Imagined Communities: Reflections on the Origin and Spread of Nationalism*. Rev. ed. London: Verso, 1991.
Appadurai, Arjun. "Dead Certainty: Ethnic Violence in the Era of Globalization." *Public Culture* 10, no. 2 (1998): 225–247.
Arooran, Nambi K. *Tamil Renaissance and Dravidian Nationalism, 1905–1944*. Madurai: Koodal Publishers, 1980.
Asad, Talal. *Genealogies of Religion*. Baltimore: Johns Hopkins University Press, 1993.
Assmann, Jan. *Religion and Cultural Memory*. Stanford, CA: Stanford University Press, 2006.
Axel, Brian K. *The Nation's Tortured Body: Violence, Representation, and the Formation of a Sikh "Diaspora."* Durham and London: Duke University Press, 2001.
Bacchetta, Paola. "Communal Property/Sexual Property: on Representations of Muslim Women in a Hindu Nationalistic Discourse." In *Forging Identities: Gender, Communities and the State in India*, edited by Zoya Hasan. Boulder, CO: Westview, 1994.
Bard, Amy C. "Turning Karbala Inside Out: Humor and Ritual Critique in South Asian Muharram Rites." In *Ritual Levity and Ritual Play in South Asia*, edited by Selva Raj and Corinne Dempsey. Albany: SUNY Press, forthcoming.
Barrier, N. G. *The Sikhs and Their Literature 1849–1919*. New Delhi: Manohar Book Service, 1970.
Behl, Aditya. "Desire and Narrative in a Hindavi Sufi Romance, circa 1503." In *India's Islamic Traditions, 711–1750*, edited by Richard M. Eaton. New Delhi: Oxford University Press, 2003.
Bell, Catherine. *Ritual Theory, Ritual Practice*. New York and Oxford: Oxford University Press, 1992.
Bergunder, Michael. "Contested Past: Anti-Brahmanical and Hindu Nationalist Reconstructions of Indian Prehistory." In *Historiographica Linguistica* 31, no.1 (2004): 59–104.
Betteridge, Anne H. "The Controversial Vows of Urban Muslim Women in Iran." In *Unspoken Worlds: Women's Religious Lives*, edited by Nancy Auer Falk and Rita M. Gross. Belmont, CA: Wadsworth Publishing Co., 1989.
Bhabha, Homi, ed. *Nation and Narration*. New York: Routledge, 1990.
Bhabha, Homi, ed. *The Location of Culture*. London: Routledge, 1994.

Bose, Sugata, and Ayesha Jalal. *Modern South Asia: History, Culture, Political Economy*. London and New York: Routledge, 2004.
Bourdieu, Pierre. *Outline of a Theory of Practice*. Cambridge: Cambridge University Press, 1977; reprint 2004.
Brass, Paul R. "Gujarat Pogrom of 2002," an excerpt from the manuscript of *The Production of Hindu–Muslim Violence in Contemporary India*. Seattle: University of Washington Press, 2003, published in *Items and Issues* 4, no. 1 (Winter 2002–03): 1–9.
Brubaker, Rogers, and Frederick Cooper. "Beyond Identity," *Theory and Society* 29 (2000): 1–40.
Butalia, Urvashi. *The Other Side of Silence: Voices from the Partition of India*. Durham, NC: Duke University Press, 2000.
Caldwell, Robert A. *A Comparative Grammar of the Dravidian or South Indian Family of Languages*. London: Harrison, 1856.
Chakrabarty, Sumita S. *National Identity in Indian Popular Cinema 1947–1987*. Delhi: Oxford University Press, 1998.
Chatterjee, Partha. *The Nation and Its Fragments: Colonial and Postcolonial Histories*. Princeton, NJ: Princeton University Press, 1993.
Cole, J. R. I. *Roots of North Indian Shi'ism in Iran and Iraq: Religion and State in Awadh, 1722–1859*. Berkeley: University of California Press, 1988.
Cutler, Norman. "Three Moments in the Genealogy of Tamil Literary Culture." In *Literary Cultures in History: Reconstructions from South Asia*, edited by Sheldon Pollock. New Delhi: Oxford University Press, 2003.
D'Souza, Diane. "Yadgar Husayni: An all-women 'ashurkhana in Hyderabad." In *Islamic Ideologies and Women's Realities: Muslim Women in India*, edited by Imtiaz Ahmed. New Delhi: Rainbow Press, 2005.
Dalmia, Vasudha. *The Nationalization of Hindu Traditions: Bharatendu Harischandra and Nineteenth-century Banaras*. Delhi: Oxford University Press, 1997.
Das, Veena. "Language and Body: Transactions in the Construction of Pain." In *Social Suffering*, edited by Arthur Kleinman, Veena Das, and Margaret Lock. Berkeley: University of California Press, 1997.
Das, Veena. *Life and Words: Violence and the Descent into the Ordinary*. Berkeley: University of California Press, 2007.
De Certeau, Michel. *The Writing of History*, translated by T. Conley. New York: Columbia University Press, 1988.
Dirks, Nicholas B. *Castes of Mind: Colonialism and the Making of Modern India*. New Delhi: Permanent Black, 2001.
Dube, Saurabh. *Untouchable Pasts: Religion, Identity, and Power among a Central Indian Community, 1780–1950*. Albany: SUNY Press, 1998.
Dusenbury, Verne. "'Nation' or 'World Religion'? Master Narratives of Sikh Identity." In *Sikh Identity: Continuity and Change*, edited by Pashaura Singh and N. G. Barrier. New Delhi: Manohar Books, 1999.
Eagleton, Terry. *The Idea of Culture*. Malden, MA: Blackwell, 2000.
Eaton, Richard. *Sufis of Bijapur 1300–1700*. Delhi: Munshiram Manoharlal, 1978.
Ernst, Carl W., and Bruce B. Lawrence. *Sufi Martyrs of Love: The Chishti Order in South Asia and Beyond*. New York: Palgrave MacMillan, 2002.
Ewing, Katherine Pratt. *Arguing Sainthood: Modernity, Psychoanalysis and Islam*. Durham and London: Duke University Press, 1997.
Fazel, Mohammed K. "The Politics of Passion: Growing Up Shia." *Iranian Studies* 21 nos. 3–4 (1988): 37–51.
Fernea, Elizabeth Warnock. *Guests of the Sheikh: an Ethnography of an Iraqi Village*. New York: Doubleday, 1965, 1989.

Fernea, Elizabeth Warnock and Robert A Fernea. "Variation in religious observance among Islamic women." In *Scholars, Saints, and Sufis: Muslim Religious Institutions in the Middle East since 1500*, edited by Nikki R. Keddie. Berkeley, CA: University of Californai Press, 1972.

Friedl, Erika. "Sources of Female Power in Iran," In *In the Eye of the Storm: Woman in Post-revolutionary Iran*, edited by Mahnaz Afkham, and Erika Friedl. Syracuse, NY: Syracuse U Press, 1994.

Gardezi, F. "Islam, Feminism and the Women's Movement in Pakistan: 1981–91." In *Against All Odds: Essays on Women, Religion and Development from India and Pakistan*, edited by K. Bhasin, Ritu Menon, and Nighat Said Khan. Delhi: Kali for Women, 1998.

Geetha, V. and S. V. Rajaduria. Towards a Non-Brahmin Millenium: from lyothee Thass to Periyar. Calcutta: Samya Press, 1988.

Giddens, Anthony. *Central Problems in Social Theory: Action, Structure and Contradiction in Social Analysis*. Berkeley: University of California Press, 1979.

Gilmartin, David, and Bruce B. Lawrence. *Beyond Turk and Hindu: Rethinking Religious Identities in Islamicate South Asia*. Gainesville, FL: University Press of Florida, 2000.

Goody, Jack. *The Interface Between the Written and the Oral*. Cambridge: Cambridge University Press, 1987.

Goody, Jack. *The Power of the Written Tradition*. Washington, DC: Smithsonian Institution Press, 2000.

Gottschalk, Peter. *Beyond Hindu and Muslim: Multiple Identity in Narratives from Village India*. New York: Oxford University Press, 2000.

Hall, Stuart. "The Future of Identity." In *Modernity and its Futures*, edited by Tony McGrew & Stuart Hall. Cambridge: Polity Press, 1992.

Hansen, Thomas. *The Saffron Wave*. Princeton, NJ: Princeton University Press, 1999.

Hart, George L. *The Poems of Ancient Tamil, Their Milieu and Their Sanskrit Counterparts*. Berkeley: University of California Press, 1975.

Hasan, Mushirul. "Imaginary Homelands." In "Partition." Special issue, *Outlook* 3, no. 22 (28 May 1997): 28–30.

Hasan, Mushirul. *Legacy of a Divided Nation: India's Muslims since Independence*. London: Oxford University Press, 1997.

Hawley, John Stratton, and Mark Juergensmeyer. *Songs of the Saints of India*. Oxford and New York: Oxford University Press, 1988.

Hegland, Mary Elaine. "Flagellation and Fundamentalism: (trans)Forming Meaning, Identity, and Gender through Pakistani Women's Rituals of Mourning." American Ethnologist 25, no. 2 (1998): 240–266.

Hegland, Mary Elaine. "Shi'a Women of Northwest Pakistan and Agency Through Practice: Ritual, Resistance, Resilience." *Political and Legal Anthropology Review* 18, no. 2 (1995): 65–79.

Hegland, Mary Elaine. "A Mixed Blessing—the Majles: Shi'a Women's Rituals in Northwest Pakistan and the Politics of Religion, Ethnicity, and Gender." In *Mixed Blessings: Religious Fundamentalism and Gender Cross-Culturally*, edited by Judy Brink and Joan Mencher. New York: Routledge, 1995.

Heidegger, Martin. *Identity and Difference*, translated by Joan Stambaugh. New York: Harper and Row Publishers, 1969.

Heidegger, Martin. *The Metaphysical Foundations of Logic*, translated by Michael Heim. Bloomington: Indiana University Press, 1992.

Heidegger, Martin. *The Principle of Reason*, translated by Reginald Lilly. Bloomington and Indianapolis: Indiana University Press, 1991.

Hirschkind, Charles. *The Ethical Soundscape*. New York: Columbia University Press, 2006.

Howarth, Toby. *The Pulpit of Tears: Shi'i Muslim Preaching in India*. Amsterdam: Vrije Universiteit, 2001.

Humphrey, Caroline, and James Laidlaw. *The Archetypal Actions of Ritual*. New York: Oxford University Press, 1994.

Ikram, S. M. *Modern Muslim India and the Birth of Pakistan*. 2nd ed. Lahore: Sh. M. Ashraf Publishers, 1970.

Irschick, Eugene F. *Politics and Social Conflict in South India: The Non-Brahman Movement and Tamil Separatism, 1916–1929*. Berkeley: University of California Press, 1969.

Iyengar, T. R. Sesha. *Dravidian India*. New Delhi: Asian Education Services, 1995.

Jakobsch, Doris. *Relocating Gender in Sikh History: Transformation, Meaning and Identity*. New Delhi: Oxford University Press, 2003.

Jakobsen, Roman. "On Linguistic Aspects of Translation," from *On Translation* [1959], excerpted in *Theories of Translation: An Anthology of Essays from Dryden to Derrida*, edited by Rainer Schulte and J. Biguenet. Chicago: University of Chicago Press, 1992.

Jalal, Ayesha. *Self and Sovereignty: Individual and Community in South Asian Islam since 1850*. Lahore: Sang-e Meel, 2001.

Jalal, Ayesha. *The Sole Spokesman: Jinnah, the Muslim League and the Demand for Pakistan*. Lahore: Sang-e Meel, 1995.

Kalra, Virinder, and Michael Nijhawan, "Cultural, Linguistic and Political Translations: Dhadi Urban Music," *Sikh Formations* 3, no. 1 (2007): 67–81.

Kansteiner, Wolfgang. "Finding Meaning in Memory: A Methodological Critique of Collective Memory Studies," *History and Theory* 41 (2002): 79–197.

Klein, Kerwin Lee. "On the Emergence of *Memory* in Historical Discourse," *Representations* 69 (2000): 127–150.

Köpping, Klaus-Peter, Bernhard Leistle, and Michael Rudolph. *Ritual and Identity: Performative Practices as Effective Transformations of Social Reality*. Berlin: LIT-Verlag, 2006.

Lawrence, Bruce B. *Shattering the Myth: Islam Beyond Violence*. Princeton, NJ: Princeton University Press, 1998; reprint 2000.

Le Goff, Jacques. *History and Memory*. New York: Columbia University Press, 1996.

Lelyveld, David. "The Fate of Hindustani: Colonial Knowledge and the Project of a National Language." In *Orientalism and the Postcolonial Predicament: Perspectives on South Asia*, edited by Carol A. Breckenridge and Peter van der Veer. Philadelphia: University of Pennsylvania, 1993.

Mahmood, Saba. *Politics of Piety: The Islamic Revival and the Feminist Subject*. Princeton, NJ: Princeton University Press, 2005.

Masica, Colin P. *Indo-Aryan Languages*. Cambridge: Cambridge University Press, 1993.

McLeod, W. H. "A Sikh Theology for Modern Times." In *Sikh History and Religion in the Twentieth Century*, edited by Joseph O'Connell et al. New Delhi: Manohar, 1990.

McLeod, W. H. *Textual Sources for the Study of Sikhism*. Manchester: Manchester University Press, 1984.

McLeod, W. H. *Who Is a Sikh? The Question of Sikh Identity*. Oxford: Oxford University Press, 1989.

Memon, Muhammad Umar, ed. and trans. *An Epic Unwritten: The Penguin Book of Partition Stories*. Delhi: Penguin Books, 1998.

Metcalf, Barbara D., and Thomas R. Metcalf. *A Concise History of India*. Cambridge: Cambridge University Press, 2002.

Minault, Gail. *The Khilafat Movement: Religious Symbolism and Political Mobilization in India*. New York: Columbia University Press, 1982.

Moini, Liaqat Hussein. "Rituals and Customary Practices at the Dargah of Ajmer." In *Muslim Shrines in India: Their Character, History, and Significance*, edited by Christian W. Troll. Delhi: Oxford University Press, 1989.

Myrvold, Kristina. "Inside the Guru's Gate: Ritual Uses of Texts Among the Sikhs in Varanasi." Ph.D. diss., Lund University, 2007.

Naim, C. M. "North and Center: Urdu." In *the Encyclopaedia of India, Pakistan, Bangladesh, Sri Lanka, Nepal, Bhutan and the Maldives*, edited by F. Robinson. Cambridge: Cambridge University Press, 1989.

Naim, C. M., ed. *Iqbal, Jinnah and Pakistan: The Vision and the Reality*. Syracuse, NY: Syracuse University Press, 1979.

Nandy, Ashis. *The Secret Politics of Our Desires: Innocence, Culpability, and Indian Popular Cinema*. London: Zed Books, 1998.

Narang, Gopi Chand. "Tradition and Innovation in Urdu Poetry." In *Poetry and Renaissance: Kumara Asan Birth Centenary Volume,* edited by M. Govindan. Madras: Sameeksha, 1974.

Nayyar, Adam. "Musical Regions: Punjab." In *The Garland Encyclopedia of World Music*, edited by Alison Arnold. New York and London: Garland Publishing, 2000.

Nehring, Andreas. Die Entdeckung von "arisch" und "dravidisch" in Britisch-Indien. Eine Erzählung zweier Städte The Discovery of "Arians" and "Dravidians" in British India. A Tale of Two Cities. In *"Arier" und "Draviden,"* edited by Michael Bergunder and Rahul Peter Das. Halle: Verlag der Franckeschen Stiftungen in Halle, 2002.

Nicholson, Reynold A. *A Literary History of the Arabs*. London: T. Fisher Unwin, Ltd., 1907.

Nijhawan, Michael. "Shared Melodies, Partitioned Narratives: An Ethnography of Sikh and Sufi Dhadi Performance in Contemporary Punjab." *International Journal of Punjab Studies* 10, nos. 1–2 (2004): 57–77.

Nijhawan, Michael. *Dhadi Darbar: Religion, Violence, and the Performance of Sikh History*. Delhi: Oxford University Press, 2006.

Nora, Pierre. "Between Memory and History: Les Lieux de Mémoire." *Representations* 26 (1989): 7–24.

O'Connell, J. T., M. Israel, W. Oxtoby, W. H. McLeod, and J. S. Grewal, eds. *Sikh History and Religion in the Twentieth Century*. New Delhi: Manohar, 1990.

Oberoi, Harjot. *The Construction of Religious Boundaries: Culture, Identity and Diversity in the Sikh Tradition*. New Delhi: Oxford University Press, 1994.

Ong, Walter. *Orality and Literacy: The Technologizing of the Word*. New York: Methuen, 1982.

Pandey, Gyanendra. "Can a Muslim Be an Indian?" *Comparative Studies in Society and History,* 41, no. 4 (October 1999): 608–629.

Pandey, Gyanendra. "The Prose of Otherness." In *Subaltern Studies VIII: Essays in Honour of Ranajit Guha*, edited by David Hardiman and David Arnold. Delhi: Oxford University Press, 1994.

Pandey, Gyanendra. "Which of Us Are Hindus?" In *Hindus and Others: The Question of Identity in India Today,* edited by Gyanendra Pandey. New Delhi: Viking, 1993.

Pandey, Gyanendra. *Routine Violence: Nations, Fragments, Histories*. Delhi: Permanent Black, 2006.

Pandian, M. S. S. *Brahmin and Non-Brahmin: Genealogies of the Tamil Political Present*. Delhi: Permanent Black, 2007.

Prakash, Gyan. "Becoming a Bhuinya: Oral Traditions and Contested Domination in Eastern India." In *Contesting Power: Resistance and Everyday Social Relations in South Asia*, edited by Douglas Haynes and Gyan Prakash. Berkeley: University of California Press, 1991.

Prasad, M. Madhava. *Ideology of the Hindi Film: A Historical Construction.* Delhi: Oxford University Press, 1998.
Pritchett, Frances W. *Nets of Awareness: Urdu Poetry and Its Critics.* Berkeley: University of California Press, 1994.
Purnalingam Pillai, M. S. *Tamil Literature.* New Delhi: Asian Educational Series, 1929; reprint 1994.
Raghavan, T. S. *Makers of Modern Tamil.* Thirunelveli: The South India Shaiva Siddhanta Publishing Society, 1965.
Ramanujan, A. K. *The Interior Landscape: Love Poems from a Classical Tamil Anthology.* Bloomington, IN: Indiana University Press, 1967.
Rahman, Fazlur. *Revival and Reform in Islam: A Study of Islamic Fundamentalism.* London: One World, 1999.
Ramaswamy, Sumathi. *Passions of the Tongue: Language Devotion in Tamil India, 1891–1970.* Berkeley: University of California Press, 1997.
Riaz, Fahmida. *Pakistan: Literature and Society.* New Delhi: Patriot Publishers, 1986.
Robinson, Francis. *Separatism Among Indian Muslims: The Politics of the United Provinces' Muslims 1860–1923.* Cambridge, UK: Cambridge University Press, 1974; reprint 2009.
Roy, Asim. "The High Politics of India's Partition: The Revisionist Perspective." In *India's Partition: Process, Strategy, and Perspective,* edited by Mushirul Hasan. New Delhi: Oxford University Press, 1993.
Roy, Parama. *Indian Traffic: Identities in Question in Colonial and Postcolonial India.* Berkeley: University of California Press, 1998.
Saksena, Ram Babu. *A History of Urdu Literature.* Lahore: Sang-e Meel, 1996.
Sanyal, Usha. *Devotional Islam and Politics in British India.* Delhi: Oxford University Press, 1996.
Sesha Iyengar, T. R. *Dravidian India.* New Delhi: Asian Educational Series, 1925; reprint 1995.
Shackle, Christopher, and Rupert Snell. *Hindi and Urdu since 1800: A Common Reader.* London: SOAS/University of London, 1990.
Shams al-Din, Shaykh Muhammad Mahdi. *The Rising of al-Husayn: its Impact on the Consciousness of Muslim Society.* Translated by I. K. A. Howard. London: The Muhammadi Trust, 1985.
Sharib, Zahurul Hassan. *The Culture of the Sufis.* Southampton, UK: Sharib Press, 1999.
Singh, Iqbal. *The Ardent Pilgrim: An Introduction to the Life and Work of Mohammed Iqbal.* Delhi: Oxford University Press, 1997.
Singh, Pashaura. *The Guru Granth Sahib: Canon, Meaning and Authority.* New Delhi: Oxford University Press, 2000.
Spivak, Gayatri C. "Can the Subaltern Speak?" In Nelson and Grossberg (eds.), *Marxism and the Interpretation of Culture.* London: Macmillan, 1988.
Spivak, Gayatri C. "The New Subaltern: A Silent Interview." In *Mapping Subaltern Studies and the Postcolonial.* Delhi: Oxford University Press, 2002.
Spivak, Gayatri C. *A Critique of Postcolonial Reason: Toward a History of the Vanishing Present.* Cambridge, MA: Harvard University Press, 1999.
Stein, Burton. *Peasant State and Society in Medieval South India.* Delhi: Oxford University Press, 1980; 1994.
Stewart, Pamela J., and Andrew Strathern, eds. *Contesting Rituals: Islam and Practices of Identity-Making.* Durham, NC: Carolina Academic Press, 2005.
Stewart, Tony K. "In Search of Equivalence: Conceiving Muslim–Hindu Encounter Through Translation Theory." *History of Religions* 40, no. 3 (Winter 2001): 261–288.

Subbiah, Ganapathy. *Roots of Tamil Religious Thought.* Pondicherry: Pondicherry Institute of Language and Culture, 1991.
Torab, Azam. "The Neighborhoods of Piety: Gender and Ritual in South Teheran." Ph.D. diss., University of London, School of Oriental and African Studies, 1998.
Trautmann, Thomas R. *Aryans and British India.* Berkeley: University of California Press, 1997.
Tulpule, Shankar. *Classical Marathi Literature: From the Beginning to AD 1818.* Wiesbaden: Otto Harrassowitz. 1979.
Vaithesspara, Ravindran. "Caste, Hybritity, and the Construction of Cultural Identity in Colonial India: Maraimalai Adigal (1876–1950) and the Intellectual Genealogy of Dravidian Nationalism." Ph.D. diss., University of Toronto, 1999.
Varshney, Ashutosh. *Ethnic Conflict and Civic Life: Hindus and Muslims in India.* New Haven, CT: Yale University Press, 2002.
Venuti, Lawrence. "Local Contingencies: Translation and National Identities." In *Nation, Language, and the Ethics of Translation*, edited by S. Bermann and M. Wood. Princeton, NJ: Princeton University Press, 2005.
Werbner, Pnina, and Helene Basu. *Embodying Charisma: Modernity, Locality, and the Performance of Emotion in Sufi Cults.* London: Routledge, 1998.
Werbner, Pnina, and Tariq Modood, eds. *Debating Cultural Hybridity: Multi-Cultural Identities and the Politics of Anti-Racism.* London and New Jersey: Zed Books, 1983.
Žižek, Slavoj. *Looking Awry.* Cambridge, MA: MIT Press, 1991; 1992.
Žižek, Slavoj. *The Sublime Object of Ideology.* London: Verso, 1989.
Zvelebil, Kamil. *The Smile of Murugan: On Tamil Literature of South India.* Leiden: Brill, 1973.

FILMOGRAPHY

Attenborough, Richard. *Gandhi.* DVD. Burbank, CA: Columbia TriStar Home Video, 2001, 1982.
Dwivedi, Chandraprakash., *Pinjar.* DVD. London: Eros International, 2003.
Menon, Gopal; Gorana, Chandana. *Hey Ram: Genocide in the Land of Gandhi.* VHS. New Delhi: Other Media Communications, 2002.
Mohamed, Khalid. *Fiza.* DVD. Iselin, N.J.: VideoSound, 2000.
Ratnam, Mani. *Bombay.* DVD. London, U.K.: Englewood Cliffs, N.J.: Eros International: Sacramento, CA: Digital Entertainment, 1995; 1998.
Sen, Aparna. *Mr. and Mrs. Iyer.* Mumbai: Modhu Entertainment and Media Pvt.; Edison, N.J.: Rainbow Films U.S.A. [distributor], 2004.

Contributors

Amy Bard is Assistant Professor of Hindi/Urdu Language and Literature at the University of Florida, Gainesville. Her research draws on literary sources and fieldwork in India and Pakistan to explore how gender, regional identity, and sectarian affiliations mediate poetic production, appreciation, and meaning in contemporary South Asia. She is especially interested in expressive traditions that gained prominence in the nineteenth or early twentieth century and still have vibrant (often religiously based) performance contexts today. Bard has published chapters in *Holy Tears: Weeping in the Religious Imagination* (Princeton University Press, 2005) and other edited volumes. She is currently completing a book about piety and poetic performance among South Asian Shi'ah women. Bard has recently been a Senior Fellow of the American Institute of Indian Studies in Chennai, India, and served as a *Journal of Asian Studies* book review editor and an American Institute of Pakistan Studies trustee.

Huma Dar recently received her Ph.D. from the Department of South & South East Asian Studies at the University of California at Berkeley and is currently a Postdoctoral Fellow in the Department of Theatre and Film at the University of British Columbia, Vancouver, Canada. She was the organizer of the feminist conference "Boundaries in Question: 2002" on the theme of *Women and War*, at the University of California Berkeley, and served for many years as a member of the Executive Board of Directors of Narika—a women's organization that runs a helpline for victims of domestic violence in the Bay Area. Dar is a published poet and has taught various courses, including "India Through the Writer's Eyes" at Berkeley and "Women and Media" at San Francisco State University. Her work is focused on the intersections of gender, religion, class, caste, and national politics of South Asia, specifically analyzing the cinematic, literary, and political representations of Muslim women in India and Pakistan.

Diane D'Souza is a Ph.D. candidate at Vrieje Universitat in the Netherlands. She pursues an interest in religion and gender, with an emphasis on Islam. She lived and worked in India for twenty years, where she specialized in ethnographic research on Shi'ah Muslim women. She is now based in Boston and is finalizing a book titled *Shi'ah Muslim Faith and Practice: a Gendered Perspective of a South Asian Community* (Zubaan Press, forthcoming). She has published numerous articles on Shi'ism in the *Bulletin of the Henry Martyn Institute, Muslim World,* and other journals and edited volumes, including "Devotional Practices Among Shi'a Women in South India," in Imtiaz Ahmed and Helmut Reifeld, eds. *Lived Islam in South Asia: Adaptation, Accommodation, and Conflict* (Oxford 2004).

Arvind Mandair teaches at the University of Michigan where he holds the S.B.S.C. chair in Sikh Studies. His recent publications include *Religion and the Specter of the West: Sikhism, India, Post-Coloniality and the Politics of Translation* published by Columbia University Press (forthcoming), and *Teachings of the Sikh Gurus* (with Christopher Shackle), published by Routledge, 2005. He is founding co-editor of the journal *Sikh Formations: Religion, Culture and Theory*, also published by Routledge.

Michael Nijhawan is Assistant Professor of Sociology at York University, Toronto, Canada. Nijhawan's research focuses on questions of translation and the translatability of violence within the realm of Punjabi performative practices. More recently, he has examined Sikh and Ahmadi transnational religious identities in Europe. He recently published *Dhadi Darbar: Religion, Violence, and the Performance of Sikh History* (Oxford University Press, 2006)," and has completed a documentary film on diaspora Sikhs, *Musafer: Sikhi is Traveling* (2008).

Christian Lee Novetzke, Assistant Professor of Religion, teaches in the comparative religion program at the Jackson School of International Studies at the University of Washington. His research interests cover the relationships among history, historiography, and religious practice, and the production of knowledge about South Asian religious performative traditions. Professor Novetzke's publications include *Religion and Public Memory* (Columbia University Press, forthcoming), "Bhakti and Its Public," *International Journal of Hindu Studies* 11, no. 3 (December 2007), "The Study of Indian Religions in the US Academy," *India Review* 5, no.1 (January 2006), and "A Family Affair: Krishna Comes to Pandharpur and Makes Himself at Home," in Guy L. Beck, ed., *Alternative Krishnas: Regional and Vernacular Variations on a Hindu Deity* (SUNY Press, 2005).

Kelly Pemberton is Assistant Professor of Religion and Women's Studies and co-director of the M.A. Program in Hinduism and Islam at the George Washington University in Washington, DC. Her research has covered mysticism, reform and revival, and Islamic networks in South

Asia and the Middle East, especially as these relate to gender issues. Her publications include "Perfecting Women in the New Age of Ignorance: Emerging Patterns of Gender Discourse in South Asia," *Gender and Language* (forthcoming), "An Islamic Discursive Tradition on Reform as Seen in the Writing of Deoband's Maulana Taqi 'Usmani," *Muslim World* (forthcoming), "Women *Pirs*, Saintly Succession, and Spiritual Guidance in South Asian Sufism," *Muslim World* 96, no. 1 (Jan 2006), "Whither Urdu?: Language, Community, and Power in India Today," in Ather Farouqui, ed. *Redefining Urdu Politics in India* (Oxford University Press, 2006), and a forthcoming monograph, *Women Mystics and Sufi Shrines in the Indian Subcontinent.*

Srilata Raman recently joined the Department and Centre for the Study of Religion at the University of Toronto, as Assistant Professor. Her research focuses on pre-colonial South Indian *bhakti* devotion, modern Tamil literature, and modern Hindu reform movements. Her publications include *Self-Surrender to God in Srivaishnavism: Tamil Cats or Sanskrit Monkeys?* (Routledge 2006), and "Soteriology in the Writings of Ramanuja: Bhakti and/or Prapatti?," *Zeitschrift der Deutschen Morgenländischen Gesellschaft* 154, no. 1 (2004). Her current research focuses on early colonial Tamil Saivism and the reformulations of religion, as linked to notions of the body, in the writings of Ramalinga Adigal (1823–1874).

Valerie Ritter is an Assistant Professor in the Department of South Asian Languages and Civilizations at the University of Chicago. She teaches Hindi and South Asian literature. She has published several articles on the noted Hindi poet Hariaudh, including "Epiphany in Radha's Arbor: Nature and the Reform of Bhakti in Hariaudh's *Priyapravas*" in Guy L. Beck, ed., *Alternative Krishnas: Regional and Vernacular Variations on a Hindu Deity* (SUNY Press, 2005), and "The Language of Hariaudh's *Priyapravas*: Notes Toward an Archaeology of Modern Standard Hindi" *Journal of the American Oriental Society* 124, no. 3 (2004). Her current project addresses poetry and poetics in Hindi within the period covering 1885–1925.

Amina Yaqin is a Lecturer in Urdu and Postcolonial Studies in the Department of South Asia and co-Chair of the Centre for Gender Studies at the School of Oriental and African Studies, London, UK. Her recent publications include "The Communalization and Disintegration of Urdu in Anita Desai's *In Custody*", in Peter Morey and Alex Tickell, eds. *Alternative Indias: Cultural Diversity in Contemporary Indian Literature in English* (Rodopi 2006), "Breaking the Mirror of Urdu Verse: Speech and Silence in the Poetry of Kishwar Naheed," *Moving Worlds* (2004), and "The Role of Family and Gender in Rushdie's Writing," in Abdulrazak Gurnah, ed. *The Cambridge Companion to Salman Rushdie* (Cambridge 2007). Her current research projects include a co-edited special issue of *Interventions* with Peter Morey entitled 'Muslims in the Frame,' a joint monograph titled *Stereotype and Performativity: Re-presenting Muslims in Britain post-9/11 and 07/07,* and a book manuscript based on her revised Ph.D. thesis, titled *Self and Subjectivity in Pakistani Literature: Narratives of Culture, Nation and Gender.*

Index of Proper Names

Thematic Index

For Product Safety Concerns and Information please contact our EU
representative GPSR@taylorandfrancis.com
Taylor & Francis Verlag GmbH, Kaufingerstraße 24, 80331 München, Germany

www.ingramcontent.com/pod-product-compliance
Ingram Content Group UK Ltd.
Pitfield, Milton Keynes, MK11 3LW, UK
UKHW022204190926
475702UK00003B/192

* 9 7 8 0 4 1 5 9 5 8 2 8 8 *